James Thomas m. Margaret Gardener

Gardner
(…ied)

James
m. Lizzie
Hanwell

William, Lord Kelvin
b. 1820
m. (1) Margaret Crum

m. (2) Frances Blandy
[Aunt Fanny. Her uncle
was Lord Blandy]
(No issue from either
marriage)

Margaret
(died in infancy)

Mary Bessie James
(no issue)

John
(died young)

Robert
m. in Australia

Anna Pearly Nelly

Anna
m. William
Bottomley

James
m. twice

Tom John Harry Mary

Frank

William
m. Annie Barlow

…m

Lawrence Jack Anna Susanna

Ena (?) Will George Hilda Constance

* She might have been a
daughter or a daughter-
in-law

N.B. On the King side were
the Henderson cousins

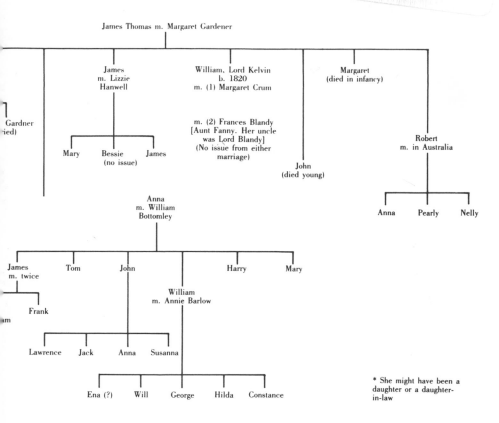

A Singular Marriage

A Singular Marriage

A Labour Love Story in Letters and Diaries

Ramsay and Margaret MacDonald

Edited by Jane Cox

HARRAP

London

For Nicholas, Charles and Olly

First published in Great Britain 1988
by HARRAP Ltd
19-23 Ludgate Hill, London EC4M 7PD

© Notes Jane Cox; photographs
and original material MacDonald estate;
Epilogue Sheila Lochhead 1988

ISBN 0 245-54676-6

Designed by Jim Weaver
Phototypeset by Falcon Graphic Art Ltd
Wallington, Surrey
Printed by Mackays of Chatham, Kent

Contents

Preface

This book is not intended as a political compilation. Rather, it is the story of a marriage which was extraordinarily influential and uncommonly happy. *A Singular Marriage* tells of the unlikely coming together of the bastard son of a Scottish peasant, James Ramsay MacDonald, and a Kensington lady, Margaret Ethel Gladstone. It also says something about the beginnings of the Labour movement in this country, and much more about the eloquent, charismatic man who made socialism acceptable and brought the working class to Westminster.

Ramsay MacDonald was a dirty word for my parents' generation. Even now, fifty years after his death, and in spite of the publication of David Marquand's brilliant and sensitive biography, all the average person seems to know about the first Labour prime minister is that he betrayed his party in 1931 and flirted with a marchioness. When I started work in the Public Record Office twenty years ago my first job was sorting and listing the MacDonald papers. For three years I lived with his letters, diaries, novels, poetry and speeches, and by the end of that time I had failed to find any hint of the swine of popular legend, except perhaps in the reading of a phrenologist's chart which gave 'love of grandeur' as his dominant characteristic. On the contrary, there emerged from the archive a passionate, dedicated man of great personal courage, compassion for his fellows and profound love for his wife and children. The other main character in this book, Margaret MacDonald, was scarcely less of a personality. G.P. Gooch, who met her in 1899, said that she 'combined the radiance of a happy child with the thoughtful tenderness of a mature woman'.

I became determined to make some small contribution towards setting the record straight. I wanted to redirect the gaze of posterity from the last six years of MacDonald's life to the sixty-five that went before, from the vain, broken old man to the creator of the Labour Party and the loving husband. It seemed best to let Ramsay and Margaret speak for themselves.

Jane Cox
March 1988

Acknowledgments

My special thanks are owed to Beryl and Gus Inglis for their many contributions to the work of putting this book together, to the late Malcolm MacDonald for suggesting I use his parents' love-letters and to Sheila Lochhead for her support and help.

I am also grateful to Noel Whiteside for historical advice; Heather Holden-Brown for encouragement; Maralyn Heathcock for typing; my husband for the dining-room table; the Keeper of Public Records, who decided that it was not worth training a pregnant lady and put her on to cataloguing the MacDonald Papers instead; and, most of all, to my son, who was the occasion of all that, and who counted the words.

The photographs of the Margaret MacDonald memorial and the MacDonalds' home in Lincoln's Inn Fields are by Robin Anderson. The photograph of the Gladstones' house in Pembroke Square is from the Greater London Records Office Picture Library. The remainder of the photographs in this book are from the MacDonald papers in the Public Record Office and are reproduced by kind permission of the MacDonald family.

Bibliographical Note

All the manuscript items quoted in the book are, with two exceptions, from the MacDonald papers deposited in the Public Record Office (PRO 30/69). The exceptions are: extracts from letters to Enid Stacey in the possession of her niece, Mrs Angela Tuckwell, and the extracts from Ishbel's personal memoirs which belong to the MacDonald family. A few minor amendments have been made to spelling and punctuation.

I have relied heavily on two biographies — David Marquand, *Ramsay MacDonald* (Cape, 1977) and Lord Elton, *The Life of James Ramsay MacDonald* (Collins, 1939) — and on JRM's memoir of his wife, *Margaret Ethel MacDonald* (London, 1911)

Introduction

Times may be hard now, but when Ramsay MacDonald was born a hundred and twenty-two years ago they were much harder. A small clique of rich people ruled the country (only 3 per cent of the population had the vote) and there was a growing body of poor and unemployed. Men either worked, went to the workhouse or starved. Wages were very low, especially in the so-called 'sweated' industries, and without the pawn-shop to keep them going until the next pay-day, many would have perished. There was no state health insurance, so furniture and other household items often had to be sold to pay the doctors' bills. There was no scientific contraception, and families were large. Education was restricted to a few, and children were sent down mines and up chimneys from an early age. The discrimination against women and the drawing of class distinctions which are now so abhorred were the order of the day. Mrs Alexander had written in her children's hymn words which no right-thinking clergyman would allow to be sung in his church today:

> The rich man in his castle
> The poor man at his gate
> God made them, high and lowly,
> And order'd their estate

But things were changing; the old order was being challenged. In 1859 Charles Darwin published his revolutionary *Origin of Species* which set the civilized world in a turmoil by challenging the time-honoured belief that God had made everything as it was. Working-men were beginning to organize themselves into unions; the first TUC, small and disorganized, met in 1868. The 1867 Reform Act had created a million new voters; radicals and a few working-men made their appearance in Parliament. And the great Victorian conscience stirred. While John Ruskin urged the 'bronzed husbandmen of England' to save their children from starvation, a thousand troubled ladies and gentlemen went 'East Ending' in an attempt to decrease the sum of human suffering. The Charity Organisation Society was established to bring order into the hotchpotch of private charities, and a whole range of cultist movements sprang up. There were temperance societies, food reform agencies, people's concerts, organ recitals, penny readings, Christian Endeavour societies and Young Men's and Young Women's Christian Associations.

Meanwhile a little fat boy — illegitimate, his mother's only child — was growing up in a bleak 'but and ben' cottage in a Scottish fishing village. Jamie MacDonald, as he was then known, learnt about the injustice of poverty while watching his mother work in the fields so that she could scrape together enough to keep them. The scorn and contempt with which he was treated by the 'respectable' members of the family and neighbours made him feel that his was 'the existence of a piece of rubbish'. But he was a clever lad, and the kindly interest of his schoolmaster and the excellent education he received enabled him to convert his pain into energy and deal with his hurt pride by writing and by interesting himself in science and politics. In those stirring times when matchgirls and dockers were going on strike and socialist ideas were filtering in from the Continent, he set off for England to 'make his pile as an agitator and friend of man'.

Margaret Gladstone, his future wife, experienced a very different childhood. She was brought up in a most respectable house in a fashionable part of London, with servants and a large adoring family. She learnt about the conditions of the poor from a gentle, enlightened Christian father, who encouraged her to do 'good works' and go among the suffering in the East End. She soon became disgusted by the 'comparative ease and luxury' of her home and began casting about for some way of serving her fellow-man. She found Jamie MacDonald, now calling himself Ramsay, a handsome gipsy of a man, already well known on the socialist platforms as a speaker of fire and conviction. She fell in love for the first and last time. Ramsay took a little longer; he was a solitary, prickly character, sensitive about his birth and — now that he was mixing with the middle-class intelligentsia of the Left, the Webbs, Enid Stacey, William Morris and the others — embarrassed about his mother's bad grammar. But within a few months his defences fell and he allowed himself the luxury of indulging a deeply romantic nature. He wrote poems to Margaret; he passed through the ordeal of the Gladstone drawing-room; he married and adored her.

It was a singular marriage for Edwardians — even Ramsay said so — a rather modern friendly affair, with the two of them working in harness and sharing the care of the six beloved children they produced one after another. They travelled the world and entertained foreign comrades in their flat, providing cocoa and bananas. Ramsay particularly disliked being away from Margaret and wrote to her almost daily when he was. In a letter written in July 1896 during their courtship, he begged her: 'to write me more love letters so that you and I may feel better and stronger'.

With Margaret's support, both emotional and financial, Ramsay was able to give more time and energy to the Labour cause. He was already involved with the Fabians, who sought to infiltrate the Establishment with socialist ideas, and had joined the newly formed Independent Labour Party. While Margaret devoted herself to the investigation of sweated industries and the exploitation of women workers, Ramsay, Keir Hardie — the Scottish miner who was already an MP — Bruce Glasier, a former architect from Glasgow, and Philip Snowden, the crippled weaver's son from Yorkshire, worked towards the creation of a new political force. All had started off as deeply religious men, thinking, (as did most of the early Labour supporters in this country) that personal salvation would solve the condition of society. Unlike the members of the extreme socialist organization, the Socialist Democratic Federation, they kept their faith in human nature and were firmly convinced that no revolution was necessary, that the reform of society could be achieved through normal parliamentary channels and that all they need do was explain to everyone about the injustices and get their men into the House of Commons.

Easier said than done. The ILP was making pathetically little progress on its own, and the support of the trade-union movement with its growing membership and large funds was essential. In 1900, with Ramsay's help, Keir Hardie managed to forge the grand alliance of all the labour and socialist bodies and the Labour Representation Committee was founded. Ramsay was secretary and Hardie chairman of the new party. Over the next ten years the spotlight transferred from the chairman to the secretary, and in 1911 Ramsay became the leader of a Parliamentary party (known since 1906 as the Labour Party) with a membership of forty-two.

It was an exciting year for the Labour movement but for its leader it brought tragedy. His 'most precious companion', his lassie, died from blood poisoning aged forty-one. He went on to fight for the causes they had championed together, to form the first Labour government in 1924 and to be Prime Minister twice again, but his heart was broken. He was forced to spend the fourth anniversary of her death in a hotel in Bristol and wrote in his diary: 'I was very weary, both in body and spirit and as I sat through the two hours of the death agony alone in my room, it was not sorrow that came to me but a sad weariness and a wonder if she was or was not, if she cared or knew or what. From time to time I have been reading spiritualist literature . . .' He felt his loss most at Christmas, and when the children did something of which he was particularly proud. When Malcolm made an unusually good speech in the House, twenty-one years after his mother's death, Ramsay went home and wrote in his diary, 'I was happy and proud and sorrowed that his mother did not hear. How her heart would have found happy peace.'

Many, including his own children, have wondered what would have happened in 1931 if Margaret had been alive. The economy was in a state of collapse and on 19 August the Cabinet was called from recess to deal with the crisis. In order to survive it was necessary to borrow a vast sum from the US and the provision of credit depended on American approval of any government scheme to raise money. Various solutions were discussed — in Cabinet, with the Tory and Liberal leaders and the Bank of England — and the conclusion reached was that only a cut in unemployment benefit would suffice as it would raise a large enough amount and be seen to be penalizing Labour supporters as well as others. The Cabinet was split twelve to nine in favour of this measure, and there is no doubt that Ramsay decided to resign. He telephoned his son Malcolm several times a day during the emergency and Malcolm was quite clear that his father had every intention of resigning both the Premiership and the leadership of the Party. His daughter Sheila remembers being sent to dust their house in Hampstead preparatory to a move out of No. 10. It was the King who changed his mind. In a series of interviews he begged Ramsay to save the country by staying in office. Bewildered and desperate, not really understanding the economics of the situation, he succumbed and split the party he had fought so hard to fashion. Had Margaret been there, she who cared so little for the pomps and vanities of the world, would it have made any difference? It is unlikely; he became convinced that he was taking the right course and told his daughter that he would convert the members of the National Government to socialism! And who was even his lassie to protect a mere 'Lossie loon' from the blandishments of his monarch?

'Some day I shall fall in love with somebody that no one approves of . . . I shall soon fall in love with that unsatisfactory man, and then I shall be exceedingly unselfish and agreeable towards him.'

Diary of Margaret Ethel Gladstone,
13 June 1893

CHAPTER 1

1866–94

Growing up

RAMSAY: SHADOWS ON A WHITEWASHED WALL

James Ramsay MacDonald was born in a cottage in Lossiemouth, on the coast of Morayshire. In the Session Minute Book for Alves Free Church an entry dated 14 December 1866 reads . . .

Compeared of their own accord John MacDonald Foreman at Sweethillock and with him Ann Ramsay residing at Lossiemouth, who being called acknowledged that she had born a male child at Lossiemouth on the 12th of October last, and she now names the father of her child John MacDonald who was sometime fellow servant with her at Claydales. John MacDonald admitted that the allegation was true and the Moderator reprimanded them both.

Ramsay's parents never married, and he only remembered seeing his father once — in Elgin cattle-market. According to one story Annie Ramsay and MacDonald were engaged, but separated after a quarrel. Another version suggests that Annie's mother, Isabella, might have intervened to prevent the marriage. Whatever the truth, Ramsay had his own dreams about the circumstances of the romance of his parents' love-affair in the cornfields . . .

And there are brown sheaves around us and the merry joke of the harvester brings its sure peal of merriment. This is the jostle of the coming cart and here's Grant's weatherbeaten honest face.

There they all come with their pitchforks, their light prints, their sun-bonnets; and we must join them and tilt up the sheaves. Listen to the swish & thud of the bundles thrown into the carts. They are talking about

1

us. We know it and are proud. How spasmodically we work, just as our hearts are beating! And how the ruddy blushes which the wooing sol brought to your cheek fade before the deeper crimson which comes when we catch each others glance. There the pile jostles off. We lean on our forks. The sun is hot and we sit down together.

Ramsay's unpublished novel, p.72

Ramsay MacDonald was brought up by his mother and grandmother, Isabella. His grandmother was a formidable woman who left her husband, a baker in Elgin, and brought up her family of four single-handed, earning her living as a seamstress. She came of farming stock, and had notions of being superior to the fishermen and labourers who were her neighbours. Her table-ware was her most treasured possession . . .

"See this tureen? Dae ye mind on't? Ah, but he never saw it used. I got it fae my Aunt Maggie afore her death an' it has never been on the table since I haed it. An' the plates! They're my marriage plates, an' they hinna been used sin the laird were here twenty year ago. The speens! Best silver. See my monniegram. My mither gae me them. My mither wis weel off, better than I am."

An old Scottish peasant woman in Ramsay's novel.

Annie Ramsay had no such pretensions to gentility.

My mother is a kind of rough diamond. She won't appreciate Swinburne nor does she know anything about a living wage nor the conditions of female employment. She was a day labourer on a farm and then made frocks for the village girls. When a raw animal on a farm, she trusted my scoundrel of a father too much. But poor soul, she has done her best for me and I am now trying to repay her.

Ramsay to Enid Stacey
28 June 1894
Stacey Letters

It was an unhappy childhood, he confided later.

My mother has never told me, but I believe from what I used to hear my grandmother say when she scolded my mother when I was very young, that there was something rather unusual about my mother never being married. All my early memories are frightfully wretched to me, but I have always

tried to do my duty to all people even when I knew they were cruel both to my mother and myself.   Ramsay to Margaret Gladstone
14 July 1896

But for his public there was a romanticized version of his past.

Somewhere about midnight in wild weather on the 12th October, I received my cold welcome into the world, and I have been told, long before Fate showed what was in her mind, that a next door neighbour who was 'gifted' as they say, showed an unusual interest in my arrival, and by signs and portents which she alone saw, announced that I was to be 'a gie lad'.

The glamour of the unknown, the weird and the frightening, was neither appeased nor circumvented, but still lay over life when I came into the world and became aware of the darkness of night, the eeriness of shadows moving on whitewashed walls and ceilings from a blazing fire, and the strange sounds which haunted the silence of night. In the North East of Scotland, Pagan beliefs and superstitions lingered long and our lives were enriched even if fear beset them. Ecclesiastical edicts were hurled against them but only after generations could we treat them with assured indifference.

Through the early days when consciousness is making life increasingly definite and ordered, certain persons and events stand out like hill peaks above indefinite memory.

Over all is my grandmother, a graceful tall stately dame of quiet commanding dignity, a beautiful face of calm resignation, for her life had been hard but had never overcome her. Her pedigree of small farmers is carved upon the table stone placed over their dust in Spynie Churchyard. They were people who worshipped God and reverenced men, and who lived honestly. Then the Disruption of 1843[1] came, her brother was a distinguished University student who had attracted the attention of Dr. Chalmers. A volume of the Scottish poets still in my possession bears his name, Alex[r] Allan, written in a fine copper plate hand, & some volumes of the classics similarly inscribed. It was said that he [?carri]ed his college books in front of him whilst he ploughed on his father's farm. He followed Dr. Chalmers and was gaining some influence when one day of cold and snow he preached by the sea shore, caught a chill, went to bed and died. He lives on in the family crowned in all the promise of his unfinished youth.

I have many recollections of the parish minister pushing his head through the door and, addressing my grandmother as 'Bell', asking if he

---

1. The split in the Church of Scotland when the Free Church, led by Dr Chalmers, seceded.

might come in, although she did not belong to his flock, and talk about his college friend Sandy. They sat down at opposite sides of the fireside, I on a stool between, wondering why they were so earnest in their conversation but feeling that it was something precious which made them so solemn and friendly. In those days people believed and their Kirk allegiance controlled their lives.

My grandmother was accepted as a 'real lady' by the neighbours, and as my mother was much away especially during the two great harvests of the districts — the herring and the corn — the former became my mentor. She sang her ballads and folk songs for my pleasure, told her stories of fairies & the unearthly, spoke of the odd characters she had come across from her youth on the farm through years of service in some of the most genteel families of the neighbourhood — one, the Robertsons who were relatives of Mr. Gladstone and who gave her on her marriage a tea set of fine China honoured above every other possession. Her mind was stored with such love and mine soon drank it all in.

But the last hour before I went to bed, especially in winter, was that when the golden foundations of the future were laid. She had a beautiful soft heart soothing voice. The fire was stirred up and the lamp was lit. The sewing was taken down and the long seam pinned to the knee. It must be fancy and not memory, but I see as I write my pink feet peeping out below my nightgown on the brass rail of an old fashioned fender which reminded my grandmother of better days, whilst I sat looking up into her fire-lit face & trying to understand what she was reading from the Bible. What matters it, however, whether I understood or not? The scene was enough. Understanding would come later: I was being taught to feel, to wonder, to know that there was a world of mystery and beauty to be drawn by affection. Thus, at those knees with a comely face crowned with grey hair parted in the middle bent over me, coaxing, urging and inspiring, I was taught the Shorter Catechism and the Psalms of David in Metre — every one of which including the CXIX I committed to memory. I believe that we have now advanced far in the half-knowledge of training and instructing young developing minds without mothers and grandmothers and the magic of glowing fires. But before we go much further I hope that we shall understand that two of the foundation stones which have to bear moral weight in life are the witchery of a fond parental voice and the creation in the mind of the mystic world of song and tale, of fairy and romance.

Soon I did know that labour and scantiness were to be my lot. Yet, the knowledge came with no feeling of depression or grievance. The community of our friends — and the whole of the village were our friends — bore the same lot. I grew up in a glorious freedom. When my feet began to carry me

4

there, the whole countryside was my playground. The moors were open to the youth of the village; there were trees to climb; I knew the farmers and there were fields and farmsteads to roam over; the fishermen mending their nets and their wives baiting the great-lines in front of their doors were fine people to talk to and I longed to grow up and join them in their labours.

But there were two scenes oft repeated in those early days the attractiveness of which hid the sense of privation & postponed my conflict with hardship. One was enacted every night. I lay in bed and watched before I slept, my grandmother sitting at a table within the yellow disc of light of the lamp stitching and stitching, every now & again lifting up her face and the garment she was making. The room was silent save the occasional crackling of the fire and the falling of the coals, and something of awe moved in me and I wondered — at what, I knew not but just wondered & yearned to help. Slowly was the consciousness of the lot of my people dawning and forming in me.

And there was another scene I frequently saw which made my understanding clearer. When the autumn & its ripened grain came, my mother was hired for harvesting and was away every week from Sunday evening till Saturday afternoon. On Saturday afternoon I was always carried until I could walk, at any rate part of the way, out to the field where she was working to take her home. How well I remember the joy which filled me when I came to the field. The standing corn was golden, the cut parts were studded with curious looking stooks leaning against each other in dozens, the happy and busy rattle of the first of the mowing machines made me shout with glee, round and round the diminishing blocks of corn they went, their long arms swinging about them. All along the track of the machines moved couples of men and women bending up and down lifting and binding the cut corn. They laughed and sang and shouted at each other. I loved the scene, & when amongst them I saw my mother who was generally dressed in a light cotton dress, I ran to meet her & be taken up for a moment in her arms. It was crowning boundless happiness. They set me at the foot of a stook and there I had to wait till her work was done & she carried me home on her back or took my hand while I trotted by her side.

But one day I suddenly grew up a long bit. I ran to her and when I opened my arms to be greeted by her, I saw her hands were bleeding. I asked why. It was her work she explained. They had come to a hard field. I pass that field frequently when I go home now, in fact I do so on purpose & I can tell almost the spot in it where this knowledge of the crucifixion of labour came to me.

An account in JRM's hand [c. 1900], possibly intended for publication.

His first experience of the world away from his grandmother's cottage was the local Free Church school, followed by the parish school in Drainie, a few miles away, where he was taught by one James MacDonald, who, when he first saw the little fat boy, said he was 'either doomed to be hanged or something worth doing'. The 'Dominie' took the fatherless boy under his wing and saw to it that his education went on until he was eighteen. When Ramsay was Prime Minister he still wore his old teacher's gold watch. A fellow-pupil, writing some years later, remembered MacDonald in short trousers.

We had to walk two miles to school every morning, winter and summer . . . we took it for granted that MacDonald would get all the first prizes. Shorter catechism, Euclid, Latin, it was all the same.

'A.T.R.' in the *Leicester Pioneer*, 30 December 1905

He read voraciously — anything he could get hold of, the Bible, novels, *Cassell's Popular Educator*, *Science for All*, the *Christian Socialist*. At fourteen his interests were religion, science, politics, cricket and bird's nesting.

Extract from Ramsay's diary, when he was fourteen:

April 6. Tuesday. Towards evening heard thunder. A little shower of rain about 5 p.m. Read in Isiah 54 and Psalms 78. Taken as a whole, the day was good. Heard that Gladstone gained Midlothian.

7th Wednesday. Day fine, like one in summer. Had a splending play at Cricket. Started a Cricket club. I hope it shall prosper. Resigned the office of Secretary of the "Thistle" of Stotfield. Was 3 in my reading class and 3 in my Latin. Read Isiah LXI, and Psalm LXXVIII 66–72, Psalm LXXIX 1–to end. Hymn 51, 57, and 58.

8th Thursday to school. Spent half day at Stotfield. Felt a little unwell towards night. Day like an ordinary day in winter without snow. Visited the mines. Saw a poor drunken woman, with boys at her. Read Isiah 62, Psalm 80th and Hymn 59. "Lord how long shall you forget me".

9 Friday. Got my thumb sprained. Day not very good. Had half-holiday for the miseles [sic]. Heard that Grant Duff gained the seat in Parliament for the Elgin Burghs. Joined in making the bonfire. Read Isiah 63, Psalm 81, and Hymn 60.

April 20 Tuesday. Day very good. Set out a bird nesting in the morning at 11. Got no nests. Went by the waterside and looked for sticks. Got some firewood. Wet my trousers very much . . . had to leave one good stick behind me.

April 25th Sunday. Sunday on which the Lord's Supper is instituted. . . . went to Church. Text Hebrews 10th 13, 14 & 15 verses. Went to Church a second time.

May 15th Saturday. Saw my Aunt Bella.[1] Took a walk up the canal side . . . Got a loan of 'Swiss Family Robinson'.

By the time he was fifteen he had begun to think there was more to life than bird's nesting and the Bible. He put his thoughts about marriage and the opposite sex into a poem.

A Wedding March

Tell me not in mournful numbers
"Marriage is an empty dream"
For the bachelor but slumbers
Taking all things as they seem
Love is real, love is earnest
And deception not its goal
Self thou art — to self returnest
Only if thou crush the soul
Not to live in lonely sorrow
Is our destined end and way
But to court that each tomorrow
Find us farther than to-day
Love is strong though time be fleeting
And our hearts fair maid to save
Still like merry drums are beating
Wedding marches to the braves
On the world's broad field of battle
In the bivouac of life
Be not like dumb driven cattle
Be a husband take a wife
Trust no future howe'er pleasant
Let cold feelings all be dead
Wed, wed in the living present
Love within and round thee shed
Lives of married men remind us
We can make our lives sublime
And departing leave behind us
Children in the joys of time

---

1. His mother's sister, Isabella Allan Ramsay.

7

Children that perhaps some others
Sailing singly o'er Life's main,
Lonely sisters lonely brothers
Wedding may take heart again
Let us then be up & doing
To escape the bachelors fate
Still achieving still pursuing
Marry or it be too late.
Tell me not in gladsome numbers
"Wives are better than they seem"
For the bachelor may-be slumbers
Yet he dreams a pleasant dream
Bachelors' lives are real and earnest
Love! they seek a loftier goal.
Just get married, then thou learnest
Sawdust stuffs a woman's soul
Not to live on endless sorrow
Is our destined end and way
Therefore go & swear to-morrow
"I'll be bachelor from to-day".
Love is ever, ever fleeting
Let our hearts be bold and brave
Let them even now be beating
"We would soon fill the grave,
Than that during Life's long battle
In our bivouac of Life
We will be as dumb brute cattle
Driven by a scolding wife"
Trust not marriage how ee'r pleasant
Let these feelings all be dead
That to marry in the present
Is the thought of each wise head
Lives of bachelor men remind us
We should try to live sincere
Leave as epitaph behind us
"John the bachelor's buried here"
An epitaph which may be others
Although bachelors can't refrain
From loving one more than their mothers
This epitaph may turn again.

Let us then be up and doing
Shun the foolish lovers fate
Warn those that are it pursuing
E'er they find it is too late.

At seventeen he founded a field club and edited its journal.

The Lossiemouth Naturalist no.3 [1884]
Every Saturday
Editor's Gossip

Leaders of excursions and private members would oblige the Editor by sending in a skitch [sic] of all excursions they take part in, with captures & anything interesting.

The inner surface of the stomach is purer when empty than when full.

A man will die of hunger when he loses 1/5 of his weight.

Some people suppose that evergreen trees keep on the same leaves for a few years at a time. But nothing is more erroneous. Evergreen trees keep on their leaves only one year, but the old leaves are not thrown off until the young shoots & leaves come forth.

A leaf dies on account of the sap evaporating, and leaving behind it mineral matter which closes the pores of the leaves.

Treasurer's Report for the week.

		S	D
Carried forward from last week	=	4.	1½
Members' Subscriptions	=		4
Tickets	=		6
Fine for keeping Magazine beyond time	=		1
		S 5:	0½

A visit to a phrenologist produced a chart which gave him outstanding scores for 'love of grandeur' and 'love between the sexes'. But as far as love was concerned, he was wary of commitment.

In short I think nothing in life approaches nearer to the level of slavery than an unconsidered, rash marriage where the husband is but a mere beardless boy, and his spouse a mere girl newly emerged from her teens.

I am rather a sceptic to marriages of any kind, but especially so to early marriages.

I would prefer the purr of a Tom-Cat however harsh and Tiger like it may be, to the everlasting screechings and scoldings of a wife who is adverse to the divine right of husband.

> Concluding sentences for a debate:
> 'Is Early Marriage Profitable?'

There was serious work to be done, and great issues to be discussed. He joined a local debating society.

Lossiemouth Mutual Improvement Association, Session 1884

SYLLABUS

September 30
BUSINESS MEETING

October 7.
Introductory Address... Rev. J. Wellwood.

October 14.
Ought Members of Parliament to be Paid?

> Aff.-James M' Donald.
> Neg.-Wm. Reid.

October 21.
Is Temperance better than Total Abstinence?

> Aff.-Rev.J. G. Duncan.
> Neg.-Hugh Ross.

October 28.
Is Emigration the best remedy for the existing Distress among the Highland Crofters?

> Aff.-John Donald.
> Neg.-Jas. Denoon.

November 4.

Lecture on the Highlands.................................... Rev. J.G. Duncan

November 11.

Local Antiquities .... Jas. M' Donald.

November 18.

Ought Capital Punishment to be Abolished?

Aff.-E. Forsyth.

Neg.-John Reid.

November 25.

Recent Applications of Electricity.............................. John Edwards.

December 2.

LECTURE.— Tea and Tobacco .... Dr. W.B. M' Donald.

December 9.

Is Competition injurious to the Community?

Aff.-R. M' Donald.

Neg.-Jas Brander.

December 18.

Remarks on the Herring Industry...................................... A. Cowie.

December 23.

Is Novel-Reading Beneficial?

Aff.-Wm. Stuart.

Neg.-John Thompson.

At eighteen he left school and decided to go to seek his fortune south of the border, where he had his first serious political encounter. He joined the Bristol branch of the Social Democratic Federation, a socialist organization founded in 1881 by H.M. Hyndman. Its members sought to put a workers' party into power to achieve nationalization.

There I was . . . not caring to go to University [chance would have been a fine thing] but wanting to follow up science if possible. I went to Bristol to help a clergyman in some work [setting up a boys' guild]. This turned out a lamentable failure and I was on my beam ends. I told my mother an untruth in order to pacify her and came to London without anything real to do she thinking I was going to a place. I know what it is to be in London with a fortnight's rent unpaid and not a halfpenny in my pocket nor a morsel of

11

food for two days. At first I got addressing to do,[1] then I got invoicing in a City firm — Cooper, Box and Co. at 15/- a week upon which I lived like a Lord, payed Birkbeck fees and sent home occasional postal orders. I also began to dream of scientific attainments. At the end of the first year I got eleven of the South Kensington certificates and was going to sit for the Queen's scholarship next May. In January I got an appointment — temporary — in a chemical laboratory and of course burnt my boats and set out for the New Jerusalem. About April I stopped going to bed and in May I was a poor miserable invalid. I had no money and did not know a soul hardly in London and the Queen's scholarship idea vanished. Still, I came up smiling. Another week or two's semi starvation didn't mean much. I was offered an introduction to Mr Thomas Lough, then beginning his candidature in West Islington as he could get no one to stay with him as Private Secretary (he had had four that year) he offered me the job (1888). My interests were always divided between science and politics and although I recognised in the new work a complete sacrifice of the old, still I had no alternative had I had more regrets than I had perhaps. We licked each other into shape during the next four years — Tommy and I. At the end of the time we winked, smiled and said 'Don't you think we have had enough of each other?' The rest you know.

Ramsay to Margaret Gladstone 1 July 1896

His London home was an uncongenial tenement building off the Gray's Inn Road. He described it in his novel.

At best Parachute [Ramsay lived in Duncan Buildings, Baldwin Gardens] Gardens might well be a suburb to a city of dreadful night, but this morning, they might have been its Citadel. They were part of the improved area of London. The model-dwellings which lay to the right and left of the Gardens at Grays Inn road entrance, completely overshadowed each other, and the sky could only be seen from the top floors. The staircase was of the kind known as 'enclosed', little air passed up and down it, and in the evening it was haunted by a medley of cooking savours which had been accumulating since morning and the remnants of which would be carried on until next day. At night when the stair lights were put out, the homeless wanderer made his bed on the cemented landings and in going upstairs in the dark, you had to proceed cautiously lest you fell over a sleeper. The narrow roadway had been named 'Gardens' as many things are in London, because the name suggests all the desirable things which they lack. If one

---

1. For the National Cyclists' Union in Fleet Street.

came there to look for trees and flowers and green grass, they would have seen bricks, and ragged youngsters and swollen women, and rough paving stones. But nothing else. The only thing approaching the aristocratic was that a scripture reader who lived on an unventilated ground floor because it was more in keeping with his position than higher and cheaper flights. He had a piano from which . . . almost every hour of the day came strains from 'Hymns, Ancient and Modern' and scraps from the popular music hall ditties of the time. Undoubtedly the improvement on past conditions had been great. Parachute Gardens had once been a collection of rotten tenement dwellings abounding in abomination and harbouring the worst thieves and vagabonds in town. But these had been cleared away. A philanthropic company had raised its brick walls there. The thieves had gone. Science had been satisfied. There were no germs there now — only ugliness, squalor, dullness and noise. But these do not send people to hospitals and certainly keep them from being discontented.

> Within two years of starting work with Lough he was well known on the socialist scene, and making his name lecturing and writing. The Fabian Sidney Webb found him a useful contact, as a Liberal M.P.'s secretary, in his attempts to infiltrate the London Liberals.

❦ Sidney Webb to Ramsay:

20 January 1890

Dear MacDonald,
   Could you, if need be, lecture at H[ammer]smith S[ocialist] L[eague][1], Kelmscott House [Morris's house], next Sunday at 8p.m. [Bernard] Shaw was to have lectured on the 'new Politics', but he must go to Nottingham to take Wallas's[2] place.

> His mother wrote regularly, sending oatmeal and family gossip.

Allan Lane
Lossiemouth
Mondon [1890/1]

My dear Jamie
   I received your not to day i went to Mrs Dean and gave hir your adress to Kings Mills Man cims to Morrow and she will give him the adress to send you a boil of mall [oatmeal]. It will be new and it is the verry best — so yu may have to pay carrage and the Mail will be paid to Mrs Doun it is handy

---

1. The League was an offshoot of the SDF, led by William Morris.
2. Graham Wallas was a leading Fabian, later a professor of political science at LSE.

fir me and Kings Mills Male is the best i get Bella [her sister, Isabella] allways gets hirs sent on frim it. My Mither is verry ill with a coff just now and is so week it makes hir wirse Hellen [her aunt, Helen Duncan] cam up on Tusday and staid all night i never saw hir looking so old and thin the people will not pay the rents and she says Willie has down them so fine out of the mony She is nearly Mad i sad i was well off fir i had frim day to day and that was all i cared fir to gev all Man his own She writ when she went hom and sad she stad a night with Aunt and Garg had sent hir 10 pun nots on Wensday last that is 20 in a short tim Annie will be hom hir man and hir will not do any thing but lay on hir father so she will not give him any of hir muny She was a fool to marry do not say to any i told you till you sea wat may hapen

Hellen saw aunt efie she is longing fir me up i connot go till the end of next week and if all is well i may go then but i do not feel well and i am verry good to my self Hellen say i am stil getting more like Aunt Annie [Annie Campbell] Writ me when you get the Meal and i will send the account of it verry cild wether (?) wit at the sea i got the premise of a small fish crell to yu to hang up and hold your laters

Love frim all to you yours Mither

A Ramsay

She promised worsted drawers and herrings.

Fridy [1890/1]

My Dear Jamie

just got fish not expecting them as the wether is not verry good only i spok fir them so the boats wos wunse out and they did them fir me so i send at wunse you will find them verry good they corst me 1 and 9 pense and i thank the carrage will be ?. . . .? but if you want more male i will pack 4 stons and send it on by the goods i am sum beter but my hands are all gon ring like Aunt Annie in Forres and i can get litil down with them only i hop that they will sun get beter

She made him shirts, inquired after his socks and made sure he had a flower for his buttonhole.

[1890/1]

My Dear Jamie

i received your later and was sorry to sea by it that you had not been well i though by your last leter som thing was ring My Mither his been wirse since Thursday Morning with pain and sekeness but i aplied the Medsin

14

again and she is verry week you will ned take mire rest fir you will be sure
to lay up yourself and that will be the end of all wirk then i will send you a
flower next week if the wether be as good as it is i had a later from Jane
Jamie got the close and they fit him so nise he is to send me som thing fir
them he has not been at work for 4 weeks but am ased on fridy the 3 and
Jane writ on the 6 the Masons was all out that morning on strich Mrs Dean
sined the acount so you can send me the mony and i will pay hir wat did the
carrage crust you i saw Jamie Petershen this morning he was asking fir you
they are all well i have not hard frim any sinse i writ yu Jane says Bella did
not writ hir this year we are geting rain and sunshin hear not i must close
with love frim all to you i remain your Mither

A Ramsay

Jamie is geting verry tired of school now i saw Mr MacDonald [the
schoolmaster from Drainie] wun night Mrs Grant [a neighbour] cald this
week to sea my Mither

> His feelings about his home were mixed; Lossiemouth meant love and
> security, but it also meant shame and humiliation. The heroine of his
> novel speaks for him:

To find peace here was impossible. Again she knew that great desire to be
away where noone knew her, and where she might live and die without
having to answer questions as to her parents or pedigree. Sleep came not.
She lay dreading the morrow when she would have to bear the gaze of
people and perhaps have to answer some of their questions. This place took
all the heroism out of her because it knew her.

JRM's novel p. 78

> London was safer. In 1891 he was chosen as secretary to the
> Fellowship of the New Life, a group of ethical socialists, with whom
> he had been associated for a couple of years. Although he threw
> himself whole-heartedly into the work, he was not really at home with
> these people, and their posturing — any more than he was with the
> Fellowship's offspring, the Fabians, whom he joined.[1]
> He described the Fellowship's rooms in his novel:

The settlement . . . was one of those that have sprung up by the dozen
within recent years in London. Its distinctive feature was that it posited no

---

1. The Fabians believed in the 'inoculations' of socialism, of 'giving to each class, to each
   person, that came under our influence the exact dose of collectivism that they were
   prepared to assimilate'.
   Beatrice Webb's Diary, 23 January 1895

dogma as the basis for its social work. The men living there had almost without exception gone through a university and were now engaged in professional work. In the evenings they met in the Common room of the Hall when they found that they did not agree on very much except that lectures and concerts and entertainments of various kinds would improve the lives of the poor, and as that was the bond of the settlement their other differences but served to make an evening pass pleasantly by supplying matter for lively, if serious, conversation. There was not a Pagan amongst them. Each one to himself was the centre of a Universe, and he had recorded his vows that that centre should be well ordered. He read his metaphysics and attended ethical discourses, and thus became acquainted with a system of principles which to him immediately became a master tailor who treated the devout settler's body as a badly fitting coat. They endeavoured to order their lives in accordance with an ethical standard in the verbal expression of which there was considerable differences; they had come by common arrangement to order their reforming action on the outside world in accordance with the organic theory of society which is dead against sudden movements of every kind; they all read history in cycles, and graphically pictured Time to the slum boys who had not read philosophy, as ascending a patent spiral iron staircase always coming back to this same point but always reaching higher levels.

These were their points of intellectual agreement, but a very respectable majority which was growing apparently like the yeast in the beer also held with the usual ardour of minorities that all these questions were intimately connected with biblical criticism, and that their best approach lay through a critical study of the fourth Gospel.

> He parted company with Lough in 1891 and kept himself by his journalism. He ran round the country lecturing, organizing and making political contacts. There was no time to spare in his frantic schedule for the niceties of courting — perhaps he kept it that way on purpose.

❧ Ramsay to Dr James Gwyther[1]

July 1891

You go away on Saturday, don't you? Jolly time to you both! I may not see you until you return. I feel very queer in all this transformation. Born and brought up a bachelor as I was and surrounded in my youth . . . by those to

---

1. A close friend of Ramsay's who had just got married.

whom the marriage problem had never presented itself, this spectacle which I have been called upon to witness is at once confusing and appaling [sic]. My mind is continually reverting to a grove of trees. I see them green and flourishing, I see the leaves seared with the breath of autumn (love) I see them scattered in the wintry wind (marriage) I alone am ever green . . .

The letter to Gwyther was never posted — perhaps he was in love with his friend's bride.

〰 Isabel Matheson (Gwyther) to Ramsay:

July 29 1891

I should like to meet you before my marriage to tell you what a lasting pleasure your letter has given me — not only a heartfelt pleasure, but a strengthening invigorating feeling, which will be renewed when I often think of your beautiful words.

So often, the beautiful pure thoughts are allowed to get soiled or left behind, but I feel that you will always be one of the foremost to help us both to prevent this, & to press forward with us — surely you touched a chord that should ever be our key-note —

I hope that our acquaintance of twelve months' (which *I* am not likely to forget as it runs side by side with the happiest year of my life,) will have even more & unexpected opportunities of becoming a lasting friendship.

If ever I can help you — you will let me?

If I do not see you on this Thursday at the Club I shall know that you will if possible be there *next* week.

I am glad you heard Lohengrin — it is very wonderful —

> ever yours sincerely
> Isabel Matheson

Will you always now call me, Isabel, it would never do to be formal Mrs . . .!

Ramsay wrote on the bottom of the letter —
Not for itself but to be a wee peg upon which to hang memories & thoughts.

There were 'modern' women in his life, like Edith Lees, who helped him run the Fellowship of the New Life. She was in love with Havelock Ellis.

∽ Edith Lees to Ramsay.

> 3 August 1891
> Cornwall
> on a "preliminary honeymoon"

Dear Old Fellow,

You will smile when I tell you that I've got you on my brain — I feel somehow that I want to take hold of your hand & shake it right hard & to tell you I'd like to have a good talk & smoke with you . . .

> But Ramsay was strikingly handsome, with black curly hair and fine features, and many worthy socialist ladies were captivated by his dashing appearance and sonorous rolling tones — like Mary Gwyther, Dr Gwyther's sister.

∽ Mary Gwyther to Ramsay.

> October 11th 1892

Many very happy and increasingly happiest returns of your birthday. Last year my good wishes were among the earliest of your birthday greetings and this year even whilst you are reading these words, I shall be awake, sad, thinking of you, with many earnest and loving longings that all good gifts and best blessings may come to you in this year of your life upon which you are now entering. Today let us leave the things that are behind us whilst we just press forward to the mark of our high calling. If you care to have bestowed upon you ALL the gifts which my heart desires for you, how rich & happy you would be, but latterly I have been learning, what in the past I have perhaps failed to realise. It is this that even the truest love oftimes makes mistakes as to those gifts, which in its shortsightedness it thinks would prove the truest blessing and happiness to its loved ones. So Mac dear, my heart's desire for you today is, that the future may have in store for you . . . whether it be by sunshine or clouds, whatever may develop the highest, the noblest, the best of which your nature is capable.

> Convinced with the Fabians that social and economic reform could be achieved through the Liberal Party, he managed to get himself adopted as a candidate in the forthcoming general election.

> Newspaper cutting, 5 August 1892

Mr J.R. MacDONALD TO CONTEST DOVER.
— Mr. Gladstone's small majority is likely to lead to immediate activity in the country to prepare for the next election. The Dover Progressive party

has approached Mr James R. Macdonald, who, as many readers will be aware, hails from Lossiemouth, with a view to his contesting that borough. We understand Mr Macdonald's reply has been favourable, and he will therefore be the first candidate in the field for the coming struggle. Dover seems to be hopelessly Tory, but Mr Macdonald can be trusted to handle a hostile majority. Already we believe he is at work on the platform. The present member is the famous Mr George Wyndham, private secretary to Mr Balfour.

> His attempts to 'arouse the labouring classes of Dover to a Knowledge of their power' were not altogether successful, but he had other irons in the fire.

> Newspaper cutting, November 1892

There is another Richmond in the field in East Aberdeenshire. His name is J. R. MacDonald. He is a native of Lossiemouth, has seen 26 summers, and is described as a London journalist. Mr MacDonald represents Scottish Home Rule, and has laid his views before the inhabitants of Fraserburgh. Like his parents, he was an agricultural labourer at one time, but he had his ambitions, and became a newspaper man. About himself, he remarks:- "I am afraid that I am a rather hum-drum personality. In pushing my way through this dear, flinty-hearted world I have always had to rely upon myself. But I look out upon things with the philosophic calm of a bachelor possessed of a room's furniture."

> Nothing came of his Scottish Home Rule enterprise. On 4 February 1893 his grandmother died.

〰 Jessie Ramsay to her aunt, Annie Ramsay.

7 February 1893

My Dear Aunt Annie

I have received the sad news today Monday of poor Grannie's death. It is a great shock to me even though it was a thing expected . . . you were a good and dutiful nurse night and day for years . . . I am wondering how Jamie Macdonald[1] is keeping. Was he able to come to see you perhaps it would not be easy but I know he would come if he could.

> Just a few weeks before his grandmother's death the Independent Labour Party was born in Bradford. Ramsay was still going along with

---

1. Ramsay was always called Jamie by the family until he married.

the Liberals, but after being turned down as Lib-Lab candidate for Southampton he decided to join the new party.

∾ Ramsay to Keir Hardie (the first protagonist of the ILP)

15 July 1894

I am now making personal application for membership of the ILP. I have stuck to the Liberals up to now . . . Attercliffe [1] came as a rude awakening.

> Lord Elton, *James Ramsay MacDonald*,
> (London, 1939).

On 17 July he launched his campaign as ILP candidate for Southampton with a great open-air meeting. He tried to establish a branch of the Labour Church there. The Labour Church movement was a branch of Ethical Socialism, designed to protect the movement from the moral hazards of politics. Congregations sang specially written hymns and listened to lay preachers who exhorted them to progress and good works.

> 20 Duncan Buildings
> Baldwin Gardens E.C.
> 4 October 1894

My Dear Scullard [his agent in Southampton]

I hope you are having successful meetings with Miss Stacey [Enid] today. She seems to have a bad cold and her voice is rather husky but nevertheless I hope she will manage to stir you up.

By this post I am sending you the Labour Church Hymn Book. It was compiled for a double Constituency Christian Socialist and Ethical Socialist, but oddly enough the Christian hymns are very rarely sung. In Southampton they need never be. I have marked those that seem to be the favourites. Before deciding upon anything formal let us first of all understand what we want to do. My idea is to get women and families to our meetings and to keep the ethical side of the movement well to the front. When Trevor[2] came to me some years ago to discuss his idea of a Labour Church I was strongly opposed to the use of such expressions as "God is our King": "God is in the Labour Movement". There is a suggestion of impudent vulgarity in these expressions which is very distasteful to me; and when I found that he insisted on keeping them, I gave him no help with his

---

1. A Sheffield by-election at which the Liberal Association refused to adopt the Labour candidate.
2. John Trevor, founder of the Labour Church.

movement in its initial stages and I have but rarely spoken from his platform. At the same time I was convinced that he had hold of a good idea. That idea we can work out in Southampton in our own way. We can say for instance:—

1. We believe that the social condition of the people must be changed before we can hope for any improvement in individual or national morality; and we believe that in this respect the over-fed and luxurious rich is in as evil a condition as the starved and pinched poor.

2. We believe that the methods of competitive industry leading to sweating, adulteration, unjust weight, and ruining the honest man can have no sanction in moral law.

3. We believe that wealth is now distributed not according to individual merit nor social advantage but according to a man's success in acquiring monopolies and in underhand dealing.

4. We therefore believe that immediate steps must be taken to radically reform existing economic conditions, so that the bounty of nature may be enjoyed by all who contribute by brain or hand to social well-being.

5. And further we believe that it is necessary to constantly keep the ethical and ideal side of the movement before the public so that character may be improved and the human material with which we have to work be of a higher degree.

Such a creed would give us a practical working basis and formed into a wing of our movement naturally suggests music, singing, exhortative readings and short discourses. The start is the difficulty. We should require at least something like £5 to begin with, as we ought to proceed as follows with expenses:—

1. Hall
2. Posters, fairly big — stuck on hoardings
3. Railway fares of speakers
4. Music — no outlay if possible

Our income would consist of:—

1. Collections
2. Sale of literature
3. Members might be made and subscriptions taken from them

If you found that you could get over the preliminary difficulties I should be very pleased to go down and give the first address, unless we could manage to get someone else who would take a good audience. No time to write further. Hope you will keep the committee up to scratch. Things will go much smoother once we start. Hope Mrs Scullard is well again.

Yours always sincerely
J Ramsay MacDonald

The Miss Stacey referred to in this letter seems to have been rather more to Ramsay's taste than Mary Gwyther. Ramsay first met her at Attercliffe, and she helped him in the Southampton contest. She was a powerful speaker and a strong personality, but she was rather a snob and does not seem to have entertained any romantic notions about him. She married Percy Widdrington, but remained a close friend of MacDonald.

Newspaper cutting [1893]

The I.L.P. at Sandiacre and Stapleford, although they did not meet with much success at the recent Parish Council elections, do not appear to be at all discouraged. On the contary, they have been again in evidence this week, having been instrumental in bringing to Stapleford Miss Enid Stacey, who gave an address on "Modern Shams," in the Baptist Schoolroom on Wednesday night. The audience was a large one, which could not fail to be gratifying to the promoters of the meeting. Those who went there expecting to see a tall, gaunt, much-spectacled female, could not fail to be agreeably disappointed. Miss Stacey is a good-looking *young* lady — with special stress on the *young* — who possesses a pleasing voice, and has a flow of language which is seldom vouchsafed even to those who are regarded as orators of no ordinary degree.

He wrote to her in the autumn of 1894:

The two things that spoil the voice are kissing and open air speaking. The former I have barely begun, the latter I am to stop.

MARGARET: THE SHELTERED GARDEN

Ramsay's son, Malcolm, wrote

My mother was born of very different stock. A daughter of an impeccably respectable, well-to-do and indeed quite distinguished pair of Victorian worthies living in the fashionable West End of London, her maiden name was Margaret Ethel Gladstone. Her father was an eminent professional member of the Royal Institution, her mother was closely related to the great scientist Lord Kelvin, and the family *were* distantly connected with the Grand Old Man. Nothing could be more proper than all that.

People and Places (London), 1969, p.15

Margaret's mother was the daughter of a wealthy, grim, depressed Presbyterian minister, Rev Dr David King. She married John Hall Gladstone, a scientific and religious widower with four small daughters, produced Margaret Ethel and promptly died. She thus had no influence over her daughter's upbringing, but if there is anything in heredity it is worth quoting some extracts from her letters and diaries.

Margaret King (a teenager) to her mother.

Belfast, 19 December 1864

The workers in some large mills are to have a ball on the 27th, no good for them I fear. One girl has spent £8 on a dress, to clog her with debt for many a weary day, and prevent her from assisting her perhaps starving family, or to lead her into dreadful temptation.

Margaret Gladstone's diary, 24 July 1869 (on her honeymoon) . . .

Before breakfast discussed somewhat heretically, total depravity, original sin etc.

෪ Margaret Gladstone to her mother.

17 Pembridge Square W
Monday August 2 1869

Dearest Mamma

I am very sorry that you should have been disappointed in the number of letters. I thought that three in the ten days when we were moving about so much and had to write to London too, would have satisfied you. I did write

THREE times, not only twice — from Perth, Blair Atholl, and Kenmore. And I earnestly hope you will not be disappointed with me after this though I cannot write so often as when away from home formerly in a visit of a month or two. You know I have a larger household than yours, in this much busier place, and far more people coming and going.

I got deep into the house-keeping on Saturday, inspecting with cook and Bynoe [the butler] their several dominions and going over the house from top to bottom with Anne the Housemaid and afterwards with Dr Gladstone and a man to arrange what papering, painting and renewing of blinds is to be done in our absence. In the afternoon I had to go around and pay all books, and be back in time to dine with Mr & Mrs Gladstone [her parents-in-law] at 5.

Today continuation of housekeeping, laying out of new garden, going over with man the house we have taken, in which I am to have a pretty sitting room for my class, John's laboratory premises, (very good) and 9 rooms are to be let besides kitchen etc.; choosing paper for all these; in town with John on business, several visitors, a great deal of packing and the day is gone. I was very sorry [to upset you] . . .

    Same to same.

September 21 1869

It seems to me a very long time since I was married; there has been so much variety. First, our ten days in Perthshire, then a little longer visit to Annaghmore as married daughter; and four or five days in London, during which I made a great dive into the housekeeping and took full possession of my new dominions. There was unusually much to do at the time for a general survey had to be made and some direction given about painting & cleaning in our absence; and the necessity of taking at once a good deal upon myself made me quite brave. Then we took all the children [her four step-daughters] with us & the nurse (a thoroughly good and judicious young woman, who has had an excellent influence over them) and spent 10 days at Ilfracombe, a fortnight at Exeter and a few days more at Westward Ho, besides shorter visits to Torquay & other places. We returned home in the beginning of September as my husband had promised to meet his boys on Sunday the 5th, but after that he & I had a run to Clifton to stay with friends during the conference of the Y.M.C.A. in which he takes great interest. So we have had a little of everything except visitors staying with us. And now all home arrangements, the children's lessons, housekeeping etc., are getting into regular order, very satisfactorily. A good deal of my time is just now taken up with receiving calls; also with shopping, choosing winter dress in which I specially miss Mamma. It feels strange going to the familiar shops now with my own carriage, and walking in all alone. Choosing too without advice, but so far, I think, tolerably successfully.

Few new mothers & mistresses find things so smooth and bright as all is for me. The servants one & all are good and thorough & obliging & not only allow, but like me to look into everything, and take my own way, which is wonderfully little different from previous arrangements. The children have all accepted me warmly and lovingly; they fully expect me to arrange things and decide everything about their lessons, dress, and all that they may or may not have and do; and are always happy and satisfied. I don't think the little girls could well give less trouble. They are very kind and thoughtful in many little ways; for instance one Sun. at Exeter when I was very tired they took the greatest care of me. All this might seem somewhat unreal or overdrawn in a book but it is less than the truth. I ought to be and am very happy & thankful.

How different was her life from Annie Ramsay's! And how different her experience of childbirth!

Diary of Margaret Gladstone,
31 December 1869

. . .after the clock struck we wished one another all good wishes and talked of the unknown year before us and what it might bring, and how I might die at the baby's birth and yet all will be well. And I felt I could leave even this intense and overflowing happiness on earth to be with Jesus. Only I would not like to leave J[ohn] sad and alone.

The baby was born on 20 July and named Margaret Ethel. It was a long, painful labour. The child was very big — and Mrs Gladstone was soon seriously ill.

Diary of Elizabeth King, Margaret Gladstone's mother . . .

August 1870

After breakfast John said to her "I think, My love, God is going to take you to himself". She said "Do you?" and after a moment added "I think today", when after lying still a little she said "Bring Baby, Mamma" When I came back with the little thing she looked to her "John you dedicate our baby to God — be short — bring in the children all" . . . John said "Will you shake hands with the servants?" She assented with a slight nod but said she could not speak to them. They were all brought in. There was a great company in the room. John said "Will you shake hands with them?" She said "Yes" and named Bynoe so he came first then she said "Cook" and cook came. The wet-nurse caught her attention by sobbing and never having heard of her or seen her, she looked enquiringly at John; He said "This is Baby's nurse". At this she tried to raise herself and with much earnestness "Do the best you can for Baby — in God's name". They said "We will" and left the room . . . Two or three days before the last she looked at clothes for baby, who was brought in with a cloak and bonnet on. She looked at her & said she thought it would grow up to be a beautiful woman. She said she liked her names Margaret Ethel Gladstone. They went well together.

John stood at her pillow and I was beside her on the bed till almost at the end she motioned me off and crossed her hands on her breast and so passed gently away.

Margaret Hawes, a family friend, remembered Margaret Gladstone.

19 April 1912

. . . a very strong, purposeful and at the same time, very sweet character. She was full of an earnest desire to help all who came within her reach, and especially her younger girl friends, whom she gathered round her every Sunday, after her marriage, for Bible readings. These readings were very clever and well thought out studies, but always helpful to the girls and inspiring and encouraging them.

She was very clever, a good linguist and I believe, a great companion and help to her father in his failing health. Margaret often used to remind me of her mother in her strong, fearless outlook on life and its many difficulties, and in her unswerving determination to do what she considered right at all costs.

I wish I could have given you a more vivid picture but after more than forty years it is not easy to recall details.

I was a very devoted admirer of hers, I can certainly testify to the wonderful influence she had. The steadfastness of her own faith was so marked it just compelled belief with her and left no room for vague doubts as to right and wrong.

John Hall Gladstone was left to bring up five little girls without the help of a wife. He was a very nice man — enlightened, rational, cheerful, selfless and lovable. He was deeply religious and it was his intention to enter the Church, but he was persuaded by his first father-in-law, Charles Tilt, to pursue the career in chemistry for which he had trained. On Tilt's death he became a rich man and gave up his lectureship at St Thomas's (though not chemistry) and spent more and more time in religious and social work: he and his second wife would entertain as many as sixty of their Sunday school boys to supper at a time. He was one of the founders of the YMCA and was on the Chelsea division of the School Board. According to Ramsay 'happiness always beamed from a face which to the end never lost its look of boyish openess and serenity.[1] In later years his son-in-law Ramsay MacDonald wrote the account of his life for the *Dictionary of National Biography*.

Gladstone was one of the founders of the new science of physical chemistry. A long series of papers — Professor Tilden estimates them at 140 by himself alone, and seventy-eight in collaboration — contributed to various learned societies through life — contains the record of his researches.

As a reformer and promoter of education Gladstone holds high rank. He was a pioneer of technical education and manual instruction, and was one of the earliest advocates of the introduction of science into elementary schools. From 1873 to 1894 he was on the London School Board, being vice-chairman from 1888 to 1891. In 1868 he contested the parliamentary representation of York as a Liberal, but was unsuccessful, and though he was frequently requested to stand for other constituencies, his membership of the school board remained his only public office.

Gladstone was active in philanthropic and charitable work, and keenly interested in Christian endeavour, organizing devotional meetings and Bible classes among educated men and women. He was the president of the Christian Evidence Society.

Margaret grew up in her father's house in Bayswater. 17[2] Pembridge Square with her four elder half-sisters, Florence, Elizabeth (Bessie), Isabella and Mary. They were looked after by Mrs Gray, the widow of a homeopathic doctor, their father's housekeeper. Margaret's holidays were spent with her mother's relatives in Scotland and after her grandmother, Elizabeth King, moved to London, Saturday afternoons

1. JRM, *Margaret Ethel MacDonald*, p.9.
2. Changed to No. 20 in 1938.

were spent in her house in Hamilton Terrace. She was close to her
father, and travelled extensively abroad with him. Ramsay wrote
years later:

Her father, one of the kindest and courtliest of men, gave her freedom to act
and think as her mind desired, and to the end never chided or blamed her
for following truth as she saw it. From him she received an inheritance of
moral directness, and ability to look at things as they are, a rare faculty of
belief in the verities, and an incapacity to elevate an excuse into a
justification. She never struggled with her reason to attain these virtues;
they were axioms of her soul. The household at Pembridge Square belonged
to a type now vanishing, where wealth, intellectual distinction and
liberality of thought mingled together, and humility reigned over all.

Margaret Ethel MacDonald, p.4.

Isabella had her own account of their childhood published after
Margaret's death . . .

The house in Pembridge Square was described by Ramsay MacDonald, but
it must be remembered that what then appeared luxury to him would not
appear in the same light to all our friends. . . The gap between Bessie and
me was three and a quarter years . . . which resulted in her coming in for a
good many interesting experiences in which I did not share. But I had, later
on, more of the things I liked, — the gymnasium, the dancing class, the
swimming bath and the pony, besides after-tea games in the Square garden.
Our horses must have known their way to Albemarle St. [John Gladstone
became a Fellow of the Royal Institution at the age of twenty-six.] . . . We
used to pick wild roses where the White City now stands. . . Hot water
bottles were unknown to us . . . we had no cream or porridge or fruit for
breakfast and no milk between meals. A fire in the bedroom would have
been considered an unthinkable luxury . . . Mrs Gray did not care to see
children on easy chairs, still less on a sofa, and we had no eiderdown quilts
on our beds or warm drinks at night . . . Dances and theatre going were not
encouraged . . . The greenhouse, a solid structure which led from the
drawing-room to the garden, was called the 'Museum', and as children we
kept sea anemones there, along with the Buhl cabinets with curios in them,
many of which were brought from Egypt by the Tilt family in 1846. There
were eight servants, seven in the house and a coachman. For 39 years the
family had a black butler, Bynoe.

I. Holmes, *The Girlhood of Mrs. Ramsay MacDonald*, pp. 6–10.

As the motherless youngest child of the family, Margaret Ethel was fêted and coddled; every step she took and every word she learnt was greeted with delight by her adoring grandmother and father. Perhaps her eldest half-sister, Florence, was the closest to her.

∾ Meg (aged eight) to Florence Gladstone.

Warwick House[1]
24 July 1878

Thank you for your letter and please thank the others especially the book from Papa and Bella as well. Here I got a good many presents too:— A Devonshire vase from Grandpapa and a mother o' pearl box that belonged to my mama from grandmama with ninepence in it, a very tiny tumbler from Aunt Elizabeth, a little doll's cradle from Aunt Agnes and a card from Miss Wickham at the vicarage.

When I came down to breakfast in the morning I found a lot of flowers around my plate from the vicarage that Mrs Wickham had picked for me and flowers in my vases.

There is such a nice little black kitten here, she and Don Pedro have such fun together sometimes when Don Pedro is out of his cage. Don Pedro pecks pussy without hurting her and pussy pats Don Pedro.

Aunt Elizabeth [her mother's sister] is painting a little baby donkey that you may have heard about from May because I wrote to her about it when I wrote to her last week.

Margaret shared a governess with Bessie, Bella and May; she then went to Doreck College in Bayswater, where she was an extremely apt pupil. Home was full of religion and learning . . .

MEG Diary (aged 14)[2]
14 June 1885

Got up; talking; doing Scripture answers to *Our Own Magazine*; reading *In His Golden Shell*; out with B. to St. Mary Abbot's, very crowded; out again in middle of service to St. Paul's, Vicarage Gardens; Hospital Sunday; walk in gardens; home; did plants, etc; dinner; talking; did Scripture for O.O.M.; talking to children; up to F.'s class; sweets and talking; tea in the garden; Uncle James T.[homson][1] came for visit; watching him at tea; talking up in the morning-room; all out but F.; did Scripture answers for O.O.M.; learning new texts for school; up to bed.

---

1. Margaret was staying with her mother's family.
2. Quoted in *Margaret Ethel MacDonald*, p.21.

There were holidays in Scotland and on the Continent. Her first journal was started in Switzerland when she was sixteen.

"I do like being abroad," she writes on its very first page. Everything is fresh to her. She is free. The fascination of the unregulated, rough life of simple nature steals upon her. "Our guide dealt round the bread to us, cutting slices of it with his clasp-knife, and we put the slices of the meat on the top of the bread, eating them together. It was very absurd and certainly not at all elegant, but it was great fun for a change, and we all enjoyed it."

That is often written and far more often felt by the schoolgirl on holiday. But it was more to her than a passing thrill. It was one of many experiences which led her back to the maternal lap of the simple and the natural where she found strength and repose all her life.

Margaret Ethel MacDonald, p.24

All the family were involved in running the Latymer Road Mission, set up by the Gladstones to service the poor of west London. But for Margaret there were no serious stirrings of social conscience yet.

ᔐ Margaret (aged seventeen) to Aunt Elizabeth King (from Manchester).

5 September 1887

I do not like the streets . . . there are such numbers of dirty ragged little he and she street arabs begging and bothering one along the street.

Ramsay concluded:

The picture which she has left of herself when she was still attending school at the Doreck College, Bayswater (a private school for young ladies) was that of a somewhat serious young person, rich in friends, methodical in habits, clever at work, a shrine of early piety, who was enjoying life. And the photographs of her as she was then are of a bright-eyed, chubby-faced maiden, alert and interested. The garden where she was nourished was very sheltered and very sunny, and she grew up where "falls nor hail nor snow, nor any wind blows loudly".

Margaret Ethel MacDonald, 22.

For her eighteenth birthday her father gave her a copy of Goethe's works. She spent time in the local church, St Mary Abbots, where she taught a Sunday school class, arranged flowers and worshipped. She went regularly to the Mission in Latymer Road to help in the soup kitchen. In the autumn of 1888 she accompanied John Gladstone on a trip to Denmark and Sweden, where they attended a YMCA conference, and was amused by what she saw.

∽ Margaret's diary.[1]

The less men understood each other, the more they smiled and embraced. It was most comic the way they all gushed at each other; every one felt so affectionate when all were united there for the same cause and with the same aims. One Swede excused himself for speaking to M. without introduction, as we all expected to meet in heaven and were making acquaintance on earth first . . . The gentlemen were fond of sitting hand-in-hand . . . Before we left, Mr. Schlumbach, a big German who had been an American cowboy, proposed a cordial vote of thanks to our host and hostess; we had prayers and addresses from a Swedish pastor, Mr. Barde (our Swiss friend), etc.; papa prayed in English; the students sang some songs, ending with an evening hymn in which one of them, a tall pastor, sang the tenor solo, the others joining in with a low accompaniment. By this time it was quite dark and the large full moon was shining.

> Science intrigued and inspired her, which was not surprising, surrounded and loved as she was by chemists, engineers and physicists. She spent a great deal of time with her father. Two great-uncles on her mother's side claimed some of her time: Professor James Thomson in Glasgow and his even more esteemed brother, the star of the family, William, Lord Kelvin.

∽ Margaret to Aunt Elizabeth.

16 June 1889

There was a delightful lecture at the Royal Institution on Friday evening, with such splendid experiments . . . The subject was quartz fibres.

> She was a serious, inquisitive girl, but full of life and laughter.

∽ Margaret's diary.

1892

From Edinburgh August '92. Uncle and Flo and I went to Dunfermline where there is a nice old church & ruined palace, but a perfect monstrosity of a church tower, with a balustrade at the top composed of the four words

---

1. Quoted in *Margaret Ethel MacDonald*, pp. 26–27.

KING ROBERT THE BRUCE one on each side in such plain letters that they can be seen from the whole neighbourhood around. Bruce is buried there, but that is no reason why they should advertise him like Pears Soap.

Monday November 4   Papa, Flo, and I went to a most interesting meeting. Representatives of different religions were invited to give an account of theirs. Mr Hoare a clergyman from Keswick spoke excellently on Christianity. Next came a Mahommedan who was most happy apparently for he said the Koran said that anyone who believed in one God would go to heaven & as there was hardly anyone who did not believe in one God he thought we should go to heaven. Then there were Hindus and a Brahmin a Christian Hindu and a Parsee. All equally interesting.

October 22   I sent off a long letter to my great Uncle Robert Thomson in Australia; he went out there as a young man and has never been back since, so I think he must feel out of things; he seems to have been much affected by Uncle James' death [Professor James Thomson]. I thought that I should like to write to him as I have seen so many of the family lately.

October 12   I had an experience which I shall remember all my life. I went to Tennyson's funeral in Westminster Abbey. Papa and May went with tickets but I waited for about 2 hours in the crowd outside and got in at the public entrance. There was a tremendous squash of people, and altogether the service was most impressive and beautiful. A very distinguished and representative set of men were gathered there and twelve were pall-bearers including Uncle William [Lord Kelvin].

> She liked men. Lily Montagu, daughter of Sir Samuel, a close friend who she first met at Doreck College . . .

. . . always wondered at her happiness — for she was motherless — but I know that she did nevertheless live in an atmosphere of affection . . . She was rather different from girls of her set, because whether she spoke to man or woman made not the slightest scrap of difference. She was not self conscious during her intercourse with men, and that is why she became a 'man's friend'.

> L. Herbert, *Ramsay MacDonald*, 9.

> There were at least four suitors; all were cousins;[1] all were disappointed.

---

1. Three of them were Andrew Henderson, James Thomson and Joshua Gladstone.

Once her formal education was finished she found passing the time being a lady irksome, and dreamed of an outrageous romance and a cause to fight for.

Margaret's diary (at the age of twenty-three). . .

13 June 1893

Sudden inspiration to write again in my journal caused by going upstairs to look for something quite different and coming across the first volume. The 'me' of that time seems such a different person from the 'me' of this time — a good deal nicer . . . but rather painfully self satisfied and apt to think everything that happened to herself of great importance. Now I don't feel interested in anything sufficiently to write long descriptions of it as I did in those days; I think every day I get lazier and less inclined to exhibition, and yet at the same time there is the restless feeling and the desire to stride out into something special. I think some day I shall fall in love with somebody that no-one approves of, including my own better self, and go to the bad. Now isn't that a horrid way to talk of what should be next to religion. The highest and best of things in a person's life! . . . I suppose I really was rather upset last June[1] . . . I think those were the most wretched days I ever spent, wretched in a worse way than all the upset afterwards about the doctoring; then came the relief just by a friendly note — well anyhow I have never been quite the same since, and it is a good thing I have not though personally I have been more disagreeable and more shut up in myself. Never mind I shall soon fall in love with that unsatisfactory man and then I shall be exceedingly unselfish and agreeable towards him . . . after June I felt very aimless and very anxious and had to have an aim . . . the Sunday after I returned from Glasgow . . . during evening service . . . it flashed into my mind that doctoring would be the most useful thing for me to do. The very next morning I went off to see about it . . . I gradually propounded my ideas to my family and a few friends . . . I hated it at the time but I am glad I did do it for I can say I was in earnest once in my life at any rate, (as I hope to be again when that unsatisfactory man comes along) . . . felt I was pottering round and frittering away my time . . . I wanted to have my work to go to in the morning and stick at all day like men or women who have to earn their living . . . I hated the comparative ease and luxury in which we live when compared with the many good things which only need a little money and attention to get them going. Yet I did not feel it

---

1. By a romantic entanglement with a cousin.

33

right to leave home and its comforts at present and did not know what to do if I should. Now doctoring seemed to me work suited for women . . . I thought probably I should set up in the slums . . . and I should be able to use the influence I got professionally for moral influence . . . I should have lived at home while studying, and been able to smile upon my family at mealtimes etc without having to go out to parties and things which I disliked . . . I had visions of a charming lady doctor speaking on platforms about religious and social questions which really in her heart of hearts she cared more about than the doctoring and I thought she could take the religious and philanthropic side, while her other interests would keep her from rushing off into all sorts of vague and wicked 'isms' . . . Seeing however that these visions were over ruled who is to blame the said charming lady if she does fling out into the said 'isms', though at present she is very good and quiet, and visits and teaches the poor in the most orthodox, and shall we say, in her case, slightly hypocritical manner . . . Perhaps one day my daughter shall be a doctor[1] . . . my children are really going to be very nice[2] . . . unless they unfortunately take after that unsatisfactory Papa who looms in the future . . . My chief idea at present . . . is to get a big trades-union and place of general mutual help, recreation and self improvement among working girls. I don't think I take to girls though, and I am too young to do the same for boys. What a lot of splendid women are at work, and how they are overcoming prejudice and distrust.

The royal wedding did not accord with a young woman's dream of love.

    Margaret's diary.

26 July 1893

London was in a hubbub at the beginning of the month. I felt very depressed, not full of joy about the wedding;[3] it was so very un-ideal, whatever the truth about it was; to marry the brother of your betrothed, less than 18 months after his death, and with such pomp and ceremony and fuss — a horrid example to the nation. I think, making marriage such a matter of convenience and social position. I should think it will hasten the banishment of royalty from the scene in England.

---

1. Her daughter Joan became a doctor.
2. They were.
3. The future George V married Princess May of Teck.

She began to consider socialism as a practical way of alleviating the suffering she saw around her.

∽ Margaret's diary.

Ste. Croix, Switzerland,
15 August 1893

. . . I am more amiable inside me than I have been for long . . . I have been going through the Fabian essays on Socialism . . . and they have given me . . . more hopeful views about socialism and the way to carry out better the love of the brotherhood and sisterhood . . .

We went . . . to . . . the meeting of the French association of science. We had various dinner parties . . . One day the healths of May [her half-sister] and myself were coupled with our future 'maris', who are to be chemists like our esteemed Papa . . .

M. Henrioud[1] and I started off at 6 a.m. for the Chasserons, the highest point in the Swiss Jura . . . M. Henrioud was telling me about the French soldiers who passed through here after giving up their arms at Pontarlier in 1870 — how ill, and cold, and wretched they were . . . He went on to say the Socialist Congress had just been meeting at Zurich, and that he thought socialism would put a stop to war; the poor suffer by it, and when they realise that they will say they will not have it, and it will be impossible. There are good things in socialism and that is one. On the other hand M. Borman, our entertainer this morning, who is a Plymouth Brother, thinks that the end of the world is near, and that the times are very evil — there are so many socialist clubs etc.

∽ Margaret's diary.

29 September 1893

I have had this afternoon a strong over-rush (is that intelligible English?) of depressed and fancied feelings about the ills of life; not my own life, but the life of other people in general. I had been visiting some of the poor people . . . and it seemed to me perfectly awful that Christian people and other good people should know of it and go on spending money on luxuries for themselves . . . Then my old friend Mrs Cowdrey said I deserved all the nice things I saw and did; when they talk like that I feel inclined to turn round almost fiercely and ask whether they think we rich people are made

---

1. Pastor at Ste Croix, the husband of a Swiss friend of Margaret's.

of different stuff from themselves that a little kindness in us should go such a long way. That really is part of the secret though; the rich think themselves of different stuff; it is kind of them to give the tiniest share of their fortune to those less fortunate, a special virtue in giving a sixpence or a ten minutes' visit to a poor person which there is not in the giving of a £6.6 present or an hour's call to a rich person; and the poor share in the delusion. But the poor are waking up to the fact that this magic gulf between them is rather imaginary, and unless the rich wake up to it too we shall have a rumpus. There is a rumpus going on at present in the shape of a big coal strike; '20,000 women and children starving' on the placards today.

Some day I shall fall in love with somebody that no-one approves of . . .

CHAPTER 2

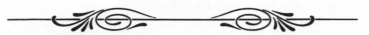

1895
The urchin and the lady

In the spring of 1895 Ramsay was twenty-eight and committed body and soul to the Labour cause. He was already well enough known on the political scene to be commanding large audiences all over the country, and was fighting for his own parliamentary seat in South-ampton. He campaigned by day and wrote stories and articles by night to earn enough to eat, pay his rent and send some money home to Lossiemouth. But, driven and exhausted, this fiery, lonely man was subject to bouts of illness and despair, and the beautiful Enid Stacey was not responding to his needs.

❧ Ramsay on desire.

But sweet desire creeps into our huts and takes its place in our chimney corners. It is blind and deaf when occasion requires. It challenges no one and accepts no one's challenges. It cannot be dislodged until it gets tired and decamps of its own will. There is nothing for the unfortunate victims of the latter except to allow their disease to work itself out in theirs. They cannot ever cure themselves.

JRM's novel.

❧ Ramsay to Enid Stacey.

from St. Thomas's Hospital
16 or 17 May 1895

I have acute Bright ['s disease].[1] Everything is up, I fear. If it becomes chronic I am dead in a month or two as it is uncurable; if it does not my life

---

1. A fatal kidney complaint; he did not have it.

will be a burden taking care of myself for a very long time . . . I am . . . rather sorry should all things end now.

Stacey Letters

Margaret Gladstone, the Kensington lady, was twenty-four and dreaming of a knight with a shining soul, a social conscience and a white charger.

∾ Margaret's diary.

19 November 1893

I wonder whether I shall meet him in this world. I mean him, my sir, my knight. I believe that each of us will meet our him or our her in some world; it may be a mistake, but if love lasts on to another world for those whose souls are married here, can we believe that GOD leaves some souls always unmarried? In all reverence I wonder why we know nothing about Jesus Christ's love for woman. I say love for woman in the singular, for of His love for women we do read, and it was chivalrous and good. I know my wonder would seem to most very uncalled for; yet He is the type of perfect manhood, sympathising with all our feelings; how can He then have been without the most sublime and most holy of all feelings towards a fellow creature? . . . When shall I have personal experience of it? . . . I know the feeling of reverence for a man . . . to them I owe many of the best impulses of my life. To one of them I owe it that I got over the foolish flirty feelings of a girl, excited over any man . . . But that is not the same as mutual love; GOD thou hast not given me thy best gift . . .

She had not met the handsome young agitator when she decided to support his cause, but she had seen him. And she had heard his thunderous rousing voice.

∾ Ramsay wrote later:

When I was candidate for Southampton in 1895, I was lying ill in St. Thomas's Hospital. One day a letter enclosing a subscription to my election fund came there with very kindly words accompanying it. The signature was "M.E. Gladstone."

Margaret Ethel MacDonald, 5.

∾ Mr MacDonald to Miss Gladstone (endorsed 'first letter').

Duncan Buildings
29 May 1895

Dear Madam,

I hardly know how to thank you for your very kind help at this moment. Unfortunately we members of the I.L.P. experience few of those generous encouragements — generous not only because of themselves but because of the kindly sympathy which they show. I appreciate your letter all the more that it is from "a stranger" and I would be very glad to believe that unknown to us there are many such as yourself watching our work with approval. It is exceedingly unfortunate that we have to oppose some with whom we ought really to be companions in arms, but I am sure it is the right thing at the moment.

From this chaos will come Cosmos.

I am glad to say that my health is improving and after ten more days of nursing, hope to be able to resume my ordinary ways.

Believe me to be,
Yours very gratefully
J.R. MacDonald

ꙮ Mr MacDonald to Miss Gladstone.

Southampton
Monday [June] 7
1895

Dear Miss Gladstone,

I am very happy to give you my opinions on the points you raise in your letter of the 6th inst. My being down here will show you that I am no longer idle and as I have come away without work, letter writing is a recreation.

I did not agree with Mann's advice to the locked out shoemakers and certainly would not have given it myself.[1] No doubt, as he explains to me, the condition of some of these people was heartrending, but although the heart is good for inspiration it is bad for guidance. Had the method of relief which he advised begun and ended in itself, I would support it. But it could not. It disturbed social order; and after all, however radical may be the changes which we desire & however strong maybe the feelings which prompt our desires, only in the most extreme cases and at a very hour are

---

1. Tom Mann was the secretary of the ILP; according to Ben Tillett, he 'oozed the energy of being'. Unlike Ramsay, he favoured industrial action rather than the Parliamentary way of achieving socialist ends. The National Union of Boot and Shoe Operatives was a militant union, resistant to technical changes in the industry. A general lock-out, which lasted five weeks, excited national interest.

we justified in laying violent hands upon the primary conditions of social existance. I fear that many of my friends, filled with the sense that we are only in revolt and in a minority and irresponsible for the maintenance of Society, are rarely inclined to take long and wide views of these considerations; but those who hold responsible positions in the Labour movement should not give advice which would weaken a sense of social responsibility in its larger issues, and which if it passed into current axioms of social conduct would place these leaders in an exceedingly awkward fix were they in a majority and in a position of national responsibility. My own desire is to see the socialist movement inspired and guided more by a feeling that it has an immediate future of responsibility before it, than that it is doomed to a guerilla warfare on the powers-that-be for generations to come. Holding these opinions, I disagree with Mann's advice believing that it was wise only in so far as the rustic was wise who killed the goose that laid the golden egg.

The personal aspect of that advice may however admit of a judgement on less austere principles. You cite your own case as one endowed with some of this world's goods, and I say without hesitation that had I a wife and children depending upon me — or even a wife alone — and I wanted work and could get none and we were starving, I would take that purse from you were I to meet you at the appropriate moment. Did my misfortune only apply to myself, I hardly think I would bother to steal, although I would not condemn anyone doing so who thought it was important that he should drag out his full tale of promised years. I make the distinction between public policy and private action because in the latter we have the consideration of individuality. An individual can — even must — recognise motive in action, a society can do no such thing, in existing conditions at any rate and except with reference to punishments. If at one street corner a professional thief stole your fur you would be justified in prosecuting him; if at the next a starving man steals your purse in despair, it might be your duty to add to the proceeds the spare coppers in your pocket. But both men are evil-doers in the eyes of society. I do not think however that it would have been wrong of you not to report the latter thief to the police because I do not think that, although if Society had his crime officially brought under its notice it was bound to prosecute, the crime until it was officially reported had any social significance.

Upon the matter of one's relationships to their family I can express no opinion of any general value. No one can. I was never faced with the problem myself and am perhaps the worse for having no positive family experience. I have been asked to advise several friends from time to time, but I have not always given the same advice. It is all a matter of circumstances. On the whole the best general advice is stay at home. Sooner or later nature brings freedom and if we are careful in the choice of our new servitudes — whether to opinions, causes, or persons — they should be but the conditions of ampler liberty.

It is just possible that I may be at the Pioneer Club on Thursday. I have had the date booked for sometime and if I find that some new work which I am starting here promises to go well, I will leave Southampton on Thursday morning. The Fabian Society is about to issue an appeal for funds to enable me to do some justice to the fight here, and attached to the appeal will be a preliminary list of subscribers. Would you object to having your subscription entered with your name thus:—

Miss Gladstone £1

It would give no clue to who or where you are, and in these Subscription lists there are many reasons why "a friend" or initials should not appear. But I will be glad to meet your wishes on the matter.

Now I am off for a drive through the New Forest.

It is convenient for a semi-invalid to have supporters who support carriages!

Yours truly
J.R. MacDonald

〜 Mr MacDonald to Miss Gladstone.

Southampton
10 June 1895

My Dear Miss Gladstone,

I have decided to fight[1] and it will be on the old register. I am sending up a volume to you as you kindly asked me. Would you mind addressing 2 sets of envelopes to MEN occupiers, service franchise and lodgers. The size of the envelopes should be such as will take that address folded once so as to save time and they should be thin and cheap. Would you tie them up in bundles, one complete street to a bundle, and address the parcel to Jno. H. Weber, 24 Oxford Road, Bevois Mount, S'ton. Also if you would not mind sending off the bundles as soon as you finish them that we may have work to go on with. We will be fearfully pressed for time and help, but will make a good show, I hope.

Yours very sincerely
J.R. MacDonald

---

1. He fought the Southampton constituency as ILP candidate.

❧ Ramsay to Enid Stacey.

[June 1895]

I am really anxious to get out of it [the Party]. Starvation is constantly staring me in the face. I occupy quite a false position as a candidate for Parliament for I ought really to be making bread and cheese, and I have made up my mind to retire whenever an opportunity presents itself after the election.

(Stacey Letters)

13 June 1895 Margaret went to the Pioneer Club and met Ramsay for the first time.

❧ Mr MacDonald to Miss Gladstone.

Duncan Buildings
14 June 1895

Dear Miss Gladstone.

It is very odd that the postman's knock announcing your letter should have disturbed me in the midst of a mental excursion amongst my friends undertaken for the purpose of finding someone who would do some writing for me. I do not know if you would care to do what I want, but at any rate I am much obliged to you for even thinking of offering to help in this way.

I want some canvass books made out from registers — a few being required at once. It only means copying names into pass books, and if you could do a few it would help me very much. Let me know as soon as you can and I will send you the register and books.

As to my method of campaign — I propose to be simply independent. Twelve months ago my chief supporters (then members of the Liberal party) went to the Liberal 350 and asked them to select a Labour Candidate as their second champion, and mentioned my name. I was still Liberal but just packing up my bed preparatory to walking . . . Nothwithstanding a strong pronouncement by Lord Roseberry [sic] the Liberal leaders tried to cheat us, my friends left the party, formed an I.L.P. and asked me to undertake the then quixotic task of being their candidate. Whilst matters were chaotic and I was holding meetings in the constituency to test the public feeling the candidate whom the Liberals selected withdrew refusing to fight us. We went on, and as I was very unwilling to fight, being heartily sick of squabbles, I offered the Liberals through my friend Mr Ellis, the whip, an opportunity of peace union if they would let matters rest for a time and then run a Labour candidate, not myself. Our negotiations did not go far, a second Liberal candidate was chosen who, when asked in public meeting whether he was a collectivist or individualist said he had never heard of the terms. Attercliffe [see p.22] came in and there was nothing for it but for me to take off my coat. In six months the Liberal candidate disappeared. During his time I never was aggressive and for the last six months (during which the field has been clear for me) I have been as mild as mild could be. Now the Liberals have appointed a committee to select another second candidate. There matters stand at this moment. My energies at this moment are directed mainly in building up our own party from both the others, and in winning sympathy within the Liberal ranks — amongst men who do not altogether agree with my estimate of the future of Liberalism. If the game is to get more complicated, the Liberals will be to blame . . . Candidly, I think it is rather inconsistent for me to help both Liberal and I.L.P. candidates, though several of the people upon whose help I rely for the final struggle are inconsistent in this respect. Several Liberal friends here and particularly at Oxford have promised to go down and work for me in Southampton during the Election. I hope that Prof. Stuart [the Liberal candidate] will be opposed in Hoxton. I have just convinced the Rev. Cartmel Robinson[1] that the I.L.P. is right, and he has joined it & is to start work in its favour amongst his folks at once. The London members are really among the least advanced in the House, and a clearance out would not be bad for the country — nor in the end for the Liberal party itself. John Burns[2] is their saviour and I may say that I do not at all agree with many of my I.L.P. friends about him. We are close friends & I respect him very much, evident faults not withstanding.

I shall be glad to hear from you about the canvass books.

> With many thanks for your offer
> I am
> Yours truly
> J.R. MacDonald

---

1. An ethical socialist who promoted the idea of a fellowship, linked to the socialist newspaper, the *Clarion* (see pp. 14-15) (18 June).
2 John Burns, a Liberal MP and former Social Democrat, regarded by the Fabians as a 'blustering demagogue'.

〰 Mr MacDonald to Miss Gladstone.

Duncan Buildings
16 June 1895

Dear Miss Gladstone

Thank you very much for undertaking canvass books. I am sending the sheets with this, and the books will follow tomorrow. This has been our system of making them up hitherto.

1. Two streets are not to be put in one book.
2. Name of street to be written on outside or if there are more books than one to a street, they must be marked I, II, etc.
3. If in the register any number of a street is omitted it should be put in the canvass book and left blank thus:—

No 2 John Brown

3

4

5 Thomas Smith

This would mean that 3 & 4 were not on the register last year and our canvassers make enquiries as to the reason. It also enables us to check the overseers list.

4. Give two lines to each number of a street — otherwise the canvasser has to crowd up his writing.

When you have finished half a dozen or so, would you kindly post them direct to:—

C.H.R. Crook

54 Howards Grove

Shirley

Southampton

and I would like if you would begin first with Chapel Street, Church Street, High Street, . . . Howards Grove, and Wellington Street. I am sending you the whole register for the district of Shirley but please do only what you conveniently can, & mark what you have done. Whatever is going down, should be in the hands of Crook not later than this day next month.

Gratefully yours
J.R. MacDonald

Duncan Buildings
18 June 1895

Dear Miss Gladstone

Thank you very much for yours with enclosure which I have just got. I only saw the Clarion last night and was annoyed to find that report in it.[1] What I said in my letter to our Secretary was that the P.O. I enclosed came from one who wished to remain anonymous but whose name suggested a relationship to the G.O.M. I am sorry that he should have taken it seriously, as at the time I had not a ghost of an idea who you were. I had not even heard of you.

I shall be only too grateful for any assistance you may be able to give me, but I should like to advise care on your part. I quite understand your position. I think God made some of us very poor that we may enjoy freedom; and we have been accustomed all our days to fight our way through the world, never spending largely without coming to our bottom dollar, and never by any possibility having friends so close to us that when we kicked we damaged them it is clearly upon us that the brunt of the fight has been place . . . Still, don't you bother too much about your inability to be an ideal Socialist, you know that passage in the Religio Medici, do you not, where it is said . . . that there will be many surprises on the day of judgment? Thomas[2] will say to many of us "I told you so". There are amongst us some who, life and health being granted to them, will make a great change in this weary world; and there are others outside of us who thought not *of* us are yet *by* us and give us just that mead of sympathy which makes it impossible for us to cry "peccavi" at the first onsets. After all, where is the possibility of any of us being ideal Socialists?

At this juncture no doubt political conviction is a precious but rare possession. But if you are at all interested in politics, don't give them up altogether.

And now the book! It is exactly what I want *only*:

1. It might be well to give three lines instead of two to each number and
2. Don't trouble to put in the register number. It is of no use for canvassing purposes. The Christian names will do as you have written them. Shirley is a mixed district. There are some very poor streets and some of the best residential quarters of S'ton included in the district. I am returning Chapel St. It had better go down with the rest.

I am very much stronger — in fact I don't like to think I have been ill at all, so well am I. I go down to S'ton next week, I hope for another campaign before retiring for a week or two into my native highland fastnesses to ruminate over some lectures I have to give in the Autumn.

Yours
J.R. MacDonald

---

1. MEG's 'anonymous' donation was mentioned in the *Clarion*, a socialist weekly paper started in 1891 by Robert Blatchford.
2. Sir Thomas Browne, the author of *Religio Medici*.

[c.20 June?] 1895

Dear Miss Gladstone

1. I am chairman of that Fabian Committee and from a hurried reading of your article it seems that you have got some valuable information on the drink traffic which I should be glad to have, if you would kindly sent it to me or our secretary.
2. I do not propose to spend any more money just now in writing out canvass books. When the new lists are out I shall then prepare my election books and would be very glad if you would help then. I shall also want addressed wrappers etc., but just now we are organising in the borough and I am spending all my spare cash on this address which I hope is to help me very much.
3. Nay! London is not to be honoured — unless I lecture in Spring at the new School of Political and Economic Science.
4. Yes, Crook[1] to acknowledge. Only for the sake of the cause don't address him as agent. He is secretary: to Socy: of Compositors and to Trade Council — a solid proud, sturdy honorary secretary to my Shirley Committee.

Yours in much haste
J.R. MacDonald

British Museum
23 June 1895

Dear Miss Gladstone

I am at a conference all day tomorrow, but could you come in on Monday at 5 p.m. There will be one or two lady friends having tea with me and I would be glad if you could join us. You will require to have no objections to having tea with me in "war paint" as I am dining out. We can talk about drink after the others go. Pemberton Gardens are in your direction, are they not? If you are going West, we might go together and that would give plenty of time for the talk.

Yours very truly
J.R. MacDonald

⮌ Margaret's diary.

24 June 1895

Tea at Mr MacDonald's. Miss Enid Stacey there!

1 July 1895

Doing up books for Mr MacD. leaving them at his rooms.

❧ To Miss Gladstone

3 July 1895
Postcard

List of Registers away has been mislaid. Would you kindly send me a list of what you have? . . . You will see I am opposed at the last moment by the Liberals. They have done it in a very dishonourable way but it will not help them except towards the bottom of the poll. Our men are fighting splendidly, but we are sadly deficient in women workers.

Gratefully yours
J.R.M.

Am up on Thursday for an hour or two to attend the Essex Hall Conference and will then get your papers.

❧ Margaret's diary.

11 July 1895

Lately. . . I have been advancing rather fast in the direction of the kind of social and socialistic work that I always want to do. So I had better chronicle some of it. We had exceptionally cold weather in February and March — water pipes frozen nearly all over London — people dying of cold etc. Personally I rather enjoyed it; I had a cold plunge every morning which warmed me for the rest of the day; but it was very awful to see the suffering it caused all around, especially of course to old people . . . I thought 'Why should GOD let this cold keep old people tossing at night with racking coughs, or little children get numb and despairing with no proper food and clothing?' . . . never had so much been given away in charity . . . only it's rather annoying to a socialist mind that people have to wait to be touched and to give of their fullness to others . . . I have been taking up more work in Schoolboard Country Holiday Fund etc. in Shoreditch; and also in the Women's Industrial Council,[1] which I am hoping will lead me on to some really useful work . . . I have also made friends with a member of the Independent Labour Party, Mr MacDonald, a friend of the Montagus. He is a Socialist and I think a very earnest one who is a good force in the

---

1. The Women's Industrial Council was set up in 1894 to work for legislation to alleviate the lot of women in industry. It was particularly concerned with 'sweating'.

movement so I have been helping him a little by writing work for his candidature for Southampton . . . I don't feel particularly interested in this election, I think if the Conservatives get in, that they, plus Joseph Chamberlain and with the House of Lords ready to do their bidding, will get on more quickly with social reforms than the Liberals have been doing . . . The Socialists won't make much show at this election . . . of course my offering to help Mr MacDonald raised the old questions which always bother me of how far I ought to do Socialist work while I live at home . . . I am very funny in the way I jog comfortably along with all these intensely interesting problems unsolved but I think it's a good thing not to bother too much but do the work that is nearest. I showed my father Mr MacDonald's election address and he said he had no objection to my working for him if I liked. I have made it an opportunity of telling rather more people my socialistic views, but then I feel such an old humbug to prate about them when I don't live them out. Of course it's a small matter that I have rather more of this world's material goods than is my share but all the same I think it makes it both important and inconsistent for me to pose as a socialist. A much more important matter is that I am so tremendously rich in friends and in being surrounded with love and goodness on all sides; only I'm afraid I should be an atheist if I weren't and I wonder how the people manage who always meet the harder colder side of life.

Meanwhile Ramsay was meeting the harder, colder side of life in Southampton.

Written on the back of Southampton candidate's Election letter . . .

1895

My Dear Mother

It is impossible for me to write. The Election is on tomorrow (Tuesday) week.

You will see the results in the Wednesday morning papers. Every hour of the day taken up.

We cannot win.

Your aff Son
J.R. MacDonald

∾ Arthur Newman to MEG.

11 July 1895, Hoxton

Dear Miss Gladstone,

I have just returned from helping J R MacDonald in Southampton in whose candidature I believe you are interested. From my observation I fancy the chances are very good if we can manage to send any help down in the next two or three days.

Do you know any socialist friends who could and would send a small subscription which is just now the first necessity. Excuse my troubling you but I was commissioned to raise what I could in the way of money, literature and helpers and send down at once — and my vicar told me that he knew you were interested in the cause.

> His campaign in Southampton was, as Lord Elton, his biographer, put it, 'the first round in a life long battle'. Although his election manifesto was bold and comprehensive, he was hounded by the SDF (the extreme Socialist body), for making no reference to Karl Marx. He was faced — in a two-member constituency with a formidable Liberal opposition — by the sitting MP, Sir Francis Evans, and a bona fide working man, the president of the local Trades Council, H.G. Wilson. The results were bitterly disappointing; the Conservatives won both seats, and Ramsay polled only 846 votes. He was one of 28 defeated ILP candidates.

Southampton
18 July 1895

Dear Miss Gladstone,

It was very kind of you to send these further subscriptions. You will have seen how badly we have done here. No one can quite understand it. The party ticket was voted quite solid, and the only explanation seems to be Hardie's[1] defeat at So: West Ham. At the last moment there was a strong rally round to the old parties. Our split votes with the other parties were very very few and the most of my 846 votes were given by voters who went for noone else. So far that is satisfactory, but still we are all very disappointed. The moral is that party is still very strong here.

I hope to see you in London sometime soon when I shall have the pleasure of thanking you personally for the kind assistance you have given me.

Yours very truly
J.R. MacDonald

Lossiemouth
23 July 1895

Dear Miss Gladstone

I am so sorry that I shall not be at home to receive you should you call. Your letter of the 18th has only just this moment found me on my return

---

1. Keir Hardie, the chairman of the ILP. His defeat was announced in *The Times* on 15 July.

from a game of golf. I do not expect to be in town again until September as I am quite run down and want rest badly. I suppose there is no chance of your coming up here during the summer, is there? It is a glorious place for talking politics (my fellow villagers are all keen politicians and are swearing at me for having knocked out a "Radigal") and for playing golf. But of course if you have to be content with an inferior place, I will not tempt you by describing the glories of 'mine own house'.

I fear Newman[1] has won your sympathies for Wilson, my opponent. A few more defeats like this and behaviour like that of the Labour Leader will send every self respecting man to strong drink and perdition, with old fashioned Sunday School teaching as a sort of purgatory between.

Thanks very much for enclosure S.D.F. did go for me. It was the one lightsome publication of a very serious election. They really meant no harm but they had been talking big for so many years that they could not stop now. They will do the same in heaven and we may find it a little awkward. I shall probably go on with Southampton but meanwhile will return to a neglected love — letter writing. I shall have a story in next month's 'Good Words' I think.

Yours sincerely
J.R. MacDonald

Newspaper cutting, July 1895

MR MACDONALD'S CANDIDATURE
To the Editor

SIR — I have no desire to raise a correspondence as to the merits or demerits of our late candidates, but as one who, for many years, has been a consistent Liberal, I trust you will allow me space to offer a few remarks respecting one of the rejected. I refer to Mr. MacDonald, whose candidature I have been conscientously compelled to support.

During the election, reports have been assiduously and scurrilously circulated that he is an irreligious and illiterate man, and my object now is to refute these base and untrue reports.

It will probably surprise many to hear that for three months previous to his campaign here he was conducting religious services and preaching the fatherhood of God and the brotherhood of man twice every Sunday, in connection with religious bodies at Ramsgate and Margate.

---

1. Arthur Newman, who worked for Ramsay in Southampton.

In addition to this he enjoys the personal friendship of such men and women as Professor Burrows, M.A., of Glasgow University, Mr. A.E. Fletcher of the "New Age", Mrs. Humphrey Ward, the authoress, Miss E. Stacey, B.A., and, I believe, Canons Gore and Shuttleworth, as well as many others well-known in the religious and educational world. It is also strikingly apparent to any ordinary intelligence that the noble and sincere band of Oxford University students would not have come down here to support an irreligious and illiterate man. No, Sir, the fact is that to a man of MacDonald's calibre the phrases "Thy will be done on earth as it is in heaven," "Bear ye one another's burdens," and "Love is the fulfilling of the law" are not the mere shibboleths they appear to be to the vast majority of church and chapel goers. Yet this is the man that the Liberals of Southampton have thought proper to place at the bottom of the poll, and by so doing have (as the *Daily Chronicle* aptly points out) sacrificed the seat of Sir Francis Evans.

> I am sir, yours faithfully,
> C.A. Woodland

> Lossiemouth
> 29 July 1895

Dear Miss Gladstone

I am so sorry that in my last I forgot to ask you to send me your stationery account. Would you please let me know what I am owing you.

The Labour Leader is Hardie's paper and so far as the I.L.P. has an official organ, the Leader is it.

We are having rather poor holiday weather here — rain and east winds. I can claim no connection with George MacDonald although he lays his scenes in these regions. The Marquis of Lossie[1] gets his name from our river.

Hoping to see you in September or October.

> I am
> yours very sincerely
> J.R. MacDonald

---

1. A novel by George MacDonald. The only peerage that tempted JRM in later years was a marquisate. According to his daughter Sheila, he had a fancy to call himself the Marquis of Lossie.

Lossiemouth
9 August 1895

Dear Miss Gladstone,

I do my best to keep up aloft but it is no good. I am a mundane minded man. Public houses still interest me, and I am always glad to see anything on the subject. The Fabian Society has a tract on half-timers on hand & I will use any information you may send me when I get the mss to look over.

I have only just got in my Returning Officer's bill and until I get all my accounts finally squared up, I cannot quite see how our Fund balances — so close have our income and expenditure been. When the matter is closed I will tell you what I did with the credit of one guinea which you put at my disposal a few days ago.

I quite envy you that complacency in which you talk of a voyage in a sailing ship. I love the sea, & when I make my pile as an Agitator & friend of man I shall build a palace on the coast & buy miles of barbed wire so that nobody may come & interrupt the long talks I can have with the curiosity-hunting waves. But I never see a boat without feeling sick — & I fear I never shall.

We are having a pretty good time here. Southampton seems to have put me off my golf but I potter around. Besides, there are a few socialists here on holiday and we are a Society within a Society — holding 'baccy' and golf balls in common, and standing mightily aloof from every visitor who does not wear a red tie. Still, would that I were within calling distance of London. I am getting tired up here and want to get back to work again. After all, one can be mad up here but in London people *live*.

I hope you are to have a good holiday. I cannot tell you how much I wish we had a good band of women like you? I mean good devoted souls — helping on Socialism. I suppose we must wait & I must meditate on the hope of the *is* rather than dream of the glory of *might be*. That's wise.

N.B. That story has not yet appeared. Its title is "Cupid in the Village".

Yours very sincerely
J.R. MacDonald

Duncan Buildings
2nd October 1895

Dear Miss Gladstone,

I shall be glad to see you here some afternoon soon — say Saturday if that would suit you. I ought to go to the Fabian meeting on Friday, but there is a Woman's Trade Union League Committee that evening & I ought to go there too or they will lop me off as a useless member. If you come on Saturday would you care to go to a socialist supper later on (6.30)? We are opening our new club and hope that Walter Crane [a socialist artist] will be chief guest.

Do you know anything of the working of the British Association? It has struck me that we might try and form a section of Political Science.

> Yours very sincerely
> J.R. MacDonald

∾ Margaret's diary.

5 October 1895

On bus in rain to Mr MacDonald's.

> Duncan Buildings
> 12 October 1895

Dear Miss Gladstone,

I thought that I might have been able to explain to you last night the enquiry you made in your letter regarding membership of the Socialist Club. You will, however, perhaps by now, receive a notification of your election from the secretary as the Committee met last night and elected you. Burrows[1] was mistaken. We only decided that membership of certain societies would settle the question as to whether applicants were socialists, we did not propose to limit our membership to members of these societies.

> Yours very sincerely
> J.R. MacDonald

∾ To Margaret.

> Telegram 19 October 1895
> Hatton Garden 6.1 p.m.

Could you meet me at Socialist Club Monday 11 morning Carmens strike committed.

> MacDonald

∾ Margaret's diary.

> Southampton
> 20 October 1895

Dear Miss Gladstone,

I fear that my paper was much too obscure, and if you are interested in

---

1. Herbert Burrows, an SDF founder member and an 'amateur' socialist.

the subject, will gladly hand over the MSS to you. Only, it is to be translated into German & published in a German magazine, the Editor of which happened to be present. So, it may be a week or so before I get it back.

We are all very busy here with Elections.

> Yours very sincerely
> J.R. MacDonald

❧ Margaret's Diary

25 October 1895

Tea at Socialist Club, Mr MacDonald lecturing to Fabian Society on Electoral Reform Discussion.

> Postcard
> The Socialist Club
> 15 November 1895

Dear Miss Gladstone,

Pray excuse my delay in answering your kind invitation for Monday: I have been terribly busy recently with many things. I would like to put in an appearance, although I always feel that the very thought of Eternal Life is a gruesome notion. One gets so tired of this life that I do not want to risk another, and I have no desire personally never to come to an end. One's happiest moments are when they are sleeping. So, I fear if I went to your meeting I would feel very wretched my self and if I took part in the conversation I would only be a discordant string that might cause pain to someone else.

> Yours very sincerely
> J.R. MacDonald

> Duncan Buildings
> 21 November 1895

Dear Miss Gladstone,

Thanks very much for the card of admission to the Annual meeting of the Women's Industrial Council. I will see that it is used, though as I am lecturing next night at Oxford on a rather abstruse side of Socialism and have to write a paper, I will be unable to be present myself. I am indeed very much filled up just now from making bread & cheese to reconstructing society. I have been lecturing every night during this and last week except Monday & I am off to Cambridge tomorrow.

I suppose it is that we are all overworked or rather over-worried that we are all in the blues, and that we would be very glad to desert our posts and shuffle off this mortal coil in the hope that there were no more of it. Understand I do not take the materialist view of the Universe at all. I call myself a Christian. As a reward I do not want a future life at all; as a mercy I hope God won't trouble me again. He has put certain impulses in me & I will try to be true to them; future life to me is, what I believe Christ taught, the resurrection of God in the race. Personally I do not want to go to heaven & I hope they will not send me to hell. I cannot form a conception of your idea of compensation without passing judgement on its immorality, so I cannot hold it. It is very pleasant to think of meeting one's dear friends again, but it is more pleasant to think of the end of Peace that is coming, and we can meanwhile enshrine the memories of friends so that they are always with us.

My one clear afternoon for some time is Saturday. Could you come here to tea at 4 p.m.

Yours very sincerely
J.R. MacDonald

Duncan Buildings
16 December 1895

Dear Miss Gladstone,

I am awfully busy just now as I suppose you can imagine, but I was in Liverpool last week, hence delay in acknowledging your kindness and these reports. Could you come to tea on Monday at 4 or thereabouts?

Yours—
J.R.M.

To Miss Gladstone

25 December 1895
New Inn, Winchelsea
Postcard

Would like to see the statement. Send to 20 D.B. where I shall be for a few hours on Thursday & Friday. Every good Christmas wish.

J.R.M.

Ramsay spent Christmas with Enid Stacey and her parents.

CHAPTER 3

January–July 1896
'Pleasant prospects'

For five months Margaret kept up the gentle pursuit, inviting Ramsay to lectures and going to visit him at Duncan Buildings as much as she could, involving herself with his political work and contacts and checking his manuscripts. By the end of May she had evidently decided to wait no longer for this proud, prickly and desperately shy man to make a move; she proposed to him on the steps of the British Museum. Much too reserved herself to admit any feelings of 'passionate worship', she seems to have suggested a union based on the practical considerations of shared ideals and common interests. Ramsay was terrified, and found himself too busy to see her.

But within a month or so they were engaged and gloriously in love.

Ramsay on love: the hero and heroine of his novel are far apart. . .

And the messengers of Love disturbed with all this commotion, fluttered about and became curious to find the other wounded one, and flew away over the snows and the long miles in an eye-twinkling. They found her in her room in the garret of the farm gazing upon a photograph that had been torn in four, and they were commissioned by these two hearts to bring messages from north to south. So for an hour they flew like light beams up and down; and lovers who see many things that other men and women cannot see, thought they saw the lightening wings of the couriers in the star and moonlight, thought they saw the flickering flash of love's messengers on the snows, and they clasped each other tightly, looked in each other's eyes and kissed, and said "All the world is love".

"My beloved" he said to her, "we shall build a palace of Beauty of our Love wherein all the world shall dwell".

❧ Margaret's diary.

1 January 1896

Received letter from Mr MacDonald.

❧ Mr MacDonald to Miss Gladstone.

1 January 1896
Duncan Buildings

Dear Miss Gladstone,

I am here to spend my new year's Day in a most unScottish (Ergo unholy) fashion. Never did London look so brutally English as this morning without a single holiday maker in its streets, and never did I feel so ashamed at having to work. One or two epistles however restore my mental equilibrium — yours for one . . .

I do hope that your 1896 is going to be a very prosperous year to you, and that in particular you are going to get more and more satisfaction out of your work. You are blessed in many ways and most of all in being given liberty to follow your own bent . . . in these days family tyranny can always be loosened by judicious pressure and wise conduct. I am so glad that worries of this kind do not trouble you. After all, what can be better work than to fulfil (sic) those obligations into which we were born, whilst we create an opinion that will revolutionise the nature of these obligations for the coming generation!

You may have heard that the Progressive Review[1] has been subscribed except £60 and that we have decided to publish on the 25th March. I am now head over ears in business, getting up the mysteries of printers' estimates and making myself versed in the Law of Company promoting . . . I wonder could you come and see me on Saturday afternoon at 4. Miss Grant,[2] whom I think you know is coming . . .

Again, all good wishes for the New Year.

Yours sincerely, Ramsay MacDonald.

I must be owing you a small fortune for postage etc. . . . .

---

1. The journal produced by the Rainbow Circle Club. Ramsay was the secretary (see p.111)
2. Miss Grant was the daughter of Baillie Grant, who taught at the established Church School at Lossiemouth. She was in service with the Montagus.

❧ Margaret's diary.

4 January 1896

Out to D Buildings. Miss Grant there . . .

❧ Mr MacDonald to Miss Gladstone

[?11 February 1896]
Portsmouth (train)

Could you do article for the PROg: Review on Municipal Gas showing:—
(1) Capital sunk
(2) profits made
(3) comparison with private companies
(4) how profits spent. I will give you what help you want & of course you will be paid. I want the article for the March issue. JRM.

❧ Margaret's diary.

12 March 1896

Read b[ible] Writing, arranging shelves, classifying papers etc., Off in carriage with Papa . . . to W.I.C. . . . to London Library. Home. Writing. Mr MacDonald calling about municipal reports . . .

❧ To Miss M.E. Gladstone

28 March 1896
postcard

In train to Leicester. I have only been an hour or two in London since I saw you & I am really ashamed to say that I have not yet exhausted the work you have already done. Could you look in at 20 D.B. abt 4pm on Wednesday. Do if you are about. By then I may possibly have gone over what you have done. My spare moments are at present taken up preparing my book for the press. I have promised to let the publishers have the MS by end of April.[1]

JRM

❧ Margaret's diary.

1 April 1896

Tea at 20 DB . . .

---

1. Possibly *Lovers Twain*, a volume of love stories.

Tea at D bgs. Mr J.A. Hobson there.   9 April 1896

In April Ramsay went to the ILP conference as the delegate for Southampton. He stood for the executive, the NAC, and was runner-up with 39 votes. An open quarrel erupted with the leading Fabians, Sidney and Beatrice, over the use of the Society's funds. There was a by-election in Aberdeen to be supervised.

〰 To Miss Gladstone
                                                    5 May 1896
                                                    postcard

Sorry it really is beyond my powers to speak at Hoxton — I am just back from Aberdeen where I had the cares of organisation, election agency, and general (?) . . . upon me & I am quite smashed up. Have to speak in Southampton today and tomorrow. Aberdeen was glorious & three more days would have put us in.[1]

                         J.R.M.

In May Ramsay was co-opted on to the NAC's publishing committee.

〰 Mr MacDonald to Miss Gladstone.

                                                    17 May 1896
Dear Miss Gladstone,
    Thank you very much for your letter and card for the lecture on banks. I am sorry that it will not be possible for me to go this lecture. Would you like me to return this card or pass it on? I would like very much to go to the Co-op: Congress at Woolwich, but I am afraid that all that time will permit will be for me to preside at the meeting for which I am booked. Tom Mann is to speak and the Socialist Choir is to warble. If I am not careful about engagements just now, I will never get my work finished. I am hurrying on with it. I wonder could you transcribe a chapter for me if I found that were possible! I am not sure yet, but the writing alone will now take two or three weeks. I am frightfully difficult to satisfy finally. I was sad to notice in a recent letter of yours that you had been upset. After your lecture to me, I thought when I read your note, 'All flesh is failings'.

                         Yours sincerely,
                         J R MacDonald

---

1. Tom Mann, put up by the local ILP, SDF and Trades Council, contested the North Aberdeen by-election. He was narrowly defeated.

❧ Mr MacDonald to Miss Gladstone.

23 May 1896

Dear Miss Gladstone,

In many ways I would like to go to the Church Congress, and perhaps I might add, particularly after your novel birthday present proposal [of marriage], but thinking it quietly over, I find it will be quite impossible . . .

❧ Margaret's diary.

26th May 1896

Down to Cooperative Conference at Woolwich.

27 May 1896

. . . to DB

28 May 1896

Off to Shoreditch . . . on to DBlgs. Reading over MS

1 June 1896

. . . to DBlgs. Reading MS

3 June 1896 (Wed)

On to DBlgs Reading MS . . . very hot.

10 June 1896
The Progressive Review

Dear Miss Gladstone

Your letter of yesterday was not altogether unexpected. I too had been thinking over what you said on Friday — would have written to you with reference to it when I got settled down at home. It really opens up to me many pleasant prospects & that you should have thought anything more about me than an interest in works that are your own as well as mine is like a spring time shower upon me.

But that is not it all. I must look behind and before.

To another it is needless that I should raise the dead just now, but looking before I see no rest and no peace. I am a man of iron will when I have made up my mind to do several things, and every day I rise and survey the forces in front of me & those about me I get more & more impressed with the presentiment of failure. All that means years of struggle, years of absorption in affairs, and perhaps a rapid & early ending. Just let me lift a corner of a veil aside to let you understand that ME which nobody knows of. Last year I gave up so much time to public work that my income was only £100 & on that I had to help materially to keep my mother. This year my income is less than ever. It is no use my even permitting myself to indulge in thoughts of a more restful life. I was born to fight & to fight single-handed. Of course, no man knows the lines upon which his destiny is cast; our duty is to work through each day and task and mood as though they were final. In all this, one, I suppose, I must get less & less human. It is the price we have to pay for our discovery of humanity — great everlasting humanity. Let us go on. If it be that God hath willed Else for Either or both of us, the revelation will come in due time. Now, upon me at least, there is . . . the spirit of strife, the thirst for the glory of going on. Read Tennyson's "Wages" and understand my soul. Still, as I have said, you have been a spring shower upon me and your words I shall reverently cherish.

It will be impossible for me to make any appointment these few days I am in town. I am going hither and thither doing a number of small things that want looking after when I am away. But after all the End of July is already at our outer gates.

Yours very sincerely
J.R. MacDonald

She did read Tennyson's *Wages* and even wrote it out on the back of the letter . . .

WAGES.

Glory of warrior, glory of orator, glory of song,
Paid with a voice flying by to be lost on an endless sea —
Glory of virtue, to fight, to struggle, to right the wrong —
Nay, but she aimed not at glory, no lover of glory she
Give her the glory of going on, & still to be.

The wages of sin is death: if the wages of virtue be dust,
Would she have heart to endure for the life of the worm or the fly?
She desires no isles of the blest, no quiet seats of the just,
To rest in a golden grove, or to bask in a summer sky:
Give her the wages of going on, & not to die.

In her diary for 10 June the column for 'letters received' has 'JRM' crossed out!

61

∾ Miss Gladstone to Mr MacDonald.

> Monday morning, 15 June 1896
> On the moors between Loch Long & Gairloch

Dear Mr MacDonald

I hope that by this time you too are in Scotland . . . we go this afternoon to Glasgow & return home on Thursday or Friday.[1]

Thank you for your letter of Wednesday. I do not think GOD will mock us by letting either of us make a mistake.

You touch a little on the practical side: perhaps I might do so too from my point of view.

I have not much of the fever of fight; my strength of will is needed more to keep me from fighting & the things I find hardest are such trivialities as meekly spending £3–£4 on a new evening dress where I would rather give it to Tom Mann's Election Fund, or giving up a labour meeting to dine with a boring aunt & cousins. But I don't bother about these: I know they have to be done. My financial prospects I am very hazy about, but I know I shall have a comfortable income. At present I get £80 allowance (besides board and lodging, travelling and postage); my married sister has I think about £600 all together. When my father dies we shall each have our full share, and I suppose mine will be some hundreds a year.

I don't know whether mine is less than my sisters? (I am a step-sister). My ideal would be to live a simple life right among the working people, spending on myself whatever seemed to keep me in best efficiency and giving the rest to public purposes specially Socialist propaganda of various kinds. I don't suppose I am a very good manager but I don't think I am careless or extravagant about money. If I married & a fixed income made my Husband & myself more free to do the work we thought right, I should think it an advantage to be used. But if you saw this differently & led me to see as you did; and at the same time we thought that by marrying we could help each other to live fuller & better lives I would give up the income & try to do my share of potboiling. I suppose I could do some work for which people would be willing to pay money. Of course, one ought to consider one's relations as well as one's self, but that is fortunately: as any who are worth considering would trust us to do what we thought right. I know your life is a hard one. I know there must be more Apparent failure in it; I don't know whether I should have the pluck & ability to carry me through anything worth doing.

---

1. She was attending Lord Kelvin's jubilee.

Grand Hotel, Glasgow. Tuesday morning.

I think I had hardly any business to write that last sentence. There is
another thing that I am doubtful whether I have any business to suggest, but
on the whole I think I have. After reading your last letter it seemed to me
that I would like you to know me more truly that you can at present. You
have only seen one aspect and that probably one of the best, since I talk to
you about the things I am most interested in. It suddenly occurred to me
that I knew of one way in which I could show you a little more of the 'tout
ensemble'. For the past 8 or 9 years I have from time to time jotted down in
a journal often at several months' interval whatever was most interesting me
at the moment or stood out clearest on looking back. I have not often
indulged in meditation in it; I have never put in it the things that I have felt
most deeply either for evil or good (some of the latter are only hinted at so
that I can read between the lines myself); but it does go a little below the
surface, and also shows what sort of life mine has been. If you cared to
glance at this you might. I never expected anyone to see it, unless I
married, & I have no right to treat even as much of my soul as appears
therein lightly; but I trust you so absolutely that I should not mind your
having read it IF we each married someone else after. The difficulty is in
offering it — it seems like pushing myself where I ought not to go: but I
think you will not misunderstand — so I will send it along after I get home,
and you can look at it as much or as little as you like . . . I have had
committees & parties, journeyings by land & sea; Trades Council Conference, and tramps over field and bog, Scotch Church & English slums;
inspection of the Family Home here, learning to bicycle playing with baby
cousins, being victimised by their grown up relatives' camera; & I have had
talks with all kinds of people, Socialists & Scientists, British and Foreign
relatives friends & acquaintances of all kinds, and ways of thinking . . .
All the jubilation is a great strain for my great-Uncle. I hope they will not
kill him with kindness; but it is refreshing to see a great man receive such
recognition & take it all so simply and courteously.

Yours very sincerely
M. E. Gladstone

〰 Mr MacDonald to Miss Gladstone.

21 June 1896
Lossiemouth

Dear Miss Gladstone,

. . . I suppose you have not sent the diary as it has not reached me. But
don't send it unless you have some special reason for doing so. Our moods

and thoughts can never be judged except in the self which is the product of them. A man's biography is not the changes through which he has gone and the influences under which he has come, the goods and the evils which he has thought or done but his self just as he went down to the grave. In that self everything has been harmonised — either to good or evil — everything proportioned, everything fitted in. So I do not want to know much of what you were, but what you are — only just that amount of were that the are may be understood. Have you really thought out calmly all that it would mean to you supposing we married, the terrible struggle in which we would be involved, the many disappointments we would have to share, the many shrines which I fear we should be fated to see shattered before our eyes? Have you thought what it is to have a husband engrossed in outside affairs, frequently away from you, with nothing settled about him, feeling very often for a breath of God-sent solitude and peace as ardently as a parched Dives does for a drop of water? And do not these two aspects of a life that is bound to be ours if we are to keep the faith and refuse the easier ways, appal you? They do me when I think of anyone I care much for. They have guided me hitherto to remember each morning that I was doomed to go through life alone, and a little tragic episode which I may tell you of someday. I have regarded as a kind of revelation attesting to the rightness of my belief. I have grown to regard you with more than ordinary esteem, but my dear lassie, that very regard prompts me to warn you against entertaining any similar feelings for me. Your own income would no doubt smooth matters for you — Don't talk of that Quixotic notion of giving it up altogether. Reduce your cost of life to a moral minimum, do service to society, hold the rest as a trustee to the community; but if you knew what it was to have ideal plans for work, a conviction of a strength to carry them out at least to a valuable point and no breakfast, you would see the real immorality of neglecting to use the opportunities you have in life. — But even with that, the life of any wife of mine must be largely a life of martyrdom. You could understand the necessity and enter into it perhaps better than any, but do not think about it as being much more than that. That is the chief thing that you have to turn over in your mind. There are also the minor things of family and other objections, and although there is nothing to be said against me, this you ought to know — I would have told it, or got it conveyed to you before had I known — that my father and mother never married. So you see all my life from the beginning has been the existence of a piece of rubbish, and only within the last three or four years when some of my relatives have been hearing about me in the newspapers have they been civil. All that has tended to make me a very unsociable being and a fighter not caring much whether I was alone or with a godly army. As far back as I can remember I had a grudge against the world rankling in me. As a youngster I had one of the most violent tempers ever known; the heat and fire of that have gone now into other qualities I hope. But that is the past which has made me and of which I am still — and shall ever be I doubt — the child.

These things you must consider as a calm wise woman and you must not allow anything to warp your judgment upon them. We care for each other sufficiently to enable us to brush aside all the formalisms of convention now I think whatever future developments may be, but do not yet permit yourself to leave the old tentative hopes or be anything but an enquirer into your own heart. When you feel ready tell me what you think and until then

I am yours ever

J.R. MacDonald

〜 Miss Gladstone to Mr MacDonald.

23 June 1896
Pembridge Square

Dear Mr MacDonald,

I had an intensely interesting talk for over an hour this morning with Ben Tillett. He put before me as strongly as your letters all the hard & dreary & bedraggling side of the work in the labour movement. — Because he has seen so many come into it full of enthusiasm & thinking they are going to turn the world topsy-turvey and then burn out in months or years . . . I have made up my mind long ago that any work that is worth doing in this world involves much drudgery and still more disappointment. What does appeal to me is that I should in any way think myself fit to undertake the responsibilities of such a life. Both your character & your work would be very difficult to give help to: & if I didn't help I should be a hindrance to you and it would be awful both for you & myself.

You ask in your letter whether I have really thought out all the change in my life would mean. The truth is I have been so frightfully businesslike about that all through that I nearly thought I had no romance anywhere in my composition. From the practical point of view the advantage seems to be all on my side. I want to be more free to do work for the Socialist movement & at the same time I don't think it right to cut off all family ties. If I can combine the two by marriage so much the better . . . Before you even knew of my existence I had a good deal about you from the Montagu girls & thought you were the sort of person I should like to Marry.

(Inserted in pencil:)
I didn't at all like you the first evening I saw you. We have a family

prejudice against long curly hair I think but I knew it was stupid to judge by that.

This sounds very horrid & cold-blooded, but I should not have let myself think about it at all or make friends with you as I did if I had not known all the time that in reality I had such a reverence in me for the love of man and wife that I would not dare to touch it afar off unless God let me.

I never troubled myself about what you thought of me — that was your business and God's: and I never pictured any particular future because that was holy ground where I might not tread . . .

I am glad you think as I do about the money: I only spoke of giving it up because I wanted to have an open mind even on points that seemed clear to me. About relations; of course that is my chief external difficulty, as none of mine care about the Socialist movement. We might have rather a bad time . . .

I can't imagine my father making himself disagreeable if I married the man in the moon & my sisters & I understand each other very well on serious subjects though we are very undemonstrative & unconfidential. There is no one else I care about much . . . I'm not one bit afraid for myself: I shouldn't like it if any of them were nasty to you. I daresay my sisters would not take to you; they are horrid (at least the 3 older ones Flo, Bessie & Bella — The fourth is May) to my mother's relations because they didn't like my father marrying again, though I believe they liked my mother personally & to me they have been kindness & unselfishness itself all my life. I just pity them for the pettiness they show . . .

I have often felt that I should like you to see them & them to see you during the past year: but I did not quite see how I could invite you specially without implying more than I had any justification in implying. They all happened to be out that day you called.

The journal is very uninteresting & unintelligible to anyone but myself — and even I got quite bored in glancing it through the other day: but it must explain itself as best it may.

It was bad taste of me to write so much last Sunday but I got into the swing and went on.

I hope your colds & headaches have disappeared;

> Yours sincerely
> M.E. Gladstone

∾ Mr MacDonald to Miss Gladstone.

25 [June] 1896
Lossiemouth

Dear Miss Gladstone

Only just an acknowledgement of your Diary to set your mind at rest.
With it has come a mass of stuff relating to politics upon which my advice is
wanted & that must occupy me first. I seem to be advising Everybody on
everything. The weather is much better and so am I. I am having such a lot
of letters that I don't feel at all out of it up here, and my friends the
fishermen will all be home next week.

Yours very sincerely
J.R. MacDonald

∾ Miss Gladstone to Mr MacDonald.

Thursday June 1896
W.I.C. Office
Buckingham St

My dear Sir,

It is only just beginning to dawn on me a very little bit, since your last
Sunday's letter, what a gift I have in your love. I can hardly write the word
— it seems too big and good to belong to me. I shall not take it in much till I
see you. I shall not take it in much then in its fulness — it will just come
gradually to us through our lives.

You told me to enquire into my own heart, but I haven't done it. My heart
is much too reserved to let me do it. It just gets cross if I ask it what it feels
about you. But I am glad that I haven't any feelings of passionate worship
because I think I have something deeper still which will wear through all
time and all circumstance, and through eternity too, for even if, as you
said, perhaps we don't have any personal existence after this life, we each
have eternity within us here.

If you could have looked at my life the last few days — it is only 2½ now
— you would have thought your letter made no difference to me — I eat &
sleep & joke and talk just as normal. I don't even have a little underlying
feeling of happiness all the time as I should have expected. As I said it is
too big & great for me to take in.

But when I think how lonely you have been I want with all my heart to
make up to you one little tiny bit for that I have been lonely too. I have
envied the veriest drunken tramps I have seen dragging about the streets if
they were man & woman because they had each other.

Perhaps after this I shall be cross and disagreeable to you sometimes. I can't bear to think about it, but I know that I may be. With people I don't care about I don't think I ever am, but I do ask your forgiveness for all my imperfections.

This is truly a love letter: I don't know when I shall show it to you: it may still be that I never shall [she did a few days later]. But I shall never forget that I have had the blessing of writing one.

M.E.G.

❦ Margaret's diary.

29 June 1896

Read B. Off to Shoreditch. Visiting St. John's Road School. Talking C.O.S. office more visits. Statistical Comtee at W.I.C. . . . up to Ham Terrace [Grandmother] seriously ill in great pain. Doctor came. D[inner] May up. Nurse in. Doctor again. Writing letter . . . Uncle G and Aunt Isobel . . . came for Evangelical Alliance. Bed.

❦ Mr MacDonald to Miss Gladstone.

29 June 1896
Lossiemouth

My dear Lassie (Do we not regard each other sufficiently now whatever happens to drop formalities?)

Your diary makes me quite despair. I have been reading it and every page has been suggesting a contrast between you and me. You were quite my lady when I was an urchin with darned stockings and patched trousers; I was one of the roughs you write about in Trafalgar Square; I fought in the Bloody Sunday row, broke my hat and got my coat torn and had I met your doughty brother-in-law, Basil,[1] would have broken his head with the same coolness as I would have broken a nut. I have felt your pages too sacred and have laid them down hardly daring to read on. The whole thing is too wonderful — that you revelling in Switzerland and being sanctified by baptism at the time when I was kicked and cursed as an impediment and disgrace should care a bit for each other, is too strange almost to be true. If I had a diary I would sent it to you, but I have none. Perhaps when you read it you would be afraid of me. A curious thing happened to-day which I will tell you. It sounded very grim to me and brought back my oldself (sic). It has been pouring here of rain today and in a pause in the downpour I started a game of golf with my dear old schoolmaster to whom I owe so much.

---

1. Basil Holmes, husband of her half-sister, Isabella.

Shortly after we started it came in torrents and he begged me to give up the game. But he was beating me and I had made up my mind to fight him out. For two hours we played in a downpour which drenched us from top to toe and I came out victor. The dear old man when we left the last hole put his hand in mine and with a lump in his throat said "MacDonald, when I saw you first as a fat little boy I said you were either doomed to be hanged or something worth doing. Our game tonight has me feel once again a babe in your hands". I am telling you that because I really think he was right. It isn't egotism at all that makes me tell you this or even think this. But I have fought a hard fight and am inclined to carry it through to the bitter end. I have a presentiment that I am not going to live to be very old, and that my nerves will rapidly wear out my body.

Something is constantly saying to me that I will do nothing myself but that I will enable someone else to do something. With all that in my mind I have read your diary, and such a terrible gulf seems to be fixed between us, I seem to stand at one pole and you at another — I the son of Hagar, you the daughter of Sarah. And in nothing is that terrible gulf more apparent than in our religion. I think over those relations about whom you have written so affectionately and I think how many of them would ever understand me. I have been trying to picture them and we have so little in common. I would cut you off, I fear, from every one you regard. They would all pity you for having married such a fellow and you know if ever I thought they did anything like that I might lose my temper, tell them I was better than they were and decline to condescend to have anything more to do with them. I know exactly how that pride of mine would flare up and how wretched you would be over it all. They would perhaps cut you off from your subsistence and then you would find me a frightfully bad husband, because when I have no money I think nothing of living for days on nothing but tea and bread. What a curious marriage would be ours! But couldn't you manage to persuade one of your sisters to come with you some afternoon to 20 Duncan's and then we might manage to meet more of your friends together. There is no hurry is there in saying anything definite? If we really love each other we will more and more love each other, we will care more and more for each other as we know each other better. And then, you know, though I am growing grey, I am much younger than I look. By the way, tell me how you knew about my birthday! And how old do you think I am? Or do you know?

Yours ever J.R.M.

P.S. But tell me, am I the 'unsatisfactory man' that diarist feared of two years ago?

❧ From Margaret.

30 June 1896
Electric Railway
Elephant & Castle

Dear Mr MacDonald

I am writing to you for the somewhat selfish reason that I am in trouble and want to tell you about it. My grandmother [Elizabeth King] was taken seriously ill suddenly on Sunday evening & we do not know yet whether she will get over it . . .

I told my father about you on Sunday. I thought you would not mind, as it suddenly occurred to me that it would be nicer to take him into my confidence while it was all unsettled & vague. I told him a good deal about you, & he asked a lot of sensible questions (Questions I mean about — what you are) He made no objection to anything & liked some of the things I said. I gave him a prospectus of your lectures & a few odd things out of your 'Young Men's Column' in the "New Age" to read. I told him that if there were any further developments I would let him know.

I did not tell him what you told me about your parents I thought you would tell me when I see you whether I should or should not. I said I thought your mother had worked in the fields & your father had died a long time ago.: That is correct, is it not?

He laughed about the minister preaching against "Socialists and Atheists". He doesn't mind my Socialism one bit, but I don't believe it has ever dawned on him that I have conscientious objections to our style of living; it's not a thing I can exactly point out to him though my sisters have some idea of it. I told him of course that you made a fuss about its being a "Hard life" for me . . .

❧ Ramsay to Margaret.

1 July 1896
Lossiemouth

My Dear Lassie

Do tell me further how your grandmother is. I am very sorry to hear that you are troubled and hope you may be able to tell me good news. Just a line scribbled in the pause of something will do.

I am awfully glad you have approached your father. Oddly enough as I was playing golf this morning, the thought of you suddenly struck me and it was one rather of reproach that I had not already told you that under the unusual circumstances, your father ought to have straws thrown up to tell him how the wind blew. Hence it was that the sadness which I felt when I began your letter was lifted at the end for a moment. You know the notes about me in the first Labour Annual and also the general kind of thumb-nail sketch of me in the Album. This is an outline of the days you know nothing of (Miss Grant will tell you all about me in those days). I was first of all brought up by a dear good grandmother who came of an old peasant family. Her brother was one of those men who grinded his Latin whilst he ploughed, went to Aberdeen University was leader amongst the students who sided with the Free Kirk in 1843 and died that year after preaching bareheaded in a snow-storm by the shore at Banff. My grannie made frocks . . . [For the rest of what he told her, see pp. 91-4.]

〰 Margaret to Ramsay.

2 July 1896
24 Hamilton Terrace
London NW.
(her grandmother's house)

My dear Humbug (I am obediently dropping formalities, I know you are not a humbug, but if you will write a letter like [that] one you must take the consequences). I feel so cocky after your letter received yesterday: I find I am much less narrow minded than you are & I was afraid perhaps I was more so. What right have you to talk eloquently about having discovered humanity, & then go and say it is wonderful that we two poor little bits of humanity should care for each other because they happen to have had rather different circumstances? Not so very different after all, either, for in the most important things we have had the same — we are under the same civilization, have the same big movements stirring around us — the same books to open our minds . . . I even have had all my life "darned Stockings" — perhaps you think that some magic keeps them from going into holes in the station of life where it has pleased God to place me, but I can assure you I have spent many hours darning my own and my father's too.

I think the contrast between our up-bringing is encouraging, not despairing. We have come by different paths to the same beliefs and aims: our interests are in many ways so much alike that I should be almost afraid of their being too much so to have a happy agreement if we married, only that we have had different experiences and I think we have very different temperaments.

There is one important thing though you say the gulf between us is more apparent in our religion . . . That point of religion was the only one about which I wondered whether it was worth while to make any explanation in sending you my diary. I have changed or developed in that as in other things; but I really know so little & care less what my dogmatic beliefs are now that I left it. You told me you were a Unitarian. I dare say I am — I leave out the earlier sentences about Christ in the creed if I think about it. But I know that whatever I do believe in is only a small & distorted part of the real truth . . . I can worship just as well with R.C.s or Jews, as with any Protestant, so long as whoever they are seem to be in earnest; . . . I never now regularly read the Bible or kneel down regularly to pray, except in family prayers night & morning and I never have a notion what they are about, though I have a sort of superstitious feeling that I like them to go on!

I suppose I am rather Pagan; perhaps you can teach me better. My father liked what I told him about your broad religious views. I told him you played golf on Sundays instead of going to service very often because you thought it did you more good.

. . . I know they won't understand you; they don't understand me & I am as simple as ABC compared with you, I should think. But they have sufficient respect for my opinion to respect you if I say I honour & love you . . . You need not mind flaring up if anyone dares to pity me because of you, only I don't think you will find they do it in my presence or after I have spoken to them on the subject. The only time any of my people saw you was my sister Bessie at that Psychical Society. I pointed you out as an acquaintance of mine & I suppose as she looked down the row of seats your curls and your red tie looked rather startling (I told you we had a family prejudice against such things & I thought they looked horribly affected at first — I don't care what you look like now) so she said "I don't admire his looks" and I replied "Nor do I, but I like him" and that was quite enough. The next day October 12th (your 29th birthday, according to the Labour Annual 1895) I had a letter from you in which you talked about the meeting & I told them at Dinner what you said & she must have seen I was pretty friendly with you for you to write to me like that, but she was as pleasant as anything (& she can be witheringly horrid if she likes) and when a few days later I said I was going to hear your lecture & told them about it at breakfast next morning she was quite extra nice & made remarks about it which is unusual in anything connected with my meetings etc. Of course my people know that since I was getting more & more in with Socialists I might probably marry one; but they had the chance of packing me off round the world with May last Autumn or Winter & yet it was they who urged me to stay at home & told me I ought not to sacrifice my interests here, while it was I who held out that it might be my first duty to go with May though I hated the idea.

. . . Yesterday through part of the time the operation [on her grand-mother] was going on I sat with my Uncle William (Lord K[elvin]) . . . I . . . knew that if ever I told him about you and he looked displeased (I think he is too much of a man — a human being, to be so, but he certainly is strongly anti-Socialist) I would be more sorry for him than for myself & you, and would give up my intercourse with him without a moment's hesitation if it involved any feeling of underlying mistrust to you. I shall be as careful as ever I can to manage our marriage, if it ever comes, without giving pain or offence to those who have the claim of relationship or friendship to me; my grandmother and aunts, I think, almost worship the ground I tread on & it would be a very great blow to them if they disliked my marriage: but since you say you care for me and my principles have the first claims upon me; and you must not for one moment talk as if I might be unhappy if they cut me off unpleasantly from some of my old surroundings. Of course they must cut me off to some extent: I shall have other work to do. After all none of those who are so kind to me & of whom I am so fond are really very much to the *ME* inside. It may sound horrid to say it — I would hardly acknowledge it to myself, but you had better know the truth, I don't believe there is a single person in the world except now yourself — whose death would mean really a deep and lasting blank to me. I really believe that the person I care most about — again except yourself — is my cousin Andrew Henderson[1] (do you remember lending him a book?) He is nearly 20 years older than I am, dull, uninteresting, exceedingly worthy but unenterprising business man most people would say: but he cared about me specially for 7 or 8 years & so utterly unselfishly and bravely that he has done me more good than anybody else and we are the very best of friends. I tell him much more about my Socialism than any other relation of mine and more about you (though that is precious little even to him): I saw ever so much of him when I was in the North a fortnight ago. If I ever got engaged to you I believe he would flare up as nicely as you could wish though perhaps not quite in the same way as you would if (I wasn't thinking what I was writing) anyone said a word in disparagement of my marrying you, though he doesn't a bit like all my heresies. I daresay you and he would never understand each other much: I shouldn't be disappointed if you didn't. I'm only talking this lot to show you that it is the human in people which appeals to me and that I can get on with all sorts of different kinds even if they are blind to what seems to me the clearest & most obviously divine teachings of the day. I think it to give me this broader view that GOD has put me among people who are good but not quite in the way that I have

---

1. His mother was the sister of MEG's King grandfather. He once proposed to her.

worked round to believing in. Do you remember at all in one of your earliest letters to me — after you had only seen me once, you spoke as if you were made poor to do the fighting and I was stuck aloft somewhere to do nothing but cheer you on a little bit. I smiled at the time & hoped you weren't right about me being kept out of the fighting for ever.

Of course if we marry people will chatter: they will all say I took with you because of Socialism or Socialism because of you. They will say hard things of you. Your Social Democrats will, I suppose, say you've married a fine Miss or that it's convenient for you to have a little more money coming in. I've thought of that ever since I first knew you, a thought that would be much harder for you to bear than anything anyone might say about me. But people who know us and are worth anything won't believe such tales, & one must not regard idle chatter though one may do all in one's power to prevent it.

But my dear sir, the only important question to my mind is, do you feel that I should be a help to you! Until you have utterly made up your mind to that, nothing can be settled; if you ever do feel that we will laugh at all other difficulties. I know you are a powerful character: I can perfectly understand what your old schoolmaster said to you, and I am all the more thankful that it is on GOD's side & not the Devil's you are fighting . . . It doesn't frighten me IF you care for me. That you or I have hardly begun to realise. I wrote you a little bit about it one day last week [28 June] but it's locked up at home & I can't get it today. I will send it you some time. It told you that it all seemed too big and great for me: I think I have felt (something like you) that perhaps I was meant just to drudge along and have lots of good things but never the one I wanted the most.

I don't feel now the slightest scrap of passionate adoration for you: but that doesn't make me waver a moment for I believe I have something much deeper & more enduring which if it gets the chance will get stronger & stronger through all our lives.

But I'm a horribly lethargic slow sulky sort of person. I've got that "Philosophic Calm" which annoys you — it is a help in times like these I have just been passing through: I think it makes me dependable & it keeps my nerves from wearing out my body; but I think too it blunts my perceptions and you might find it a drag upon your fire and quickness. I think I should know if I were very likely to get tired of you; until I see you I shan't realise in the least what I do feel for you, & then only a little bit; if now or then I felt the least shadow of a doubt whether I cared for you enough I would tell you however it would be kinder to both to draw back however deeply I had committed myself, but I think that is not likely to happen unless all life is a farce & a mockery & then it doesn't matter whatever happens.

. . . But I don't mind how long you are making up your mind one way or the other — only I would like you to take me on my own merits & not on what my esteemed relations might think of you or what particular kind of summer holiday I had eight years ago. If you want it of course I will bring specimens of my relations to B. [Duncan Buildings] or you can come to us & I'll have a selection for you to inspect — like animals at the Zoo. But I can't introduce them to you without their having some idea of the relations between us, and I certainly at present don't relish the idea of this sort of thing. "May I introduce you to Mr. M, who will condescend to marry me (or whom I will condescend to marry) if you speak respectfully to him". I'd rather tell them straight out (I mean if we do settle anything definite) "Here is the man I am going to marry" & take it all as a matter of course.

What a lot I am writing . . . You talk about there being no hurry: of course there isn't. But, one thing is troubling me. I couldn't at all be pleased to promise to marry you without making the acquaintance of your mother & your home as soon as possible; & I should think your mother would want to see me too, would she not? I do hope she will like me; if you ever say anything to her about me I wish you would, if you like to & if she would not mind, give her, well I don't know what — love would sound too gushing and kind regards too stiff — tell her I want to see her & hope she wants to see me. But I can't see how you will have time to take me up to Lossiemouth when you get back to work for ages & it wouldn't be the same to go alone. It did cross my mind that if you at all liked it you might spare 3 or 4 days to come up (I'll spare the cash if you spared the time) — say next week and then if we didn't quarrel you could see just the most important of my people and I could be with you if you invited me & could take me anywhere for your last week or so. But it would have been a great rush for you & I suppose it is quite out of the question for me now that my grandmother is so ill . . . Now I have to go to a committee: I feel as if I had been sick nursing for weeks instead of 3 days.

P.S. I can't bother to read this over — nor have I time!

> Yours
> M.E. Gladstone.

❧ Margaret to Ramsay.

> [3 July] 1896
> Pembridge Square

. . . I don't know what to do about Lossiemouth. I talked it over with my father and then I talked it over with Aunt Fanny & Uncle William [Lord and Lady Kelvin] . . . & they all think with me that I cannot well disturb my grandmother now with talking about it, & I can't go to Lossiemouth without telling her why. I am really awfully sorry on your mother's account . . . I shall send you some photographs for HER, only I'll address them to you as I don't know whether you will want to tell her just now. When you do come up we can think it over & if we do quarrel — well I haven't compromised you with my people.

Yours M.E. Gladstone.

❧ Ramsay to Margaret.

3 July 1896
Lossiemouth

Don't count the 'buts'

My Dear Detractor,

What a horrible twist you have given my words and thoughts about our difference of position — so horrible that I suspect you have joined the S.D.F. What I said (don't reply that I expressed myself badly please — I know you won't because you are already becoming quite obedient!) was that I was odd (not intellectually but accidentally) that etc. etc. etc.

Now, I have told you all the reasons I can think of why you should *not* marry me. You still stick to it. Now in my heart of hearts I have a conviction that with all my manifold shortcomings there are some virtues left that you will care about and that you will make better than they are. Yes — you will help me — help me in every way. When you spoke that day at the Museum,[1] it seemed to me as though I had spoken that way to you before . . . I believe we shall face life better together, in our own quiet way. I am philosophically calm as I write, but were you sitting by me here with the sea — so dear is it that I might almost say *my* sea — almost below my window and a beautifully clear sky overhead, I would stop and would find that rare blessedness of soul which all men desire by drawing you close to me. We would say nothing perhaps, because only in silence do we know each other best. Like all sane men and women we will find faults in each other, but like all true lovers we shall harbour none of these secretly so that the discovery will be but a new bond of our love.

I would gladly run through to London next week and undergo the terrible ordeal of talking serious matters to unsympathetic people (Please don't write me a terrible letter that I called you unsympathetic. That is really too

---

1. The suggestion that they marry, generally referred to as Ramsay's proposal on the steps of the British Museum, was clearly Margaret's.

S.D.Fish for you) Then you could come up for the last week or so. I would really like you to come up. I can, imprimis, have nothing whatever to do with a girl who cannot swing a golf club. Then my little place here is a blush of roses. You must be generous with my mother. She will not at all object to my marrying — quite the opposite — and of course I shall assure her that it will make no difference to her — but still, poor body, she does fuss over things. But I should like you to see my friends here very much and then finally, it will be really an excellent holiday for you. Only — if we fight in London! or if I discover that I am the unsatisfactory man! I have shaven the curl and promise to buy a new tie (Of course you will) sneer and report me to Hyndman! (Did you see my article on him last week's *New Age?*) Glad to hear of your Grandmother's progress. Command me re your arrangements. I am sending two sermons of mine — they will give you part of my religious point of view. Paper is done.

Ever
JRM

❧ Margaret to Ramsay.

4 July
Hamilton Terrace

. . . My brother-in-law (Basil) has tried for years to make us decently demonstrative; but the more he tries, the less he succeeds, especially with his own wife. Up here I am a little more so because they like it . . .

About the "unsatisfactory man": I was wandering in the abomination of desolation when I wrote that [in her diary] & longing for anything to really rouse & interest me: but even then I had too much belief in myself & my fate to really expect it.

I suppose you had better have the enclosed [letter of 28 June], though it alarms me rather. I wrote it one day instead of Committee notices.

MEG

❧ Ramsay to Margaret.

6 July 1896
Lossiemouth

My dear Madam (for I see that with your 'Sir' you are an eighteenth century spirit, and I verily believe you will receive me in brocades, give me tea in blue china, offer me a cheek with a little black patch upon it and read me nothing but Alfred Austin and Andrew Lang with a yawn of Goss between) I am sitting at my old window with the scent of roses and mignonette around me, thinking of my fate. A game of golf with a dignified Dean is past and another with a Professor of Church History is ahead of me. So you may imagine how difficult it is to write anything like a love letter. I am rather in another mood and am sighing that I cannot give you a Royal Insitution lecture on moral beginnings 'Beware of the leaven of Mrs Bosanquet'.[1] But there is a red rose — ribbald thing! — tipsily winking at me. You cruel creature, what a frightful ordeal you are preparing for me! Do you remember I have nerves and that I blush sometimes and often lose my head. You have no idea how glad I am that one of your sisters knows me to look at. How *am* I going to face you all! And why was it not my fate to have seen the family in the calm of an unsuspected relationship! I hope the sister who does not want to examine me will talk about Mrs Pyper of Boston, ghosts or anything else entertaining until the fearful crisis has passed. I expect no sympathy from you. During these days you will not be 'madam' even, you will be Lady Macbeth. My dear lassie, say you pity me. (The red rose guffaws at the appeal.) This heart disease is a waefu' thing. If you were a Lossie lassie it would be simple aye even if you attained to the heights of being a minister's daughter. (Still that red rose teaches me wisdom.)

I have hinted to my mother that if an impending quarrel does not come off, I am a doomed bachelor. She remarked that that was rather an old story. 'Can she cook a decent meal?' was her Meredithian enquiry. I had to confess that I have never asked you. 'Can she keep a house clean?' Again I was in a fix. 'Can she darn?' Joy! I could say yes. 'Is she a leddy?' 'Middlin' kind' (Pardon) *Reynolds Newspaper* flashed in her eye. 'I wid jeest hae been as weel pleased if ye'd taen an ordinar' servant. She'll nae be pleased wi' me. She'll be turnin' up her nose at everything, an' aifter ye're mairrit ye'll never come here again'. I did not dispute your vices but took the liberty of adding a few of your virtues. You being a member of the I.L.P. pacified her. She said you were decent looking in your photograph. Really she is quite nice. It means more to her than we can imagine. She only wants you to promise not to take me away altogether and sends many kind thoughts and words to you. Poor body, she does not know you.

Pacify your relations who want titles by the assurances that you will become a Duchess when I become respectable. Tom Ellis [Liberal Chief Whip) has promised to create me Duke of Lossie when the Liberals return

---

1. Helen Bosanquet was the secretary of the Hoxton and Haggarston Charity Organisation Society where Margaret worked two days a week.

to power and when I whistle a Whiggish tune. Limited Liability Companies are started on poorer prospects.

But, I feel with you, how good all your people are — and how wise. I *do* wish I knew them all better. There is so much to be known and so much to be explained, and outwardly I am such a stranger. I can't go to them in the ordinary way and prove that I can pay your rent, buy frocks for you and all that. I can hardly believe that they in their position and with their ideas, can have the faith to enable them to believe anything but that you are being sacrificed to a self-seeker in one of your quixotic moods. But we shall convince them all the same that we love each other and that we can in a worldly sense scrape along quite as well as though we had much outward show and, what is better, that our common work will bless us.

At present the *Dictionary of National Biography*, the *Echo* and the *New Age* are the only things I write for. I don't want any more work because, as you know, I am doing an extra lot of political work. I propose to continue this policy at least until another general election, and the great essential is that I should be pretty free as to times and places. The *New Age* is turned into a Limited Liability company and Mr Stapley refused to subscribe unless I was appointed Secretary. So that is a new duty but I have stipulated that they do not pay me more than £15 per annum. Up until I joined Mr Fletcher on the *New Age* I was chief leader writer for Mr Fox Bourne on the *Weekly Dispatch*. That I got shortly after I left Mr Lough. Stories to the *Peoples Journal* etc. with a long article or two for the *Scottish Review* are about the most I have published. But I have never tried to get much potboiling literary work. I have no *Echo* poets by me just now. But this morning I had a cheque by which I know that three went in last month — Aubrey de Vere must have been one and a criticism of Swinburne's last volume must have been another. If you are passing the office before I return you will see a file there.

. . .But now, my dear lassie, we are going to be equals and there's to be no 'sir' which means that we are not to go arm in arm through our work. And you are going to write me more love letters so that you and I may feel better and stronger and life may be brighter and purer for us.

Ever thine (barring the possibility of a fight)

J.R.M.

Poor old Macrosty[1] has lost his baby. He has written me a very sad letter. I wish I could look at the old boy in the face and say, 'Old Man, the back's

---

1. Henry Macrosty was Ramsay's chief ally on the Fabian executive.

made for the burden'. He would know the old Scottish saying and it would be a stay to him.

❧ Ramsay to Margaret.

[8 July 1896
Lossiemouth]

My Dear Kumrid (you see you are drifting me into the beastly SDF), . . . I have been writing incessantly on Fabian matters since I came up. The Liberal and Eighty Club lot are doing their level best to circumvent us and I am awfully sore at having to lie up here. . . I am now afraid that my mother may let slip that you and I are talking of ending spinsterdom and bachelordom. The sweet photographs are far too much for her. Miss Grant is coming up here this month and if she hears it, she will be sure to tell Lily Montagu.[1] If I had a chance of seeing Miss Grant, I would put her on her honour to say nothing in London until she heard whether she was permitted or not . . . The bond of silence — if I may infer anything from numerous engagements and love affairs in which I have been behind the scenes — is always religiously broken. Hints and half statements are made and one day the miserable couple concerned awake to the hum of gossip. I don't mind. I shall laugh and trail red herrings on the upper lips of the gossips. For instance, if you should hear at the Socialist Club that I am going to be married to an Auchtermuchty fisher girl, know that Mrs Sammie Hobson[2] has been telling them a story that I wrote as an excuse to her the other day. We *must* have fun with them — if we don't row and I pass my exam.[3] (Deary me! that exam!) We shall deceive them, tickle them, tantalise them; humbug them, swindle them and enrage them until they have lost all sense and can be easily persuaded that they are standing on their heads. But at present it is awkward for you, isn't it? . . .

❧ Margaret to Ramsay.

9 July 1896
Hamilton Terrace

Dear Mr MacDonald (Obedient again I drop the 'Sir'. I think it politic to be occasionally douce at first, but it won't continue long.)

How can you talk about your being frightened of my relations when I know within myself that I can't cook a decent dinner or darn a decent darn

---

1. Miss Grant was in service with Margaret's friend Lily Montagu.
2. The Sam Hobsons were Fabian colleagues.
3. Meeting the Gladstones.

or do any thing (my grandmothers room) decently that a woman ought first & foremost to do — only in an amateur fashion at which your mother would most certainly look in scorn . . .

I daresay /my home people/ would be rather shocked if they knew how often I had been to your rooms . . .

If you find my father very vague about you, you must take for granted that I omitted every important point in telling him about you. You are quite right in hoping Bessie will talk and keep you going . . .

. . .Flo will probably "put her ears back" a little at you; but I don't think you need flare up if she does: . . . She often does it to visitors — I mean puts on some manner which exactly reminds you of a horse when it is cross & puts its ears back . . . We openly bewail her peculiar ways to her; last Sunday at dinner I roused even my father to defend her, by describing to May how, after she opened a sort of pious dissenting bazaar, the Court Circular of 'The Times' described how "The fascinating Miss Gladstone in a lovely bonnet — and with her small delicate ears laid back" etc? . . . I have had that nonsense about my heart being cross knocked out of me by the sorrow & anxiety of the past days. I don't say it will never return: perhaps it may: the heart is deceitful above all things & desperately wicked: but the deep waters I have been passing through & they have been deeper even than you know I will tell you some day — have made my love for you deeper and stronger & more tender — as I hope it may go on getting always.

My grandmother is not progressing much: The doctors were disappointed and grave this morning — she has had a bad night.

. . . What I am really afraid of is that the Queen will hear you are a vagabond & lock you up; for Uncle W & Aunt F [The Kelvins] dine with her next Monday. I saw them this evening & they were more affectionate than ever — I suppose to try & make up to me for your shortcomings. I'll tell Lily Montagu. When are you coming up and what your project? . . .

I have just been up to see my grandmother. She was dreadfully down about the pain she has to bear·. . .

I have been very serious this morning: I wonder if I can tell my sir anything about it. I was reading some German Social Democratic & Working Women's papers before breakfast, & they made me hop out of bed & kneel down & think as I have done hundreds of times before, how I could best work to help in the Socialist & labour movements . . . I feel just as vague and powerless about helping as I always do — but not in the blues: only I need much more determination and down-rightness to do any good.

Yours till the quarrel

〰 Ramsay to Margaret.

10 July 1896
Lossiemouth

My Dear Lady,

After two days! I have been seeing uncles and aunts unto the borders of Inverness and have been taking the liberty — and the privilege my dear lassie, too — of asking their opinion of a photograph — my uncle [Annie Ramsay's brother, Alexander], a guard on the Highland Railway who gave me £10 once to do anything with I liked and a good square headed chap, looked at the *Punch* one. 'What does this mean?' he asked. 'Will she pass for forty?' I evaded. 'Well she looks a bit young for forty. I would take her to be about thirty-eight'. I shall probably marry her daughter when she grows up', I said. Wasn't it horrid of me? Do forgive me! You can punish me in any way you like and I shall not murmur. Then I showed it to a great-aunt, a sister of my grandmother's [Annie Campbell], a woman of whose qualities I am secretly proud. 'She's a nice modest lassie' was her verdict. And tears came into the poor old body's eyes and she told me to tell you some things but I said I hoped she would be able to tell you herself.

Then I came home and found my mother rummaging a dictionary because her spelling is shaky; and I have been laughing ever since about the cooking and my name.[1] Again fine me for being horrid and ease my conscience. You have many alternatives — James, Jeems, Jamie, Jim and goodness knows what else. Do give me a sample of my new baptism . . .

〰 Margaret to Ramsay.

10 July 1896
The Socialist Club

. . . I've written to Lily Montagu. She will be pleased. I told her if all went smoothly I should be indebted to her for the greatest blessing of all, because she introduced us.

Nobody has asked me yet if I am engaged to you: if they do I shall say "I daresay, but there is no hurry".

Mr Toke has been telling me all about the Fabian Row tonight:[2] I wish you were going to be there. He wants me to join the Fabians & help make

---

1. See Annie's letter to Margaret, 13 July.
2. The row was over Bernard Shaw's submission to the International Socialist Congress which implied that the Fabians did not want a socialist party. Ramsay led the revolt of the more radical members of the Society against a policy of manipulation and permeation.

rows. Shall I? I told him it was too painfully respectable for me; but seriously I've been thinking for some time that if I could help make it less so it might make it worth joining. I am in Mrs Webb's good books now: I might go to her tea-parties & get converted to the old gang & then you and I could fight nicely.

Altogether I have been getting all the Socialist news, which is very refreshing after having hardly heard from any Socialist but yourself for so long.

M.E.G.

〰 Margaret to Ramsay.

11 July 1896
Pembridge Square

. . . I told you in my yesterday's letter that I had been passing through deeper waters than you knew. I think I must tell you now, though it must give you pain. It has given me more pain than I ever had in my life, before, but pain of a purifying and ennobling kind.

Read the enclosed[1] and then tell me whether my conscience is guided by a good GOD, or by an evil demon. . . The only things on my side are that for all these years he has never dared to propose to me — this letter I am sending you is the most definite love making I have ever had from him (there was a funny sort of hubbub some years ago which I will tell you of someday in which my father — not I — spoke to him & I think he was rather hardly used — I apologised to him for that 3 years ago — I didn't suspect I was going to treat him ever so again so much worse). . . I never read anything like his friendship & mine in books: I don't think it could often happen — but oh! to think what a mess I have made of it. He was a little haughty sometimes, for which I liked him better under the circumstances . . . yesterday I saw him again at Hamilton Terrace (I forgot to explain that he is up this week on business & so I wrote to him on Sunday about you & said I especially wanted to see him — I meant it to be to tell him more about you) . . . After all this do you think you can trust me still, or do you think that an evil demon may be making me think that I love you when I don't, or that I can help you when I can't? I haven't prayed more earnestly about you than I did about him.

---

1. A letter from a cousin, Andrew Henderson, who was in love with her.

  Ramsay to Margaret.

11 July 1896
Lossiemouth

My dearest Lassie,

I am so very, very sorry for what has happened. But why regard it as you do? These things will happen without a demon ruling either you or the universe. Your cousin's letter is really difficult to understand. It surely could not have been in reply to one of yours referring to ourselves either directly or indirectly, or even referring to the possibility of your being engaged, otherwise I do not believe a word you say about him. You have probably been protected from a knowledge of the life of the feelings. I have not and I shall ever thank God and reverence my fellow man for the sturdy heroism I have been privileged to be present with. The one was a man and the other was a woman and I never see them now but I know I am unworthy to loose the latchet of their shoes. My lassie, we shall probably have many of these dark clouds on our way through life. You and I are not going to walk rose strewn paths. Your love only makes me set my teeth harder. It is but a new spiritual baptism this to both of us. We are doomed to be often sad in our happiness — only in this way can we help others and do the work which I think we may be able to do together. I would never have loved you unless I felt pretty certain that it was neither romance nor passion that has hold of me but a firm conviction that you were of the stuff that would come through the fire purer than when you went into it. God has blessed me by directing broken hearts to me already. We have talked together and even wept together; and I know it all. What I now know has not touched my affection for you in the least. Nay, nay yours (sic) fears give no explanation of these mishaps.

A hitch in *Progressive Review* arrangements will probably shorten my holiday, and I shall be in London this day week (Saturday). It will really be very odd seeing you, you will be so different. Could we lunch at the Club? Wouldn't it be fun to walk quietly in as though nothing had happened! Of course I would hardly look at you and you could flirt with the Toke as much as you like and I would reprimand you in a fatherly kind of way . . .

  Margaret to Ramsay.

17 Pembridge Square W.
July 11/96

It is such a long time since I last wrote to my dear Sir; (more than 28 hours since I did up for him the zoological specimens [family photographs]

84

which I posted this morning) that I can't get to sleep for planning what I shall say to him first thing tomorrow morning. I wish you would make haste & come to London because I am getting so atrociously fond of you as long as I don't see you that I am quite longing for that quarrel to bring me to my senses. However I am not lackadaisical. I managed to make frivolous remarks to a girl next to me in the midst of my own pet sentimental song which my sister Bessie sang specially for my benefit at a dinner party — we had this evening . . . Kyerulf's Nightingale.

. . . Miss Grant seems to have spoken very nicely of you personally — only that you are turning your capabilities in the wrong direction! and that you are conceited — she always says that. On that point my sisters and I have a difference of opinion. They say that you are sure to be conceited both as consequence and cause of having made your way as you have: and I say that you ought to be able to think you have some brains without being uppish about it and that if you are I will knock it out of you. Was that right?

Now there's another thing. I told my sisters yesterday that I had suggested to my father last Sunday when he said something vaguely about finding out more about you, that I thought Mr Hobson would be a good person to ask . . .

So I daresay I will spur my father up to call on him or something, as I am almost sure you wouldn't mind.

. . . My father wouldn't care to ask Sir S.[1] or Lady Montagu; he hardly knows them, — I don't think he would go for their opinions much.

. . . to think that I have a romance of my own is so laughable. By the way my niece Edith[2] has been here today & I was, so I did not feel free to ask her advice about you. as my matrimonial prospects have weighed on her mind for years. Only a few weeks ago she gave me a royal command to supply her with a new uncle, & when I asked what he was to be like he was to be a 'funny man'. That will I am sure frighten you more than any of the other requirements of my relations, but don't be downcast because I am quite supposed to be 'funny'. Visitors are always told by the children that I am, & it's most embarrassing to live up to. Today Edith was explaining to me why she liked me & to my disgust 'funny' was the first virtue and 'kind' only came in second best — I do hope it is not because I am a buffoon that you imagine you like me!

Goodnight, dearest.

---

1. Sir Samuel Montagu was a friend of the Gladstones who moved in socialist circles.
2. Daughter of Isabella and Basil Holmes.

Sunday 6.30 a.m.

Now I can say that you will be home next week; I'm afraid your mother won't be so pleased with the flight of time as I. But perhaps I shall be shy and grumpy by the time you are due.

Marian & Lily Montagu came here after Synagogue to see me, and they were so very very pleased about what I had told them that I began to think there must be something nice about it myself. They told me my sister Flo had been to see Miss Grant the day before. I hope you don't mind. I thought it very sensible of her; she might perhaps have asked me first, but I should have said she might, and of course I had talked about Miss Grant to her. So in the afternoon I asked her what Miss Grant had said: Bessie was there too, and we had some talk. Miss Grant had told her about your mother; neither she nor Bessie made any fuss about it. They said of course that it made no difference to you personally except in the effect it had upon your character & I told them some of what you had told me about that. Miss Grant seemed to have told my sister what she knew about you, but said she would write to her father & that she knew he would keep it quite dark even from her mother, and she would send Flo his answer. Flo had been waiting to speak to me till she had got this letter & had said nothing to my father. I said I would speak to him when the letter came, but I will wait also to hear from you in case you have anything you would like to tell me. I don't suppose my father will make a difficulty & if he talks it over with Flo and Bessie they see the matter exactly as I do.

I do hope I didn't do any harm by addressing your mother as Mrs MacDonald. Miss Grant said she is called Miss Ramsay. I do wish you would tell me how much she is entitled to be called an agricultural labourer, because Miss Grant will hold out (she did to me once before) that she never worked except in her own garden, and I told my sisters that you must know best & that you had told me she had worked in the fields at ordinary agricultural work.

1 p.m.   You must think I am a funny mixture from my letters. I hope I am not taking too much for granted that you will try to put up with me after the way I have treated Andrew Henderson.

I recalled my father to his parental duties and responsibilities this morning by giving him Mr Hobson's address. He seems to have got Sir Samuel Montagu on his mind too . . . I should like to set my father down to write an essay on you!

He gravely informed me this morning that your mother had wished you to go into the ministry; and that you had dined at Sir Philip Magnus'. Both may be true for all I know & my father may have the gift of second sight: but

I had to tell him that I had given him no foundation for either statement except with regard to the latter. I told him you knew the Sydney Webbs, & he said he had met them at the Magnus'. I am in terror now that he won't remember your name when he gets to Mr Hobson's & will come back fortified with the character of some different party.

I told Uncle George Gladstone about you last Tuesday; he smiled and said it was the way of the world, so I said it was a nice way if it was the right man, & he looked and said "Yes". He and his wife were very devoted. I don't think I told you, as I meant to, that she was the nearest approach we ever had to a mother: that is why I sent you her photograph though it was not a bit like her.

My grandmother is very, very weak today. Do you think your mother would mind my sending her my love: if she would not I would like you to give it to her please? I do want to see you very much, and I hope we shall not quarrel.

Yrs Margaret E. Gladstone

❧ Annie Ramsay to Margaret. . .

13 July 1896
Lossiemouth

My dear Margaret

Many thanks for the book and letter i shall read it and return it. My dear Gural i am sorry to here of your Grandmothers ilness i do hope she is better i now wat nursing is i my Grandmother My Aunt and then My Dear Mother My Mother was confined to bed for 4 years & 6 months and a Dear person in trouble she was. . . My dear gural you ask me for My young Mans Christian Name it is Jamie Ramsay MacDonald we call him Ramsay[1] My own name is Annie Ramsay My son is a good Son to me and i trust if it please God that you and Ramsay be happy i trust god will go with you in all your ups and downs in life and i shall be verry glad to sea you in Lossiemouth My dear gural you spake of Milking cowes i have milked cowes and mad butter and all that work but for the last 29 years doing little but sowing in My dear little home now My dear i will not forgoet to pray to god for you as i have doun for him in the past that god may be with you both and that you may be happy

---

1. In fact, in her earlier letters she addressed him as Jamie.

Ramsay will soon be back in London and i will be all alone again with much love And i hope you will writ me soon

From your friend
Mrs A Ramsay

Thank very much for your Photo by the time this reches you you will have my hom and do writ me and let me now wat you think ofit My Dear gural

with much love

❦ Ramsay to Margaret.

13 July 1896
[Lossiemouth]

My Dear Duchess of Lossie,
   . . .The place is now getting merry. The summer visitors are just arriving, two old friends of mine have just come today and my old pupil teacher with whom I have just been having a bathe. The water is exquisite and so refreshing. It is very odd to find these old fellows turning up in exactly the same clothes as they had on last year, playing exactly the same style of golf and taking up the old topics of conversation at exactly the point where we left them when we bade each other 'goodbye' twelve months ago. Sir William Gordon Cumming of baccarat fame, who owns a good deal of land up here, is now in the neighbourhood and his swears go further than his balls across the links. The last two days have been boiling hot, the sea has been calm as a mill-pond, and the sands have been glistening as though myriads of armed fairies had been marching along them.

   . . .The Webb business is really very painful to me. I opposed him because I thoroughly disagreed with him first as to the position which he imagined the will gave him, and then on how he was spending the money.[1] He took the opposition in very bad part and made it a kind of personal quarrel. I never meant it as such. . . I fear that I am very much in the Black Books at 41. Only I very rarely went there, as somehow or other the set was never very congenial to me, and I mortally hate all this advertising that goes

---

1. Henry Hutchinson left £10,000 for the 'propaganda and other purposes of the Fabian Society'. The Webbs used most of the money in the founding of the London School of Economics. Ramsay regarded this as misuse of the funds, and was perhaps piqued because Beatrice thought him 'not good enough' to be a lecturer at the School. He did not, however, bear grudges and had Sidney in his Cabinet in later years.

on from there. Still I am exceeding vexed that a difference in opinion should have put Webb (apparently) in the sulks. Only perhaps he thinks I am. . .

Yours ever,
The Duke

〜 Margaret to Ramsay.

14 July 1896, 6 p.m.
Pembridge Square

. . .What is the good of asking me for instructions: if you can't evolve your behaviour out of your own head I'm not going to do it for you? I've told you a good deal about them, so that you can perhaps judge a little. It would be an awfully jolly way to meet first quite casually at the club — if we didn't explode with laughing in the middle . . .

. . . I gave Mrs Hicks[1] a hint of the news yesterday: I could not resist it . . .

Yesterday morning I had a letter of "advice" from Aunt Fanny, talked over with Uncle W. I am just going to answer it; It is much the same advice as you insisted on pouring on my devoted head, only less forcibly expressed, and I am not sure that you laid quite enough stress on the sadness of my giving up my life to chimerical notions. They have been kind and courteous to me far beyond what I should have dared to expect knowing how much they dislike & disapprove of anything Socialistic & unorthodox . . . We have great jokes about their dining with the Queen. Uncle Wm has had to have trousers made on purpose — buttoned up at the ankle & he is to have socks without clocks: Aunt F was not quite sure if she had been able to get the latter, if not I suppose the Queen will spy the clocks & say "Avaunt Lord K."

. . . Do you know what my sisters are doing? Looking for a nice house near London where we can settle down for our holidays and you can come up & down sometimes to see us. Isn't it sweet of them? . . . I hope you will feel flattered at having the Laws of the Medes and Persians (which reign in this house) broken partly for your benefit. We always wander about far from London for our holidays. Certainly my father is less fond of travelling than he used to be, so the settling down will please him, though what on earth he will do with himself all day if he doesn't move about & sight see we can't imagine.

---

1. Margaret had recently met this lady, a working woman and a socialist, and had been much influenced by her.

. . . Do you know, I have omitted to tell you about one of the most important members of our household — dear old Bynoe, our black butler (only he's bleached a good deal) who has been in the family about 33 years, and takes a most fatherly interest in us all & in all our friends. You should hear him welcoming an old friend in the hall: everyone looks forward to seeing Bynoe again.

The Laws of the Medes and Persians also are safe in his hands; most of us don't know what they are but we should know if we broke them. Flo and Bessie ordered tea in the garden one Sunday lately & found it was a very very naughty thing to do . . .

∾ Ramsay to Margaret.

[July 1896]

[First page of letter missing]
I wish you were with me.

You really are making me quite foolish — and I am glad of it. Do take a house with a donkey in it and I'll make a second. If you are away flirting . . . there must be golf and a post office, but if you are about I want no more recreation than a church. If the glory of all — a visit to Lossiemouth — can be accomplished, then the cup of my happiness will be quite filled. Why don't you all come up here? . . .

I shall be glad to hear from Lily Montagu. She is a sort of mother to us [she introduced them] and if we don't fight we must stand her a spree out of our combined purses. I'll also observe old Bynoe and his ways and shall order myself accordingly. Shall I ask for 'Massa Gladstone.'

. . . My mother is very sensible of the shortcomings of her letter she says. She has been thinking a lot about you. I showed her the *Scotsman* paragraph [reporting on Lord Kelvin's jubilee]. 'Is that her uncle and aunt?' I said it was so. 'I'm sorry', said she, 'for you and that chap won't get on well together'. Democratically refreshing, isn't it? She thinks you are a brick and would lecture me on my duties to you if she could muster up courage. Only I was always a bit of a puzzle to her, and she had learned to trust to Providence. So perhaps you'll get the lecture. I know she would like to see you. She said that she had made up her mind to accept such as you. She has been specially busy sounding my praises to the neighbours as a kind of preliminary I suppose to some other announcement. In fact she is as happy as we are.

Now it is midnight and my hours here fly past with lightening speed. I'm loathe to part and yet I am keen to go. One more letter from this place which

90

is now twice as dear to me and then the scene will be changed. But here or there *I am thine unsatisfactory man.*

Ramsay was deeply hurt that the Gladstone family found it necessary to 'take up character references' by interviewing the Grants as if he were about to be employed as a cook.

🙰 Ramsay to Margaret.

14 July 1896
Lossiemouth

My Dearest Duchess,
 . . . THE DUKE AS COOK OUT OF EMPLOYMENT.
In a way the Duke was a little disappointed that Miss Grant should be approached and told why information was wanted. (I understand that she knew why she was being quizzed.) As to my mother, she is altogether out, as I believe my mother has already told you. Her gardening experiences only came after I was able to give her this house just after my grandmother died three or four years ago. My mother did both outside and inside farm work before I was born and for years afterwards used to go harvesting in order to make ends meet. Indeed she only dropped going out in Summer when I was able to come in with something. My father was an ordinary ploughman. I can just remember having seen him once long long ago leading some horses out of a cattle show in Elgin. I never saw him before and never again . . . If these clouds are to come up again between us two, I shall bow as I have done before, though it will be very very hard. And yet I know it is right that everything should come up. If you would write to my mother you are entitled to know everything. She will tell you I am sure everything about herself & myself — only I would like it if you never show me the letter. I am tired of these things. They have so often raised their heads when I felt happy. God knows, though, I have done penance for them. If the lash is again to be laid on my back, I am ready for it. Your sister, you say, suggested character! To me it has been a furnace. If I have a good quality in me it comes from these dark hours & bitter experiences.

I am also rather sorry that Mr Grant[1] is to be written to. The fact is that the Grants were always a mighty stage above us. I never went to his school because he taught at the Established School & I went to the Free Church School & when the Board School came in, so bitter was the opposition in the town to Mr Grant that a lot of us walked out two miles into the country to

---

1. Grant taught at the Established Church School in Lossie, and Ramsay went to the Free Church School. There was bitter rivalry between the two institutions.

another master. Latterly Mr Grant was degraded for inefficiency and as I was taking some interest in local affairs by that time & worked against him (I still think he was grievously inefficient though I am ashamed at my youthful enthusiasm) he blamed me amongst a few others for being his particular enemies. I never called upon them until I met the Miss Grants in London and found them nice. (I do not remember them at all in Lossiemouth.) Still, Mr Grant now knows me very well & though I do not believe for a moment that he harbours any ill-will against me, yet he can only give present impressions, & I am sorry he should know that anyone is enquiring about me. I shall try & see him, I think, and say it was quite a mistake — a gratuitous act of kindness. What is it exactly that is wanted? Is it a proof that my mother worked in the fields constantly for a living for some time — years and years in fact? There is at least one of her farmer masters still alive & you can write to him. I can send you his address. Or what is it? I wonder how all this will read to you or your sisters if you care to let them see it. Perhaps not well.

But it has been my evil shadow & ugh! that it should be the subject of silly corespondence between Baillee Grant and his daughter. It is one of the places where my skin is very thin — where in fact there is no skin at all, just raw flesh. But you satisfy yourself & everybody to be entitled to be satisfied. Only let there be no gossip. My mother knows it all. Get day and date, place and person from her. Check everything she says a la Women's Industrial Council Stat: Comm:[1] I abide by the result . . .

Next morning with a dull grey sky, a peaceful sea & an impending horror for the examination.[2] I almost think I shall remain here for ever so as not to risk that fight & so that you may always be atrociously fond of me.

. . . The day after tomorrow & gracious I am spinning South again! I don't believe we will have a hearty word for each other. We shall be as awkward as possible & the grand result of it all will be that we will laugh at each other. I once wrote that Nature made men fools & created women to give them a chance of exercising their natural endowments. It was abominable & you can put it down on your fine list if you like, but my dear lassie, this old stager as a swain will be a sight for the gods of sad visage. What will my Southampton "Comrades" say? They will put it down to softening of the brain.

Why didn't you give me further notice about your father's visit to Hobson? What I have laughed over that! I would have sacrificed a week's

---

1. Margaret was active on the Statistical Committee of the Women's Industrial Council.
2. By the Gladstone family.

holiday to be behind the door of a cupboard or something when poor J.A.H. was being cross-examined. You don't know the poor old book-worm with his funny twitches. I know how he must have been exploding inwardly.

But don't bother Sir S & Lady M. They don't know anything about me except that I now refuse every invitation to sprees that they send me. Hobson can stand for bookishness. Mr Richard Stapley of 33 Bloomsbury Square (Messrs Stapley & Smith, London Wall) and member of the Common Council or Mr Mackensie, manager of Edwin Jones & Co, the Whitelys of Southampton will tell you if I am satisfactory from a business man's point of view. Fletcher late of the Chronicle will certify as a Journalist, Tom Ellis, Sir Francis Evans, Sir Barrington Simson & Tommy Lough (I know them very well) will put in word as politicians, W. Whittaker F.R.S. will give a scientific opinion, the Lossiemouth fishermen know me as a smoker & the Southampton people as a gentleman. Keir Hardie and many others will certify as fools. When these are done I have another pack up my sleeve beginning with Lady Russell (Lord John's widow) with whom I used to stay occasionally until she got too frail. If my old friend Mark Wilks had been alive he could have told your father everything about me. I took him home with me for his last holiday. I was in a laboratory belonging to Sulman & Berry near Gower Street Station (I think the street is called George Street). Sulman has just discovered a new method of precipitating gold in washing & Berry (Edward E.) took some disease in the lungs and is now an exile in Bordeghera. He and I are still close friends and always meet when he comes over here in August. I also know the family well & when they were at Much Hadham used to visit them a great deal. One of the sons was Senior Wrangler & is now Fellow of Kings, but I have seen nothing of them since I met them last year in Surrey when I was staying with Miss & Mrs Toynbee (Arnold's sister & wife). We had a delightful party then — Miss Thackeray (Thack's daughter) Miss Ritchie, Miss Sichel, Mr Herbert Paul & his wife. We read Greek plays in the woods & had glorious music in the evenings together with L.P. discussions, literary talk and so on. I'm going to note what you say about chemists, (I always hated chemistry — geology & biology were my pets) and particularly the Queen's Scholarship & shall pay you out some day.

Your sisters are binding me to them with thongs & if they will only let me, when they know me, be their knight I shall be a most devoted champion of theirs in every cause they have in hand.

Of course your friends MUST feel objections to me. My mood at the moment is that I'm as good as they are and a darned sight better. Now Margaret just think of that. Tell your Aunts & Uncles all and sundry, that I am one of those odd people who think a peasant better than a peer & that I will act my opinion in their presence perhaps.

I think the best thing I can do is to go down to Southampton and make a violent attack on the intellectual quality of Scottish Liberal Unionism with special reference to Lord Kelvin's spinning of raw eggs before his class.

Yours
J.R.M.

〰 Margaret to Ramsay. . .

16 July 1896
11.30 a.m.
4 Hamilton Terrace

My *dear* Sir

My dear cook, I think I may tell you that you will very probably be engaged — only a personal interview is required: & I should be much obliged if you would let me have the refusal of your services & not take another place until I have decided. I will promise on my part not to let the place be filled at any rate until I know finally whether you would like to take it.

No further references will be required (what a lot of paper you did waste on them to be sure.)

I shall never ask your mother anything. I should not wish to. I will reverence your relatives & try to get as near them as they will let me & as I can; you must do the same with mine.

I read to Flo this morning all that you said about your past history & about the Grants. Of course she will not breathe to Miss Grant anything that Miss Grant does not know about — nor to anyone beyond the four walls of our house.

But I disagree with you on one point. A peasant is NOT better than a peer. It may be more easy for him to be good and worthy; but they are both men before anything else & must be judged equally as such.

. . . What a blessing laughter is: I can't think how people keep their strength up who think it is harmful to be bright when there is sorrow. Only this morning I nearly broke down over telling my aunts my grandmother's words. [Margaret dear, I am wearing away.]

. . . Now — thank you for the letters. I took them up to my grandmother's room to read them quietly there . . . it was especially good of you to send me that very nice one from "Mary" [Gwyther] I have MUCH nicer ones from Tom Mann than that. So gushing that I don't think I shall ever dare to show them you. The best way is to give each other cartes blanches. We are both so marvellous.

1.30 p.m.

I am sitting watching in charge of my grandmother.

What a mystery it is — the spirit so present here, now with all its memories & its thoughts, its struggles & its longings & perhaps in a few hours beyond our reach all together.

. . . Just now my grandmother was talking to me and about what my mother said of me when I was a baby. She said she would tell mother about me — and I said "Tell her GOD is very good to me."

Your Loving
Margaret Gladstone

PS I'll try to send a scrap at any rate tomorrow — & your letters.

  Ramsay to Margaret.

16 July 1896
Lossiemouth

My Dear Limb of the Aristocracy

The Scotsman of today announces that your Uncle & Aunt were dining with the Queen. That is one point in my favour. I have not yet condescended to dine with the mother of a blackguard like the Prince of Wales. I have selected my friends with better taste than that — up to now at any rate. If they dine wtih her it shows that any objection they may take to me is purely artificial. This is a growl in bad taste; but, my lassie, you must see all my sides, good, bad, and indifferent. I am glad that others are urging common sense difficulties on you. You must look round everything they say without passion or prejudice & any doubts you may have must be given against me. Unless after all that, you can say to me that you are prepared to face life with me, our marriage would be a failure, a lamentable failure. I am very, very fond of you. This has been the happiest holiday ever I have had; I am fearing indeed that I am too happy. But notwithstanding all that unless WE are going to throw a light upon the paths of our friends & the causes which are ours, I have strength of will still left to bow before a decree of separation. If our home could be made a place of solace & refreshing experience to all whom we love then, my dear lassie, we shall face everybody & our worth will break down opposition. But to attain to this, the only success of such a marriage as we contemplate, you must listen to all that your friends have to say against it & make up your mind on their case point by point. Above all, for God's own sake, do not marry me for my opinions. I am not proposing to do so for yours.

〰 Margaret to Ramsay.

17 July 1896
Hamilton Terrace

. . . I hope you will not find them (my folks) all very unresponsive and dull when you are making up your mind to like them: but you deserve to after the horrid letter I got from you this morning. And after I told Aunt Fanny I had been thinking over the pro's and con's of you for more than a year for you, ungrateful creature, to write to me as if I didn't know my own mind.

Flo and I have been settling the time and place of the duel. Will you call at 17 P Sq about 6.45 tomorrow (Saturday): if you are sleepy & cross it will be all the easier to fight. Only ask at the door for Miss Margaret & if I'm not in you will know that my grandmother or aunts have needed me so much I did not feel it right to leave. In that case, a thousand apologies for troubling you, but could you come at 12.45 pm on Sunday. The programme for either day is — fight with me — for thirty minutes, examination by my father for 15 minutes; meal with us and my charming sisters 38½ minutes — after that you can stay as long or as short as you feel inclined.

. . . Flo says that Miss Grant read her a good deal of her father's letter & that it was very straightforward & nice (again — I'm so sorry) & spoke most highly of you and your mother. Flo says that only she and Bessie & my father need ever know about your parentage. As far as we are concerned, & of course she and Bessie will never refer to it & you and I don't suppose my father will. Of course it may come up as you say, but we won't be afraid of that.

Farewell — not for very long now; and don't expect too much either from me or my people or your hair will turn grey with disappointment.

Yours at any rate till tomorrow.

Margaret

〰 Ramsay to Margaret.

[17 July 1896]
Lossiemouth

My also very dear Margaret Ethel Gladstone of that ilk. — I was very sorry to have the bad news of your grandmother this morning. Isn't this a very grim world, the music of which is the whisper of the lover and the gasp of the dying? I wonder will we be able to throw some sunshine across it. And so I am again packing for my home, for London is that now. Another glorious sunset and a bad game of golf have bidden farewell, and I go out into a new life. I am very happy. God is good. These past few days have been equal to years of deferred hopes and thorny paths. My dear, dear sweetheart!

But jealousy is in my heart. If every letter my mother writes to you means a lost train, a missed station and a midnight trudge through London streets I must prohibit her. Then, just to think that a possible mother-in-law has more effect upon you than a possible husband!

I sadly fear there is no chance of meeting you at the Club on Saturday. I would have liked a look of you before we met at 17. I really believe I love you because you are, first of all, funny and then because you are kind. And still that cold self-examination does not make me wise. My folly increases with the days and your letters. Do you know I was the patent joker amongst my friends about love making and the writing of love letters. Such old hands as Samuel Hobson and Enid Stacey etc. (they have suffered poor things by my tongue) will simply explode when they hear that I have become as big a fool as they have been. My philosophy of marriage to them has been: when a man gets tired of the paradise of bachelors he enters the wilderness of marriage, when he gets tired in the wilderness he commits suicide. When a woman enters into league with the evil one she makes love, when she is saved from her sins she dies. How can I look them in the face and say 'I love Margaret Ethel Gladstone', what have you wrought! That nether lip and that fringe in the bridesmaid photograph! Do have a fringe when I see you. You really *are* funny. I quite understand your reputation. The Duchess does not know herself. But what Duchess does? She requires a Duke to hold up a mirror for her. My decision is: you are funny.

I have a tiny spark of hope in me that you may manage to come to Lossiemouth and that you will persuade me to chaperone you. In August it will be Paradise — particularly the last week. I'll take you out for a sail and let you catch fish for my breakfast.

Now I'm off to bed. Tra-la-la.

Ever yours,
James Donald Ramsay [sic]

Your unsocialist socialist, why have you started an Esq.

❦ Margaret to Ramsay.

18 July 1896
postcard

Last Confession of one of the Kilkenny Cats.
Saturday, eighteenth of July 1896
17 Pembridge Square 8 a.m.

You told me yesterday not to marry you for your opinions.

P.T.O.

If you become a Tory, a Liberal Unionist, or a Liberal who dined regularly
with the Queen,
I would not marry you but I would LOVE you still.
WILL THAT DO?

❦ Margaret's diary.

18 July 1896

. . . over to Chancery Lane to see Mr. Macpherson . . . Home JRM Came.
Introductions . . .

19 July 1896

. . .JRM came [to] D[inner] . . .

Some of Margaret's friends were concerned.

❦ Florrie Kemsley to Margaret.

19 July 1896

. . . I don't seem to know merely about him [Ramsay] except that with you
he is a Radical & Socialist, Independent Labour Candidate, Fabian, Trade
Unionist, Home Ruler, a writer of revolutionary articles in newspapers —
and is in fact all these things and many more (if there are any) that I entirely
disapprove of and I expect before long he will be teaching you to steal the
family silver from under Bynoe's nose.

〰 Ramsay to Margaret.

20 July 1896
Duncan Buildings

My Dearest Lassie,

A kiss to greet you on your birthday morning. May this new mile be crammed of everything that profiteth the soul for you. Not even in Lossiemouth with the bridesmaid photo by me did I think you so sweet as you were last night and as I am sure you are going to be today. I *did* try to show you how dearly I loved you but I laugh at my performance. I have been so long accustomed to consume my own feelings, that I am a frightfully bad subject for an angel confessor. But you know tha, and I'll come out of it in time. You'll teach me to be spry. Everything is so changed to me that I sometimes wonder if I had died and left my body at home and am now in a new state of existence. But that can hardly be as I seem to have known you for some time. Only they say such delusions happen in heaven. Now you see I ramble all over existence to tell you that I greet you on your *dies natalis*. My dearest sweetheart you have made a fool of me. I am so happy. Under this you will find the tiniest wafer of a kiss — so tiny that only your heart will know it is there. Take it as my offering this morning at your shrine. The little book may remind us both in years to come of these early exquisite moments of true love.

Every thine, my dearest sweetheart,
Ramsay

The Dook
X
His kiss

[On the outside of the envelope.]

Sweet seventeen has been praised by poets
For beauty and for bloom
And forty laughed at till we know it's
The gathering shades of doom.

But he who'd fix the happy age
When bloom and shadow mix —
When youth is joyful still yet sage —
Will vote for twenty-six.

❧ Margaret's diary.

20 July 1896

My 26th birthday . . . Ramsay in. [to Hamilton Terrace]

❧ Margaret to Ramsay.

20 July 1896
Hamilton Terrace

. . . I took the Dook's birthday greeting kiss and felt all the better for it — like a pill. But the Dook makes me feel very bad when he says nice things & then pretends he can't. It makes poor little me who can't even write ½ or ¼ of a line of rhyme feel so very very prosaic & dull & matter of fact. But what a blessed thing it is if my love has helped you already it has given some sunshine to those around us.

As far as I remember this was meant to be a business note in case I don't get to the tea-party or am so entranced by Mrs Webb's tea-party that I don't get on to you! I know my aunts would like to see you here ANY time; if your Fabian committee is over early enough and you care to come for a few minutes before 10 p.m. tonight do or tomorrow morning early. I have made no plans for tomorrow yet — I have a committee at 4.30 but I think it will get shunted.

Also I wanted to say, why don't you ask my people to your rooms this week if it suits you: only you must include my father or he will be jealous. I don't know their engagements — except that Friday afternoon is not a good time. I would come or not as I could or not . . .

P.S. You passed your preliminaries awfully well everywhere and it was very nice and dear of you.

❧ Ramsay to Margaret.

20 July 1896

My dearest Margaret,

I must tell you what a happy day I have had with you. It is all too good. The best of all your friends are your aunts [Elizabeth and Agnes King]. I know them. They are Scotch. When they told me of all their family love and loyalty I almost felt criminal to endanger it. But it all only makes me more sensible of the great and good treasure I have been blessed with in you. If only I had the old religious beliefs I would be happy in being so chosen by God; but my feelings are those of awe for that unknown power in whose hands we are and whose thought is fashioning us in love, and in fulfilment of whose purposes we have both had our disciplines — you yours, I mine — so varied and yet so harmoniously blending now. I really wish I could show off better for your sake. But do tell your aunts how kind and good and sympathetic I felt them to be and how sorry I am, at such a time, that my Scottish nature sticks so closely to me and that when I try to say anything that would give them an idea of my feelings I wish I could creep away out of sight into a mouse hole.

When I came in, *The Album* was staring me in the face and seemed to say 'Send me. I may help'. Perhaps what is in it may just enable you to say that it is not only your (blind?) eyes that see any hope in me. But all these things are of small matter. *We* understand each other; and *we* love each other; and our love is to make us *work* together. Everything is comprehended in that. You make me feel a strong man. If ever I could do anything, I can do it now. And now, lassie, I am off to bed happy and hopeful.

Ever your sweetheart, Ramsay

∽ Ramsay to Margaret.

?21 July 1896

Dear Sweetheart,

What a fool I have been to live for so many years as I have done today without the glimpse of a face I love. And yet I was wise, for at the end of the long dark way there the Duchess stood. I got a wire from Carpenter[1] this afternoon saying his wife was ill and asking me not to go to supper. I missed Miss Grant this morning and as she wanted to see me very specially I went to 12 K.P.G. in the early evening and had a long talk with her. She was troubled about what she had done and wanted to know what she was to say when she went home. I am glad I saw her as it settled some anxieties. Then I thought I would see my Margaret but remembered her preference for Mrs Webb, stood in the pavement a moment, shut my teeth hard and muttered 'No, not tonight', and went to Hobson's to do some Progressive Review business. Now you see how independent I am. How happy we were last night! Oh for a year of those hours! As you have added to my self-conceit, I will add to yours. Hobson is gone upon you. He thinks you will make an excellent wife. But everybody likes you.

Give my love to your aunts and your uncle George. Tell your aunts my tie was much worse than usual today. It would not behave itself and I

---

1. Edward Carpenter, the Fabian poet and Simple Lifer.

abandoned it to its own freedom and walked about with a streamer over my shoulder. Were it God's will to relieve you all now, your poor grandmother included, it would be a blessing.

> Ever thine with love,
> Ramsay.

∽ Annie Ramsay to Margaret.

> 20 July 1896
> Lossiemouth

My dear Margaret,

Your very kind letter came all right My Dear gural. Many thanks. How is your grandmother? I am sorry to see by your letter she suffers so much pain. My Dear Mother suffered a gret deall of pain. Now My Dear Margaret i am all alone now and i saw Ramsays heart was in London and not at home. i am glad to sea by a Post Card i got to night he is back to London and is so happy. i do hope god will bliss you both. i now Ramsay is good and kind and i trust with god's blissing the wone will be a good help to each other. Dear Margaret I do hope you may soon com to Lossiemouth and we will sea each other and that love may dwell in our hearts. You must now the love i have for my young man and i do hope i may get you My Dear girel to love too. But you now we must set god before us and all ouer ways and then we are sure happy ness will folly

Dear Margaret when we sea each other we can tauck to over many things.

Now My Dear may god be your gide and gard you. With much love from your Frind,

> A. Ramsay

∽ Margaret to Ramsay.

> 22 July 1896. 12.30 p.m.
> My grandmother's room

My dear Ramsay (I must get accustomed to that horrid new fancied way of addressing you)

My grandmother is very much weaker than yesterday morning. The doctor says no one can tell how long it may be, but we feel as if it must surely be very near, so I am not going to stir far today. — not even to 17 P S. I have a good many engagements, but as you know I think quite lightly of breaking engagements of any kind. Dear Sir, you know it is only because I am so absolutely sure we love each other truly that I can joke about it at all . . . How good "Mary" was to us last night & didn't we have fun with Tom? If we had been able to foresee two years ago that Mrs Hicks & Mrs Webb & Tom Mann would be among the first persons I should confide my engagement to, I should have stood on my head with joy . . . & I do hope we shall both be really fitter for our work and have a better "personal influence" (see a letter I send you) from our love. The letter I send you — besides May's — is one I think you will like to send. It is from Aunt Matilda's second son: one of those cousins I so mercilessly call uninteresting. He has been in love with me for a good long time, & been rather a self-conscious ass, I always think; but with good feeling as this letter shows. I really gave him a hint about you, without telling your name and saying we might never be engaged — even a day or two before I told my father — because I happened to get a letter from him just then which I couldn't quite stand under the circumstances (only saying he hardly dared to pray that I might ever marry him) — & I thought he had better not even think of daring to do so.

3.30 p.m.

P.S.

Since closing this, I have had such nice talks, first with Flo alone, & then with her and Bessie that I must tell you a little about them. They really are bricks. I knew they were. We are all three very indignant with my father for not taking a more intelligent interest in it! but then it gets more difficult every year to get him to take an I.I. in anything but Athelstan Riley.[1]

And Aunt F & Uncle W. are kindness itself you know (I'm sure they think you nice & it's awfully good of them when they are so fond of Duchesses (or Aunt F. is). Flo said to me in the mildest of voices, "Well, it is rather unfortunate to distress your relations" and I said that of course it was but I thought it the only thing to be done if I cared about a man & thought him the right man . . .

You should have seen Uncle William & Aunt Fanny too, kissing their hands to me out of the Hansom as they drove off (I had walked down the terrace with them to tell them) & looking so bright & kind. Aunt Fanny says, & I think very wisely, that you had better have got to know my father and sisters and been about the house a little longer before I tell my grandmother (that is assuming that she goes on improving as at present); it

---

1. Athelstan Riley (1858–1945): Eton, Pembroke College Oxford. Traveller in Persia, Turkey and Kurdistan in 1881–8. Member of House of Laymen of the Province of Canterbury to 1932.

would be less startling for her. She is so clear headed: she would want to know every detail & would think it all over even now if I told her, & she is so very weak that freedom from every possible excitement is her only chance. And I couldn't possibly go off to Lossiemouth without telling her why. It is rather hard on us, but perhaps it would have been quite too like heaven to go to Lossiemouth so soon: the only thing I really mind for is that I shan't make the acquaintance of your mother so soon. Will that wretched old Review really take up all your time hopelessly after you get back? Of course if my grandmother got on very well I might tell her, but I can't quite imagine doing it within a fortnight as it would have to be if we are to go to Lossiemouth & be here for the International & I'm not going to miss that. I daresay she won't worry about it especially if the Aristocracy (Uncle W & Aunt F) remain on my side; I fear my grandmother is rather painfully fond of grandees; but she couldn't fail to be excited over it anyhow.

I must go down stairs and tease Flo soon. (Have I told you yet that she is the family butt and we all get our share of teasing but she much more than her share.) She is generally last down to breakfast but today is her grand day where she goes with lots of Notting Hill Mammas to the seaside, and she has to have breakfast at 7.30, poor thing. It's Bessie's birthday too & I don't think we have got enough presents for her so I must see if I can get some. Do you know anything about fines and deductions in shops? I don't but I have to read a paper on the subject & spout it in a hall in October that holds 1500 people in Manchester. I never promised to spout in public before, but Mrs Hicks and Mrs Webb are to speak at the same time and it was quite too tempting though I can't imagine myself coming out alive. It's only to philanthropic ladies, so you won't think much of it (I can get plenty of information, I think). I've never told you about my two most intimate girl friends — they are about as different as different can be both from each other and myself.

One is T[eenie] MacKenzie who has quarrelled with her people and come to live with strangers & does nothing much but society & knows lots of stagey people & has a new love affair nearly every time I see her (I get the benefit of them, & I suppose it doesn't do her harm if she wants to talk. I don't remember ever mentioning your name to her). The other is Florrie Kemsley who lives in the depths of the country — her father is a farmer — and sees hardly anything of the world except when she comes to stay with us, and then we do rush around, but who is the honestest & best & nicest girl who ever lived. Neither of them are the least inclined to Socialism. The Montagus you know: I like them very much. I don't suppose I shall tell anyone else (I shan't tell the girls) about you till I see you & have a chance of that quarrel, except perhaps my Uncle George Gladstone, the Salvation Army one, because I do like him so very much. I flirt systematically with him so you will be jealous.

Oh Sir, under all this I feel as if I ought to be hiding my face & not daring to look up. It is all too big for me.

Yr MEG.

∾ Margaret to Ramsay.

22 July 1896
Hamilton Terrace

Dear Ramsay,

We hardly think my grandmother will live through the night: we are going to sit up with her in turns . . . Don't feel an intruder even in this sadness; they won't expect you to say much, so long as you sympathise. It is really only these three cousins — A.H. [Andrew Henderson], James Thomson and Joshua G. who have ever had to be refused . . . I have been to get a ring out of my aunts as a pattern: but my fingers are too fat for their . . .

yours
Margaret

Letters received on becoming engaged.

To Ramsay.

From Margaret's father

22 July 1896

My Dear MacDonald,

I must acknowledge your warm-hearted letter. No doubt in assenting to your union with my daughter Margaret, I do show my public faith in you; but from all that I have heard and seen during the last fortnight I believe that you are worthy of that confidence.

I pray that by God's blessing your union may, indeed, be for the good both of her and yourself, as well as those in whose welfare you are so much interested.

Hoping to see you tomorrow.

I remain very sincerely yours,

J.H. Gladstone

105

❧ From Florence Hobson.

I am alone in sea-side lodging & have lost my pen on the sands! There is not time before post to get another. So please forgive a pencilled scrawl to wish you joy on your engagement & warmest congratulations — We are delighted at the news & think you and Miss Gladstone stand a far better chance of being happy than most couples in the like predicament.

❧ From Emma Brooke.

I do not feel inclined to miss a post in congratulating you on the happiness I hear has come into your life. It was from Miss Gladstone's own lips I heard it and have her permission to write, and I am sure you are much to be congratulated on the wife you have won. I heard you were suffering from insomnia; but perhaps it is only the insomnia of Joy!

❧ From Mary Gilbrand Husband.

I have been refusing to believe my ears for some days, but now my eyes have taken sides with their discredited brethren and the citadel of scepticism is stormed. "Oh you!" . . . What about "The pipe of yr soul"? What about "La vie bohème"? What about . . .?

❧ From J.F. Husband.

I am delighted to be married. With all the wisdom of 15 months' experiance of this full and happy state, with all the developed insight of a developed relation, I warmly welcome you as a valuable recruit into the cosmic-domestic army. No preaching about the simple-sanctities, the home-humanities. May goodness and mercy follow you all the days of your double life!

❧ From Enid Stacey.

24 July 1896

I am maliciously chortling at the idea of your being married in correct form and in a church!! And oh you renegade and traitor — you even refused to come to ours "on principle".

❧ From John Stirton.

23 July 1896
[Southampton]

If I am right the future Mrs JRM was known to us by her kindly help at the General Election. When a young lady comes out and helps us workingmen to fight for Labour we think of her as we think of the angels.

❧ To Margaret.

From her half-sister, Isabella Holmes.

22 July 1896
5 Freiland Road
London

My dear Margaret,

I don't think there is much to be said — as you seem to have settled up matters for yourself — than to assure you what you must know already, that we hope you will be very happy. As for the "political and social views" being "rather different from those of the rest of the family" I must say I always thought our family was singularly free from "views" — and yours will no doubt be modified with age and experience.

Don't be one-sided in your choice of friends.

I am afraid it will be some days before I shall be able to get about the house — and until then I am much too lazy to be properly dressed. You shall know as soon as I can receive visitors.

These are rather "trying times" for you I fear, what with your engagement and your grandmother's illness.

With best love and all good wishes

Yours affectionately
I.M. Holmes

❧ From Beatrice Webb.

[22 July 1896]

My husband and I were immensely interested in your news (about which we will be absolutely discreet). We have always had a warm admiration for Mr MacDonald & steady faith in his future career. That faith will be heightened by the knowledge that he has secured such a helpmate: it is exactly what is needed to supplement his fine qualities.

❧ From Annie Hicks.

[?22 July 1896]

Dear Miss Gladstone,

Will you accept this hot water bottle from Mrs James, Claire and myself. With all good wishes for your future happiness and prosperity.

Yours ever sincere
Annie Hicks

❧ From Ernest Gladstone.

22 July 1896

Dear Margaret

We are most pleased to hear of your engagement and I congratulate you most sincerely.

I feel sure Mr MacDonald is just the cousin we shall like; and now that you have chosen to make him happy, hope he will add greatly to your life. I hope too you will want to make your home near London, so that we benefit by the new cousin and shan't lose you.

Believe me

With best wishes for your future happiness
your affectionate cousin
J. Ernest Gladstone

❧ Ramsay to Margaret.

23 July 1896

My Dearest Sweetheart,

I wanted very badly to see you tonight, to kiss you and hear what had happened. But I thought and thought about it with the result that it seemed best not to intrude. Your father also agreed. Then I was to wire you but found that it would be ten and perhaps after, before you would get it. So here I am unhappy and dissatisfied with myself. The day has been troublesome. The few minutes in the garden were a blessing. Tomorrow I shall be at the Museum, my old place, or in the Newspaper room from 10 to 12.45; then I shall be at the club, then at the Prog: Rev: Office and at 4.30. at the Fabian Executive. Couldn't we meet somewhere in the evening and have a walk rather than sit in drawing rooms? I had no opportunity of talking to your father tonight. I'll look in here about the middle of the day for messages.

I am confounded to hear that poor Carry Martin is dead.[1]

My dearie, how mysterious are our births, our loves and our deaths. Just now I have no heart for anything. God bless you my sweetheart for the light you throw around you.

Ever,
Ramsay.

〜 Margaret to Ramsay.   23 July 1896
                                                        Hamilton Terrace

. . . Now I have just been in the garden reading my letters. My dear love, the 'little fat boy' is just precisely like what I thought he would be. I believe I must have taken a trip from my cradle to look at him — I seem to know him so well with his sturdy boots and his top-knot. I've just shown him to the housemaid — no other sympathetic soul being about . . .

A comparatively gushing letter from Bella . . . ending with 'best love' . . .

〜 Margaret to Ramsay.

                                               24 July 1896, 12.14 a.m.
                                               postcard
                                               posted Paddington

My grandmother died 9 p.m. . . . I could meet you a few minutes anywhere if you telegraphed here quite early.

M.E.G.

〜 Margaret to Ramsay.   24 July 1896
                                                       Pembridge Square

My dear Sir,

. . . Would it be possible for you to come to St Saviour's, the church we went to, for the funeral service at 3 pm next Wednesday? . . .

Yours lovingly
Margaretta.

P.S. Dinner at George King's 7.30 pm Thursday, is that right? Oh dear Sir, Don't break it off: I won't always be inflicting my relations on you (and you on them) . . .

---

1. Caroline Martyn. Ramsay took her place on the NAC.

〰 Annie Ramsay to Margaret.

27 July 1896
Lossiemouth

My Dear Margaret

I received your kind letter and was so pleased to hear from you i am glad everything went so nice wat a fue days i spent before i got Ramsays not i now wat it was all but we propose God dispossess and many a dark day have i spent since then but God has given me more then i every thought of. A good son and a Honourable win and i do trust god will make you both happy and now My Dear Margaret i will be looking forward to seeing you by other 4 weeks and that we shall like other and be verry happy to gether as fir as me i will do all in My power to make you both happy.

Now Dear Margaret how is your Granmother i do fell fir you it is so traying i went to Forres in Wendsay and saw my Aunt Campbell that is My Mothers only sister Alive now

Now my dear i will close with god to bless and keep you both

And May every good Atund you from your

Mother as it must be

A Ramsay

if god spares you i will hae 2 for won.

CHAPTER 4

August–December 1896

'Learning how to do our lovemaking'

The wedding was planned. For Ramsay there were the Gladstone and King drawing-rooms to be faced, forbidding and grand, with aunts and sisters snobbish and suspicious of the radical rascal who was about to make off with their beloved Margaret. She too had to go through the family examination, and went up to Lossiemouth on her own to show Annie Ramsay that she could make porridge. Ramsay was house-hunting in Bloomsbury and Holborn while Margaret nursed Aunt Elizabeth in Berkshire. Together they went to the International Socialist Congress and to dinners and parties with their friends and her relatives. A few weekends were spent at Chilworth, where John Gladstone had taken a house for the summer.

As far as work was concerned, Ramsay was writing, speech-making and organizing with renewed vigour. He was nursing Southampton, supporting socialist candidates throughout the country and squabbling with the Fabians, who caused great offence to the ILP by publicly attacking the putting up of 'frivolous' candidates for Parliament. Most of Ramsay's working hours were taken up with the launching of the *Progressive Review* of which he was the secretary. The journal was the organ of the Rainbow Circle, a radical discussion group composed of liberals and socialists. Margaret meanwhile was finding it difficult to concentrate on anything except her 'sir'.

~ Margaret to Ramsay.

Sunday 2 August 1896
Pembridge Square

Dear Ramsay,

I suppose you are just going off on your train. I am not having such a complete holiday as I might, because I have been thinking about you, and wondering if you are getting on nicely with thinking over your speech and whether that nasty cold has developed, & why you love me, and all sorts of other questions difficult to answer. And through it all the thing that I think most of all is that I love you very much & you are a very good Sir!

10.40 a.m. Just off with my father to church (the lot has fallen today on St Peter's, our parish church). I suppose we shall talk about Lossiemouth. How is Ramsay getting on in the train?

8 p.m. I wonder now how Ramsay is getting on with his speech: I do so wish I could be there to hear — I am sure it would do me good. But I have been very happy reading Blake in the garden — and receiving confidences from Flo about HER old romances! I think I shall be able to work Lossiemouth all right in a day or two, without upsetting anybody. They will be pleased to see you on Tuesday evening if you can come. So will the Duchess — though she is not pining for the Duke one least little bit. Only she thought he would have looked rather nice in a chair in the garden this evening . . .

Flo says she is sure my father is really pleased about our engagement. I mildly suggested to her that I was aware how you & she are flirting.

I enclose a ring (the nobbly one) which fits me. I don't know what it is or where I got it from. The other is for you from me: You will not I am sure mind the name being wrong: I can't afford to get a new one, each time!

Dear Sir, I mustn't run on any more: you know I love you.

Yours
Margaret.

~ Annie Ramsay to Margaret.

5 August 1896
Lossiemouth

My Dear Margaret

i shuld have writen you sonner My Dear Gural i was sorry to here of your granmothers death we feel sory to part with frinds near and dear to us but we have a good hope that we shall meet them and My god lead us and prepare us for we now not the houre the calls coms i have not been so well for sum days back but hopes will soon be all right again My Dear Margaret i am looking forward seaing you and Ramsay Now in 3 weeks if all is well Miss Grant called last week & gave me all the nuses but it is yourself i am thinking to sea My Dear Margaret till Ramsay he did surprised the people of Lossiemouth When the courant came out on Tuesday with the engagement in it so now won new of it till then but near Frinds Now my Dear Margaret i do trust you are none the worse of your nurseing and may your happyness brighten you in the midst of greff My Dear giral May god gide and keep you both and with much love to Ramsay and yourself with i hope soon to sea you My Dear Margaret

From your Mother

A Ramsay

i winder wat you will think of me When you sea me My Dear Gural

∾ Bessie Gladstone to Margaret.

7 August 1896

Coutances

. . . I feel decidedly doubtful about the happiness of the event (the engagement) myself, & I think you must by no means hurry on your marriage. Mr MacDonald is evidently a man of good nature, & good capabilities & honest & sincere. But he is crude — & certainly must develop in cultivation & refinement if he is to rank as a gentleman. I think you can help him to this, if you choose; but it will not be by lowering yourself & you can help him best by retaining every inch of your own dignity & 'lady like ness'. This latter quality is not superficial, it goes down to the very root of the being . . .

∾ Ramsay to Margaret.

10 August 1896

The Socialist Club

Holborn E.C.

Ma très Chère Margaretta

The paper betrays my whereabouts & the letter my thoughts. Yes 'twas a grand day yesterday. Chilworth must be our Mecca in days to come, when the bloom is on the heath & the sand makes dirty shirt tails and the sudden evening shades make it improper for us to sit alone in the smoking room even with "Paracelsus" and the "Barrack Room Ballads" handy to deceive an intruder.

113

. . . Are you going to the Trades Union Congress in Edinburgh? I have had an invitation this morning to speak at the Women's demonstration but I hardly think I can afford to be away . . .

With the very pleasantest memories of Chilworth humming in my soul and the very best of all love to my sweetheart whose ever I am

Ramsay

3 August 1896
Birmingham

My Dearest Lassie

Just a line before breakfast to show that even here you rule my thoughts. What were you doing yesterday? We had a pleasant day. On my way to Euston I looked in and saw Mary Gwyther. They want to see you again. Then when I got up here I had a nice welcome from Sammie [Samuel Hobson] and his wife & a bad scolding that I was only to remain a day or so as they had planned a week's entertainment. But I pleased your broken heart & we came to a compromise. I am to leave this on Wednesday morning (so the Tuesday dinner will have my place by you vacant unless Uncle George fills my shoes for the time being). To-day we go to see the opening of Australia V. Warwickshire & to morrow we go on a spree to Stratford-on-Avon. Could you come to Stratford? . . .

Contemplating the bliss of two young silly creatures in front of me, words fail me & I can only fill the remaining space with hosts of invisible kisses.

Off to the cricket match.

Ever thine with love.

∾ Ramsay to Margaret.

[August 1896]

My Dear Sweetheart

Hobson says we must leave in 10 minutes so have no time to relate MY problems. Off to Stratford-on-Avon to wusship at William's tomb.

Ever thine
Ramsay

Hobsons send love.

Who is my love? Indeed I cannot say
She's in the earth, the heaven & in the sea,
She is the whispering of God's mystery,
She is the notes of Love's Eternal lay.

I only know that on a certain day
I felt a guardian angel's watching care
And ere I scanned her face knew she was fair
And ere I told my love, had heard her "yea".

My love is but a door through which I've passed
Into a life & world that are both new,
I yet am at the threshold & the vast
Meads, dells & hills are scarcely yet in view.

> A congratulatory letter (annotated by Ramsay) from Helen Bosanquet. She was the secretary of the Haggerston and Hoxton Charity Organisation Society where for some time Margaret had been spending two days a week arranging both chairs for invalids and outings for children.

7 Cheyne Gardens
Chelsea
12 August 1896

[A LOATHSOME CREATURE & A LOATHSOME HUSBAND.]

My Dear Miss Gladstone

I had not heard your news: thank you very much for writing to tell me. I am sure you know that you have my very good wishes (HOPE NOT) and I cannot wish you better than that you may be as happy as I am (GET AWAY). We know Mr MacDonald by name (THANK GOODNESS YES, ONLY) and I believe I met him once at a meeting of the Fabian Society (WHEN SHE MADE AN ASS OF HERSELF & I KISSED AWAY HER TEARS). You will let me say that I think he is very fortunate; I think that your well earned experience should be invaluable to him, interested as he is in social matters. Does it mean we shall lose you in Shoreditch? I hope not (BUT I DO!) but of course you will have other claims on your time now (AND HIGHER MORAL STANDARDS). You do not tell me whether you are to be married soon, or whether you will live in London. (NONE OF HER BUSINESS.) I should very much like to know more about you if you have any time to spare. We have come home earlier than we expected because of bad weather (AND THOUGHTS OF EXTRAVAGANCE.) But we are not taking up work yet (LAZY BRUTES). I am trying to learn to bicycle (FOOL ENOUGH FOR ANYTHING) in the rather far off hope of being able to get to Shoreditch without going through the horrors of the underground; it would make the work much lighter. (PERSUADE HER TO WEAR KNICKERBOCKERS). . .

Believe me

> Yours affectionately
> Helen Bosanquet

[UGH!]

❦ Margaret to Ramsay.

14 August 1896
Chilworth, Surrey

Dear Ramsay

Charing Cross	10.55	2.5	4.25	5.14
Chilworth	12.54	3.50	6.20	7.9

I think these are alright, but of course could not say for certain.

. . . We are all very jolly here: I am so glad Bella is down: we see so little of her now-a-days. Edith pretends to be enraptured with you — has been telling May she likes you awfully. I can't imagine why, but May says it's affectation. I told Edith you were going to bring her down a story book, & she said "Oh, he IS a good man — I do love him." Isn't it horrid when girls are so forward. She says she likes girls' books better than boys' books — I expect you have something neutral in that bookcase of yours.

I hope you are seeing your way to go to Edinburgh. I have often wanted you to go to the T.U.C. Congress, and more than ever after the International C. It is rather appalling to think that you and I have to 'live up' to the Webbs & Bosanquets! Thanks for "New Age". I think you said right things in it.

Hope the Berrys are nice.

> Ever thy Margaret.

17 August 1896
Alnmouth, Northumberland

My dear Margaret Ethel

. . . I want to give you our best wishes on your engagement, & we hope much that it will bring you all happiness. — Of course we know that it is not such an engagement as your friends could have wished for you but if you feel it is the right thing for you and if it brings you *true* happiness your friends cannot wish more for you than that. Your love will be put to the test,

116

as no doubt you will have to give up something for the sake of your Fiancé but I suppose love is not worth much unless it can stand being tested . . .

With our much love, believe me,

Yr affectionate Cousin

Annie E. Bottomly

~ Margaret to Ramsay.

18 August 1896

Chilworth, Surrey

My dear Ramsay,

I have just woke up, & of course thought of you. It is pelting here & personally I am rather glad as I want to write about 30 letters today besides having other writing to do, & it will give me a better chance. I believe you must have transferred your want of sleep to me last evening. I kept dozing off over the "Cooperative Movement" in the drawingroom, and when I escaped to bed could hardly keep my eyes open through the necessary preparations. I was wide awake enough though to hope I was transferring my sleepiness to you, and to send a little blessing — the biggest and best I could think of — travelling up to London.

. . . My *dear* Sir, I have been very happy since I saw you (since we parted) . . . I was going to say but that sounded too near the truth. I am just very gradually finding out how much richer in meaning & in beauty every thing is to me because of our love. That is not an idea stolen from your poem, it is quite my own as well as yours. It has struck me specially just in reading books and newspapers; it all seems nearer to me & more human than it did before.

To think of those 29 letters I ought to be writing!

It is a month today since that historic meeting when I wore a golden halo & you a malicious grin.

10 a.m.

No word from the Montagus yet. I am writing to them about Friday & Sunday & Monday.

I enclose letters from Mrs Bodes, from another old C.O.I. [Charity Organisation Society] pensioner, and a nursing friend of mine — for you to read at your leisure; don't lose Mrs Bosanquet's, please: you haven't returned it! I do hope I shall see Stirton at Southampton.

I'm gradually getting through the 29, I hope you are doing ditto with the "New Age".

Margaret the Faithful.

  Ramsay to Margaret.

18 August 1896
Duncan Buildings

My Dear Best Girl

. . . Then there was that mysterious transference of your blissful sleep to me. I slept last night like a top, despite a hard day. When I awake tomorrow, I shall think of my lassie and the way she can lead me into the Land of Dreams just as she led me over the hills of Surrey. I really do not know now what I should do without my lassie. She has turned me a nice Topsy-Turvy and I would not be sane again for anything. It is so pleasant to think that someone is thinking sweet things of you and even more pleasant to return sweet thoughts in exchange.

I have written to my mother telling her that you may after all be able to go up to see her before you run away with me and no doubt you will hear from her. She has not been very well she says but is apparently getting better. My aunt has written asking if I had forgotten that I promised to run down to Shoreham and see her and I have written her explaining to her why I had said nothing . . .

Yes, it is one long month since you came sailing into the drawing room holding up your cheek in a most forward way and making it quite impossible for me to quarrel with you whether I had made up my mind to do so or not. But what a nice month it has been and what a sweet new spring time has come at the end of summer?

I am very sorry that we are to be in different places in Southampton, but you see if you will have a man who has other than domestic interests and who only thinks his dear lassie one of the great blessings of life you must put up with him, faults and all . . .

Ever thine
Ramsay.

  Ramsay to his mother.

[c. 18 August 1896]

Professor Gladstone was very kind . . .

I know you will like her when you see her and she will not make you feel uncomfortable in the least. Only please get flower pot saucers and abolish those hideous plates you have got under the pots at present. Also take down the photographs of me on the wall beside the Alma Tadema. It is exceedingly bad taste . . .

∾ Annie Ramsay to Margaret.

19 August 1896
Lossiemouth

My Dear Margaret
    i received your king letter i am keping much beter i had a letter from
Ramsay and he tells me you are comming to sea me i shall be so pleased to
sea you and make you as comfortable as i can and i do hope you will get
good weather when you am North and if all is well i shall be able to show
you lossie
My Dear Margaret Lossiemouth never had so many visitors as it has just
now but the wether is verry sweet now my dear gural i have not much nues
to give you but if god Sparies us both we met and now each other we shall
love each then and now and more of the things that will interest us i have
writen Ramsay to night so may god bless you both and mey he spare you
both to be a comfort to each other for my dear Margaret i feel i have left
charge of him now as i now you will be nearer to him than ever i have sinse
he left hom Now my dear Margaret God bless you and i trust soon to sea you
from your Mother A Ramsay
    i had Miss Grant with me on Sunday for a good while and giving me all
the nues

∾ Margaret to Ramsay.

20 August 1896
Chilworth: Surrey

. . . I tell Winnie Unwin [a socialist friend] she has the cranks of Socialists
without their principles, as she is a vegetarian and wears sandals, but she
rather thinks she has got their principles too if she knew more about
them . . .

∾ Margaret to Annie Ramsay.

23 August 1896
South Stoneham House[1]
near Southampton

My Dear Mother
    I am so glad to be able to put those three words together: I never have
before, and I have felt the blank all my life of not having a mother.

I was so pleased to get your last kind letter, and to hear that you are keeping better and that you will let me come and see you at the end of September. I am looking forward to it very much indeed; and I shall not mind much what the weather is like, if you take care to keep nice and well yourself when I come.

I am staying here with the Montagus, and Ramsay was over here to lunch and dinner yesterday, and in the afternoon he and I visited several of his friends in Southampton. Today some of us are going to one of his meetings and then I will have tea with his I.L.P. friends & he will come back here to stay the night & go off to the New Forest tomorrow morning if it is fine . . .

> Your loving
> Margaret E. Gladstone

❦ Margaret to Ramsay.

24 August 1896
Chilworth

My dear Sir

. . . Good morning to my love & a happy day to him. It is really half an hour or so since I sent him my first greeting — I have been lying and thinking of many things. Amongst others of those at Southampton. I don't know which seems to me the most sacred — those quiet times in the moonlight and by the holly leaves of the New Forest — or the opportunities I had of getting nearer to you (and your 'comrades') in your work.

It is a lovely morning & the heather and the trees & the sky look so beautiful. I suppose in November I shall consider it specially charming that yellow fog should exist.

Do you know that I and you if you come on Thursday — have splendid opportunities of learning at last how to do our lovemaking? Mr and Mrs Frank Gray carry on together in the most pretty and loverlike way after 12 years of matrimony (in 1908 I don't suppose you and I will have any poetry left in us). I must say he ground forth a love song to "Margaret" last night while his wife glowered at me from a corner; but still we brought him to see how wrong that had been. Now there is a fact that you and I will have to take quite a back seat as old stagers & watch the young couple[1] (who converse in French — you'll get quite a French-lesson for nothing) with patronising superiority and perhaps envious thoughts . . . Seriously however my father explains to us that we are to treat M. Bach not as future brother-in-law but as a family friend — so I flirt with him at my ease & you mustn't

---

1. Her sister Bessie and her fiancé Henri Bach.

congratulate any body unless I tell you, though I suppose they are practically engaged to be married.

Now I shall go out to the woods & take a book with me to help the heavy hours away.

10 a.m.

I didn't — I slumbered again & then went a walk over the heather; I have a fellow feeling with Mrs Gray — yesterday she passed a donkey cart (with Lady Magnus) & she murmured shortly after "I have fallen quite in love with that donkey — as usual". It was hard on Frank. Charing Cross 7.17 — Chilworth 9.1 if you miss 5.10.

Thine
Margaret Gladstone

❧ Annie Ramsay to Margaret.

25 August 1896
Lossiemouth

My Dear Margaret

i received your kind letter this morning i am glad to say i am better i cannot tell you how Much i admire your present you sent me My Dear gural i have had a grat love for poker work my frend Miss Shoolbrid has sum of it so i always admired it so many thanks you will be surprised to sea how i love every old thing. have so menny of them. My garden just now is like summer and i am sorry you did not cum and sea it only i do trust we shall be able to meet soon. the weather here is verry sweet just now . . . and Lossiemouth is full of visiters just now My Dear Margaret i expect soon to sea Miss Grant so i shall give your massage to hir

Dear Margaret do not think i for get but i now you are near him whill i am far from you both remember me to Ramsay i am sending his papers to day now my gural may you be happy in all your wolks in life and i will look forward to met you soon with much love to you both from your Mother

A Ramsay

❧ Ramsay to Margaret.

26 August 1896
The Progressive Review

Margaretta Mine

How dull London is after the moonlight & the Holly leaves! How sweet you were at Southampton! How rich I am to be permitted to take your arm and — etc! I have been at a Director's meeting of the 'New Age'; correcting proofs of the two signed P.R. articles; having . . . a gossip with Sandy Stewart of the 'National Observer' & Mudford of the 'Standard' & now here I am, or rather we are for your letter has come. I shall study the twelve year's old love as you bid me & all the other things shall be observed. I am trying to get to my sweetheart tomorrow but it is really impossible for me to say just yet whether I can or not. If Margaretta has nothing better to do than guide her Sir up the hill past the monastery she might come in faith to these trains . . .

❧ Annie Ramsay to Margaret.

> Friday
> [?] September 1896
> Lossiemouth

My Dear Margaret

i have kept the house to tray and get beter of my cold but we have so cold wither and snow showers and i connot get it away i send you a nightgown and a petticoat which i hope will plase you so you will get more next week then i will have your warm stockins down i am glad you saw my sister[1] i had a fue lines today from hir and i am glad to say i had a letter from America frum Jane[2] they are all well Falcaner has had little work this somer by post only the General Election year is verry dill and Allan Ramsay his little boy has not been well since he was a little boy the tonsils of his throat was swollen and now he had a gatherod throat and after it was beter the Doctor cout out the Tonsils he has 5 days be nerer spark poor boy so my sister would send him hom if she got any chance of him coming the way but she is verry busy in the store My Dear Margaret let me now when you get the things i hope Ramsay and all the others are well your father will be thinking the tim is coming verry near to part with you both[3] May God be with you and make you both happy in your new homes i have been asking about a dog but have not hard of wun yet before I send the cottage to Amaric i will writ Miss Duncan Buckie to get me win of the 4 of us every wun says they are so good and my sister will like to get wun Your latter this morning My Dear Margaret Many thanks Many thanks you make me to prod only i will do my best for both of you and so i may wirk Mrs Moor says when you cum back

---

1. Isabella Ramsay, 'Aunt Bella'.
2. Ann Ramsay's sister in Philadelphia.
3. Margaret's sister, Bessie, was married a week before the MacDonalds.

you must cum and milk the cowes often i was wonse over in the old town and saw a good many people asking for you here i close with much love frin your Mother

A Ramsay

remember me to Ramsay and i am glad you have fisted on a house It will be nice to see gardens i feel a gret deall beter today and the day is better with frist this morning

Aunt Elizabeth was ill, and Margaret went down to Berkshire to nurse her.

~ Margaret to Ramsay.

2 September 1896
Hamstead Marshall
Newbury, Berks.

Dear Dr Ramsay

I have pleasure in informing you that your prescription of hot milk was followed last night by the patient; but you omitted to tell me what should be done to cure its after effects, which took the form of ravenous hunger in the early morning. We thought of telegraphing to you today to see if you have any further suggestions: but I think that if we put a good hunk of bread & cheese by the patient's pillow it might do. She intends to try your prescription again tonight.

. . . Cousin M[argaret] is very busy over our photographs. You are very good in all, but I spoil most of them.: however some are decent & you shall have some copies. But I have specially hurried this one to send you today . . . they all say I look utterly sick and disgusted with you & am breaking off the engagement, saying I can't stand it a day longer & it is no use your saying anything though you are trying to. I want you to have it as a warning of what I can look like if you are not always submissive & sweet to me. We think it would be nice to have an enlarged copy for our house when we marry, only they think it would be best in your private study.

I have told Aunt E. that we are thinking of the end of November. She was rather disappointed because she seemed to think she and Aunt A. could not come in their deep mourning, but I have assured her we expect them black dresses and all. So I think it will be alright. . . . I feel as if I should come to the end of a long pilgrimage then — and begin a new one. Only my Sir has helped me through the end of this one, & will be with me in the new one.

Do you remember the words of Browning that you quoted at the end of your Hutchinson lectures? I think they ran "To other heights and . . . GOD willing". They kept ringing in my head those few days before I spoke to you at the Museum, but today I can only remember the thought & not the words.

> Yours always lovingly
> Margaret Gladstone

✺ Ramsay to Margaret.

> 2 September 1896
> The Progressive Review

My Dearest Lassie

. . . You will be glad to hear that Gore [Hugh Holmes Gore, a friend] has consented to be best man. What a comfort! I have come away without his letter, or I would send it to you, but you will see it. Sustained by you and him, I'll go through twenty marriage ceremonies.

I hope Aunt Elizabeth got out yesterday though I almost fear she did not. Tell them both that it was such a pleasure to be down with them & that I sighed when I got into the train — and that, I fear, the sigh was not altogether & absolutely that I left you behind. Hampstead Marshall itself & its hosts came in for a share.

But I had a spree last night — quite unexpected. When I got home I found a letter awaiting me asking me to dine with the writer — a grand bouncing American girl — and two of her friends. We four, I being the only man, had a regular good uproarious time (Why aren't you American?)

My pen cannot describe these hours — the talk and the laughter & the (?Savour). So I leave it a blank here. Tomorrow we are going to a concert together. They do want to see you so much & went into tears when I told them it was quite impossible. They sail on Friday evening. So you see I have given you a quid pro quo for your Reggie flirtation and added interest at the rate of "schent per schent.". . .

Now I wonder what my lassie is doing whilst I am here writing letters and posting up my cash book etc. etc. I wonder is she in the park, on the tree, leaning over the gate, by the canal; I wonder is she thinking of me or of her dickey, or of Reggie; or what! Never mind! it's all the same . . .

> Ever thine
> Ramsay

〜 Annie Ramsay to Margaret.

3 September 1896
Lossiemouth

My Dear Margaret

I received your kind and wilkim letter to day & will be so glad to sea you any tim you can only let me now the day before and i shall met you at Elgin i feel sorry for your aunt 3 years past in July i had a operation but i soon got round but was verry week and only geting strong when i took Inflenza so now i feel alright as far as the operation went my old complaints never trabels me and i hope your aunt may soon get strong again i saw Miss Grant and she says will be hom by the 17th so that will be befor you cum North i am writing Ramsay at the sam tim the weather is verry weet i do trust we will get good wether when you cum North i am glad to here the good nues of your sister and may every good atend them bothe Now my dear Gural i hope the tim will soon cum now when we will met and cum to now each other for night and day your and Ramsay is in my thoughs and prayrs that God may gide you both & as i love him may i love you and never cross wun of you but try to plase you in every way as long as i am spared to you now My Dear Margaret i close with love to you and Ramsay

From your Mother A. Ramsay

〜 Ramsay to Margaret.

3 September 1896
The Progressive Review
Temple Avenue E.C.

Dear Miss Gladstone

If it is permanently registered that it is off, so be it. However I'll wink at one of the Americans. I'll whisper in her ear, I'll take a ticket to New York —

SO:— Fare thee well sweet Margaret!
      A heart like broken bones, can set
      And Phoebe will be mine een yet.

Don't cry & don't come up by special train. I'll wait however until I see the photo before doing anything rash, so you have still a bare chance of being a Duchess.

Meanwhile, I am too stern to write more. Thou art a trial, as the wives of all great men have been to them.

Until a day or two settles things

I am

Ever thine with love
Ramsay

125

❧ Ramsay to Margaret.

4 September 1896
Duncan Buildings

My Dearest Lassie

The night is far gone & I have to get up at 6 tomorrow morning to catch my train & yet I must just tell my lassie that I am thinking of her — dreaming ere now I hope. I vanished in laughter when I saw myself looking at her & made up my mind to withdraw all promises to fly to the States, for if my lassie stuck to me after that, how much must she be willing to bear with!. . . Do you know what I was doing? Well, I'll tell you. I'm insuring my life. 1. So that you may kill me for a profit. 2. So that you may have something to bury me if I die. 3. So that I may have the benefit of a thorough medical examination for nothing. I am negotiating with Scottish Widows.

Last night again was divine. I thought of you and Brother B [Henri Bach] & goodness else & in pique I asked two American girls to dine with me. It was the previous evening over again — only more so. You were pronounced to be "a vur sweet girl", I pledged myself to go to Washington D.C. next year and to marry my second wife out of Amurrka. We wept to think that today the briny ocean would begin to stretch between us & that it would be perhaps five years before we would meet again.

. . . I would like you to read Carpenter's "Loves coming of Age" I know you will understand it all, & whether you agree with it or not, it is rather appropriate just now . . .

Finally, don't hurry with that *Progressive Review* — paper. We find we can do without it this time after all, and the fines will do next time. No word from Moon though I wrote to him on Tuesday. If you laugh about that Bazaar I'll . . . kiss you! This is the opening sentences of my speech tomorrow at 2.30 sharp.

Ladies and Gentlemen, Ever since you did me the honour to invite me to perform this ceremony, I have been at a loss to discover the reason. I have a girl to whom reasons for honouring me, especially when my appearance may be regarded as an influence, are never wanting, but I am too modest to ask you to believe that I am good-looking; I have friends (sarcastic this) in common with every agitator who believe me to be rolling in wealth but I cannot cheat you by making you believe that this cheque for £100 which I have drawn in your favour will ever be honoured; the short speeches which I am told are soul not only of wit but of eloquence at opening bazaars, are alas! no characteristic of those who are expected to point the way to the New

Jerusalem & give valid reasons why Tom, Dick & Harry should join the pilgrimage — all in one oration. I am still, Ladies and Gentlemen, in the attractive toils of the problem, & I am to do myself the pleasure of giving it up. A wise man makes it his duty not only to enjoy life but to accumulate pleasures against the day of his death.

My friends, the problem of why I was asked to open this bazaar will be stored away in my memory to add a new attraction to death when we are assured all mysteries will be cleared up. And so on.

AH! Why do I want to marry you. It is too ridiculous to think of this heart of mine being in love. But it is.

You ridiculous old thing.

Oh; that photo! Ph-up-uph-uph-ah-ha!

> Ever thine lovingly
> Ramsay.

～ Margaret to Ramsay.

> Thursday 4 September 1896
> Train to Reading

. . .I was leaning through the calf's window watching Bailey (our friend of the broad smile who drove us in to Newbury) milk the cows when I read my love-letter. And in simulation of you & your American girls I immediately went off & discussed the crops with the farm-labourers & bicycles with the potato boy & had a real good time.

But nothing is so nice as getting a letter from my laddie except seeing him himself or thinking about him . . .

I am anxious to get home & hear for myself how brother B is progressing. But I was anxious too at leaving Hampstead Marshall for Aunt E seems no better: She had a bad night. Do you think GOD sends me all these extra family excitements in case I got too wrapped up in our own happiness?. . .

Do you know we got into a lively Socialist discussion late last evening: It was very naughty of us because Aunt E went on with it in her head after she got into bed. Poor thing, she *has* got a horror of Socialism . . .

I am thinking of you & simply exploding with laughter at the[?] times of your bazaar on Saturday. Ridiculous man. WHY do I want to marry you!

> Yours ever
> Margaretta.

〰 Ramsay to Margaret.

5 September 1896
Stafford Station
11 a.m.

My Dearest Gel

Here I am yawning and tired, having just finished three speeches — one of them the bazaar oration — and a chapter of Borgeaud's "The making of Constitutions". Of course between the flights of imaginary eloquence & the learned paragraphs of Borgeaud I was thinking of somebody down on a sunny heath who was flirting very likely with some relative more or less remote and breaking the heart of some blood-relation. I had to come away this morning without letters & so feel bereaved of being two ways distant from my gel. (Bother it! this train do shake & I'll read some more of Borgeaud)

STOCKPORT. Here I am like a wise man running further & further away from you. But the journey is now about over & I shall be received into the arms of my comrades. I wonder if you have any good news from Newbury today. Now we are off again & I stop.

ROCHDALE. 11.30 p.m. Dead! This is only my ghost that is writing. Crowds! Handshakes! Talking shop! Nigger Minstrels! etc! etc! not forgetting scientific Exhibitions. The speech was delivered & my traditions are broken. I have opened a bazaar. There was such a crowd of ladies. They presented me with a sweet button hole. It was like a funeral — so decent, so respectable, so absurd, so much a closing of my old life. When I rose they smiled, but I saw the 23rd Nov. and, I swear, I did not smile in return. I kept true. I apologised to all the nice looking girls in private and explained why I was so dignified. I am covered with the decorations of my commiserations. I talked like a father to them for twenty minutes, handed over the young men to the care of the girls, recommended the girls to fleece their charges & declared the bazaar open. There was an excellent turn-out. but that was not what pleased me most. I must begin another paragraph.

J. Hope Allan came all the way from Sheffield to see me. A gentleman came up and shook my hands. I had not a notion who he was. "I came from Sheffield" said he. Then the wily spirit of the politican flashed in me & without a pause I beamed "Ah yes Mr Hope Allan of course." Bull's eye straight away. "What a marvellous memory you have. (I bowed) you only saw me once. I heard you speak at that tremendous meeting in the Attercliffe Hall. I was in the body of the hall." I beamed only more so . . .

Ramsay.

Sunday morning with bells ringing and Salvation Army bands playing. It was 12.40 before I could get to bed. I came here hoping to get upstairs by 10.30. Found the bed stripped and my hostess had a stall at the bazaar. There was nothing for it but wait for her return. I wrote advertisements for the *Progressive Review* and a love letter, until at last I got away . . .

∾ Margaret to Ramsay.

5 September 1896
5.30 a.m.
Chilworth

. . . You don't want to be married the same day as Brother B. do you? You can if you like, but not to me!

May nearly broke her (engagement of course) to Papa yesterday. Poor wretched man. I do wish he wrote novels: he would have so much fresh material, would he not?

I have had one or two or three talks with May about hers: I brought in your opinions a little as she asked me what you thought. She says she was really very nice and democratic out there [she had been in Australia] & hobnobbed with everyone in a nice Socialist way! And when I told her I was distressed the way she told me she wouldn't marry him if he felt it his duty to be a missionary, she said she meant that she did not feel to be a missionary's wife.

Flo discussed November dates with me & all went smoothly. She thinks I am too cold to you, so you won't mind my sitting with my arms round your neck at breakfast, will you? . . .

Goodnight XX

Sunday 6.9.96 3.15 p.m.

My beloved old Donkey, what is the use of writing to you when 1) I am always thinking of things to say to you & tell you about & couldn't possibly write them all down. 2) You give me no address to write to. It is very mean of you — you know I am stuck here & can't get away from your [?Dear] letters, & so you write away to me and give me no chance of answering.

But all the same I can't help writing to my sweetheart, just because he is my sweetheart & I love him very much more than I can tell him.

Every day the delight & beauty of it all comes over me — and every day it seems new & fresh & wonderful . . .

Brother B. and I spent such a happy half-hour tête à tête in the smoking room this morning — talking all about Protestant Church Government in France & my wedding dress and other similar subjects . . .

This day 3 weeks I shall be in Lossiemouth: Hurrah: I had another kind letter from our mother . . .

Mind you give my love to Mrs Hicks. Your letter was so nice. It almost dissipated my anger at your sitting up so late to write it, bad man.

Monday evening 7/9/96 6.30 p.m.
Dear Ramsay,

I only sent you a very scrubby card today, together with a budget of stale news; but I was rather busy with Social dates, & of course they do & always will come before my sweetheart.

More than half the time has gone of our separation — it seems long but it WON'T when I see you again. Then we shall be separated for longer still (unless you come to read a geological paper at the B.A.) but I shan't mind because I shall have Uncle George & our mother to keep me going. In some ways I realise the change you have made in my life better when you are not there, because it is all just the same only with the great difference of a satisfactory man in the background: when you are here, it is all different but all so utterly natural and so . . . what's the good of adjectives — you know much better what I mean without putting it in clumsy words.

You have been jabbering — I hope you said some sensible things by accident — I wish I could see you and (all the other people) at the TU Congress — I should enjoy it all . . .

We shall only be four at Dinner tonight — quite a relief; we are all tired of a houseful. Poor Bessie is seeing the last of her beloved in London & returns tomorrow — May is with Bella for a few days: so Papa, Flo, & I are left with Mr Ormonde Crosse (a bachelor who is much interested in you — & said that about the photo for which you ought to throw me over) and with Effie [Johnson] who is an invalid & doesn't come into meals & Marion [her niece] whom I must go off and put to bed.

I hope you won't come back a wreck from Edinburgh — Give the dear place my love. Only keep some of your still more dear self. — as much as you like.

Thy Margaret

〰 Ramsay to Margaret.

7 September 1896
Edinburgh [at T.U.C.]

My Dearest Lassie,

. . . We had very good meetings in Rochdale . . . Edith Lanchester was there and was a bit of a draw for the SDF opposition show. I hear she *is* living with Sullivan . . .

. . .Now, blow business! How is my dear Lassie? I wonder if she always knows when I think about her and when I wish she were not hundreds of miles away . . . They were all very interested in Rochdale . . . There is a general impression abroad — chiefly amongst married men which is very suspicious — that you will make me give up the ILP and that I will not be able to stand out against your wishes. There was a sigh of relief when I recounted your many virtues from the Socialist point of view. But I do wish you were here. Wouldn't we be happy looking across upon the lights of the old town and letting all the Ghosts of Edinburgh steal like cold winds across our souls. My dear sweetheart.

> Ever with love
> Ramsay

∾ Margaret to Ramsay.

> 8 September 1896
> Chilworth
> Tuesday morning again!

My father has just taken my letters to you & others to the post when he came back and hung around. I began cutting a pencil so that he might give forth what was on his mind & he began talking quite spontaneously about business (at least he began with Bessie's but it was mine he was aiming at.) Money matters came on quite swimmingly. Apparently my mother's marriage settlement is £.5000 which brings in £160. Then Papa has left me £10,000 in his will and an equal share with my sisters of what is over when other things are paid: he thinks it will come to my having about half what they have. He thinks of giving me £300 a year now: that is less than he gives Bella and will give Bessie but as I shall have less ultimately, there's no harm in that. Then he will give me something now for furnishing. Of course if I had made any objections of any kind, he would have increased or decreased the allowance to order; but as he had an idea & it suited me all right I thought it had better stay as it was. He says I may as well have a marriage settlement, but that won't be any bother — our solicitor can see to it when we get back. Papa seems to want us to get our own place as soon as possible: I said you could be looking out & if we found anything that just suited us we might get in straight away after the 23rd November: but we can see about that later, of course. I wonder what my money is invested in: I hope it is in respectable sort of things. The £5000 is not mine, we suppose, till he dies, but he will give me the interest of that now & make it up to £300: at least that is what he suggests. Does that suit your Highness?

Then Papa said how all these excitements had tired his brain so I gently suggested that he had heard of May's too and we talked together as a grandfather and grandmother over that. I gave the young man a good character as far as I could judge from his letters. I also said if May cared about him it would settle her happily and Papa said he thought it had helped already. He said if she went to Australia he would probably not see her again. I suppose that is true, and he is fonder of her than of any of us.

〰 Ramsay to Margaret.

8 September 1896
Edinburgh

My dearest Second best Lassie

Your long and very very very welcome letter has come but really I have no time and no inclination to answer it. I am off to a Lord Provost's reception to meet Miss Tuckwell.[1] Burrows[2] is here, smiling as usual and has invited me to stay with him in December when I go up to Glasgow.

Thanks my own sweetheart for your nice letter to Gore. He will like it & so do I.

Ever thine
Ramsay.

〰 Ramsay to Margaret.

9 September 1896
Edinburgh at TUC

My Dearest Best Girl,

For so I doubt it must be, Gertrude and my heart having decreed so, Unto thee my love. I am down waiting for breakfast & am throwing my morning thoughts away to Surrey. I am thinking of a gate, a dickie and a lassie, and I wonder how they all are. As to the writer, he is gloriously well. I have been having talks with some of the TU leaders — a long one last night with John Wilson of the Lanarkshire miners. The Socialist resolution is to be lost. The miners are all to vote against it. They always vote in a body & as the Socialists are in a minority they have to vote against their own opinions and the British public will be asked to believe that there is not a single Socialist in the Miner's Federation. As a matter of fact, however, Wilson tells me that there was only 3 or 4 of a minority amongst the delegates so the backset

---

1. Gertrude Tuckwell, trade unionist and campaigner for women's rights.
2. Herbert Burrows, a civil servant associate of Hyndman.

is more apparent than real. Beyond attending to the Congress I have been able to do but little.

Today, the Women's Industrial have a lunch & the big meeting is over as they have billed me to speak, but as they never asked me I am not bound to them. If I stay I shall have to travel all night and I am not very keen about that. I cannot say just yet when I shall be able to get to Chilworth — maybe Friday night, maybe not until late on Saturday night. But I'll let you know when I get to London.

By the by — wrote to Gore that you were already in search of a second husband and I have also told Burrows. I do think it mean of you not to send the objectionable photograph of yourself. There I am consumed with fear lest that thing I have is a sort of Röntgen discovery of my heart, and it would be so comforting to have proof that you are equally bad with myself.

I was as interested as an old wife in hearing about May. Your poor father must be in a very poor way. Tell Flo that I like the coldness — especially when everybody's back is turned & when the chimneys of the cottage disappear below the ridges of Blackheath.

I lost my soup because after these long days, I preferred reading your letter to going through the proper dinner course. I really do not know what will happen unless someone cures me of my joy in loving my lassie. And the cure must be very drastic as the photograph is beginning to lose its effect already. Cannot you help me out of my difficulties!!!!!

I suppose we will not see Annie Matheson when I am down. I thought possibly that she would get excited — only, and you be wise, don't take her estimate of my virtues & warn your family against her descriptions. How am I to receive Effie? Fall on her neck and weep? Kiss her cheek? her brow? Or how? Please tell me. Brother B & you for a whole morning in the smoking room! That won't do. He is not on the list. I'll tell Bessie.

The postman was drunk.

Now I'm off to the Congress. If your thoughts are mine, you are very very happy.

Ramsay

〰 Margaret to Ramsay.

9 September 1896
Chilworth morning room

My dear dear Sweetheart,

. . . Here we had a terrific storm of thunder and lightning & rain last night, & the rain and winds are continuing I had to get up in the night to rescue 3 of your letters & one of your mother's which were sitting by the window with my purse & other contents of my pocket and all calmly getting drowned together. I shall go out for a blustery walk by myself as soon as I have posted this letter and one I have written to our mother. That will put me in a good temper (necessary after thinking about you, you see). No, thinking about you puts me in a good temper. I never knew time go so slowly before. Isn't it horrid & mean & discontented of me to grumble when I have got you to think about. But it's human nature — the more one has the more one wants; and I have a very great deal, my dear, dear sweetheart.

Thy Margaret.

꩜ Margaret to Ramsay.

Tuesday 15 September 1896
Chilworth
6 a.m.

Goodmorning to you my dear love. May you have a successful and peaceful day.

You gave your Lassie yesterday the best day she ever had in her life, because her love for you grows deeper and stronger and better the more she knows you. She knew it would, wasn't she clever?

But the journey home last evening was a poem — a love poem with my dear love as its subject. I wanted to tell it all to him, but I have no words, perhaps he knew it without. It all seemed like a sacrament — the railway journey and the walk up the dark lane, and the opening out on the heather beyond. It was dark & cloudy when I crossed the common, and the stormy wind made me glad as it has often done before, but this time it kissed my lips and found them consecrated by your kisses.

There is one love poem that I often think of, & that puts into words a little bit of what I feel, and that is one you wrote and sent to me from Birmingham.

I had a sudden thought yesterday towards the end of my train journey — that that day ten weeks I might be going on another train journey which would seem a sacrament — when you go to Cornwall & I to Monte Carlo.

I did a naughty thing through that. I was very ashamed of — it was stupid and selfish of me to keep you from going for that paper for Papa, and I must never, never be selfish over my love.

I couldn't see a bookstall at any of the stations except Redhill & there I was reading Carpenter & forgot to look out till too late, so Papa had to do without his Westminster. That was not very important, but it was important that it was my fault because I was greedy about seeing an extra half minute of my sweetheart . . .

Thine ever
Margaret

∾ Margaret to Ramsay.

16 September 1896
Liverpool
Adelphi Hotel

My dear Ramsay,

. . . I have just left Papa to go to a Committee & Flo to frivol round the Reception Room till I return to meet her, (after a visit to the Women's Industrial Council here), & frivol again myself. We have seen heeps of friends already. Uncle joins us this evening. I haven't seen my relations yet: if the Bottomleys & Thomsons come as well as the Kelvins it will be awfully jolly. Last night I spent 1½ hours at the Committee of the Shop Assistants' Trade Union — very interesting. We talked about all sorts of things, socialist work here included . . .

Bessie and I both wrote to Mr Glyn yesterday. I told him about Mr Lilly [the curate at St. Mary Abbotts] and about wanting to have some of the service curtailed [I didn't say what points) & I said I would like him to be there. but was not particular (only I put it nicely). It would be such a joke to have him pairing off two red revolutionaries and he's very jolly personally. Shall we ask (Dea. . .er) if he doesnt come.

I've been thinking muchly about our home. An idea struck me early this morning, but I havn't thought it out very fully yet, so only mention it to you in a casual way. It is that if we take a house we might set aside part of it for a family to live in, the woman element of which should come and do our housework at stated times. Otherwise we should be independent of them and they of us; but of course it would be convenient to have them there when we were gadding round. A widow with one or two children would of course be most convenient as we don't want to have any overcrowding under the shadow of our roof — it is bad enough to have it elsewhere where we can't help it. Mrs Spence has rather a large family I believe . . you wouldn't like it at all, so don't scruple to object. Only it would answer my prejudices against living respectable and orthodoxly in a house to ourselves with more room than we want and with one or two outsiders imported just on purpose to attend to you & me. It would also, (& if we got nice people this

135

would be nice) bring us in touch with their lives, & yet I think we could be as independent of them as we liked. And of course it would save us some expense. Don't bother to answer about this. I do feel so lazy about the house-hunting: & I should rather enjoy poking about if only I were in town. Unless you can find something nice without fagging yourself. I think it is better not to be in a hurry: we can always get rooms somewhere for December even if that flat is let . . .

❧ Ramsay to Margaret.

> 16 September 1896
> British Museum

My dearest Sweetheart

Once again it can only be an impressionist love message . . . I have been all the morning and early afternoon at the *Progressive Review* office and have just got here to hunt up something about John Timbs and write an *Echo* article on Jean Ingelow. I got your nice little poem last night and loved my lassie more & more for it, & wondered why it was that I was so blessed as to have her writing to me

Tom Mann's arrest will probably mean that I shall be in London on Sunday . . .

❧ Margaret to Ramsay.

> 17 September 1896
> Liverpool
> British Association

Messrs Hollibone
Wine Merchants
19 Southampton Street
Bloomsbury

The above address was given to me by Howard Unwin as a suggestion for our abode . . . He says the Hollibones are very trustworthy, and the old housekeeper there saw to Buxton & did the cooking in a kitchen down stairs. [He] didn't tell me how many rooms — I daresay Flo knows, but I would rather have your opinion than hers. So if you are passing call in!

. . . Kelvins & May Thomson are here. I am showered with congratulations every where. I am writing to your mother to ask (see enclosed) if she would rather I went by Aberdeen as she seems to be going to pick me up at Buckie . . .

❧ Ramsay to Margaret.

17 September 1896
The   Progressive
Review

My dearest Lassie

On the whole, the time seems to be passing fairly well. I am so busy I have no time to brood upon the distance of Liverpool & my own bereavement; indeed, so prone am I to make the best of a bad job, that when I read Sir Joseph Lister's address this morning over my porridge I was under the pleasant delusion that somebody — sweet, fair & twenty-six was sitting by me. I hope you are enjoying all these sprees, and that ere now you have been bountifully kissed by your relatives — except the youthful male cousins. I am living very mildly in your absence. I was out dining last night — one of the farewell dinners some of my batchelor friends are giving me. And, so again, with the soup, the fish, the claret the old problem comes up — "Why do I love my lassie?" & I can get no other answer than a whisper from something inside — "Go away, donkey". That makes me feel it is real. Now, Good Afternoon, my dear Donkey! I sent you the New Age to make you dull, & to tone your wayward enjoyment. Don't come back on Saturday. It will be no good as I have a meeting of New Age shareholders to attend before catching a train to Norwich. Besides, how do you know I want to see you? Love to the family and ever so much more to yourself.

Ever
Ramsay

❧ Margaret to Ramsay.

18 September 1896
Liverpool
British Association Meeting

Dear Sir,

Another nice letter from you. Do you know this is one of our red letter days — 2 months since that would-be quarrel so ignominiously failed — and next Wednesday will be two months to something else that will be red letter day.

But I'm much too busy & too scientific to write loveletters. I only think continually of my dear love & wish he were here . . .

I . . . let a dark curly haired vagabond sit beside me at lots of sections and social functions. At present he is quite interesting himself in Röntgen rays and gases & currents & electro motive forces, & laws of conductivity, while his lassie's thoughts, I am sorry to say, stray something to her two new homes — the Lossiemouth one, and the little nest home in London. Is it for Dickie or me that you want to get a nest? I am going to make a new grey silk dickie for Lossiemouth: may he come to the nest too? . . .

Ever Margaret

P.S. Since the above I happened to find myself next to the Hon W.P. Reeves[1] and talked to him. He wants to explain to me the Domestic Servants Half Holiday Bill (New Zealand) because it has been so ridiculously misrepresented in the papers, & he has the only copy in England, so I'll go & see him when I return to London. He sent you his congratulations!

❧ Ramsay to Margaret.

18 September 1896

Can't do more than a good night Dear Lassie. Off to meet Hobson; Clarke etc., etc., Everything came alright this morning and I am as happy as a lark with you.

Ever
R.

❧ Ramsay to Margaret.

19 September 1896

. . . Does the gaiety of scientific surroundings still inflict you to go gadding about like a may-fly, or have Röntgen rays and half pennies in boys' stomachs sobered you to a proper appreciation of the dignity which is becoming in one about to change her past by a visit to St Mary Abbots?. . . I got hold of a place in Staple Inn this morning, where alas and alas I found that Staple Inn will not do for married people. I had another look round Gray's Inn down St John St. and Bedford Row and round Mecklenburgh Square. There is the most beautiful house in the square half the full size with a glorious outlook across the Foundling Gardens . . . It is perhaps just a very little too big, but in appearance it is ideal — 4 small rooms e.g. servants bedroom and boxrooms at the top, 2 good bedrooms on the second floor, 2 rooms on the first floor and two on the ground floor, with a servants'

---

1. William Pember Reeves (1857–1932) New Zealand politican, historian and Liberal collectivist.

room kitchen, etc., in basement. The rent is £95 exclusive of rates but a 7 years' lease is wanted. If it were £20 or £30 cheaper it would be ideal for a house. I am still unable to say that any flat I have seen is worth anything except one at Ridgemont Gardens which however is on the fourth floor & has a rent everything included of £110. Still there are other places to look at although I was dreaming last night that I was living in the suburbs and went to tennis parties — that horrid creatures called respectable men and women came in and talked 20 to the dozen about parish work and bazaars. Two more hairs have gone grey this morning. Enid [Stacey] has written me a very doleful letter . . . There is some thought of her postponing her marriage yet again . . . My Dearie why has everything gone so well with us? Do you ever fear that someone is grinning behind us?

I do sometimes because you have changed everything so much that I can hardly believe it to be real . . .

❧ Margaret to Ramsay.

> 20 September 1896
> Liverpool
> Adelphi Hotel
> British Association Meeting

Dearest Friend — and Sweetheart
   . . . It's all very well for Miss Irwin to blarney you in the Clarion but the sentiments she put in your mouth were exactly those which she rammed down my throat when I saw her in June as her own pet scheme, so I can quite see that you were only the cat's paw.

Do you want your curiosity solved about what I have been thinking lately? Well my heart has been annoying me very much by its vagaries. It got tired of being sentimental about you . . . It wanted to know what on earth I was going to bore myself with a man for, and a man with myself, & it very properly explained that I knew very little of you and could not say in the least how you would behave under all sorts of circumstances for instance what would interest you at the B.A. and what people you would care to talk to & what sort of things you would say. And it insisted on feeling no interest in anything & looking upon the last 3 months as a beautiful dream (it graciously allowed that they had been beautiful) and all the rest of things in general as absolute nothingness . . . And all the time I smiled serenely and waited for my heart to come back to its senses & write a loveletter — which it is doing at the present moment.

And dear Sir, I loved you so much all the time that I didn't care how many strange moods I had, and didn't even desire to commit suicide as I should have done a few years ago: because I knew deep down that the new duties & responsibilities need not oppress me or make me afraid because they all came as a good gift to me for me to use & enjoy — a gift from love. — your love & GOD'S. You asked me in your letter this morning whether I ever fear that someone is grinning behind us. No, I don't — never. My philosophy is very simple — it is only that the Power which made you & the other good things in my life must be greater & not less than they — therefore good. Certainly one might apply the same reasoning to the evil things: but then I know in my life I always either find Good behind things that seem sorrowful — or else see that they are bad because of some fault in ourselves & that if it made us see it & remedy the fault the badness would be worth while. And so I believe GOOD is more powerful than evil. And I don't believe I should feel differently or want to be rebellious even if things seemed to go all wrong with us. But I am ever so sorry about Enid. How can we help her? I don't feel as if I could even write. I have no excuse to do so.

Papa & I did go to church after all. — the sun came out and he said he was too restless to stay at home, so we went and heard Profesor Ryle: I think he was rather nice, but I was thinking mostly about my dear Sir: I do wish I could hear him this afternoon & evening: I hope he will be nice.

About that breach of promise . . . I don't remember either of us ever promising to marry the other: we have said we wanted to marry, & that may come to the same thing in the end, but I feel perfectly free to throw you over at any moment . . .

I thought Staple Inn was too good for the likes of us. But please don't land me with about 13 rooms to look after & such an awful name as Mecklenburgh Square for my address.

We went to "High Tea" and "High Supper" yesterday with some most respectable & typical middle class relatives of ours — the Halls — they asked you too — and I wanted Uncle to pose as "Mr MacDonald" & offered to sit hand in hand & call him Doodles & let him call me Trotsy Pootsy if he would . . .

The poverty of the people is much more evident here than in London, and there are hundreds of underground dwellings and shops. The docks are busy — we went all along them Saturday.

Thine ever with love
Margaretta.

〰 Margaret to Ramsay.

> 20 September 1896
> Liverpool
> Adelphi Hotel

My dear Sir

. . . You shouldn't dream about suburbs: you know if you want to live in a suburb I should take a tent & pitch it in an East End Slum & forsake you. And if you find too respectable a house anywhere I shall do so most assuredly. And the S.D.F. will laugh and I shall cry. The only thing about that Mecklenburg Square place is that it sounds nice & healthy and open, & our precious healths must be considered, as of vital importance . . .

I wonder how you are getting on at Mansfield.

I wonder — lots of things.

〰 Ramsay to Margaret.

> [21 September 1896]

. . . It will not be necessary for you to go by Aberdeen in order to pick up my mother at Buckie. She can join you at Elgin. I doubt if she means quite what she says, as I do not think she will stay so long away from home. She is a bit mixed up in her journalism sometimes . . . Who *is* that fellow you say sits by you at the sections? I *do* hope you show him your ring. I shall be jealous, as by your descriptions he is nice looking . . . Gray silk dickie — scrumptious! Mind Lossiemouth is a community with nerves.

. . . I was flirting with Mary Gwyther last night & it was very pleasant to feel the freedom of old days. Alas they are gone. Love has come upon me. I melt into tears & hence stop writing to the girl who has left me behind her . . .

〰 Margaret to Ramsay.

> Tuesday, 21 September 1896
> 11 p.m.
> 88 Telford Street
> Inverness

More kindness — more relations — more beautiful scenery — more thoughts of my dear love in London — and another nice letter from him.

Such is my diary: a list of good things which I owe to my sweetheart; and I am proud of the debt.

My heart has been singing inside me at the thought of this day week — and the two committees I shall have the privilege of attending! Goodnight, dearest Ramsay, a VERY, VERY good night.

11.30. Been to the station — brought "Uncle Sandie" [Alexander Ramsay] back in triumph — just left him at his breakfast to write a line or two to you. I like everybody — & am beginning to think I must be a most sociable creature, not to say bumptious, for I seem so at home at short notice.

It was LOVELY along the river yesterday. Autumn hues reflected in the water — how I wished you were there to enjoy it. But we will be back together, I hope, dear sir . . .

Thy sweetheart.

Effie told Flo one day at Chilworth that one of my characteristics which struck her most was my loyalty to my family, and she said that Flo seemed pleased. I am glad she said that, because I never manage to show it to them at first hand much. I was just as off-hand & cranky at Liverpool as usual — perhaps I'll be meltingly emotional for the last seven weeks. I'm quite sure I shall cry myself to sleep every night at the thought of leaving Bynoe.

May wants me to tell her how to write love-letters. I feel quite an essay on the subject simmering in my brain.

Now for the honeymoon — My dear Sir by Nov 24th I shall have promised to obey you, so why make a farce of pretending to consult me beforehand when you know I shall have to go wherever you make me? But if it is YOU that makes me I shan't be nasty partickler? Why don't we stay at home the first week and do our furnishing — go off to Scotland on the day after the NAC: Rainbow and stay over Aberdeen & Glasgow? I suppose we might run up here for a day or two, but I won't say a word about it as you are quite certain to change your mind sixty times before that.

Look at me meandering on, and I have the whole weight of lighting the fire on my mind tomorrow morning. I've extracted a sort of promise from Mother to leave me to my own devices till 7 a.m. so I want them to be as manifold as possible. At 9.50 we go to Buckie.

I don't believe she ever trusted you to sweep the room out before she appeared.

Mr Wellwood did not preach tonight, but the assistant. In 5 (or 6, my mathematics are shaky) weeks our banns will be howled — awful thought — I am going to object. I shall say "The man is a vagabond" The woman a treasure! They must not wed!

M E G

➣ Ramsay to Margaret.

21 September 1896

My Dearest Gel

I am repenting my choice every day from the point of view of respectability though from that of love — alas! alas!

But we are quite famous now — nothing but review, review, review! . . . I have turned advertisement canvasser! . . . I sallied forth today & got 4 pages of advertisements [for the *Progressive Review*]. Everything is now finally fixed, the machines are running like mad & the first copy is to be posted to me tonight in Southampton.

I had the Canning Town Hall crammed yesterday for the afternoon service[1] — 1200 people — & about 800 filled the Mansfield Hall for the evening lecture on "Thrift". I am taking the chair next Sunday at Holborn Town Hall for Hardie; & yesterday — Sunday though it was I pulled off a good political bit of business about Canning Town. Now I'm off to Southampton to the "at home". Up tomorrow! Why do I walk on my heels thus? Don't know! Can't you guess? Because I never felt stronger & happier. Long long days ago I used to think in a surly way that the world was an oyster & that I would try my hand at opening it. But that WAS long ago, and now again the springtide feeling of power comes over me. I daresay it too will go & we shall laugh at it when it is gone and say "how silly!" Nevertheless thanks ever so much to my dear dear lassie for recalling these old grand feelings . . .

➣ Margaret to Ramsay.

22 September 1896
[Liverpool]

My dearest old Donkey,

I want to write you a nice letter & can't think what to say. But perhaps the pretty pictures on the margin will make up for my shortcomings. I wonder how that old Progressive Review is getting on & whether you had a nice time at Southampton last evening.

Now I'll tell you something touching. Yesterday afternoon I went with my Uncle and sister to survey the big ship Teutonic (sic) in all her gorgeous array. I walked through painted and carved saloons; I feasted on tea & chocolate cake in an armchair sumptuously upholstered. I marched up and down winding greasy stairs and looked at the latest marvels of engineering.

---

1. Ramsay preached for the Ethical Church.

I also looked at the stokers, and thought that if I were an engineer I would invent means to let that horrid work be done by machinery. But amidst it all, the chief thing that touched my emotions was — a donkey engine — because it reminded me of my donkey man. (Not that I need reminding for I had been thinking of him even over the chocolate cake) And I got home to find a lot of stale advice about trains & a bad tragedy, which proved he was a donkey man.

In little more than two days I shall be making the acquaintance of our mother and our home. I feel so strange about it, as if I had no right & was a horrid intruder. Only I don't think I will feel like that when I get there. And it is only sometimes that I feel it now . . .

I am dining out three evenings running, & cramming myself with knowledge all day & yet I waste time in writing to you . . .

Just got your silly letter about an oyster — which was what I was waiting for really — But dear sir, I don't deserve such nice letters — only if you want love you have got it from your ever devoted lassie Margaretta.

Ramsay is still hesitant, and obliquely suggests a postponement of the wedding . . .

22 September 1896
The Progressive Review

My own Lassie
   Cheerless and dull is the world in rain & my heart pities it & I sing.

> Why run ahead of Spring so far?
>   Why wed in midst of winter time,
> When orange blooms but brown buds are
>   And Nature's clad in shroud-like rime?
> Why wait not till the wood and lea
> Have hearts as gaily tuned as we?
>
> It is not fair to pipe and play,
>   It is not right to love and woo
> When in the bush no linnet's lay
>   Tells Nature's folks are loving too, —
> In winter days let's pass to rest
> To sleep in Nature's sleeping breast,
>
> But spring-time is the hour of love,
>   When bush and brake are filled with song,

And Nature's voice trills to approve,
   And sings & gossips all day long, —
When every leaf and twig and tree
Awake to love's witch melody.

The Spring will come & we will blush
   To think we piped to dancers few,
To know we wooed in Winter's hush
   To feel we kept from Earth her due —
Her due to watch us woo, and fuss
And skip & dance around with us.

And so my lassie — like a rose —
   Late blooming when the days grow chill —
Shall we wait on till Nature knows
   The boundless joys & hopes that fill
Our hearts? Shall we wait till the dew
Is kissed by Spring's sun — and then woo?

This is because I love my lassie & when the sun breaks out I will write her her reply.

                Ramsay

  Margaret to Ramsay.

                       23 September 1896
                       Liverpool

   . . . 3.30 p.m. Waiting for Papa & the Garden Party: Alas, my time of charming independence is slipping away: & the funny part of it is I can't squeeze out even half a tear on the subject though I've had such a happy time of it.

Why, Oh Why?
I care for nobody, no, not I
And nobody cares for me.

Vide Bessie's letter which may amuse you[1] and cannot harm you. The bit about matrimony is ever so much nicer than one she wrote to me from Brittany on the same subject, so we are getting on. I didn't trouble to

---

1. It did not. See letter of 24 September.

answer the first; but today I quietly assured her we weren't marrying on a political basis but for something rather better.

I do wish somebody would give you a white bouquet. And do you know, Flo says the Frenchies give their fiancees a lovely basket of flowers every week — ever so expensive from florists — so mind I have them regularly, please.

Why didn't you tell me I was going to see a nice second cousin James Thomson (I've got one already) . . .

About marrying in November — you say you are going to write my reply to your poetic wish to put it off. But, curiously enough I was going to write to you myself on the subject. It occurred to me yesterday that I had overlooked a most important objection. Don't be afraid — I don't want to break it off all together — only put off for some years, because on going over a cigar factory yesterday I suddenly remembered that the dream of my life was to be a factory inspector. But if you are nasty about it I will wait until I am a widow — it would just do then for I should want drudgery & yet something I was interested in.

I've been to lots of bookshops about the Progressive Review. And I love you so very very very much that I can't express it one bit.

❧ Ramsay to Margaret.

24 September 1896
Duncan Buildings

My Dearest Sweetheart

I wonder how you fare. You have not quite stated yet but you will soon be on the road & I am sending this — the second, for the numbers to mount up — to our home. Give my love to all the people there. I hope our mother will be kind to you. I never asked you to overlook some of her ways. I knew it was unnecessary. How does my sweetheart like this for her reply to my warning? It is for her eyes only!

> In Winter, Nature does not die
> But lies enchanted in a sleep
> Afar in Northern mountains high
> Where Frost close guard doth keep,
> And now and then she almost wakes —
> When sun through winter's snow clouds breaks.

When every little brook is still
And brake & lea are under snow —
When earth's fair face from plain to hill
Lies wreath on wreath below —
Then, Nature's dreaming dreams of death —
"She dies", Death laughs & merrily saith.

And when the brooks their tales renew,
And songsters pipe a broken lay,
When lovers blush & lovers woo
And wed in Winter's day
Death sees on Nature's face a beam
Sighs he: "She dreams a pleasant dream".

Oh! Nature lies in Northern lands.
She dreams of joy, she dreams of woe,
She smiles and sighs till Spring commands
Cold Frost to let her go.
Till then, we'll send her dreams of bliss —
We'll wed in Winter — Sir, a kiss!

❧ Margaret to Ramsay.

24 September 1896
7.30 a.m.
Dalwhinnie

My dear Highland love,

This place that the train is now carrying me through has always dwelt in my memory as one of the most weird and fascinating spots I ever knew, since I spent a night here eleven years ago. This morning that wild Loch Ericht & its mountains around looked splendid. It is sunny yet there are a few mists & heavy clouds to give mystery & rich colouring. And it all appeals to me now as it has done since I was a child, only with this added — that you come from the Highlands & my new home is there. I suppose Lossie is Highland, isn't it?

I wonder how you are in pokey old London. OH, there is such a splendid mountain up at the head of a bleak valley. I'm not feeling a bit shy of my examination [by Annie Ramsay] — perfectly brazen. Indeed I'm not thinking of anything except how fine the Hills & the heather & the sky & the peaty burns are. It is rather an effort even to write to you: only

Dalwhinnie has such a hold on my affection & I thought I would like to send you a message on paper to my own dear love from there.

. . . Why can't the train stop & let me have a scamper up the rocks and over the heather? Why do I feel bound to write to a stupid man in dirty London when I am enjoying myself so much. I always used to enjoy these things quite to myself, & why it should add to the pleasure to tell you about it, I can't imagine.

Perhaps it is because I am your Sweetheart.

12.50 p.m.

. . . I've been so busy indoors I've not much time to write to you; indeed I ought to be laying the dinner now, but your mother knows I am writing to you.

I have been helping with housework & seeing all the old treasures in the presses & the things your grandmother spun, and it all seems so real I nearly had a little lump in my throat.

Then our mother has started me with some stockings to knit for myself (I've learnt the porridge) and I've been teaching Cousin James [Thomson, Ramsay's cousin, who was staying with Annie] the ordinary notation & hearing him fiddle. He says you can fiddle Home Sweet Home.

This afternoon we are going to call on Miss Shovelbred. I can't tell you all your friends that I have had a welcome from. I must talk about them when I see you, but I'm afraid I won't remember all their names. Such dear hearty fishermen and fishwives — oh and all sorts of people. We went to get the milk from the Moores this morning. Mrs Moore asked if I would like to live in Lossie & I very nearly said yes without thinking: only I just remembered that perhaps we would rather stick to London after all. Our mother says that I am to tell you of young Mr Slater's death. You will see it in the *Courant*. It is very sad, is it not? Miss Innes & Mrs Macpherson were in to call last night. We were going down to the harbour to see the steamer come in (on the pilot's invitation, Mr Stewart). But it was too wet. I've been reading your *New Age* aloud: Thanks for it.

> Your ever loving
> Margaret

❧ Margaret's diary.

24 September 1896

Highland Railway. Mrs. Campbell at Forres. Mother & James Thomson at Elgin. Lossie. Walk. Visitors etc. talk . . .

🙰 Ramsay to Margaret.

24 September 1896
Duncan Buildings

My dear Sweetheart

You are in Elgin I hope & have just met my mother. I do hope you like her . . .

. . .The S'ton folks were half expecting you — as if you had any interest in them — at the dance on Monday but I assured them you were much too superior for that. Thanks expecially for showing me Bessie's letter [of 7 August]. Whilst we have some slight cause for feeling vexed, at the same time we should admit that the way we conducted ourselves at Chilworth more than justified them, with their notions, in prohibiting a speedy marriage.[1] I really think we were both rather to blame because we ought not to have asked them to take so much for granted as we did without any slight approach to an outward sign that we were in the marrying state. I rather feel that your father has his suspicions similar to those that Bessie has expressed, and I am rather sorry at it. I also feel sure that that is Basil's[2] opinion & of course he will talk. I do not care much one way or the other, except that there is some danger of it leaking out sideways into the world where it will be one more thorn prick for a short time & that it is not pleasant to feel that people with whom you are in more or less intimate contact have to recognise our marriage whilst they suspect its real genuineness.

We know it all ourselves, but the world is in the position of a jury & wants at least *prima facie* evidence.

I suppose you do not treat such letters from Bessie with any approach to elaborate courtesy, but seeing that we rather share her fault she is entitled to a reminder that she knows nothing about me & that she is in a position to express an opinion on our marriage in no way better than that in which I am to express an opinion upon hers. As a matter of fact I am in a better position for M. Bach & she — particularly she — are so transparent. Now I have this little regret off my mind & here I am, emerged.

My lassie must tell me all about Lossiemouth, how she likes it, & whom she sees & how she likes them . . .

Ever thine
Ramsay.

---

1. Evidently Margaret and Ramsay, who both had difficulty showing their feelings, had been so cool to one another during the weekend at Chilworth that the family concluded he was a fortune-hunter.
2. Basil Holmes, Isabella's husband.

∽ Margaret to Ramsay.

24th September 1986
1.15 p.m.
Lossiemouth

My dear Ramsay

Thanks, ever so many, for your nice kind welcome to my new home. I found Mrs Campbell[1] at Forres, & she was as sweet as could be and sweeter, & came on with me here . . . Cousin James went to the post to telegraph to you, & brought back the Progressive Review which looks very swagger — and — and — and — it is all perfectly lovely.

I am really awfully glad you are not here with me. Because it couldn't have been nicer, and as I suppose your being here must have made some difference it would have had to be less nice. But why did you have such a nice little home & why did you say I might come here & be so happy.

Now you'll want to know about our mother. Why didn't you tell me she was young and pretty? The photographs don't one hundredth part do her justice. And she's ever so kind to me, but then I knew she was going to be that . . .

Our mother called me "my dear lassie" once just like you do only with a far prettier accent.

We have just been laughing at you in the Southampton photographs. You are a ridiculous man, but you have a very nice home. Your mother sends a message that we are all well & if it is fine weather we are going about a great deal.

Your Lassie

P.S. I am happy.

∽ Margaret to Ramsay.

Same day
10.45 p.m.
Lossiemouth

My dearest Ramsay

Pardon, I am using your red ink, and what is more I am using your desk. This is where you used to write me love-letters sometimes — in the days of long ago. So if anything of your influence lingers about it this love letter of mine ought to be a very sweet one.

---

1. Annie Ramsay's Aunt Anne.

But my dear Sir I don't think it will be very sweet, for the simple reason that I'm much too happy to tell you about it. Only I can't go to bed in my new home without just thanking you from the bottom of my heart for giving it to me.

It does seem quite like a home already — & our mother is so kind to me. And I have been all about & your friends have been welcoming me for your · sake & I have been looking at the things you looked at when you were a little fat boy & in later days when you began to get unsatisfactory — and our mother has been talking about you & I have loved it all for your sake, and you for . . . well, what I love you for I never make out, but I do.

What a gushing young party you will think me: Only dear Sir the gush is only a little froth on the top of a very real and deep feeling of love and gratitude.

Yes "we'll wed in winter" if I can tear myself from Lossie; and if the daughterly feeling which is getting strong possession of me doesn't turn out all Sweetheart tendencies.

Goodnight dear love, & many blessings be upon you.

X

7 a.m. A first good morning to my dear Sir from my dear home. It all seems too good to be true — too good for me at any rate: but it's very, very nice. I hope you are getting good news of how the Progressive Review is going off. I am glad you sent our father one. I felt horrid leaving him all alone in Liverpool on Wednesday night, though it was his own choice to stay there another day after we left.

༄ Margaret to Ramsay.

25 September 1896
11.40 p.m.
Lossiemouth

Now look how very wrongful our Mother & I are — we have been sitting by the fire talking to this time of night, while James is out gadding at a supper-party at Mr Glennies. But late as it is, I must just give my dear Love his Goodnight and tell him that Lossie is still a Paradise and our Mother an angel. And as for your poor little lassie, she is sad — quite melancholy — because she knows she will never be able quite to show you how much she loves you, & what a privilege it is that that one is going to be your wife.

Good night, dear lad. XX

151

10 a.m. Just time to write a little before we go off on a picnic to the Covesea Caves.

Yesterday afternoon we had tea with Mr Shovelbred. Jack was in fine form, & Miss Flora S. was there too, who is a niece of Mrs Paton at Southampton. Then Mother and I went to I don't know how many fishermen's cottages & they were all so fond of you & so glad to see your "young lass". They sent you lots of messages, & so want to see you . . . Mother is beginning to think we shall not need to keep a servant because I do the housework so nicely. So There — you needn't turn up your nose at me again. I was to be sure to tell you I made the porridge myself this morning. But alas, I fear me I am no true Gladstone, for I am so clumsy with the axe that when I am chopping the wood Mother has to come every few minutes to see if my fingers and toes are still on.

∾ Ramsay to Margaret.

25 September 1896
Duncan Buildings

My Dear Lassie,

And so you are up there flirting with other cousins now are you? Ah! well! It doesn't matter. You don't know what a jolly time I am having — the only fear being Nov 23rd [their wedding date]. I got your wire & now comes your letter. I am awfully glad that everything came off without a hitch, & now I expect you will have a rare high time of it. Only please do not undermine my good character up there. If, for instance, you were to flirt with our Free Kirk minister he would think that I had gone wrong. I expect you to sit with a demure face all day in the usual & natural "butter wouldn't melt in my mouth" style. That is how ladies behave up there — and of course you are a lady with a marriage settlement. Pray do not do much, washing the dishes & clearing the table. You will break so much, & I shall have to pay for them that, once again, you will be a frightful expense.

. . . *The Southampton Times* is getting out a special wedding number & this picture is to be the poster. Won't you feel flattered & won't Bessie retire to private life in Lyons with her back up!

But it is really very very nice to think of you being up there in our rooms, in our garden & amongst our friends. Do tell me whom you see & what you think of them — and generally · . . . what you think of the dear old village . . .

Thine
Ramsay.

P.S. I have given up househunting. I have seen a flat or two but they are never vacant a day. They put up posters, visitors come by the dozen & the place is taken. There is one now in Southampton Row, 2nd floor, 4 rooms, kitchen, servant's bedroom & bathroom for £115. It is vacant on Monday & we would have to take it straight away. I think we can wait for a fortnight.

Kindest love to my mother & Thomson.

Yours is up above.

R.

∾ Ramsay to Margaret.

26 September 1896
Duncan Buildings

My Dearest Lassie,

. . . How does Lossie air & a Lossie welcome agree with you? How does your household education proceed? Can you boil potatoes? Can you eat pickled onions? Are you any good at all? Of course you will pass examinations on all these things before you come and keep house for me.

The *Review* [Progressive Review] is now staring you in the face on every bookstall. I think it looks well e.g. striking like Enid. Now we are all head over heels into the second. I have given them due warning about November. Would you be very much annoyed if I proposed to cut the honeymoon a little short. The letter I sent you from Dr Beveridge of Aberdeen is really important & I am trying my Portsmouth date until the 20th December. But going to Aberdeen means a few more days than going to Portsmouth and they must be made up. If we came back from Cornwall say in six days, we might manage the whole week from Dec. 5 to Dec. 14th in Scotland. But of course I can hardly say anything definite yet on that. You are already beginning to experience the finesses which your unsatisfactory man has to perform. If you had only known in pre-bauble days!

Last night, Trenwith, leader of the Victorian Labour Party, lectured to the Fabians with Webb in the chair and preached the Webbian faith "Be Liberals!" I went for him tooth and nail. Shaw was put up to smooth over my attack & altogether we scored heavily. Still, we are going to be beaten on the 9th I fear unless I can manage to detach some of their present support; so if you find me twisting and wriggling in my opening speech — I am starting the ball — don't be surprised. I know you propose to vote against me, but I am to appeal in public to her who loves me etc., to desert rascals . . .

Ever

R

Wednesday

I will not be there in person, but here I am in spirit offering the heartiest welcome home to my dear lassie.

R.

Your nice letter has come — the last this week — but it is much too champaigny to take any notice of ————!!!!!

❧ Margaret to Ramsay.

Saturday 26 September 1896
11.30 p.m.
Lossiemouth

My dearest Ramsay

Does my own dear love want another goodnight in red ink? Because I want to give it to him. Does he know how often I have thought of him today, & how I have wanted to rumple his hair and give him a kiss? And how much I liked his letter, and all his nice kind thoughts.

Don't we keep late hours here? I'm frightfully sleepy; but you ordered me to give you "generally what I think of the dear old village". My dear Sir, what a silly order! I should have thought the Black Hole of Calcutta nice if you had lived there . . .

Sabbath morning

12.30 p.m. My first Sabbath in the new home has not been spent in quite such a godly way so far as I should have liked, for the rain is pelting so much that we have been gossiping over the parlour fire instead of going to the free kirk. But we are going to the Established this evening whatever happens to hear Mr Welwood or Mr Slater, & if by any lucky chance it clears up a little we are going to see Sandy Brown this afternoon.

I hope you will have a good meeting at the Holborn Town Hall.

We had tea last night with the Stewarts: how charming & hearty & utterly courteous & gracious they were. They sent lots of messages to you, & nearly rung my hand off with their welcome to your intended. I assured Mrs Stewart I was not "a bicycle lady". I must tell you more about every thing when I get home? if we have time for talking about anything except pots and pans & orange blossom bouquets before the honeymoon. I envy all these people for having known you as a boy, & then I pity them because they do not get loveletters from you.

Those letters you sent interested me. Thank you for them. If you like to go to Aberdeen for your honeymoon, I'll speak at Portsmouth for you & let you go off North.

It doesn't seem very long now to the fatal 23d. But it seems a very very long time since I saw you.

Thy Margaret.

∾ Ramsay to Margaret.

26 September 1896
Progressive Review

> I saw old Boxall, weird & thin,
>   Sit in the club dejected, wet,
> "Old chap", I said "You're out of tin?"
>   He sighed: "I'm lonely — Margaret".
>
> I saw old Jokie throw him down —
>   A pair of haggard eyes, mine met.
> "Hullo, old chappie, why that frown"?
>   He gasped, "bring back my Margaret".
>
> The Clock is stopped; the books so blue
>   Are thick with smuts as black as jet.
> The Tom cat whispers in a mew —
>   "Oh, where! Oh, where is Margaret."

My Monday morning greeting. Prog: going like wildfire. *Morning Advertiser* has leader on us this morning. Liberty Review is shrieking, declares that I will answer everything in its next. *Morning Daily News* & *Daily Telegraph* also notice us. We only sent out press copies yesterday. *D. Chron* will likely have leader on Monday.

All this with infinite love to my lassie whose existence gives colour & energy to my pleasure.

R.

∾ Margaret to Ramsay.

Sunday night 11 p.m.
Lossiemouth

Dear beloved Sir,

I meditated deeply in church. A shade of sadness stole across me — in eight weeks I shall be having my last day in the home of 26 years. And it is a home that I wouldn't change for any other in the world — except yours — Just to think of my nice school-room desk, and my dear little window looking out over the sun-rise. And the breakfasts when Flo comes down late, & the Sunday suppers when we all take second helps of the other pudding. It is a good thing you are nice, (or I think you are) or I should be in a bad temper. But you know, don't you, that I would give up every pleasure in life to have you say I helped you at all — for that would be more pleasure than all. And I am so spoilt that I have the pleasures & your love too.

But I fear Papa and Flo must be feeling rather dreary: I wish they would move to a smaller house. I wonder if we'll be able to cheer them up much. I had a letter from May today which I liked better than any I ever had from her before & made me happier about her future — I'll show it you some day, but I must answer it first. I hope you remembered when I sent you that letter of Bessie's how much Papa & Flo interfered with her plans & said she wasn't suitable for Brother B. I don't wonder that she thought I got off easily and deserved a dose.
P.S. I don't think I mentioned love anywhere, but
cela va sans dire!

∾ Margaret to Florence.

27 September 1896
Lossiemouth

My dear Florence,

I suppose you will be back in London when you get this. I hope you have had a nice time at Carnavon & that your conscience allowed you to stay over Sunday. I am having a very good time indeed and can hardly imagine I have only been here three days. — I feel so much at home & have seen so many of Ramsay's friends. His mother is very kind and nice, & the cousin James Thomson who is staying here I like. Just now he is writing a lot of committee notices for me, as it is raining too hard for us to go out.

Everyone here seems to know and like Ramsay & give me a very hearty welcome for his sake. Yesterday evening we had tea with a delightful old fisherman & his wife. They talk such broad scotch that I can hardly understand it when they talk fast among themselves.

We had a picnic yesterday and a most lovely walk along the seashore & visited some very interesting caves. In some of them there are tinkers, and we came across a woman with a baby only 8 days old — just living there in the cave, but they seemed to find it warm and comfortable & had made a pretty little garden outside.

This week we are going to Inverness, Forres, Grantoun & one or two other places. I will return on Monday week & see about my trains later.

Ramsay has given up house hunting as the things get snapped up so quickly and so it will be better when I return.

Love to all

> Yr aff. sister
> MEGladstone

❧ Margaret to Ramsay.

> 28 September 1896
> Monday evening
> Lossie

My dear Ramsay

. . . Off at 9.50 tomorrow to Inverness: then to Grantown and Forres. Hamish [James Thomson] leaves us at Inverness.

I expect to leave our mother behind me an absolute wreck: but then she shouldn't have a son sending a strange daughter-in-law to worry her.

I am sorry to trace tendencies towards luxury in your family. There was your mother this morning lying in bed sipping her tea & listening to the fire crackling in the kitchen & saying "Eh, What'll I dee when ye ging awa' " and my private opinion is that she will engage a French cook, two housemaids, and a buttons. And Miss Duncan wants to come here & have her tea in bed too. Hamish, however, is a brilliant exception: he has turned into my private honorary secretary & sends out my committee notices for me . . .

> Thy Lassie.

157

❧ Margaret to Ramsay.

[September 1896]
[Lossiemouth]

. . . I don't believe you guessed what we were doing today: we often thought of you and how you would have laughed to see us, for we have been the three giddiest donkeys you ever heard of. We set off for our picnic, and we climbed rocks, & ran races on the sand & visited the tinkers in the caves where there was a baby 8 days old, & James and I crawled on all fours down the Robbers stable, & we lost Mother's gloves out of the lunch basket, and we dragged her on to places she had never been to in her life before, right on to Hopeman & we dined in the Station Hotel there & thought of you in some pokey stuffy London office, and we drove back in a dog cart & passed Drainie Schoolhouse: only we were all much too ramshackle to go in & call (I mean to go another day). Only I thought of my dear Sir going along that road every day & felt very very glad that he is my dear Sir: and now we are all back & going to have tea, only we laugh so we can hardly turn our minds to business.

Now dear Sir! I rather thought perhaps you were getting some ideas like you put in your letter about what my people think of us. But I don't think you need be uneasy: only I'll take the hint & be careful. Basil's a donkey, though a very good fellow: However I shall be writing to Bella & I'll put things nicely.

It is only the old tale which I suppose has been my mistake all my life — that I show my feelings least to my home people when I really care about them more than anybody else, but you. Still I think we understand each other better than we show, & I'll be as careful as I can.

We were too engrossed by tea to post this before 5 p.m.

Since then and washing up (I always take charge of that now) I've been having a lesson in wood chopping (see how Scotch I am) & find I have some of the old Gladstone blood in me still & I am improving in my handling of the axe though Hamish did suggest I should make a good stonemason because I hit the stone so much instead of the wood. But I am going to have a wood yard on our roof at Mecklenburgh Square and practice there every morning before breakfast.

I daresay there is a letter from you kicking about the town for me somewhere, but we were out when the post came.

Your mother is sending a perfect geological Museum which she picked up at Covesea for you and which I have to bring you.

Thine ever
Margaret.

∽ Ramsay to Margaret.

28 September 1896
Duncan Buildings

. . . We had a good meeting last night in the Holborn Town Hall. The Fabian meeting on the 9th is to be lively. I suppose as usual you are going to vote Webbian and against me. The interest of the meeting, however, apart from the voting will be so considerable, that I can overlook your sins this time.

I can record no jolly picnics — no Covesea wanderings — no sprees — no dogcart escapades. I have been a very decent well-behaved citizen, doing my painful duties like a martyr & thinking of my lassie like a lover. I have lunched at the club & smoked my pipe of peace with my friends & talked business with my colleagues. But I thought you were engaged on these tricks — and didn't you see the form of an unsatisfactory man mirrored in the pools in the rocks, & sitting on the driver's knee? I assure you the form was there & it was very happy because you were. Now I must away to the office. I hope my mother keeps well & is not too oppressed with your breaking her dishes & destroying her axe.

Kindest love to her & Thomson — who apparently has been deceiving you into the belief that Hamish is Scottish — & ever so many more to your own dear self from

Yours ever
Ramsay

∽ Annie Ramsay to Margaret.

Monday ? September 1896
Lossiemouth

My Dear Margaret

Many thanks fir your last letter i will be most happy to trim your nightgown or any thing i can do fir you i have your Stokens down and i am dowing Socks fir Ramsay i am beter but nothing like myself but i hope i will soon be all right again i will send you a parsel by the eand of the week yesterday was the frist day fir weeks the son was quite no boats could go to the sea som of the people could not be well off they got so little fir the Herring in sommer we never had 2 howers of dray wither since you left No My Dear Margaret Now the tim is passing and now soon you will have to change your life May God go with you both and make you happy how often i

159

think of you both night and day though absent my mond is present with you in my quite hom and i am so glad to get a letter with all the nues now my dear gural i close with much love from your Mither

A Ramsay

∾ Ramsay to Margaret.

30 September 1896
Duncan Buildings

True as the magnet pointing to the poles my morning thoughts are turned up against the North wind & towards my dear donkey girl. I hear she is behaving nicely — so very sweetly, & that all the Lossie people are pitying me, because there is a healthy prejudice there against a girl that is perfection before marriage. Such girls, they know, turn out demon wives. Still, I must risk that now & try to make the best of you. It is so very pleasantly strange to think of you being up there, going to tea with Jock Stewart, and sitting in the Established Church listening to Wellwood. It makes me so sweet tempered & happy when I try to picture it. The oddest thing of all, however, is that you have never said that you met me there. I am often about there, particularly within the last three or four or five days, & just in the places where you are most likely to be. Have you really never seen me?

Nevertheless, Bessie is right in her fears as I am now going to prove. I said I could not see you on Saturday because I was much too interested in the *New Age* shareholders meeting. That was one for Bessie. But I have got an appointment with you for Tuesday — which I cannot keep. It is all very well of you to say, "Breakfast on Tuesday morning". But behold! On Monday evening I speak in the Norwich Town Hall on the Political Situation & that means that I am not up in town until about 10.30 on Tuesday. I was to meet you at Berners Street & dine with you at Pembridge Square but a meeting of the Fabian protestors has been called for 8 at *The New Age* office. So that's off. Now amn't I unsatisfactory & isn't Bessie right? She may be. There's no saying; but whether she is or not, I am only thirsting for work because I love my dear lassie. So once again I leave off with a sweet, sweet, X to that other party in L. who is coming to keep house for me. R.

❧ Margaret to Ramsay.

> 30 September 1896
> 11.15 p.m.
> Louisville — Forres

Here I am under the roof of our dear kind old Auntie [Anne Campbell] — in a room where she says you were once frightened in the night.

I am sending all sorts of loving messages to my laddie . . .

> Margaret.

> October 1st

Next Month . . .

I wonder how you are & what you are doing. Did you dine at Pembridge Square? What happened at the Club Committee? I have another notice for this week. Please convey my apologies to Mr Toke & Co: It is entirely your fault that I am not soberly at home pursuing the daily round, the Common task.

Bessie wants me to be bridesmaid to her. My first thought was "Catch me": it wasn't until the fifth thought that it occurred to me I might play the buffoon if it pleased other people. I'll see when I get back. I'm sending Brother B. a Review with our love (?) . . .

Miss Jean Dewar wished to have her good wishes conveyed to you: We met her at the station.

Mrs. Campbell has given us a splendid old blue china bowl that has been in your family for six generations, perhaps 7 . . . and your mother is going to give a blue jug & wants to ask you about whether she shall send the cups with the squirrel to us & is going to give me one of her grandmother's wedding rings. How do you like our rifling the Establishment?

I get to King's X on Tuesday at 6.45 a.m. but if by any chance you are coming to meet me, would you prefer Euston at 7.30 or St Pancras at 7.55? Because I would obey you if you did!

> Always Margaret.

❧ Ramsay to Margaret.

> 1 October 1896
> Bradford
> The Midland Hotel

My Dearest Donkiest Lassie,

Now, this morning I will have nothing from you & perhaps tomorrow morning the same desolation will reign. I am up here attending a meeting of the N.A.C. and imagining your surroundings at Liverpool. I am sure all the virtues which blossomed forth in the early days of your Lossiemouth sojourn must have worn themselves out by now, and so I am sending you a few familiar pictures to enlighten your graces.

Flo wrote me yesterday saying that 17 was again tenanted, regretting that I had given up househunting and bemoaning your long stay in Lossiemouth. I wasn't very much concerned on the last point for the simple reason that I can so well picture you up there, & when I do your surroundings have such a stamp of home feeling for me, that you do not seem to be away at all. You must try and see me on Tuesday at lunch or in the early afternoon & then we shall have such a big talk.

By the by, a bit of business! I suppose your father will now be seeing after your marriage settlement. Will you write to him & say that I wish it to be drawn up that in the event of your death, I get nothing. I want to make it quite clear that I do not want your money. £100 a year will always be enough for me and I can always make that.

And now, with my very very very kindest and sweetest love to my lassie I am ever her

Laddie,

∾ Ramsay to Margaret.

1 October 1896

Bradford

Central Commercial Hotel Westgate

My Dearest Lassie,

Another deep deep love message to you. I have just finished "Paula", Victoria Cross's last novel & I have been understanding somewhat the meaning of a woman's love & despairing more than ever of being able to understand it all.[1] I have been in one of my sad moods (why do people always imagine that sadness is the opposite of happiness) — when happiness is so blended with love that it becomes sad. And I am thinking of the dear soul that is trusting me, & am praying that I may be worthy of her & that we may both be worthy of our humanity. I wish you were with me here, sitting by me. We would not say much, because words are poor things. We would simply feel, & love would reveal many secrets to us & our hearts would wonder at the mystery of it all. My dearest Lassie, you are a

---

1. Victoria Cross was a popular romantic novelist of the 1890s. *Paula* was the tale of a clergyman's daughter; an actress and playwright who sacrificed love for a 'casting couch' marriage. She eventually committed suicide.

treasure that grows in its preciousness every day. It is booming out twelve & I'll be away & try to sleep. My good night & blessing to my dear lassie

Ramsay

I go to London again tomorrow & am getting impatient for your letters.

◇ Margaret to Ramsay.

2 October 1896

Dear beloved Sir,

Behold me lying full length on the heather to prevent myself being blown away by the Highland breezes — thinking blissful things & solemn things and ridiculous things . . . I am in my glory now — up a wild heathery blowy hill before breakfast. I've been tramping through bogs and climbing wire fences in my Sunday best frock & relieving myself of my hat (which at present is sitting under five blocks of granite by the cairn to keep itself from blowing away, cocky feathers and all) & kicking my heels in the air, & doing all sorts of delightful old-maidish things which I suppose will be forbidden when you are my Lord and Master. Don't you feel your bachelor days drawing dreadfully near to a close — I've been wishing the old free days back again — and laughing at myself because I know I am counting the very hours till I see you again. There is dear old Cairngorm winking at me from behind a cloud, and reminding me of the time when I sat by his cairn for nearly an hour, shivering in a storm of snow & hail for the view he never vouchsafed. But I've loved him ever since, so take warning & be cold & proud to me if you want my affection.

But this is a glorious place and I have glorious things to think of — you had the fine scenery to prepare you for the bustle of our engagement (not that we did bustle over it) — I have it to prepare me for the bustle of marriage.

Once I came to Grantown nine years ago — passing through on a drive. I thought it a stupid towny place after the freedom of the moors. — But how pleased I should have been if I had known that on a little hill behind I should have a nice little consecration service all to myself on the eve of my marriage.

Sometimes the thought comes across me that this happiness is not for us after all — well — sorrow can strengthen & purify as well as joy. Probably we shall have both. Whatever it [?is], we love each other & we mean our love to be an unselfish one — & it is all very, very blessed.

And the wind and the heather and the clouds are lovely: & down below there are my kind new relations ready to welcome me back to breakfast.

Margaret

∞ Ramsay to Margaret.

> Friday night
> 2 October 1896
> The Progressive Review

My Dearest Lassie,

Back from Bradford. Every thing gone wrong except your comforting letters since I went away. So only a thought in passing amidst a mass of letters — a loving one all the same. You know I cannot get up from Norwich until Tuesday morning & the Fabian protesters meet in the evening. Where can we meet?

> Ever thine
> Ramsay.

∞ Margaret to Ramsay.

> 2 October 1896
> Friday, 11 p.m.
> Lossiemouth, not to say Home, Sweet Home.

How very nice to be home again, and how very nice to go down to the post & get two letters from you. I hope the N.A.C. went well . . .

. . . What a joke to see the marriage settlement when I get home — I shall feel 2 inches taller & borrow Wilfred's wig. BUT:

1. Nobody imagines that you marry me for the filthy lucre as everyone knows how charming I am in my own sweet self.

2. I don't intend to die, yet awhile.

3. I suppose you will allow me to do what I like with my own & leave it to you if I wish — only I don't know yet how much of my own comes into the settlement: I'll give you nothing if I can manage it . . .

---

1. The NAC held their quarterly meeting at Bradford on Thursday & Friday 1st and 2nd October — there being present Enid Stacey, J. Keir Hardie (in the chair), Frances Littlewood, Pete Curran, Fred Brocklehurst, H. Russel Smart and J. Ramsay MacDonald.

You are quite mistaken. I never meet you about here . . . I only wish I did — I feel so jealous when people say they saw or heard you here or there about the place.

But sometimes I meet a dear little blackeyed boy with sturdy boots on his way to school — or more often lurking round & up to pranks — & this evening I met a youth in a potato field — & he was a nice youth. And he had a sweetheart waiting in London for him X

M.E.G.

〜 Ramsay to Margaret.

5 October 1896
Monday morning
Wronham Broad
Norfolk

There is a dear little sweetheart of mine away about Lossiemouth a sobbing and a sighing at this moment because the fates have decreed that she should come back & see a very unsatisfactory man and a very matrimonially minded family. That same man is now scribbling a line of love to her so that she may be get it when she comes home to-morrow morning . . .

Ever thine
R.

I have opened this to put in this slip saying that the Scottish Widows Assurance has accepted me at normal rate. That little cloud has therefore gone as it means that so far as their doctor could say I am alright & he examined me specially for my possible diseases.

X

Once Margaret was back in London they saw one another as often as they could — house-hunting, choosing wallpaper. Ramsay spent a few more days in Bradford preparing for the by-election.

10 October 1896
The Labour Leader

The visit of the NAC is an event that is now past and gone and Bradford still stands where it did . . . owing to the death of Mr Bryon Reed MP . . . is the candidate to be Tom Mann, Keir Hardie* or Fred Brocklehurst?

* choice fell on me.

~ Margaret to Ramsay.

10 October 1896
6.30 p.m.
Pembridge Square

My dear Sweetheart

Why does my love for you make me feel restless & lazy, instead of urging me to work like you say yours does? It is naughty in anything concerning you. Otherwise I'm not in the least particular. But I ought to be writing to Lady Salisbury & Lady Frederick Cavendish & other folks for subscriptions to the Nurses: and instead I only want to kiss you & say nice things to you & take away your nasty headache . . .

~ Ramsay to Margaret.

?11 October 1896
Saturday night
Bradford
postcard

My Dearest Little Donkey —

This is the very first note your present has ever written. So isn't it a happy pen to begin life by telling a new lassie that she has been making a poor man feel very sacred because she loves him. I have really been thinking these last few days especially, whether I am worthy of you at all. I fall short of so many things & I feel I am only beginning to know you & like one who has become possessed of great riches, I feel that I want some good justification for my blessings. But I'll try my best. I have been in the mood when I see many difficulties ahead these past few days. When I heard your father refer yesterday to Westminster & so on, my heart felt sore. How little do they all know the weary way that lies between me and that, & how little do they know our hearts. I never knew what & how much you are to me until last night when I failed so miserably at a supreme moment. That walk up Chancery Lane & along Holborn was our marriage. It was much more sacred than any ceremony can be to me. It settled all sorts of problems. Someone, I forget who, has said that the man is blessed who in success or failure can lay his head on the breast of one who loves him. I felt that blessedness for the first time in my life last night & I knew that I had really passed the confines of an old world into a new . . .

Ever
R
X X

∽ Ramsay to Margaret.

[11] October 1896
c/o J. Lazenby Esq
Claremont
Bradford

. . . We had a good time last night & of course talked politics by the dozen. Mr Lazenby is a splendid fellow & is now one of the Hon: Secretaries of the Bradford Liberal Association besides being Ex-this & that throughout the whole range of offices. They seem to have some dark horse up their sleeve (or should I say in their stable?) He says none of the mentioned as possible candidates will be selected. I find that he has filled me up every night & so I will not be in London until mid-day on Wednesday. To-night I have supper with Mr Varley the leading Congregationalist parson here. Tomorrow we sup at 10 pm with the Illingworths, & on Tuesday there is a supper here at 10 pm when I meet the President etc. of the Liberal Club & Association . . . When my lassie gets this tomorrow she will know how fondly I am thinking of her & how I am wishing that that beastly ceremony were over and we were going out into the world together.

Ramsay XX

∽ Margaret to Ramsay.

[11 October 1896]
Sunday 12.45 p.m.

How art thou? Frivolous as ever? Your sedate lassie is in a good temper with herself because on the way to church she had a talk with Bessie, about you and cleared the air . . .

∽ Ramsay to Margaret.

12 October 1896
Claremont
Bradford

My Dearest Lassie,
. . . I have been lunching at the Liberal Club and have met the leading spirits of Bradford Liberalism. Of course, even to you our talk and arguments must be unknown — except that the general result is that I am infinitely better pleased with myself than I was on Friday; & at the moment, if our fellows would only be reasonable East Bradford may surprise some people . . .

Tomorrow I play golf with Arthur Illingworth, on Wednesday I am going to kiss my sweetheart.

Ever thine
Ramsay

〰 Margaret to Ramsay.

12 October 1896
7 a.m.

A very warm birthday greeting to my dear love — I wonder whether he has got it yet, or whether he is still asleep. I hope the latter for I am quite sure he kept his kind hosts up last night by chattering late. Or was he reasonable & good & sensible & off to bed in good time.

I have been lying awake for two hours thinking a most curious medley of birthday wishes to you, fines and deductions in shops, and most of all thoughts and plans for our dear, dear home which is not many weeks off now.

Just as I thought I had got my attention nicely concentrated on fines I danced up quite without permission of my reasonable self to send you a message though I don't know where to send it yet. But I love you!

X MEG

8.15 a.m.

My dear love, I have got your letter now, & your Saturday night card. I can't answer you in writing: the only answer is to love you more and more and to pray that I may be more worthy of the trust you give me.

I think that last night at Lossiemouth I felt as strongly as I ever did how utterly unworthy I am of you. I even had mad thoughts of writing & trying to explain to you how stupid & shallow & small I am: Only my better self knew that we loved each other, and that that love could brave all seeming failures & shortcomings.

I too have been wishing the ceremony were over. When we have been so patient, you for 30 & I for 26 years, Why are we so impatient over the last few weeks? My dear, dear love X

Fancy me with a husband! As if I wasn't quite nice enough alone! And Honnor (sic) Morton saying I am going to disappear. Does she think you are going to eclipse me? The converse is <u>much</u> more likely, and would be much more profitable to the world at large.

Talking nonsense means that I am happy. That I am happy means that I have a dear man to love me & to be loved by me. And that means — more than either of us can say.

Why do I like your being away? Because I get letters from you. Why do I dislike you being away? Because I don't see you, and I do long to do so.

In pencil:—

Many, many thanks for your letter

Margaret.

Monday evening

. . . After a committee today I went flat hunting — why, I haven't a notion, as I am not going to let you take any of the places I looked at — they were all pokey holes near the music halls of Shaftesbury Avenue. But it was so nice doing it alone — so much more interesting than going with you; and I built castles in the air of how I was a spinster lady going to live there alone with a screeching parrot — and it was all so exhilarating that I finished my spree by having a birthday tea at a certain A.B.C. shop where I had tea the day before I went to Liverpool. Why I chose to call it a birthday tea I don't know, seeing that my birthday is in July; nor why I chose to sit at a corner table & imagine what a rowdy he & she would look like sitting opposite to me. It must have been the parrot I was thinking of somehow . . .

. . . I may go and look at the Finsbury flat & at this one Basil mentions as you are not to be back till Wednesday: but my affections are entwining themselves round Lincoln's Inn Fields. [They finally settled on a flat at 3 Lincoln's Fields.]

12.45

. . . I knew it would all come right.

And so it has, especially as far as the unsatisfactory man goes. I've just been writing rather a nice letter about you to Florrie Kemsly. I somehow felt as if I should like to tell someone beside yourself that I was considerably gone, (in a reasonable and dignified way) over you: I told her that she knew I had a pretty high ideal of that sort of thing, but that so far the real was better. Now, don't feel cocky or I shan't like you.

MEG.

❧ Annie Ramsay to Margaret.

12 October 1896
Lossiemouth

My Dear Margaret

i am glad you got hom all safe and sound i stad over night with Aunt in
Forres and got hom all well My Neighbour got a baby boy next morning so i
met Doctor Brander he was verry sory he did not met you when in Lossie i
saw the other baby yesterday she is quite well we have verry bad weather
here and a sea storm Miss Shoolbrid and Mrs Grant called yesterday Mr
Grant leaves fir hom to day i had a letter frim Ramsay have you settled on a
house yet i have not been out much for the last two or three days i have
taken a cold so i am bissy at the needle and hopes soon to get over it i hope
your none the worse of being in Scotland

Now my Dear Gural may God go with you and guide you both and make
you happy with much love from your Mither

A Ramsay

Your letter to hand this morning Many thanks for you kind offer I have had
2 pounds 12 shillin so that leaves 7 pounds but My Dear Margaret i cannot
ask you to pay so much fir me i got it to pay part now and again so i new
Ramsay would be willing to help me but you muse plase your self and i will
do wat way you like frin yur Mither

❧ Ramsay to Margaret.

12 October 1896
c/o J. Lazenby Esq. J.P.
Claremont
Bradford

My Dearest Sweetheart

I am feeling very old today although your kiss has kept every trace of
sadness out of my heart. . . I am sure there is a troop of invisible
messengers flying between us and bringing us news . . .

I am attending a meeting of the Bradford East I.L.P. tonight, & am now
away to see about things.

Ever Thine with love
Ramsay.

∾ Margaret to Ramsay.

13 October 1896
8.15 a.m.
Pembridge Square

My dear Sir,

Men were deceivers ever and poor woman has to find it out for herself gradually . . .

Such a nasty bumptious letter . . . I don't in the least believe you do any good with all your diplomacy. At least if it is like your lovemaking it must be very poor sort of affair.

I've absolutely nothing more to say to you: Possibly breakfast will put some ideas into my head. I daresay in any case I shall have thought of something to say by tomorrow when I see you.

I've been planning all about our cupboard & things this morning: as I do not think there is room for any at L.I.F. [Lincoln's Inn Fields]. It was very easy to plan: I just said to myself do without. You won't mind having my ball-dresses on your bookshelves, will you? There will be lots of room in the study, you know, & I'll let you hang your surtout on the kitchen dresser if we can find a corner for such a luxury.

9.30 a.m.

Breakfast has suggested no remarks that I wish to make to you except Mary's thanks for your letter to her.

I suppose as a matter of form, I had better end as

Your affectionate sweetheart
Margaret Ethel Gladstone

P.S. I don't intend to kiss tomorrow. I have a cold & am trying to cherish it.
P.S.2 Just remembered that I love you very much. XX

∾ Ramsay to Margaret.

[Late October 1896]

A line to my love because we [were] both a little vexed tonight. There was such a pretty lamp cloth waiting me when I came home from Leonard & Mrs Matheson of Hendon.

> We talked of gifts tonight, my love
>> How you had those & I had that —
> How I had only few, my love
>> How most had gone to you, my love
>> And I but smiled thereat.

171

Now, why my careless sniff, my love
　　Why have I no regrets thereat?
Why? — Why, I thought you knew, my love
　　My richest gift is you, my love
　　　I can't own more than that,
　　　　　　　　　Your love

XXX etc., etc.

〰 Margaret's diary.

17 October 1896

Down to Shoreham with Ramsay to see Aunt Bella.

〰 Margaret to Ramsay.

18 October 1896
Sunday afternoon

My dear sir,

I broached the L.I.F. decision to my father this morning, & he made no fuss — only he said he must talk to you before we settled. (As far as I can make out he wants to tell you to curb & wisely guide my youthful enthusiasms & obstinacies & to keep me from weighting you down in a slough of unsatisfactoriness to which I heartily say Amen.)

So you must somehow let him see you tomorrow: He is not quite sure of his engagements . . . He might meet us at L.I.F. but I rather think it would be better if you could see him here, & I shall try to arrange accordingly. I shall make you give up the Statistical Committee if you have no other free time! Perhaps you had better make no arrangement with the Chancery Lane man [their solicitor] till you see me. — at Temple House . . .

Thy Margaret.

〰 Annie Ramsay to Margaret.

19 October 1896
Thee cottage
Lossiemouth

My Dear Margaret

Many thanks fir your kindness i am quite ashamed to think my dear gural any wun should be so kind to me only all i say is god Bless you both and every good atend you my dear gural my cold is not beter but we have such wet and cold weather not 2 hours the same Wat a pity you did not here C. Tuloch on Sabbath night We went to Mr Mcdonalds on Socialists i may have the chance of hearing more about it litter on i should have liked you had hard him No wird from Jane nor any but Miss Duncan Grantown i had a verry kind letter from hir The Mars is always esking about you and says you will milk cown yet . . .

A Ramsay

On 19 October 1896 Margaret was bridesmaid at her sister Bessie's wedding and later in the month she and Flo went to the NUWW (National Union of Women Workers) Conference in Manchester and stayed in the Grand Hotel.

Ramsay to Margaret

28 October 1896
24 East Park Terrace
Southampton

My Dear Madam,
I do not know at all why I am wasting my time thinking of the Grand Hotel, Manchester . . .
I saw a beastly little inquisitive man yesterday before leaving London. He is called a verger and he asked my age & if I was a bachelor & one or two other impertinent questions. Then I gave him half-a-crown and went away. I also saw a chap without an arm, who is known in the classics as a British workman. He had sponges & pumice-stone, paintpots & batter dishes & he had come to build and decorate a nest for a silly couple aged 26 & 30 respectively. I saw him begin his work & went away. Then I met a brother-in-law going to 3 Lincoln's Inn Fields to see his solicitor & we said "Ow de doo" & other intelligent things; & I felt that a brother-in-law who had a solicitor was a possession . . .

Ramsay to Margaret.

28 October 1896
24 East Park Terrace
Southampton

My Chere Marguerite
Nothing to say except that I am in town tomorrow morning & lunching at the club. Thence to Lincoln's Inns Fields. I would like an invitation to our

marriage sent to Mr & Mrs James Mackenzie, "Melrose" The Avenue, Southampton Mr Mackenzie was president of the Chamber of Commerce last year & is a director of Edwin Jones & Co. Quite respectable you see!

Ever my dear love.
R.

∾ Annie Ramsay to Margaret.

[October 1896]
Lossiemouth

My Dear Margaret

i like the lace could you send me sum more for the next one i do not think i shall go to Inverness i feel the cold verry much and i now my frinds here would be very disopented so i will let the Inverness people now i am verry bissy dowing a little bit of work fir you i hope you will like it and ware it

Miss Shoolbred tells me i never could send the tea set with geting all broken so i will be glad if you are cumming you can carry them hom with care fir they are so old[1] . . .

Jackie is to put flags on the lady Margaret on the Wednesday that is wat he calls your ship My Dear Margaret nothing will give me more plushare than a vessel of you both with much love and may God be your gide from your Mither

A Ramsay

∾ Ramsay to Margaret.

5 November 1896
The Progressive Review

My own dearest lassie,

. . . I should like the following to be asked for the 17th — should you agree: [he lists 20 friends]

. . . Things Kelvinese I wanted a word with you but could not have it. I have a very strong objection to calling upon the Kelvins [Margaret's great-uncle and his wife] until they ask me. They have never asked you to bring me even, I believe; & after the letters you showed me and also — *pardonnez moi ma chère*: their undoubted priggishness, I am inclined to be quite stiff & haughty. I have several times thought about it and then made enquiries in Glasgow, so I know quite what they think. You know, my dear lassie, how pained I am to write in this way . . .

---

1. China which had belonged to her mother.

❧ Margaret's diary.

6 November 1896

Call on Kelvins with Ramsay. Dinner at Gwythers.

In the Bradford East by-election on 10 November Keir Hardie lost the Liberal candidate the seat by splitting the vote.
R.H.F. Greville (Con.) 4921
A. Billson (Lib.) 4526
J.E. Hardie (ILB) 1,953

❧ Ramsay to Margaret.

18 November 1896
The Socialist Club
St Andrew's Street
Holborn EC

My dear Lassie,

This is the invitation you sent to Lilley.[1] He was going to write to you day after day & forgot. Hence, he knew nothing of last night. He knew nothing of the Monday hour either — which I suppose was my fault. I daresay you want him & his wife to lunch with you on Monday. Would you drop him a line if you do. He is to deliver no address but when the prayer book affair is over, the ceremony is done. He wants you to explain to Flo why he was not present last night. He thought indeed that it was for a Monday reception & was waiting to see me for particulars.

Do say if you don't want the ring I bought. I can easily change it & would like to do so if you prefer another.

Also give May my love & my regrets at not having said goodnight. I am saying it tonight instead & hope she feels it.

I am also sending you — by special messenger — a kiss of the best quality. May you have it.

Ever thine my dear lassie
Ramsay.

---

1. Rev. A.L. Lilley, who was to conduct the marriage service.

23 November 1896
Newspaper cutting

MARRIAGES

MacDONALD-GLADSTONE. — At St. Mary Abbot's, Kensington, London, W., on the 23d instant, by the Rev. A.L. Lilley, Holy Trinity, Sloane Square, assisted by the Hon. and Rev. Carr Glynn, Bishop-Designate of Peterborough, James Ramsay MacDonald, late of Lossiemouth, to Margaret Ethel, youngest daughter of Professor J.H. Gladstone, F.R.S.

After the wedding there was a lunch for thirty at Pembridge Square. Annie Ramsay had a party at Lossiemouth.

Tom Mann to Margaret.

23 November 1896
telegram
Ludgate Circus 11.49

Every good wish to Both was at church compelled to leave re Hamburg.[1]

Elizabeth King (Margaret's aunt)
to Mrs McLaren (a friend) . . .

24 November 1896

And now I must tell you about our dear little Margaret's marriage which took place yesterday. The day threatened to be very foggy but the air cleared somewhat as the hour of noon approached. By the bride's special request we joined her in the old home before the ceremony and found her happy, calm and bright. She spent a good while with us and we spoke of her

---

1.   5 December 1896
                                                               Labour Leader

HAMBURG DOCK STRIKE
Appeal for funds
To the public — The situation at Hamburg is of so serious a character as to merit the attention of all who are really concerned for the cause of labour. In Hamburg there are some 18000 port labourers of all kinds, 15000 of these, at least are now out on strike including the lightermen and tug-boat men.
The demand of the Hamburg dockers is for a minimum 6d per hour as against 5¼d they have been receiving.
On behalf of the Central Council IFSD & RW . . . etc.,
Tom Mann Chairman

mother and her grandmother and she shewed us with pride all her pretty and useful presents. It was with difficulty we induced her at last to run away and get into the simple grey frock in which she was to be married. She looked very sweet in it, "a little quaker" as she called herself. She wore a black hat and carried a large bunch of beautiful white flowers, the gift of the bridegroom. The wedding was a very quiet one with no bridesmaids and very few invited guests. It was very touching to us but we [she and her sister Agnes] have great hope that it is the beginning of a truly happy life.

Ramsay MacDonald looked both manly and gentlemanly and won golden opinions from all present.

CHAPTER 5

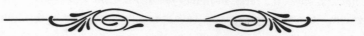

December 1896–February 1900
'A stranger in a
strange land'

From their marriage to the birth of the Labour Party at the Farringdon Street Memorial Hall on 27 February 1900.

Ramsay was brought up in a household without men – there was no father and no grandfather. Margaret was motherless. Neither had experienced normal family life. Margaret had always dreamt of an enveloping partnership while Ramsay conjured up stories of his parents' glorious passion in the cornfields, but they had never seen their parents together, struggling with the practicalities of life.

How would they fare, with their romantic notions, the urchin and the lady? Margaret's father drove off in a carriage to the British Academy most days whereas Ramsay's mother worked in the fields to scrape together enough money to keep the family. How could Ramsay cope with a wife who was used to a butler, and Margaret deal with a man who was used to his women gutting herrings and making porridge? Their shared dream of a new Jerusalem would have to see them through.

After a brief honeymoon and a trip to Lossie, they settled down to work. Mrs Gurling looked after the domestic arrangements while Margaret spent as much time as she could at Ramsay's side. He was working for the ILP and fostering his potential constituencies, while she was busy with the compilation of statistics for the Women's Industrial Council. Their modest but assured income released Ramsay from journalism and allowed them to travel. A trip across the Atlantic in 1897 was the first of many holidays which were more like political progresses. A baby arrived in May 1898, was cherished and sentimentalized over, but was not allowed to interfere with things. At the end of their first three years together the Labour Party was born, and Ramsay became the secretary.

The Labour Representation Committee, as it was called until 1906, was a union of the extreme socialists, the SDP; the moderate, but active and proselytizing ILP; the permeative Fabians; and working-men, represented by their unions. Hitherto there had been virtually no co-operation between any of these groups, and the essentially middle-class socialist organizations were not doing very well. In the 1895 election none of the ILP's candidates were returned. Ramsay was the architect of what Hardie described as the 'great alliance'. The socialists needed the unions, with their huge membership and considerable finances. It was Ramsay's task to bring the four bodies together as a party of Labour, not of doctrine. He drafted the resolution (ostensibly from the Railway Servants) which declared that the unions and socialists were in favour of direct independent working-class representation in Parliament. He was appointed secretary – perhaps only he could have done the job – a moderate, a manipulator, a gentleman by marriage. His powerful eloquence, his commanding presence, his intellectual vigour and his private income made him the obvious choice. Perhaps without Margaret's money the Labour Party would not have been born.

Malcolm MacDonald (the second son) wrote:

A . . . fact about my mother's and father's partnership deeply impressed me in my early years. This was the superlative affection which bound them together. Their profound love for one another made them ideal companions in their private life, whilst their zealous joint political work made them perfect comrades in their public lives. For a while the relationship caused me to suppose that human existence is invariably blessed with supreme life-long joy . . .

People and Places (London) 1969, 16.

But the two families were uneasily yoked.

∾ Margaret to Dr Thompson.

> Lincoln's Inn Fields
> 12 July 1909

. . . Mrs Bottomley (. . . Aunt Fanny's elder sister . . .) is the only one of my relations who *quite* cut me after our marriage . . . when my uncle was alive I don't think my aunt dared not to be friends with me . . .

∾ Margaret to Annie Ramsay.

> 24 November 1896
> Golden Lion Hotel
> Ashburton, Devon

My dear Mother,

It is very nice to feel that now you are really my mother-in-law. I think Ramsay has written you a good long letter, so I suppose he has described something of the wedding. It all went off very happily and everybody was very kind. We were so glad to get your telegram, and hope ours reached you in good time. I will not write much just now as I want to catch the post, and must finish a letter to my father also.

> With very much love,
> Your affectionate daughter,
> Margaret E. MacDonald.

∾ Ramsay to Florence Gladstone.

> Wednesday November 1896
> The Golden Lion, Ashburton

My dear Flo

In great haste & on a very shaky table. We are just starting to drive across Dartmoor to Princetown and Tavistock, but whilst the geegee is being made respectable (how this old table does shake) we are writing sundry notes. We said at breakfast "Poor dear Flo!" and it was with reference to all the trouble you are taking and have taken with us. I am sorry to have given you an unnecessary journey to Maples. But I had other impressions. Under the trying circs, pardon & forgive. My usual luck, I may say parenthetically, has followed me here. We had hardly left the train when I was faced by an old friend of mine who is "professing" agriculture for the Devon County Council. He looked and I walked on. He knew I had no sister & was absolutely certain I had not married. I am expecting a letter from him expatiating on a double of me which he saw at Ashburton.

Now about your good kind thoughts about Lincoln's Inn Fields. Don't bother to do anything except to have the top bedroom straight with a fire laid. We can place a chair or two in the sitting room & will devote the four days when we are not at home though in London to getting things quite straight. If you would just do that & get Mrs Smith to be quite certain as to locking up things, you will be doing the work of an angel. Tavistock tonight & then Tintagel until Saturday morning: Bristol Saturday & Sunday.

With love & every good and grateful wish to you all

> Ever affectionately your
> Ramsay.

∾ Margaret to Annie Ramsay.

> 3 December 1896
> 3 Lincoln's Inn Fields
> London W.C.

My Dear Mother

You see we are in our new house now & I am writing you the first letter on our stamped paper. We found it in fairly comfortable order when we returned as my sisters and some friends of theirs had been working very hard to get things unpacked & put out. But two of the rooms were not ready to be used so we could not put the furniture right and of course it was difficult at first to arrange everything conveniently. I feel quite amused at my first attempts at housekeeping: however we will tell you more when we see you. We hope to arrive on Tuesday next at Lossie at 12.44. We will not stay at Buckie, but I am sending a card to Miss Duncan to tell her we shall pass through at 11.45, & shall look out in case she can be at the station . . . I enclose the trimming for the third nightgown.

I do hope we shall find you better & without neuralgia next week.

We were very glad to have your letter of welcome to our new home. With love from both

> Yr affec ate daughter
> M.E. MacDonald.

After the honeymoon there was the first of many trips to Lossie together. Work started.

∾ Margaret's diary, Aberdeen.

> 7 December 1896

Writing out R's lecture . . . on 'Fallacies of Socialism'.

❧ Ramsay to Margaret.

Tuesday, 5 January 1897
Livingstone Hotel, Norwich

My dear Lassie,

. . . I am sorry that as the N.A.C. sat from 11 a.m. until 6.10 p.m. today I cannot get back tonight so there will be another accumulation of love debts upon my shoulders. I have been thinking in all kinds of sweet musics of my little lassie looking out upon the hills and perhaps working at my lecture & I have been longing to see her again. I have also promised myself not to make remarks about smuts on her nose – that indeed I would be a reformed man when my exile was ended. Now I have to speak tonight & as I met some two or three nice eligible second wives at last night's dance, I must make a good impression . . .

❧ Ramsay to Margaret.

24 January 1897
East Park Terrace
Southampton

My dearest Wiffie,

A nice good morning to you. How is my dear lassie in her solitary state? I wish she were here. Did her little heart burst out again? She is a dear little thing. Her Unsatisfactory was very loath to go & leave his Satisfactory behind but he hopes she has felt all the blessings he left for her & the kisses he sent to her by the new Electric method. He is trying to think what she is now doing and wondering if she sees him. Two more days yet & home! Bless my dear lassie!

. . . Now there's a kiss for one side of your lips and here's a kiss for the other to prevent jealousy; there's a blessing for your heart, and here's love to fill the cisterns emptied by your tears. And there's a little formal-looking but very, very real

Adieu from your ever-loving sweetheart

R

X X X
X X
X
& an odd one to Floretta [Flo]

❧ Ramsay to Margaret.

> Monday, 25 January 1897
> 24 East Park Terrace,
> Southampton

My dearest Wiffie

. . . I was skating yesterday & wished so much that my lassie had been with me. She & the frosty air would have made the day, which was very pleasant, quite divine . . .

> your loving
> Poultice
> X X X

At the general meeting of the [Socialist] Club, held on February 15th, the following members were elected as the Committee for the next six months: Miss Armstrong, R. Wherry Anderson, Mrs. Paul Campbell, Rev. Percy Dearmer, J.F. Green, Mrs. J.R. MacDonald, and J.R. MacDonald; Herbert Burrows was re-elected Treasurer, and John Penny was elected Secretary in place of Leslie A. Toke, resigned.

In April Ramsay was re-elected to the NAC, the ILP's executive.

Margaret's first 'Mrs MacDonald' speech was given at a bazaar in Southampton. She wrote it on the train on the back of a letter to Ramsay — after reading the *Echo* her thoughts turned to 'Billy Doos'.

❧ Margaret to Ramsay.

> 28 April 1897
> Southampton

Well I have delivered my maiden political speech . . . I remembered all the points all right, but I started on one leg and was very bashful.

❧ Ramsay to Margaret.

> 28 April 1897
> 3 Lincoln's Inn Fields

My dear Lassie,

Your bachelor husband is miserable. He sat in solitary state at dinner wondering many things about bazaars, muddy skirts & orators; & he only got a tiny telegram with a tiny cross upon it — no information you see. It is very pleasant however to be at Duncan Buildings again because Saturday is coming & a little bit of personal happiness adds an exquisite touch to life. Now tell me about yourself. Your skirt, your shoes, your jokes & your arguments. How did the ladies in your carriage behave? How did your audience? How did your hat? How did my curate? I am waiting to hear & can now only just give you a goodnight . . .

Goodnight my dearie & bless you. And good morning & a good day. Ever thy poultice.

R.

∾ Ramsay to Margaret.

29 April 1897
3 Lincoln's Inn Fields
London W.C.

My dearest Lassie,

What a very rich husband you make me. Two very special thoughts from you today & a little thought to be taken like a powder with my oatmeal tomorrow morning. Why have I a lassie whom I like so much, & why are we lucky enough to be separated for a day or two? It is beastly lonely here & even the smiles of Flo will not keep me up tomorrow night. I must speak to Mrs Moon[1] for encouraging your vanity by arranging you in her tea-gown which is very pretty. But I am glad to get good news of the hat & promising ones of the skirt . . .

Ramsay thought that

[Margaret] was perhaps a little too indifferent to dress. It was supposed that she made it a principle not to dress better than the wife of a workman. The thought never entered her head. She would have regarded that to be pandering, and if she had ever thought of a standard at all it would have been one of her own. She had a blind eye for externals of all kinds. Never did medieval saint of primitive habits pay less attention to the flesh and its decoration than she did. It is told of her that when about to take a leading part in some important deputation, friends insisted upon her buying a new blouse. When she appeared and rose to address the powers who were to be persuaded to do righteously, it was noticed, to the horror of those friends, that the new garment had been put on with its back to the front.

Margaret Ethel MacDonald, pp. 38, 9.

---

1. She stayed with the Moons in Southampton.

∞ Margaret to Aunt Elizabeth.

23 May 1897

I should like to say something to you of the blessedness I feel in [my marriage]; but it is difficult to express it in words: only it is a growing happiness as all true love ought to be.

∞ Ramsay to Margaret.

29 May 1897
The Progressive Review

My dearest Wiffie

I am very wretched for this morning. I forgot myself – why? I do not know, & would give anything to undo it. This is a special day with us too. But I have been sending telegrams all morning & think I have been receiving them. Ever, my dearie, your own unsatisfactory man.

X X X X

P.T.O.
Love to our aunts.

∞ To Ramsay.

4 August 1897
Southampton I.L.P.

. . . I think you would do wisely if you resigned your I.L.P. Candidature here and sought another constituency, although this is merely my private opinion & not the result of any discussions with the members. I think you altogether fail to grasp or understand the temper and material of the I.L.P. today, & I am sure you would never have made up your mind to spend your last night in England with the local chief of the Liberal Party, did you foresee as clearly as I foresaw, how it will destroy the confidence of many of our I.L.P. members in you . . .

Faithfully yours
Joe Clayton[1]

---

1. Secretary of Southampton ILP.

෨ Margaret to Annie Ramsay.

7 August 1897
South Stoneham House
(Home of the Montagus)

My Dear Mother

This will be our last letter before we get to America – as we leave the docks here today. You will get a telegram from Toronto about the 19th or 20th of the month. As we are allowed only ten words we have a code, and we shall if all is well, just say Well, & then Good for good passage, if we want to add anything special.

It was <u>very</u> good of you to work so hard at those nightgowns, and they are very nice; but I wish you had left me to sew them as I asked: it was too hurried for you. Ramsay sends £3, for the 7/6 and 8/- we owe you and the rest to take you to Edinburgh if you are able to arrange to go there . . .

Yours with much love from us both

Margaret

෨ Margaret and Ramsay to Annie Ramsay.

Friday 13 August 1897
S.S. "Paris"
near New York

My Dear Mother

. . . We have not had a very rough crossing but both of us have been rather sea-sick & Ramsay has felt seedy all the time . . .

We have not done anything very exciting on the way across except seen a few whales and porpoises . . . We do not know anyone on board except one of the stewards who is a member of the Independent Labour Party at Southampton, & the Countess of Aberdeen & her children who are in the first class & whom we have just been over to see. We shall land early tomorrow morning, spend Sunday somewhere along the Hudson river, & then get on, probably by Buffalo & the Niagara river to Toronto. Continue to address us to British Association, Toronto till you hear differently. [In Ramsay's hand.] There is just an inch or so for me to add a word, but I think Margaret has given you all the news there is. We hope to have a very good time over here. We are choosing a place for Saturday & Sunday amongst very fine scenery & shall then rest after our sea trip going further on Monday & Tuesday. We hope to hear from you at Toronto. With kindest love from us both

Your affectionate son
J.R. MacDonald.

∾ Ramsay's diary.

14 August 1897

Saturday – Awoke 3.30 in harbour. Thick haze. Curious continental effect of the deep red & ochre of houses on the hard green of the hills which lay along the narrows on Staten & Long Islands. At 5 the gun at Fort Wordsworth boomed and the "Stars and Stripes" was run up. It was interesting to note the Yankee enthusiasm on board at their flag. Looming ahead was "Liberty".

16 August 1897

Monday – Pack and prepare to say farewell to our kindly host of the Mansion House, but first of all in the morning we went to see the representative of the Federation of Labour in the district. Oddly English in his manner but apparent a little more independent. Had just started a tobacco factory on his own account, was cigar-maker by trade.

17 August 1897

Tuesday – 9 a.m. Appointment to meet Dr Jones at Capitol & he showed us round the museums, libraries, governor's chambers, Senate and Assembly Houses, and introduced us to various of his colleagues. The public walk in anywhere. They sat in the Senator's and Representative's chairs with their hats on reading their newspapers, in the corridors, the lounges and smoked. Spitoons lay in plenty on the fine crimson velvet carpets with the laurel wreath patterns. The Capitol is an example of American public bodies' waste "kept going as not finished to give work".

18 August 1897

Wednesday. Left Buffalo & came via Niagara Falls (the Falls from a distance are disappointing) and Lewis Town to Toronto. Professor Armstrong, whom we met on board the boat, had been West, was disgusted at the lack of culture shown by the people, and had learned nothing but superiority!! Very wet night. President's address delivered in an almost inaudible voice to about 1200 people, in a hall seated for 4000.

21 August 1897

Saturday. Niagara. American side blemished with factories, flags, towers, lager beer, and merry-go-rounds. [Professor] <u>Goodwin.</u> Economics in Canada human; education much valued, though "Practical". Professor

MacAlister's conversation with Sir John Alexander MacDonald[1] the benefactor of McGill. He endowed "practical" education.

〰 Margaret to Annie Ramsay.

23 August 1897
British Association
Toronto Meeting 1897

My Dear Mother

Ramsay & I are having a very good time here, and enjoying the meetings of the Association, & all the kindness of the Canadian people very much. We got here last Wednesday & it seemed quite homelike to get into British Territory again after a few days in the States, although of course everywhere we are amongst English speaking people & they are very like our home people.

We are in very comfortable lodgings here, but are out all day & every evening also, attending meetings, lectures, garden parties, etc., Ramsay is to read a paper tomorrow before the Economic Section on the Workmen's Compensation Bill. We have a great many English friends here, & have made many acquaintances among the Canadians, who are very kind and hospitable, & anxious to show us everything & make our stay pleasant . . . We spent the day on Saturday at Niagara Falls, which are most marvellous. It was a lovely sunny day & the Sun made rainbows in the spray. The water looks so green where it rushes over the rock, and then it dashes up in spray, so that you are almost blinded by it. We went in a little steamer right below the Falls, in all the spray & rushing water, as near as they dare to go, and that gives one a very good idea of their tremendous height. We also did a still more exciting thing – we went, dressed up in funny mackintosh costumes, right down on the rocks, where you can get behind one of the smaller falls, as it pours over & leaves a cave behind it & we had the roar of water all round us & the spray dashing down upon us. It is very grand to see such masses of water falling & the rapids above & below are very beautiful. We go on from here on Thursday to Ottawa & Montreal & back along the St Lawrence, & then shall take a little time quietly among the woods & lakes: but as our address is not quite fixed please send to Hull House, Chicago U.S.A. they will forward letters. We hope to hear from you soon, good accounts of yourself. Love to all the friends and much to yourself from your affectionate daughter & Ramsay

MEM

---

1. The first Prime Minister of the Dominion of Canada.

∽ Ramsay's diary.   25 August 1897

Wednesday. Moore told me of the Young Canadian movement centering in
the Patriotic Clubs, chief of which is that of Hamilton with 1000 members.
Leading man is Evans of the *Mail* with whom I was very much impressed &
had a rattling good discussion of political and social democracy. They hate
the U.S. and are only loyal to Britain if B. will benefit Canada. It is said to
be a new Conservative movement but I think that a somewhat narrow
criticism. Evans is Conservative but is to fight Hamilton next election as
Patriotic . . . The circle impressed me as having a belief, energy, youth
and power.

∽ Ramsay to his mother.
                                                    1 September 1897
                                                    c/o Professor Goodwin
                                                    Queen's University
                                                    Kingston Ontario
My Dear Mother
    We have both been disappointed not to have heard anything from you
since we left England. If you have written, your letters have missed us
somehow. We have been sending you a newspaper or two & one or two other
things which, we hope, have reached you all right.
    We are having very good times of it here. This country is much more like
home than the United States are. The people are very kind and hospitable,
we are being shown everything there is to see. Since we have left Toronto
we have travelled a long way, very long, and a great part of our journey
having been through wild forests where nobody has settled yet. We have
also been in such towns as Ottawa & Montreal; now we are here in a very
nice place standing on the north side of Lake Ontario. The lakes here are as
big as our seas & people get seasick on them. Indeed everything here is on
a very large scale, and we spend a good deal of our time in trains and
steamboats. We leave this the day after tomorrow and are going up further
north and then west. We shall take two or three days to do the journey but
when we get to its end at the place called Rat Portage, we shall settle down
for a few weeks & then cross the boundary south again into the United
States. Rat Portage is the centre of some most beautiful scenery of wood and
lake & the country round about is very wild. We cannot tell you all we have
been seeing because we have been seeing so much. But in Montreal we saw
a great political demonstration in honour of Sir Wilfred Laurier[1] who has
just returned from the Jubilee celebrations to Canada.

---

1. Prime Minister of Canada, 1896–1911.

We are just starting to look over the University here & so I must close. Margaret joins me in sending her kindest love with mine. We are still in hopes that we may hear from you soon, & I enclose an envelope for your next letter. Kindest regards to all enquiring friends.

Yr affectionate son
J.R. MacDonald.

❧ Margaret to Annie Ramsay.

9 September 1897
Rat Portage
Lake of the Woods

My Dear Mother

We have not yet received a letter from you, but hope to find one today at the Post Office or we shall be quite uneasy about you . . . I wish you could see some of the enormous Lakes we have been passing – they are so big that we cannot see across them, & they seem to us more like the sea than fresh water lakes. Most of them are dotted with pretty little wooded islands & are wooded all round their shores, & in coming here we passed through hundreds of miles of country which was nothing but forests, lakes & rivers, with hardly a house to be seen anywhere except an occasional log hut for men who were engaged in cutting timber, or sometimes a Red Indian Encampment. The Indians live in tents, or in huts made of birch bark, and it is funny to see them squatting outside these & cooking their dinner. The women sometimes carry their babies or papooses, as they call them, on their backs in baskets, or wrapped round in a shawl & tied on, and the little things look quite happy. They almost all wear *English* clothes however, so do not look quite so fierce & picturesque as one sees them in pictures.

I enclose the programme of the British Association showing Ramsay's paper down. I hope you got all the papers & illustrated books which we have sent you, to give you some account of our doings. I also enclose a piece of the birch bark which the Indians here strip off the trees & make up into baskets & all sorts of things. One day we had a picnic breakfast in the woods & they made our sugar basins & salt cellars out of this, twisted up & skewered with bits of twig . . .

With best love from both of us

Your affectionate daughter
Margaret M.

 Annie Ramsay to Margaret.

27 September 1897
Thee Cottage
Lossiemouth

My Dear Margaret

just a fue lines to sea if som of them will find you i saw Mr Mcdonald Drany [Ramsay's schoolmaster] asking for you on Saterday they are all well Davie West got his plase all burned on Saterday night i have not hard nothing more about it but that he had lost all his things

My Dear Gural are you not thinking long to cum hom tell Ramsay that i here Charly Allan is on the way hom i have not much nues to give you i do not now if Miss Duncan is hom or not only i hard hir sister is now better i have a verry sore eye with Iflemation and could not stand the cold but i hope it will soon be beter. The nights are getting dark now and i feel beaing alone just a frist Now i must close and i hope you get som of my letters and papis as i have sent you so many the plase are getting winter like and all the peaple are going hom give much love to Ramsay and the same fir yus self and i do trust you will get good wether when you are coming hom

from you Mither
A Ramsay

 Margaret to Annie Ramsay.

3 October 1897
Chicago

My Dear Mother

We were very glad to have another letter from you this morning, but sorry to hear from it the bad news about Miss Duncan of Buckie. We shall be anxious to get your next letter and hear further. Ramsay has been meaning to write to you but we have been very busy meeting new friends and seeing new places & he has had to speak several times (we sent you a Hull House Bulletin from which you would see something of what we are doing) & to prepare his lectures, so has not managed to write yet . . .

Your affectionate daughter
Margaret E MacDonald

∽ Ramsay to his mother.

24 October 1897
New Haven, Connecticut

My Dear Mother,

You will be surprised to hear that we have been taking tea this afternoon with one of your Lossiemouth neighbours, Mr Ritchie, who is over here seeing his son . . . We had Scotch scones . . . which seemed very nice and homelike.

We are still having a very delightful time, though we are looking forward to getting home & settling down again. We cross back in the same vessel we came by, the *Paris*, to Southampton & have secured a nice cabin.

One evening at Boston we spent with a son of William Lloyd Garrison who was one of the chief movers in the anti-slave movement, a splendidly brave and good man & we saw all sorts of relics of the agitation and portraits of those who had taken part in it. I think I will keep this to post at Philadelphia after we have seen our Aunt there.

I had an exceedingly good time of it, meeting old friends & making many new ones.

On its money side my trip has also been a very great success – much greater than I expected, as in two cases I got paid double fees for my lectures. I am also bearing away with me invitations to return from various quarters & as each invitation is accompanied by considerable financial temptations, it is very likely that my visits to America are only beginning. I am already feeling quite at home in a good many of the towns & we take great pleasure in thinking of our kind friends over there . . .

∽ Margaret to Annie Ramsay.

3 November 1897
New York

My Dear Mother

there is so much to tell you that I shall have to crowd it into small spaces & write you longer on board ship if I am not too seasick.

We had a very nice time with Aunt Jane & her family at Philadelphia, and saw a good deal of them though we were only there from Wednesday to Monday. They have quite a comfortable little house & Aunt's shop is going on nicely. We are bringing you from her one of the American Wrappers and we also got you an apron which she made herself . . . Allan looks rather pale and delicate but they say he is growing stronger; we offered to bring him back with us to stay with you as you suggested but they did not like to part with him. Aunt has kept her Scotch accent & it sounded like a little bit of Lossiemouth to hear her talk. She wanted to know all about the old country & Ramsay and She had great gossips about folk I do not know.

We have just been through a great election here for Mayor of New York, & the party against whom all our friends are working because it stands for corruption & bad government has got in by a huge majority, so all the thoughtful people & honest people are very distressed. They have not paid enough attention to politics here & let them get in the hands of rich people who make them just a game of plunder, and it will take hard work to get a healthier tone into them . . . We send you a paper showing what an impressive funeral was given to Henry George[1] who died during the fight suddenly. He wrote "Progress & Poverty" which was one of the earliest books which turned Ramsay's attention to Socialism, & we had letters of introduction to him and were hoping to meet him here . . .

We shall be in London November 18th I hope

> Your affectionate daughter
> M.E. MacDonald.

〜 Margaret to Florence.

> 3 November 1897
> 265 Henry Street
> N.Y.

My dear Flo

Ramsay thanks you for your letter to him. I made a stupid mistake about Mrs Sedgewick's introduction & thought all you gave us were in New York, and as Ramsay had the slip in his pocket book and once or twice when I remembered and asked for it to put amongst our other introductions it was not handy and we did not turn it out till too late. We did go to Boston before instead of after Philadelphia because some lectures at the latter place were fixed for a later date. I wrote to Wanamaker[1] at Philadelphia but he had just sailed for Europe, and there were two Horace Smiths in the directory & I did not know enough about ours to distinguish him! I have written to apologise to Mrs Sedgewick. I met someone who knows her.

We are in the midst of mourning and woe now & shall be amongst friends in the blues for the rest of our visit for Tammany and corruption came out with a huge majority at the New York election yesterday and all our various friends were working against it and counting on victory. We are in a Nurses'

---

1. Lewis Rodman Wanamaker (1863–1928)

Settlement here (we shall know much more about settlements here than in London!) by special invitation to be in the midst of the campaign and we saw lots of the election excitements yesterday and went out at night to see results coming in. It is evident that the thoughtful folks here will have to work harder at public affairs before they gain the influence which they have let slip: but it is sickening to hear how everybody talks about corruption & "boss" rule as the great thing to fight for or against & have hardly time to have any constructive programme for improving the city positively.

We are going to dine with my cousins the Bottomleys tonight: the general hospitality of everybody continues and we seem to live in a state of having to refuse kind invitations because we have too many. This time next week we shall be on the boat & it will be delightful to turn homewards. I expect we shall be in London on November 18th, as we shall probably spend one night at Southampton, but we will send you a p-card when we land. Tell Roger that Ramsay & I often talk about him & are looking forward to making his acquaintance.

The "New Age" office boy must have lost your address! It is very silly, as R has written a lot about our doings for it and sent Papa H. George's funeral as it was so impressive: unfortunately we were in Philadelphia.

> Yours with love
> M E MacDonald

❧ Margaret to Florence.

> 16 October 1897
> Boston
> U.S.A.

* Address will be Nov 1-10
   c/o Miss Burke, Jersey City

My Dear Flo

I am doing a little writing before joining Ramsay who is pow-wowing with the Mayor & going to lunch with the Principal of Harvard & on to spend Sunday at Concord. First of all we have given an introduction to you to one of the Hull House residents, Miss Starr, who is coming over to London to study book-binding under Coburn Sanderson (Auntie Jane's brother-in-law) if he will take her. He is rather unwilling to take many pupils and she may have to go to Paris to get what she wants, but if not perhaps you could help

---

1. Henry George (1839–1897), journalist, economist, reformer.

her about lodgings or something, as we shall not be back till 3 weeks or so after she expects to arrive. A letter to the City Bank, Threadneedle Street to Miss Ellen Starr, would find her; she will arrive about the end of October. She is Yankee and artistic but very pleasant. She and Miss Addams were the first to start the Hull House Settlement 8 years ago and now they have 22 residents and all sorts of outside work. They were kindness itself to us. Though Miss Addams is the centre of all the work there, she seemed as if she had nothing to do but entertain us and arrange for our seeing everything we wanted to see and inviting everybody to meet us who would interest us; so it was a splendid centre. I had a bilious attack there – like I used to have when I travelled in the heat & went to bed for a day or two (it was sudden heat down at St Louis that upset me) and they got in a Doctor who could not discover that it was anything worse than a bilious attack & the trained district nurse, who tried hard to find out that I wanted special attention. [She was expecting her first child.] I am alright again now, and as you see we have got to the East again. Here we are being entertained at another settlement & Ramsay is the only he crittur with a number of charming young University ladies! The autumn colouring is just gorgeous now & we had a most perfect day & night at the seaside with a friend of Fisher's (T.F.U.); the dearest and sweetest old lady, Mrs. Fields,[2] who has been an intimate friend of Lowell & Holmes and all the best Boston set & of Dickens, Tennyson etc. She had the most lovely old things in her house; it was most refreshing to get some place where things seemed old.

Did we tell you that we got for your birthday an Alaskan sable from the historic Hudson Bay Co. centre at Winnepeg to keep your lovely throat warm this winter?

You will be sorry to lose Jane, but she will like Toronto, I should think. We thought it a charming city. Will she feel lonely there? We could ask Mrs Hutchings with whom we stayed there to be friendly to her if she would like it. At New York we are going to another settlement, whose head we met at Hull House and our

Love to all
Your affectionate sister
Margaret M

---

1. She was two months pregnant.
2. Annie Adams Fields (1834–1915): hostess, author, wife of James T. Fields, editor of *Atlantic Monthly* 1861–70.

The American trip was the first of their many foreign excursions. Ramsay wrote that

On these journeyings we found many friends and received much hospitality and kindness, but these friends will not misunderstand or be aggrieved when I say that we enjoyed one another most of all.

Margaret Ethel MacDonald, 12.

They had been married a year.

✍ J.H. Gladstone to Margaret.

23 November 1897

Just a line to congratulate you on the anniversary of your wedding day. I cannot tell you how happy I am to see your happiness, and only pray that it may increase – and your usefulness too, as years go on . . .

✍ Margaret . . .

14 December 1897
3 Lincoln's Inn Fields
W.C.

Dear Mr Pease

Please put down the following resolution which I shall move at the next meeting of members.

Yours very truly
M.E. MacDonald

"That whilst married men sit on the [Fabian] Executive young unmarried girls be inelligible."

P.S. The resolution is aimed I may say at that giddy young piece from Richmond who wunk at my husband last Friday.

Ramsay to Margaret.

19 December 1897
Leicester
Sabbath

My Dear Lassie,

You are very annoying. I had several telegrams whilst I was speaking this morning which made the big drum chuckle to its lady the trombone. Do be proper. One of Enid [Stacey]'s hosts says he will never have her again because she is so vulgar. Little did he know of my lady. I am well but lopsided feeling like a man whose leg is off – whole but queer. The last telegram was alarming "Your wife suffers from an illness with an ache but she has eaten a magnificent dinner" Ethel! I do hope that something more moderate is true. Meanwhile here I am well looked after as at sea.

Yours faithfully
Sir
X X X X X X X X X X X-
X X X
Design *for* trimmings

[Early 1898

Ramsay stood as ILP candidate for South Hackney in the LCC elections; he was defeated by Mr Browne.

Newspaper report

SOUTH HACKNEY COUNTY COUNCIL FIGHT.
THE RADICAL SPLIT

'London,' the official Progressive paper, says: In the adoption of Progressive candidates "friction has occurred in two divisions (South Hackney and Central Finsbury), and in both cases it seems to us, the Liberals are in the wrong . . . South Hackney is now represented by Mr Alfred Smith and Mr Humphrey . . . Two progressives have been selected for the second seat. The Liberals have chosen a Mr Browne, who is, we believe, an Irish politician, and is unknown in connection with municipal work. The other Progressive organization in the division, the Independent Labour Party, the local trade unions, &c., have chosen Mr J.R. Macdonald, who is well known as a broadminded Progressive of the advanced school . . . We are informed that the Liberal Association declined to hear

Mr Macdonald, who was ready to address any representative assembly of the Progressive forces in the division in competition with any other candidate. He will be supported, not only by the advanced labour organisations and the Fabians, but by trade unionists, Christian socialists, and other enthusiastic workers on the Progressive side."

We learn that Messrs John Burns, G.N. Barnes and Fletcher, and the Hon. G.W.E. Russell, (a member of the late Radical Government), will support Mr Macdonald, and he will also receive the assistance of the 'Daily Chronicle' and 'London'.

Mr MacDonald and his friends have been suffering from a new mode of blackballing lately. They have applied for the use of several chapel school-rooms in which to hold meetings. In every case, except the Hampden Chapel, they have been refused because they are the Independent Labour Party.

∾ Ramsay to Margaret.

> 7 January 1898
> The "Oxford" Temperance Hotel
> 16 St James Street
> Sheffield

Oh lassie, Lunnans far awa'
    An' you are left in Lunnan town.
Nae sang lilts fill our bosoms twa
    An baith our hearts are casten down.

Bit madcap April greets in showers
    An' lauchs tae hide the smiles o' May;
So, Lassie, thae heart aches o' ours
    Bit hide in fun the bonny day

It's better gangin' South than North
    It's better gangin' up than down
Though my auld name's a yon the forth
    My heart's awa' in Lunnan town.

Enclosed

Your aunts want you to dine with them tomorrow evening & if I return I shall go there & fetch you in a jewel case.

Lost 2 but taken the 3 p.m.

❧ Annie Ramsay to Margaret.

> Saterday [16 January 1898]
> Thee Cottage
> Lossiemouth

My Dear Margaret

Many thanks for your kind letter i saw wat was cumming and told Aunt the day she was frim Buckie that i though you were 4 Mounths so i did not like to say anything to you but told you to tell me wat you wanted and to keep free of damp feet be sure and move about but not weary your self i had no trible more than you but plenty greef and you have happiness my dear gural i went up to my draws on Fridy to sea how many of my own baby gownes i had and som of Ramsays so you sea i wos not to firget you i will do all them things you ned only they will be Scoch and if you cannot cum to me i will go to you and i do trust god will give me helth to nurse you and god will spare you both and i took it verry kind of you to ask me to nurse you but i will let you now more later on only my dear gural take car of your self did you get the persol i sent on Friday give my love to Ramsay and if god spars me i shall do my best for you and with kindest love frim yur aff Mither

> A Ramsay

❧ Ramsay to Margaret.

> 24 January 1898
> 24 East Park Terrace
> Southampton

My dear Wiffie

I have just got yours & am astounded to hear that this is the Boro' Poly night. I have posted the tract off to the Secretary.

And how are you *four*?[1] [Margaret and the 'triplets' she was expecting; *see* next letter.] It was naughty of it to raise the little row in your throat & I shall wallop it when I get back. I just managed to get off two articles last night.

The lecture went all right. But everybody here was disappointed that somebody was not with me. I have got a few notes re America & never mind. Glad you went to Lily [Montagu]'s affair as I sent a few telegrams there on chance. You will have noticed that one was for Lily. I suppose you passed it on. I have been telegraphing all the morning to you & the three, but have been having nothing very decipherable in return.

---

1. Margaret and the 'triplets' she was expecting, *see* his letter of 25 January 1898.

I left on my desk the unfinished mss of the leaflet I am to publish on the Progressives and Labour. What I want you to do is to get me a few more samples of what I refer to in it. Look at it & you will see what I mean. The cases in point I remember are:- Leasing trams instead of municipalising; Stedmans motion re hours of tram employees a few months ago; ditto re wages; the municipal steamboat service; & last July there were several divisions on the works Department bearing out my point.

Ah! that naughty poem. Who would have thought of it poking its nose in that forward way?

Love from us all, especially from me to my mother in law & my cousin.

Your Mannie.

〰 Ramsay to Margaret.

25 January 1898
24 East Park Terrace
Southampton

My dear Missie Ethel,

I am glad you have a new friend. Thanks for telling me about it. I am *so* tired of you. You are such a worry. You would not stay away these two days leaving me in comfort, peace & quietness. You came and broke a vase. I didn't know what people were saying to me. You *are* a worry. Liberty is now a sham. I have given up its pursuit as an impossibility. I am returning to bondage. My youth is passed. There is the shadow of triplets on my soul & the sound of bottles in my ears. Things are not as they were. I am a stranger in a strange land.[1] I know not the bus routes nor the street names. The very policemen are unfriendly. I wander. Adieu! Whether you be Marg. or Ethel or Maria I have no opinion, but just a shade of a suspicion. But you have a friend to whom I think I may send respects

Thine or him or hers
Whether or which or why

My marriage lines are gone
& my name is forgotten

---

1. Four years before he had written to Enid Stacey: . . . I congratulate you in being freed from the gentle attentions of a baby. I was nursing one on Sunday. They are horrid cusses. I just managed to call it a cherub to its mother and whispered 'a devil' into its own ear. Its father, silly fool, was very proud of the booing torture machine.

Stacey Letters, 3 November 1894

∽ Ramsay to Margaret.

24 March 1898
The Progressive Review

    I'm wae & sad & lone
        Ochone – aree – ochone, ochone
    For far, far off's my own
        ochone
    The north wind blows sae cauld & raw
    The driving showers in torrents fa'
    But my heart's wintrier than them a'
        For wantin' o' my lassie
    Ochone – aree – ochone, ochone

THE TIMES
LONDON, SATURDAY, MAY 21 1898
BIRTHS.
MACDONALD. – On the 18th inst., at 3 Lincoln's Inn-fields, the wife of
J.R. MacDonald, of a son. [Alister]

∽ Ramsay to Margaret.

Saturday 12 September 1898
Labour Institute
Norwich

My dear Love,

The people here are awfully nice. There is a delightful sing song going on in the next room, there is a well-stocked bar downstairs, there are many young ladies about who have a proper estimate of the position of a member of the N.A.C. Why is it then, I want to know, that I should rather not be here at all but somewhere else? It is a funny feeling & one that I cannot quite understand. My heart says that I am not at home, & yet how can that be? My dear love, I think you are to blame & I must talk seriously about it to you when I get to London on Monday by the train which leaves this at 7.30.

The dark lady opposite me was very nice & was probably a daughter of the sunny, sunny South. She kept the window closed the whole time & though I cried & cried like the little man it was no use. She was as heartless as the little man's mother, & I roasted, stewed, & boiled by turns.

How is the little man? Is he going to have a good night, I wonder; and is he going to let his mammie have a good night? Also, I wonder if his mammie has sent that nice telegram I have just had. I thought at first it was the result of the Darlington Election when the rat-tat came to the door of my heart, but behold it was something else. I have sent reply after reply to his mammie on the off-chance that the telegram did come from her.

I am going to think of somebody tomorrow & who do you think it is to be? I don't believe you can guess. The most unlikely person imaginable! Kiss the little man for me and tickle him on the ribs & say I told you.

And now my dear love I am sending 'good night' telewags & tomorrow I shall send 'good morning' & a good many other ones. When Monday comes telewags will not be necessary.

Ever your Laddie

X   X   X

❧ Ramsay to Margaret.

1 October 1898
Cobden Hotel
Glasgow

My Dear Lassie

The Laddie's little joke of a letter came this morning & has set his daddie agoing too. Glasgow is a lonely place. Littlewood[1] & Snowden[2] are both here with me, but still – Scotland is a lonely place. The L.N.W. Ry is a bad line. Billie is to preside over a Duke of Devonshire meeting here the week after next. What a long way off Tuesday is.

That is all the news.

Instruct Timothy [Alister] in his capitals.

I am sending by parcel post a pound of little crosses x for him & two pounds of bigger ones for you.

Ever thy Laddie

---

1. France Littlewood, ILP activist and Labour councillor.
2. Philip Snowden, ILP activist.

∾ Ramsay to Margaret.

Monday 24 October 1898
3 Lincoln's Inn Fields
London W.C.

My Ladie Faire, [at Norwich, attending a midwives' meeting]

The day of desolation number one has all but flown; one lunch & one tea are behind me & one dinner is timed to pass in an hour. Italiana & I have been comparing notes with that wholehearted friendship which springs up between two bereaved souls mourning the loss of the same treasure. But I have no little cause to be thankful. Providence has permitted me to resort to that universal cure for all vacancies in the heart-&-another place – work & I have finished Aristotle's *Constitution of Athens* & Sir William Wyndham.[1]

There has been one little annoyance. Natural it was that I should often find myself in imagination hanging on a door of a carriage at Liverpool Street filled with a desperate sense that time flew & that no man, nor woman could make him dally. But I also saw in those moments, a long and terrible & irresistable stream of austere people in petticoats.[2] They had come from the North, from the South & from the West & had left their babes at home that their looks might be hard & their lips thin. I became in spirit as one who had many sins reddening my soul & who knew that his day would come. For I beheld the beginning of the second matriarchy. I saw the flag of man rent by graceful fingers sheathed in lavender kids. Beneath the poetic sway which comes of wearing high-heeled shoes & the gracious smile which is born of many generations of affectionate oppression, I saw the furious flames whose tongues are to purify the world. I feel like the one who folds his arms, bows his head & waits. The tyrant in me palpitates to but one hope, as in the camp of all divine missions there was a traitor – a little one [?Alister] – but one nevertheless. He had an intelligent eye, a firm muscle, & a great voice. When he lowered it was like the clouding of noonday, when he laughed it was like the gurgling of many waters. I thought I saw in his eye that somewhere in his luggage he had the flag of man, & that he would keep it flying.

There are no telegrams, no sensational news in the evening papers & so I presume the stream flowed on to Norwich without impediment & that it is now surging, eddying, swishing, whirling, gurgling in Sheepshank's drawing room.

---

1. Article for the DNB.
2. Midwives and other ladies off to Norwich.

But here I am pulled up. A tellewag boy from Alister's old home has arrived with a bundle he could not deliver before as I was out, & so I must close this now & turn & read them.

Love to Flo & Little It [Alister] & much love of the Nth power of quality to Maa-Mee

Ever thine

Big It

    Ramsay to Margaret.

25 October 1898
3 Lincoln's Inn Fields
London W.C.

Meesus,

The morning and the evening are the second day. It has been dull & grey & has been greeted gladly by no one – except myself, who greet days just now for reasons unknown at the Metereological Office.

I suppose you have all been in great style today. Did you talk or did you content yourself by having thoughts. I read of the proceedings of yesterday and my soul was satisfied. I want to know how everybody is dressed but I suppose you will [think] my curiosity feminine & do nothing to satisfy it. So my thoughts remain hazy & unskirted, unbloused, & unbonneted.

Even were I to fill my record with my imagination I should be but an unromantic mole & an unprofitable butterfly to the mothers, wives, aunts & old maiden friends of the coming race of the gods. I had breakfast in a Sahara. Like de Rougemont I picked up a newspaper in my solitude & behold! I knew I was in a strange world. I had lunch & of the company was one who had to hurry off to see his beloved – round a corner comparatively speaking. I sighed me much. I had tea, and the silence of the desert again reigned. Alach! a me! Why was I born? I have read all the Plato & Platonism I want & have gone far into the Greek Constitutions book. I have put the finishing touches upon the Wyndham article & have been arranging my papers to begin on Sir Charles Wolseley. But I cannot go on exhibiting my farthing dips to the effulgence of Norwich illumination. I turn to my correspondence & sink myself in it . . .

Between the land of darkness through which I have been going & the point to which I have now come is a pleasant country whither all hungry men are led by the many sweet sounds which announce the preparation of dinner. I had my lassie's letter this morning & was glad she had been so lucky as to come across a lady in a state of decay, & I hope that further experience has confirmed first impressions. I knew that Little It would be

worthy of the confidence reposed in him & that Flo would go to the Mothers'
meeting. The letters which have come here all related to the Monday "at
home". The date seems to be rather unfortunate. It is the day before the
municipal elections & the Canning town and Tonbridge Wells people are
all "off".

I hope you are all enjoying yourselves. Kiss Little It & bless him for me
& the same over & over again to yourself. Love to Flo & affections to all my
friends. I hope Mrs Hicks is amongst them by this time.

> Ever thine
> Your long lost

❧ Ramsay to Margaret.

> 26 October 1898
> 3 Lincoln's Inn Fields
> London W.C.

Mine Own (at Norwich)

I am contemplating the passing of the days in my own den still . . . Mrs
Gurling [the housekeeper] ministers unto me with affectionate solicitude –
your assurances that Timothy receives the world with a universal smile as
before calms me immeasurably. That Flo should behave I took for granted
from the beginning – as I did that you would go to the midwife's meeting.

After reading the morning papers the day has been uneventful. A letter
from Ada was a gleam of sunshine; an epistle from Norwich a flood of divine
splendour. I hunted after your derilict property and found it in the I.L.P.
office. I put in my book mark two hundred pages in advance of where it
rested yesterday; I completed my draft of Sir Charles Wolseley. And now I
have just come from a peep in Exeter Hall (to show my sympathy) at the
meeting in favour of peace. It was rather Christian; the Bishop of London
was wise, Dr Guiness Rogers was moved to call Canon Scott Holland a
"holy man"; F.B. Meyer was slow & mild; Cousin John kissed Guiness;
then I came away & left them singing. May I not pronounce of the evening
& the morning – "And behold it was very good"?

To-morrow May has asked me to dine at Pembridge Square. I hardly
think I shall go, but I may. I want so much to finish my Greek things next
week.

I have had a letter from the Marot. The Philadelphia University in
conjunction with School of Economics will arrange for three lectures. The
price, however, is rather disappointing but they promise to supplement it if

the tickets sell well. They cannot take me until the middle of February so I must make my arrangements accordingly.

And now the little guardian that keeps my arrangements orderly says "times up, gent" & so does my note paper. But I am permitted just to say "How d'ye do" to Timothy, and "How d'ye do" to Meggie; & to ickle Timothy's cheek with my moustache & the same to you; also to say "How d'ye do" to Flo without the sequel. I hope you are still winning the golden opinions of the matriarchy, but whether you are or not you are Ever mine own.

℘ Robert Thomson to Margaret.

> 14 December 1898
> from 193 Torrack Road
> South Yarra, Australia

. . . may [Alister] grow up to be a great David like his grandfather to slay the Goliaths of unbelief and man's machinations begotten of that "littel knowledge" leading up to presumption "is a dangerous thing" and a great grandson of your grandmother [Elizabeth Thomson] my sister, worthy of his descent and a strength and support to you in later life.

℘ Ramsay to Margaret.

> [1 January 1899]
> The Kosinestie
> 3 Lincolns

A good New Year! A good New Year! A good New Year!
  My love!
O could I bring the Evidence my heart desires to prove!
But souls, alas! are strangers in this half-created world,
When they would pelt with roses, lo! 'tis brick-bats that
  they've hurled.
The only proof I dare to bring – it's shaky too at that
Is that about three years ago I did "put on my hat".
And so in this New Year, my love, may every evil flit
And leave you only with the good

> Yours
> Me and Little It*

In January Ramsay went to the USA on a lecture tour organized by the London School of Economics.

❧ Ramsay to Margaret.

> 5 February 1899
> Royal Mail Steamship
> *Etruria*
> stuck off Liverpool
> in a snow storm

My own Dearest Dearie,

> Ochone for somebody,
> For little It & somebody
> My heart is riven in twa, in twa
> Because I have na somebody.
>
> Little It & somebody
> Bonnie It & somebody
> Ochone the sea is runnin' wide
> An' I hae nae my somebody.

I do wish you were here my dearie. I am so lonely and thirty-five days are so long. I shall count them on my fingers & send kisses by tellewag & everything else. A little white angel is whispering, though, that due compensation will be paid when we meet again. X X X X to you & Little It. Bless him for his daddy every night and kiss him for me & I will pay you when I come back.

Now for the material things. I wonder if you noticed in time for the post that I left my waterproof. I have wanted it already. When we were within about half an hour of Liverpool it began to snow & it has been snowing ever since, & at the moment of writing we are stuck off New Brighton so thick is it. We may not move for a long time.

This ship is as far removed from the *Paris* as Lincoln's Inn Fields is from Grays Inn Road. Our dining room is nice & bright with warm white paint & the waiters and other attendants look a decided cut above the American liners. It is well worth the extra money. I have a seat by the door & as there are no benches but swivel chairs it is very easy to clear out if necessary. There was a companion in my berth & so I spoke to the Cunard Representative before we sailed. I have consequently changed into a very large outer berth which I share with an exceedingly dear looking man with whom I have been having some conversation. He is very much like

Matthews of Grays Inn, so he is pleasing. There are some books here but I have not looked at them yet.

If you come across Allen's[1] knife will you post it? I am not sure if I took it after all. Be sure you send me the Library photographs. Had you not better buy at 'Taylors' drugstore a small bottle of 'Talcotone' (fixing & toning both combined; & print some yourself & send them to me? Talcotone was what I used first & gives no trouble. Print somewhat darker than you want (compare some of the right ones I have got), wash half a dozen or a dozen together for ten minutes in running water – until that creamy fog in the water which you will notice has completely gone. Eight ounces measured in the measure glasses (an ounce is the bigger figured marks, not the smaller ones) should do for twelve, six should do for six. But I think there are directions on the bottle. You might do this by Wednesday's post if you can and send them. I want to have them with me. You might try and let me have one of each but if you cannot, let me have yourself with him & him in the Library. Of course after taking the prints from the Talcotone you will wash them for an hour to an hour & a half. Use the smallest bath for the Talcotone.

I have taken all precautions against illness – two hours short of Liverpool I had Sanitas. On coming on board I had Sanitas. But so long as the boat is stationary I am perfectly safe.

And now I want to write to Mother and they tell me that all letters to be sent off from Queenstown must be finished by half past ten. I am thinking of your wavings at Euston. Bless you my own dearie & my own Little It. It will soon be time for "In Memoriam"

> Ever your own Sweetheart
> R
> XX   XX

❧ Margaret to Ramsay.

> February 1899
> Saturday 8.30 p.m.
> 3 Lincoln's Inn Fields

My dear dear love

This is the first good night of our 35, & I do hope it is a real good night with you. How I wish I were with you to see that you are as comfortable as possible. I hate the thought that you are perhaps ill & wretched & I am not

---

1. Perhaps his cousin, son of Aunt Jane in Philadelphia.

there to help you. I was awfully sorry when I found your macintosh hanging in the hall. What asses we were to forget it. It was only sentimentality which discovered it, for I was looking to see what signs of your being still here were in the hall & lo and behold there was this naughty old macintosh winking at me. He was awfully angry when I bundled him up & carried him off to the post-office tied up with white tape as the first thing that came handy. But I found he could get in the train at Euston, so I took him there myself to make sure that he didn't run away again & I do so hope that he & all the other parcels & letters will reach you there. I have been busy writing & reading and washing Little It's unmentionables. Little It went upstairs while I went to Euston and at the request of his lady loves was left there till bedtime; and I could hear him downstairs talking away in a half patronising half lordly way like his father will do tomorrow week. Now I am going to bed early & I daresay you will do the same tonight. In memoriam is by my bed. Goodnight.

Sunday

I have just been for my lonely little walk to the post. It is 35 hours since we parted so 1/24 of the time has gone. It has been wet and horribly muddy again, but little It went to see his (?) – and she squealed at him & he – in a dignified way at her & he sat in her high chair & looked very grown up.

I got a letter from S. Hobson[1] which he asks me to send on. I have written. The N.A.C. minutes have come & some book catalogues which I am not forwarding. I do hope you have not had it wet like we have, without a macintosh to keep you dry. I wonder whether you got all the parcels at Queenstown this morning – Dear Love Goodnight.

Monday.

Your letter has just come. It was so exciting to get it. And such a funny feeling to know that you are going further & further from me. Ah! but 2½ days of 35 are gone. Hooray I fear you must have been late at Queenstown I do hope you won't be delayed again. Here we have the most awful rain and winds. I went to dine with Honnor and the Oakshotts at a Swiss Café by Broad St Station & was drenched. Since then I have been wasting by the fire & reading up Campbell Bannerman & Macedonia & Samoa & New Foundland. I expect you will find the Yankees excited over the Philippines. Everybody who wrote to me in business or otherwise sends good wishes for your voyage. So do I & so does Topsy. He has been so good today . . . He looks for your greeting when he comes in the study in the morning, but also he looks in vain. Goodnight & bless you 10,000 times. I am so glad the boat is nice.

Tuesday

Just going my little walkie to the post. Tomorrow I shall walkie to the post with this letter. . .

. . . Hendry & Rickett have paid (latter £5) & Bank took my signature without any hesitation, so I have got enough to have a nice fling. Mrs Gurling is back but not better; doctor says she may go about if she likes & seems to be attending pretty thoroughly to her . . . Her roof lets in rain so I shall write to the landlord . . .. Several people asked me if you were well this evening & I said 'no!' seasick. Osmonde Crosse was coming to hear you at Ishmaelites but was ill. Dear Wilfie [Cousin Wilfred] was there flirting with Floey.

Wednesday

. . . I am beginning to feel very queer at the thought of having to address an envelope to you so far far far away. Topsy is sucking his thumb & squealing & singing.

I enclose his photographs. The sun kept coming in and out while I was printing them so it was difficult to do them right. It told me on the bottle not to wash them before toning, so I thought I had better not. They are nice but you must get them with better exposures when you return. Now I am going off to see Mr Wolstenholme Ebury at the House of Commons & I shall try & see Sir J.S. Maxwell & also get Sammy [Hobson] or somebody to let me in the Ladies Gallery. I have got lots for my letter & shall write most of it today? but not type it. I have been doing some other typing. I won't send the *Spectator & Outlook* today as I may want to refer to them. I can't find the corrected Homework Bills and have written to ask Mrs Webb if we left them there. You haven't carried them off in your pocket have you? . . .

Now I must close. Hoping that this finds you well as it leaves me at present & with love from Alister & Mrs Gurling (at least I haven't asked the latter)

Your Ever Loving
Lassie

P.S. Just put away the Halma! I asked Mother to send yr Scottish papers direct.

---

1. Samuel Hobson, a Fabian friend.

Top: The memorial to Margaret in Lincoln's Inn Fields. Centre: The Gladstones' home in Pembroke Square. Bottom: Annie Ramsay's cottage in Lossiemouth.

Top left: Margaret at nineteen. **Top right:** 'The little fat boy'; Ramsay at six. **Bottom left:** Margaret's parents, John and Margaret Gladstone, c. 1869. **Bottom right:** Margaret aged about ten.

Top left: Ramsay aged
sixteen, poet and pupil
teacher. **Top right:** Margaret
(*centre*) with her four half-
sisters, February 1880.
Bottom: Margaret, aged
fifteen, with her father, 1885.

Top left: Margaret aged seventeen, taken by her aunt, Agnes Gardner King. **Top right:** Margaret with her father, John Gladstone, 15 June 1896. **Bottom:** Annie Ramsay (*seated right*) and Margaret (*standing right*), probably taken in September 1896 when Margaret paid her first visit to Lossiemouth.

Margaret in her thirties.

Top: 3, Lincoln's Inn Fields, where the MacDonalds spent their married life. **Bottom:** Margaret (*on roller*) with her father and aunts Agnes and Elizabeth, c. 1896.

Top: The Gladstone family c. 1896. *Left to right*, seated: Florence, Marion Holmes, Henri Bach, Isabella Holmes, May Gladstone; *standing*, John Gladstone (?), Bessie (?), Margaret.
Bottom: Margaret with her first child, Alister, 1898.

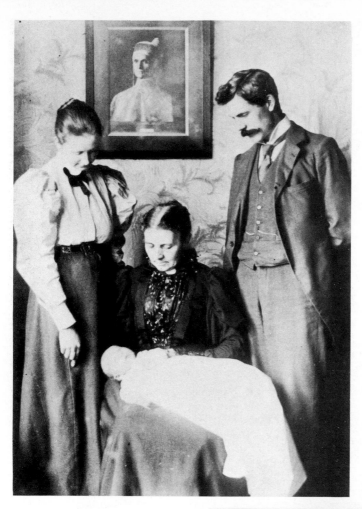

Top: Margaret, Annie Ramsay and
Ramsay with Alister, Lincoln's Inn
Fields, 1898. Bottom: Margaret with
Alister, 1898.

Top: Margaret with her first baby, 1898. **Bottom:** Ramsay with Alister, c. 1899.

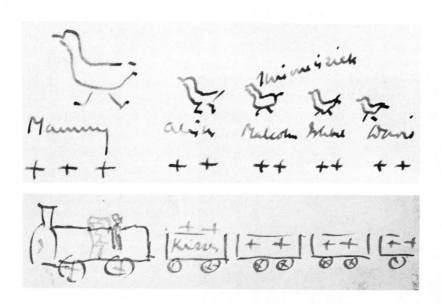

Top left: Margaret and Ramsay with Alister, c. 1899. **Top right:** *Left to right*, Annie Ramsay, Annie Campbell, Alister, Ramsay, Lossiemouth, 1899.
Bottom, above: Ramsay to Margaret, 1904. **Bottom, below:** A train load of kisses. Ramsay to Margaret, Jan 1906.

Candidate for Leicester – Ramsay in 1899.

Top left: Ramsay aged thirty-four. **Top right, above:** Ramsay to Margaret 1904. **Top right, below:** Ramsay to Margaret, Jan 1906. **Bottom:** Working together on the dining-table in their flat, c. 1903.

Top left: (*left to right*) Malcolm and Alister with David and Ishbel in the foreground, c. 1905. **Top right:** *Left to right:* Alister, Malcolm and Ishbel c. 1905. **Bottom:** Annie Ramsay with (*left to right*) Ishbel, Malcolm, David and Alister c. 1905.

Top left: Margaret and Ramsay with (*left to right*) Malcolm, David, Ishbel and Alister, c. 1907. **Top right:** Margaret in 1909. **Bottom:** Margaret and Ramsay setting off for India, September 1909.

Top: One of David's letters. **Bottom left:** Margaret with Mary Middleton at a meeting of the Women's Labour League, c. 1910. **Bottom right:** Alister and Malcolm with their mother's portrait, c. 1912.

Top: The Hillocks, the house Ramsay had built for his mother in Lossiemouth. Rams is in the doorway and Annie stands behind the pea supports.

Centre: The ILP council in 1899. *Back row, left to right:* MacDonald, J. Burgess, Parker, J. Penny, F. Littlewood. *Front row left to right:* Bruce Glasier, Keir Hardie, F Russell Smart, Philip Snowden.

Bottom: Sheila and Malcolm, 1934.

❧ Margaret to Ramsay.

Wednesday 8 February 1899

Just a little good night kiss & I am so glad you have not much more than 2 days more, & I do hope it hasn't been too horrid & have you been counting the hours till you land like we did; because if you haven't I have for you. And I've been . . . in the Lobby of the H of C. Mrs Webb has found the Bills. And I have been reading newspapers till I can think of nothing but Campbell Bannerman's Common Sense and sonorous voice. And I've sketched out a good deal of my letter. And I am so frightened of making lots of wise remarks which I want to make because they might not be so wise after all. And Little It had Mrs Oakshott & Mrs (?) to call & he wouldn't smile at them but only stared rudely at their hats. And he helped Mrs Gurling stick on lots of stamps for me. And he's not a *nice* little boy. And Halma made me so sad sitting and looking at me that I nearly had game with Topsy but he wouldn't play so I put it away instead.

Friday morning.

. . . I fear you will hardly make out my letter. The matter is practically the same as I gave but I changed some of it in copying & made it more forcible & terse in style, I think. It made 9 pages & I hadn't time for more so have held over some nice bits which will do next week. (I did all that is here) I see it is awfully cold in New York. I have been thinking of your landing. Here it is so hot that I feel oppressively warm on the top of a bus in strong wind without a jacket.

Bless you a thousand times, dear heart.
M.E.M.

❧ Ramsay to Margaret.

[c. 12 February 1899]
Monday
Royal Mail Steamship
Etruria

My Dearie Onnie

What can you be thinking of us? I suppose we are reported overdue, & it will be tomorrow night with you before you hear of us. There has been a Jonah on board. When I wrote to you a week ago, we were stuck in the river at Liverpool. Early on Sunday morning we passed into the Channel in a gale. At Queenstown we were twelve hours late. We left again in a gale. On Monday it was worse & we were running about 300 miles a day instead of 480. With the break of a single day this went on until Saturday when our misfortunes seemed to have reached a head. The wind was blowing a hurricane & mountains of water danced around us & broke over us. All day long you heard nothing but the groans of passengers and the smash of crockery. I never saw anything like the storm. Sunday was a little better but when we got up this morning expecting to see land in an hour or so, we were in the midst of a fierce blizzard. Ice lay thick on the deck just as though we had come from the Artic regions & snow and sleet were driving down in masses making progress impossible. Nor did it end there. Suddenly when we were all huddling in the smoking-room, the propellors danced and kicked & we were joggled off our seats. We rushed outside & stretching our heads over the bulwarks saw a huge ship just swinging clear of our bows. She came along and passed so close that I could have thrown my handkerchief on her deck. I saw the eyes of the sailors upon her. She was the U.S. warship *Marblehead*.

It was a marvellous escape – for the *Marblehead*, they say with us. Like the rest of the fleet she was painted white & was apparently carelessly navigated. Now here we are, hove to & not moving an inch. We have not gone twenty miles today & the blizzard still continues.

It is spelling ruin to me. Of course I have lost the £15 for the lecture I should have delivered to the Ethical Society yesterday and tonight there will be no People's Institute Lecture. What can I do? Blank miserable failure stares me in the face. We may get in tomorrow & I shall do my best to recover losses.

And you, you will be worrying, thinking, (here the shaking got so bad I had to leave off. I got sick).

Tuesday Morning. Another day of violent gales, snow, frost & now a bright morning and land is at last in sight. Shall send this off by sea-post. It may get you sooner that way. The morning is magnificent. We are ploughing our way through ice floes. But oh that Somebody & Something were here. They have my love & thoughts & blessings all the same. I wonder if my spook is telling them that it is all right.

Ever thine
R.

∽ Margaret to Ramsay.

13 February [1899]
6.30 p.m. Monday

My dear Sir,

Why did I leave my home where it is warm and cosy and go to the
horrible arctic regions? I am trying not to be in a state about you; but the
papers are horrible and I can't find your arrival in the *Daily News*. It says
all the steamers arriving never had such bad times before. Oh Sir, it is
dreadful. I do wish I had been with you. It is horrible to think of you ill &
tossed about all alone. The only comfort is that Miss Bradford is so kind and
nice and will comfort you up, but then I don't know whether you will be able
to get across to her. They say every place is blocked. And even if your boat
has arrived & I have missed it I don't think you will have good audiences &
you won't be able to get about and do your work & the houses are so horribly
heated & you will get cold going out of them. Oh dear Sir, I hope you will
telegraph when you arrive (I didn't ask you to because I thought it so
expensive) and tell me you are alright. I wonder if the Evening papers will
have anything. I must go out and get one. 7.15 . . . The latest evening
papers have not got you either. I wonder what is up. Perhaps I missed it. I
do hope so. I will look again but have not got the earlier papers here just
now.

I was laughing at Mrs Eweling the other day because she heard that a
boat had been lost in the Atlantic & sent out for an *Echo* in an awful state;
and now I am fussing too. But when you get this I hope you will be all warm
and cosy & halfway towards starting home again, & perhaps you will be
pitying me because we shall be having this cold weather here, sent over by
you in your telegrams. *7.30* . . . Now the Saturday paper has just come (it
was in my bag coming by Carter Paterson from Hamilton Terrace) & you are
not announced in it – I didn't look before because I didn't imagine you
could be. Never mind.

When you get this it will be alright, so let me talk of something pleasant.
Topsy (see how naturally he occurs to me as "something pleasant") was so
good at Hamilton Terrace that Sarah, the housemaid, thought him too good
to live and was rather anxious. Lily [Montagu] has been here to lunch
today. Her article is out in the Jewish quarterly – about making their
religion more spiritual & less antiquated – & she is deep in thinking out
how to follow it up. Miss Grant left them this morning in floods of tears &
affection to go to Macclesfield to a new place to look after a child. She
seems to be happy about the place. Mrs Bode seems happy here. And I
wish my Sir was here, looking out at the lights with me. It is nice to be home

again, though it was very pleasant at Hamilton Terrace. Bless you, bless you, dear Sir & come back safely to your Lassie.

Tuesday evening . . . Would you like to know what is my favourite newspaper & what is the very nicest piece of print I ever read in my life? It is enclosed in a little piece of paper and you must kiss it & send it back to me. And since then I have had your telegram and am so glad that you were at any rate able to drag yourself to some telegraph office. You poor dear – how I do so wish all the time that I were with you to laugh at you & comfort you & be miserable with you & listen to your bad words and say others of my own. I nearly jumped into the train going to Queenstown with your macintosh & only stopped because I thought you would be so cross when you saw me, & I didn't know quite what to do with Topsy & the Indian letter; but if I had guessed what you would have to go through I would certainly have come along & left Topsy cosy in England to look after himself. I shall look anxiously for your letters and keep imagining what you are doing. We won't talk of the agonies of yesterday & today now, but keep them to smile over together. Only little Timothy was very sweet & nice & comforting & he knew all about it, because when he & I went to the shipping office to inquire about you he asked quite as many questions of the clerk as I did & quite as intelligently. He said "Ahahah?? ("How is my Daadie") & "Haave yooou heard of his arrival?)" only he said it all very cheerfully & in a downright commonsense way to show he didn't mean to fuss. When I got the *Evening Standard* I telegraphed to Mother as she would be anxious. And now dear heart how nice to think you are reading *In Memoriam* on terra firma again. Good night and bless you a thousand times. And I do hope you are not very cold. And I do wonder if you were able to get across town to kind Miss Bradford.

Wednesday. . . In haste for post. Papa sends love and condolences. So does everyone. All serene. Are you going to stay longer to make up?

A thousand million blessings
Thine
Margaretta.

❧ Ramsay to Margaret.

17 February 1899
Thursday Morning
Whittier House
Grand Street
Jersey City

My Dear Little Wiffie,

. . . It was pleasant after the nightmare was over. "A summer night in Greenwood spent is but tomorrow's merriment" I am sending a newspaper or two about us. The illustration in the New York Journal is not one [bit] exaggerated. Imagine us! Well, I got here on Tuesday afternoon dead tired, ill, cross. But the light, the warmth! And I recovered. New York was under two or three feet of snow & the ferry boats could hardly get up to the landing stages. Cars were not running. And yet the brave Miss Bradford, another and myself went back to the Social Reform Club to hear a debate on the Eight Hours movement and a Mr J. W. Martin of the London County Council being advertised as the chief speaker. He was not there & I had to take his place. Got to bed at midnight.

Yesterday began work. Owing to the fearful nature of the blizzard the Monday night Peoples Institute Lecture had been put off & I fixed it for tomorrow (Friday) night, so that is not lost. I saw Dr Adler[1] in the morning. They were rather prepared for the breakdown & Adler wants me to take Sunday next & following & wishes me to stay until Wednesday 8th March & sail by White Star instead of Cunard.

. . . I have not yet decided but after the loss of those days I am almost afraid that that will have to be done at any rate if I can at all arrange it. I shall know perhaps before this is dispatched.

I lunched with Miss Wald [Lilian] whom I had seen the night before at the Social Reform. She is lively as ever, & sends her love, kisses etc., etc., to you direct and through me to Honor. She isn't coming over after all. She is determined to have H.M. stay with her & I think H.M. should. There are no cheap boarding houses. £50 won't run to it. The £50 was the chief topic of conversation at lunch. I told Miss Wald that H was wild no longer – that she was placid, docile, domesticated. They were interested.

Friday. Have been in Philadelphia & found Miss Marot and Innes so nice. Timothy attracts them. It was an awful day & noone could venture out so I must stay until March 9th as no lecture was given last night. Saw

---

1. Fritz Adler, an Austrian socialist.

enormous fire. Out I must go & that means I must close for the mail. Off to see Whitlaw Reid etc., etc.

There are no letters from you. I am longing for home.

My love's awa', awa, awa,
Echone! Echone!
Great seas are ragin' 'tween us toa
Great storms atween us rave an' ola
I'm sad an' weary, wae au' love
Echone! Echone!

Kiss my dear little one every day & bless him from me and the same to yourself.

Ever
R
X X X X X Ad infinitem

∽ Margaret to Ramsay.

Saturday morning
18 February 1899
17 Pembridge Square

My dear Sir

What a lot I have been thinking of you & how you are & where you are. I wonder whether you got to Philadelphia & how Helen was, & whether any ferries are going across to Cornelia; and whether you have had to be taken in as a destitute and homeless one by the New York Salvation Army. I am afraid I must wait some time for the answers to these questions, as Flo says she saw in the paper that the mails didn't start from New York on Wednesday. But we were all glad to have a message from your Captain in the *Daily News* to say that you were "comfortable" on the voyage. We hadn't been thinking that you were.

This is little Timothy's 9th Birthday counting by months. He asks me to tell you that he is a very nice little boy & that his grandfather is specially struck with his intelligence. He joined his grandfather in leading family prayers this morning & did it very nicely – Cheerful yet quiet.

I had such an excitement for my Indian letter this week. President Fauré's death on Friday morning. Fortunately Mrs Bode was able to give me a little local colouring from Paris & I managed something. I'm afraid you won't be able to read it. I had to scribble & I alter phrasing a good deal in copying.

Yours with tons of love & kisses from
Wifie & Sonnie

❧ Ramsay to Margaret.

Wednesday 22 February 1899
Whittier House
Grand Street
Jersey City

Mine Own Little Onnie,

Just a good morning and a line for the present. I have a quarter of an hour before I go to Philadelphia & I shall think of you. The days are flying splendidly; we are half way back again. And I wonder how they are going with you. I am thinking so long to see & hear you & little It. Otherwise things go well with me.

I felt in fine style for Adler's people & I am told I have won their hearts. Carnegie is a huge hall – about the same size as the Queens & it was three parts filled. I am told it will be quite full next Sunday when I speak on "Democracy & Imperialism from the British point of view". Was it your spook that was in me last Sunday? Or Little Its? I have finished my People's Institute Lectures & on Monday night after all was over I received an ovation, the crowd standing up and cheering. I have been going it. The financial result has been that I asked Sprague Smith a fee of $12 a lecture as arranged & he said "Nonsense! we must give you at least $20" & today I have had a cheque for $40 sent to me. Now I am off to Philadelphia. Thursday. Another good morning to my two little ones.

. . . on Saturday I went to the Bottomleys. They were very friendly & send all good family greetings to you & our Aunts. Later on that day I looked in to see my special friend Nellie Carrigues & my jealousy was roused by finding five or six young men there. They send all sorts of greetings to you & the little stranger. At seven I dined at Adler's. There were 14 leading men present including Carl Sturtz, Mr Warner, President of the Reform Club, Prof. Seligman, some of the leading Jews of the city & Professor Geddes of Edinburgh who is over lecturing . . . That night I went on to Boston, getting in at 6.30 a.m. After breakfast I went to Dennison House & was asked to come back to lunch which I did and met Miss Addams again, Miss Withington, Miss Dudley & one or two others. They all send love . . . We had a little meeting at Doctor Everett Hale's church about Peace & it was very successful. A Boston *Herald* man interviewed me but the paper has not come to hand yet so I do not know if it is good, bad or indifferent. The great nuisance of the visit is that camera. It opens of its own accord, the plates stick, it is an ill-tempered woman & I am inclined to buy a new one here. I took it to Boston and after the first picture it refused to act. Hang it!

Yesterday I came on here as I was guest at a little reception given by the Library of Economics . . . It is so homely here & wherever I go I really think we were the great successes of America. Today I am lunching with a Mr Mercer, a lawyer & city alderman, at the big Philadelphia club & am meeting some of the public men of the city. I have seen Aunt Jane [Annie's sister], her husband is as lazy as ever. She . . . has bought her house freehold & will have it rebuilt during the Spring and Summer. I cannot find Allan's knife in my luggage. Did I leave it? I lecture tonight & then leave for Jersey City & early tomorrow I go to Cape Cod, getting back on Saturday. On Monday I have an appointment with Roosevelt at Albany & go on that afternoon to Niagara. I cannot get away before Wednesday by the White Star & I hope it isn't a slow boat . . .

I could do nothing whilst in Boston about the sweating shops . . . I tried to go to the State House, but found it impossible. I wonder how you are getting on with the [Homework] Bill? and with every thing else. Will it be possible for us when I return to get away together for a few days' rest in the country? . . . The trip I think, is it be a great a gret financial success, but in order to cram everything in, I have to be active day and night. Still I like the weather. The air is so clear, clean, fresh and invigorating. But I am longing for home again. It will be grand to get back – and in that respect this knight (?) will also have been a success . . .

Bless you and little It. Any toophies yet? Love to our Aunts. Flo, Cousin John and the rest.

My stock of kisses is enclosed herewith

> Ever thine Own
> Laddie & Daddie

❧ Ramsay to Margaret.

> 28 February 1899
> The Stafford
> Washington St.
> Buffalo

My Dear Best Girl,

There was such a scene here today as Topsy might have created. A gentlemanly looking man came down to breakfast & said to the headwaitress; "May I not sit at that table there? There the wife of my bosom who is now in heaven sat with me in the happy days gone by." He then burst into tears & didn't eat much breakfast. I had a few words with him when he

---

1. space left here for a footnote p.358.

calmed down. He said he had been overstrung; that he had been travelling a good deal; that he had had an interview with Governor Roosevelt which rather upset him as he had got on so well; that he had had a quarrel with a young lady named Cornelia about railway trains and dessert spoons; that he had met an Astor & was invited to dine there because the said Astor liked his "bully speech"; that on the back of it all he had made a pilgrimage like a brother-in-law of his to the scenes of tender memories and that it had proved to be too much for his gentle nature. He seemed an exceedingly nice fellow & I gather that he had two children – one Timothy, the other Topsy. He was reading a long scrawly letter with blots on it. In his moments of absentmindedness I gathered that he was over here on some miscellaneous business & yet seemed to be very well pleased with the result. He was leaving this morning for Niagara & was to travel to New York again, back to his Cornelia, I think – late in the evening.

I also gathered that he was to sail for England on Wednesday the 8th March by the *Majestic*, so I saw in a letter he was writing to his best girl – a sister I daresay. He seemed to belong to an extensive family for he sent love to cousin Johns, Mays, Flos, Florettas & two of three more lines of proper names. I also saw Joshs & Matildas scattered about. Funny I should have taken such an interest in him, but having taken it, I could write of nothing else this morning, for indeed I had nothing else to say. And now as to myself I just send the usual consignments of love and kisses to mine own two to whom I am ever Laddie & Daddie.

P.S. There was something of the rascal in my friend I fear, for he seemed to be writing a good deal about a Miss Honnor I think she must be a bit of a minx who has acquired undue influence over him. He seemed so nice.

꙰ Ramsay to Margaret.

> 3 March 1899
> Dr George M. Gould,
> 1129 South Seventeenth Street
> Philadelphia

My Dearest Lassie,

In a hurry. Off to catch train. Writing impossible if I am to get this, the last post. Hurrah! I start Wednesday & my best message will be myself. The *Majestic* is my boat; send letters to Queenstown, c/o *Majestic* White Star.

To my dear Timothy & yourself many kisses.

〜 Ramsay to his mother.

8 March 1899

H.M.S. "Majestic"

My Dear Mother

I intended to have written to you whilst I was in America, but my time was so short & so much filled up that I find myself once more on the sea before having an opportunity to send you a letter.

We left New York at noon today, & if the whole of the voyage is to be like its beginning we are to have none of the excitements which we had in crossing the other way. Of that crossing I suppose Margaret has told you. It is very pleasant to think of now, but it was far from that whilst we were going through it. I suppose you have seen some of the pictures of our ship. When we got to New York we were covered with snow and ice & the harbour was frozen over. I was so busy in America lecturing that I could not go far afield in the country & most of my time was spent in going between New York and Philadelphia. But I managed to get as far north as Niagara Falls and found them covered with ice and snow. I walked across the river on the ice bridge.

Whilst in Philadelphia I saw Jane for a minute or two three different times, but I really saw very little of her & I was not able to go and see Mr Irving whose address you sent. Jane was just as usual. Allen is growing quite a young man now & Jamie has not changed either for the better or the worse. Jane has succeeded very well with the little shop and they have bought the house they are in. They are going to make it into a much better place & have added an outside kitchen already & when I was there on Monday, Jamie had begun to pull down the inside partitions so as to enlarge the shop. They all send their kind love to you, & Jane says that the purchase of the shop will now prevent her getting home for a long time to come. Jamie however, seems bent upon coming & I should not be surprised if he started.

〜 Ramsay to Margaret.

15 March 1899

Telegram

Handed in at Queenstown Spa

Arrived shall wire from Liverpool

Ramsay

❧ To Ramsay.

20 April 1899
58 Clovelly Mansions

My dear MacDonald

Probably some one has sent you the *Southampton Times* with report of Liberal Council's arrogant rejection of I.L.P. proposal. I think the I.L.P. courted the snub but I hope it won't calmly submit to extinction.

It's no business of mine but I hope under the circumstances you will contest the seat. A good deal could be done in two years & I will very gladly give you all the help I can . . .

Yours very faithfully
Joe Clayton

❧ To Ramsay.

24 May 1899
39 Cranbury Avenue
Southampton

Dear MacDonald,

I laid your letter of the 15th inst before the Executive Committee and I am to inform you that the Committee receive the news of your retiring from Southampton with keen regret but wish you every success in your contest at Leicester . . .

With most sincere regards

Fraternally yours
Henry S Phillips

❧ Annie Ramsay to Margaret.

6 June 1899
Thee Cottage
Lossiemouth

My Dour Margaret

i got the box all right Many thanks i also got the little present for Aunt Annie and myself it was verry kind of you to remember me and hir the farns looks fresh and i have put them in pots i do hope they will do well i will send on the box as soon as i can and i Am sure Alister would be plased to see you back again Mrs Wellwoods father is dead and was from hom the tim of Mr Grants death i met Dr Gran and Miss the other day Miss sad she was

leaving on Thursday give my love to my dear little boy and i will be looking
to sea him soon if all is well the tim will soon pass by with love to you also
and many thanks fir your godness to me frim your Mither

A Ramsay

〜 Honnor Morten to Margaret.

30 July 1899

I saw Corrie G (?) yesterday and he says J.R. would be an excellent
candidate *if he would stick to it* – [a place on Chelsea school board] – but he
wouldn't have anyone else using it as a stepping stone to L.C.C. or
Parliament . . .

〜 Ramsay to Margaret.

5 September 1899
Richmond Hotel (strictly tee-total)
Mount Pleasant Terrace
Plymouth
T.U.C. Conference

Meesus,
There's nothing to say. Except that I am here . . . a lot of Scottish miners
are here too but I have not seen much of them yet except dancing. I looked
in at the Congress . . . First impression is that the chairman is poor & that
the Congress is, in consequence on the verge of slipping out of control.
Now how is my Biggie She and my Little It? Have they akes of heart and
tooth? Some of the delegates were asking if the person was down and
regretted she was not . . .

R.

Newspaper cutting . . .

I have just had a run down to Plymouth where the Trades Union Congress
– the great annual parliament of labour – has been sitting. I was curious to
feel its political pulse, because although Congress resolutions do not always
mean very much, Congress itself is attended by the flower of the working
classes from John o'Groats to Land's End. Politically the great question
before the Congress was contained in resolutions sent in by two or three
different Trades Unions instructing the Committee to take steps to call a
conference of labour bodies for the purpose of considering a course of
political action which shall be conducted independently of both the Liberal

& the Tory parties. Those resolutions originated in the socialist sections of the Trade Union world, especially in the Independent Labour Party, & it was frankly recognised all round that they were the gage of battle boldly thrown down. The terms of one of them were extremely foolish & it looked at first as though they were to wreck the Socialist's chances. But this resolution was adroitly withdrawn & the battle began in deadly earnest, several of the working men who sit in Parliament as Liberals being bitterly attacked, & being as warmly defended. It was difficult on the platform to hear the arguments as the Plymouth Guildhall appears to have the worst acoustics of any place in the country but the great point insisted upon the one side was the need of independence & on the other the futility of isolated action. The excitement was of the most intense kind for it was evident from the beginning of the debate that the Congress was pretty evenly divided & the issues at stake were tremendous. At last the drama drew to a close and the tellers went round counting the votes. Amidst a painful silence the Chairman announced "For the Resolution, 546,000: against 4-". Nothing more could be heard. A yell of joy filled the hall. Old men rose and waved their arms wildly over their heads. For a minute or two the Chairman's voice & the Chairman's bell were equally ineffective & when comparative quiet was restored "Against 434,000" was announced. The Victory of the Extreme men was totally unexpected & when I went out I found the Liberal Trades Unionists wild with fury & disappointment. There is no disguising the fact but that this might be a serious thing for the Liberals at the next election. But it all depends upon how the Parliamentary Committee interprets its mandate. It should be noted that the two most powerful nations at the Congress, the Miners and the Cotton Operatives opposed the resolution & that detracts somewhat from its importance. But all the same, the Trade Union Congress drifts more & more under the influence of the more extreme men and the leaders of the workers are beginning to adopt continental methods of political work.

❧ Ramsay to Margaret.

10 September 1899
White Bull Hotel
Blackburn.

Ma chere Weevie,

I fear you won't get this letter in time. I have been terribly busy. Shall go down by the 5.15 as you say but I am not clear by your instructions whether I get there or leave London at that time. I'll look at the time tables however and put myself right. I have had Dreyfus nightmare last night. What a fearful thing it is.

But adieu until tomorrow.

> To Little It & thee X X X
> X X Thine

∽ Margaret to Lady Mary Murray.

Apologies for not giving you longer notice of our Legal and Statistical [Committee of the Women's Industrial Council] which meets at 12 Buckingham St. Strand Mon. 25th inst. 3 pm . . . travelling about wanted to write . . . days go by. In Lady Carlisle's letter said we shall be discussing the Factory Bills of last sessions, census statistics and a new scheme of investigation that we are starting. The TUC passed a resolution in favour of the principle of our Homework Bill & one on the lines of the outwork clauses in Mr Tennant's bill was withdrawn.

I want to ask you if you would allow me to nominate you as one of Vice Pres. of the Nat. Union of Women Workers. The election comes off in October at the annual Council meeting. As Vice Pres. you would be summoned to the Quarterly Exec. meetings. – Delighted if you would – for the N.U.W.W. represents a large number of active women. . .

In October Ramsay was adopted as ILP candidate for Leicester. Both he and Margaret had resigned from the Fabians over their refusal to denounce the government's declaration of war against the Boers.

∽ Ramsay to Margaret.

> [? October 1899]
> Sunday
> S. Mark's Vicarage
> Belgrave Road,
> Leicester.

My Dear Missus,

The "chockies" came alright. I left them lest you should neglect me. This is a nice place. Donaldson[1] is of the Church Catholic & so is Mrs Donaldson, and so are the pictures & so is the library, so is our conversation. When a man gives you his pipe & makes you ill fearfully and shamefully ill so that you spoil his floor, you cannot help feeling subdued next day. But they are very nice. They have seven children in ten years & I

---

1. Rev. F.L. Donaldson, Ramsay's host.

am surrounded by these cherubs . . . We have had a very good meeting this morning and I am supposed to be contemplating, free from wordly distractions, the message I am to deliver this evening.

I expect that Hooligan offspring of yours is as aggressively robust as ever & that only in moments of satiated bliss does he think of his departed parent. I also hope that Mr Tandy is behaving himself.

And now to the mother & the son be the blessings and the kissings of the father.   Thine

       R.

❧ Ramsay to Margaret.

          October 1899
          Wednesday
          16 Princess Street
          Leicester.

My dear Lassie,

How is the family, its It, its heart & its chilblains? We are well here and getting on nicely. But this weather is fearful. It has been snowing for two days and last night the meeting in point of numbers was a fiasco. There were only about 70 present. Several important officials, however were present & it was worthwhile; & then the *Post* gives me a column – with the spicy bits left out, e.g. The d--ds etc, etc. Our men are very buoyant, they think that things are going well and that we are making friends. Taylor is very nice & so is his wife. I saw *Mrs* Harris yesterday. Invite them to dinner . . . They are coming up for the Fabian dinner & are to stay a week at the Thackeray Hotel. There is no excursion up here tomorrow, but even if there were the weather is so very bad that you had better not venture.

I have been around the Equity Boot and Shoe Works today. The machinery is most extraordinary & you must arrange to see it when next in Leicester. This afternoon I am going round the Wheatsheaf Boot Works with Richards and I am hoping to drop in & see the Harrises for tea. So you see I am enjoying myself.

I don't think there is anything else, except that Mrs Lee has sent her aged love & Mr Mackintosh is wanting to know about the young ruffian & so on. I am looking forward to tomorrow – the meeting, of course; & I suppose that I shall find my way home again after the affair.

For Little It & you many of the ordinary crosses.

      Ever
      J.R.M.
      X X X X

❧ Ramsay to Margaret.

4 November 1899
The Labour Leader
1 & 3 Queen's Parade
Glasgow

Ma chere Luvie et Littleitio

Here I am safe and sound and sleepy having called on Margaret [Irwin] & having found the door shut. The train was crowded & I had to sit bolt upright all the way. It was an awful day here yesterday. Every low-lying tract through Lanarkshire was flooded. The streams have overflowed their banks and at several places the houses were standing up in the midst of broad & apparently deep lakes. From this description you will have an idea of salt sea breezes & in imagination you will be able to hear the roll of stones upon the beach.

And how are you? And how is Little It? I hope he is looking carefully after you as every time I go away I fear more & more for your character. So many young angels are going wrong. If you like you can meet me with the pram at Euston on Monday. I get in at six by the 10 a.m. from Glasgow. If I can get up in time to-morrow morning I am going to see the Scots Greys off. They march through Glasgow. Hardie does not allow more paper & so adieu & bless you

Ever He
X X X X X X

❧ Margaret to Lady Mary Murray.

14 November 1899

Sorry you not able to stand for N.U.W.W. JRM up in Glasgow last week saw members of council – we are hoping to co-operate in some schemes for a very thorough & extended investigation of women's work trade by trade – which we want to publish in a series of volumes.

❧ Ramsay to Margaret.

[? 1899]
Angel Hotel
Cardiff

Mine Own,

Here I am. The Co-op Congress is a much poorer affair than I imagined. The type of man is not nearly as strong as you find at a T.U. Congress & his outlook is much more circumscribed. But I have met a good many & am having a very pleasant time – the Women's Cooperative Guild being well represented. Some of the cooperators I have been talking to are a little disappointed themselves. The crowd is too big for debating purposes. Our special matter comes up tomorrow morning, but I do not know how it will fare except perhaps that it will be defeated.

The weather is delightful and the country is splendid. I find that Burrows lives a little bit out of town & I have not been out yet but I have seen him.

How is Timothy? Well, I hope, and singing. I also hope he is keeping you straight. Now I must off to a meeting. We had a good time in Gloucester.

Ever Thine

R

X X X X X X X

〰 Ramsay to Margaret.

Tuesday 1899

The National Union of Women workers of Great Britain & Ireland

Our dear Mammie,

At 7.30 a.m. the Biggie one was startled by a nightmare. Bales and bales of cloth were down in his stimmik and the voice of a whispering angel came into his ear:- "Mammie gone?" It was the little one. The said little one was very offended that Mammie should have gone without explaining matters a little more to him, & insisted that she must be coming "back soon" & kept his eye on the window. But when, late in the afternoon a post card came saying that she had left important papers the little one giggled with satisfaction, for by putting two and two together he saw that Mammies insides had been more troubled at the parting that he had imagined; when the further p.c. came this evening he roared with laughter & tried to say: "Poor Mammie, must have been bad." He found time to post the papers immediately yesterday afternoon & were told that you should get them today by twelve o'clock. Along with this, the other papers go.

Now Mammie, don't think we are not getting on without you because we are. We have ballies and gee-gees and baths and we feel very happy. Perhaps we are looking forward to Thursday, but only just a little. Then, of course, we quite understand that the rights of the other sect must be looked after and asserted in the teeth of ourselves. So we understand. We are sorry that our loyalty to ourselves will not allow us to do our two Aunties and our Mammie justice, but we look upon them all the same with encouraging friendliness.

227

Our paper is coming to an end & we should like to send our dutiful love to Uncle George, to Aunti Flo ("you know") & Auntie Bella ("queer fella") & to yourself. We hope you are not forgetting your duty to your home, and that if you hear of any good cooking receipts you will remember them. With one accord we sing "Come back again, Mammie From over the foam, and me and my Daddie will welcome you home."

Thy two

∾ Ramsay to Margaret.

[?23 November] 1899

> November, too, my dearest love.
> To me of months is best
> For then it was, my dearest love,
> We built a little nest.
>
> And ever since, my dearest love
> Wherever we do roam
> We think and speak, my dearest love,
> Of our own comfy home.
>
> And so it is, my very dearest love,
> Though dirty fogs me choke
> November can't, my dearest love
> Obscure her smiles by smoke.

In early December 1899 representatives of the Fabians, ILP, SDF and the TUC's Parliamentary Committee met to prepare an agenda for a conference of labour bodies, as proposed in the Railway Servants' Resolution, to devise ways of getting all labour members to take part.

Ramsay:

Are we ready to witness the birth of a genuine Labour Party on the House of Commons?. . .

Ethical World, December 1899

Ramsay to Margaret.

6 January 1900
Hotel Manhattan
New York

My Dearest Wiffie,

. . . We got in this morning after a very good voyage, my poor body, however, exacting the due penalty for my follies. Mrs Langtry [Lily Langtry, the famous actress] was with us, but I mistook a very pretty lady for her & so did not catch a glimpse of real person until in the dock here. But my opinion of Jersey Lily is not so high as of ordinary lillies. We had some good sunrises and sunsets & some very long days & some very, very long nights; & now here I am & everything looks so ridiculously familiar that I wonder if I were not brought up in the midst of this regal shantydom. Somehow New York seems more barbarous than ever. The carriages, the dresses, the tone, the style are more gaudy, violent, gorgeous than ever. It was a study in prehistoric civilizations which I had this afternoon in looking at the crowds dispersing from the theatres after the matinees. And as further evidence of the pristine creative force of this raw crowd there is now the Dewey Arch apparently, (for I have not seen it closely yet) a remarkable effort of barbaric creative power. It is simply Force enthroning & encrowning itself & holding high revel in its own honour. And the living here in a Byzantine palace of colour & glare & marble & copper, the genius of America seems never to depart from my elbow. Like a Mephistophole, it whispers of occult powers, of powers of heaven & hell which are to rule the Western World & carry the sceptre of civilization, as they carried the America Cup, across the Atlantic. Of course I believe more than ever that the sceptre will take sick on the way & that when it lands in New York or gets to Chicago it will be feeling rather funny in the head.

I really have not had time to read up the papers yet but I see that some complications have arisen owing to our seizure of vessels. I think that on the whole, opinion on the boat was with us. People got it into their heads that we are fighting for democratic liberty, but I am told since I came here that swinging is going on & that opinion will not keep long with us. Of that I cannot say as yet. But here I am without an introduction & I have to paddle on my wits. "Faint hearts etc" as you know to your gain. White came along in the boat & is here, so I shall make a beginning with him and then go independent.

I went over this morning to see Miss Bradford but as I dreaded she had gone to see her father. I am so uncertain now regarding my movements that I do not know if it will be possible for me to see her again, but I saw the charming Miss Cossard, the nice Dr A (a lady of course) & the smiling Miss B. They fell upon my neck & I kissed them but they didn't offer me afternoon tea and I was offended.

And now to come to what is at the bottom of my mind all the time – le thought domestique. How are my Wiffie and my Little It? They look very nice in photograph, but not so nice as in themselves. It was very good of them to come both up out of my bag under my bed & read Kingsley with me even hours after they in ordinary circumstances would have been fast asleep. Little It did his best to follow us but he *was* rather sleepy. At the present moment they are both snugly up in my room on the 11th floor. I wish I were back to them again. That wish is one of the great reasons for going away, and I am hoping so much that when I return it will be at an hour when they can both come to Euston & say "Ow-dee-doo".

With very much love and very many kisses which Mammie must not keep all to herself.

I am ever
Thine

❧ Ramsay to Margaret.

14 January 1900
The Shoreham
Washington D.C.

Mine Own,
 . . . I wondered how your many functions went off. Sixty-five sounds very successful; Fifty sounds very poor. Did any one who smoked my cigars sicken? What happened to the pamphlet? You said nothing about that. Has anyone except Dodd been nominated for the Fabian Executive? Oh you are a poor newsmonger. You have told me nothing. As to my own mission [Anti-war propaganda] I have nothing striking to report. I have seen several people & they are thinking I go every day to the Senate & House & listen to the debates but I have heard nothing very striking. The Senate Library is a fraud. It has got nothing yet worth speaking about.

I wish you had been here on Sunday. It was a most magnificent day and I walked out into Virginia about 10 miles to the National cemetary at Arlington, took some photographs, viewed the land from hill-tops, listened to a niggers' revivalist meeting & heard the genuine nigger spiritual songs. But, generally I get more and more disgusted with America and more and more impressed that it is the greatest of things which man and nature have made. I saw Dr Harris Commissioner of Education this afternoon and had a very pleasant half-hour with him. Did I tell you I have also seen Fowderly the famous head of the Knights of Labour, now a Washington politician. We got very friendly & I must stand him a dinner.

Well, the time flies, & much as I am seeing & doing & mightily pleased as I am that I came, I shall be very glad to get better the day before reaching Queenstown & still mightier pleased to saw "Ow-dee-do" to you and Little It at Euston on Saturday fortnight.

Ever thine
R
X X X   X X X

Ramsay to Margaret.

19 January 1900
The Shoreham
Washington D.C.

. . . Somebody doesn't think much of her poor husband. He has been looking for letters & there are none by Wednesday's mail. The poor husband will not write any more . . .

Ramsay to Margaret.

Thursday 29 January 1900
The Shoreham
Washington D.C.

My Dear Lassie,

I have reached Mecca. This morning I went down full of expectations that I should find waiting for me a voice from across the water. But I was disappointed. I have heard nothing from [you] since I left Queenstown — now twelve days — & it'll probably be Saturday before I see your hand. Of course no introductions have come either. It has been rather unpleasant and my work has been done under difficulties. So far I have seen Abner McKinley and Senator Mason to talk over matters . . .

But I am glad I came. I have seen into things a good deal. We are altogether mistaken regarding the American feeling on our war. It is almost unanimously against us, so much so that those reasonable people who see how absurd it is for the Anti-Philippine folks to say a word against us, are changing their opinions about all American policy rather than accept the responsibility of supporting us. Even amongst business men the anti-British

231

feeling is spreading & the newspapers are cooling in the support they gave us a month or so ago. The Democrats make no secret of their intention to raise the anti-British banner this year & the Republicans are afraid of the consequences. The war has undone all the work of the good feeling which sprung up between the two countries after the Spanish War. In Washington here the friends of England have to hold their tongues whilst our opponents are loud in their condemnation of us. The administation is all right but this being the year of the Presidential Election McKinley will not venture to go very far in supporting us . . .

I am feasting on oysters and grapefruit. The sons of the burning plains of Afric minister unto. The magnificent wives of undistinguished senators keep my eyes busy. This country gets more and more wonderful. Here you see the essence of Amerika, its business, its bounce, its society. The great question agitating Washington just now is: "How much should the wives of Ministers receive the wives of senators etc" Women are breaking down, fainting in the streets, dying as with the Yellowjack because the social life of Washington is so exacting. Washington is two things – a lobby and a reception room. It is wonderful to see the bosses bossing, to sit and eavesdrop in the smoking room. "Ah, Mr Senator," I heard this morning in the Senate lobby. "I should like to tell you before I go, how often I hear my wife speak of you. She always says when we speak of politics "Well, you stick to your Senator. He is the right sort" He wanted an invitation to functions. Last night I walked up & down the city after nine o'clock and every street was a stream of people in evening dress rushing along to receptions. It is equality with a vengeance which rules here. Everybody wants to be as good as everybody else; the representatives of the "plain people" are determined to have their money's worth out of American principle; and so every evening the streams flow & every morning the hurrying drops are minutely separated and named in the Washington *Post* and *Star* . . .

ɷ Ramsay to Margaret.

> 22 January 1900
> The Shoreham
> Washington D.C.

Mine Own Dearie,

Two letters came today, one having been very lazy. I gave it a whipping & stood it up in the corner when it came but it only laughed & said Little It told it to be naughty. Hurrah! This is the last I shall have to write to you because by Saturday's mail I come myself.

I am very very busy, but not too busy to read your letters – oftener than once. But I have seen my American girl only twice, have not been able to go to see Carroll D. Wright[1] yet, but I have seen Gompers,[2] Fowderly & a few other Labour men. To-morrow I see the Secretary of State, today I have been interrogated by the Chairman of the Foreign Relations Committee of the Senate. I went last night to a demonstration here in favour of the Boers. The meeting was held in one of the largest theaters in the city & the place was packed from Orchestra to ceiling & scores were turned away. They yelled at us and jeered at us. References to our friendship were howled down. There were about ten speakers & they prayed & prayed & prayed that the British Empire would pass away and that in God's hands the Boers might be the means. They told lies about us & they told truths. I never felt so pro-British in my life and today I have let out at them in an article in the New York *World*, which however, may not be published until Sunday. But still, the tide of anti-English feeling is rising here. Paper after paper is swinging round and the administration is beginning to recognise that the agitation is spreading away beyone the mere Hibernianism with which it started . . . I believe the popular agitation has caught on & unless we are speedily successful America will be stirred from the Atlantic to the Pacific. I hold the people who are doing the stirring in contempt; but they are wise men & know the real affections of the people . . .

❧ Ramsay to Margaret.

23 January 1900
The Shoreham
John T. Devine
Washington D.C.

My Own Biggie One,

I wrote last night but I am waiting half-an-hour for White and as I have nothing particular to do (mark the words) I am writing to you another letter which may or may not find you before I do. It is a glorious morning. I wish you were here. We should go out a walk and wait for White in a rational sort of way. I have just come from the Secretary of State. He was very genial, very attentive, very pleasant, somewhat confidential. We had half an hour together. He put questions, told me of the feelings of the Administration,

---

1. Wright (1840–1909) was an American statistician and social economist.
2. Samuel Gompers (1850–1924), born in London, became an American labour leader.

promised to lay my information before the proper authorities and so on; talked about London & Scotland; shook hands most cordially. I think something may come out of it. The administration is watchful. It sees that it cannot go too far. It knows, the Secretary said so, that the vast majority of the people here are opposed to us and that those who are most friendly to England view the present situation with regret and recognise that it is now impossible to take up openly the English cause. I told the Secretary that Hibernian demonstrations would only do harm. We despised the black-guards. Nor should we tolerate any interference until Ladysmith is relieved and the Boers are practically out of the Transvaal, but that after that, friendly offices might be effective – at any rate they would not be regarded by the intellectual and the better classes in our country (who are all but unanimous against the war) as an attempt on the part of America to interfere in a hostile spirit. He wanted to know about the effect of the Resident's message, of Mr Chamberlain's position, of the government's hold on the country. I told him of my 'political prejudices' & with that warning proceeded to talk straight. I also explained about how the worthless people in our politics were exploiting the good feeling which had grown up between the two countries. In short he had it; & I finished up by expressing my ideas about how our good feeling should be worked. We really had a fine talk. Now I am going to see Senator Lodge & when I have written a statement for the Foreign Relations Committee I shall be practically finished. I don't think I shall trouble the President. Then hurrah for Saturday! A kiss or two has been found in the corner of my box overlooked last night in clearing out & I send them to you and little It.

R

In February Ramsay stood for the LCC at Woolwich as a 'Labour and Progressive candidate'.

26 February 1900

Daily Mercury. . .

Mr. J.R. Macdonald has cut a poor figure at Woolwich, after all. The County Council election took place there on Saturday, and the "Moderate" candidates were returned by votes approximating to those recorded on the previous occasion. But there was no unity among the Progressives, despite the efforts in that direction. Mr. Marsh stood as an independent and received 2,402 votes. Dr. Lindow came next with 1,907, and Mr.

Macdonald was last with 1,405. We regret that the negotiations for united action among the Progressives should have failed, but it must be acknowledged that the temper shown by so many Socialists makes unity very difficult.

The great conference of socialists and trades unionists, planned three months earlier, was finally convened in the Memorial Hall in Farringdon Street on 27 February. The SDF, inevitably, wanted the new alliance to be a party 'based upon the recognition of class war'. This was rejected, as was the 'influencing' of Liberal MPs and a suggestion that Labour candidates should be drawn only from the working classes. Keir Hardie's proposal for the basis of the new party was accepted; there was to be 'a distinct Labour group in Parliament who should have their own Whips and agree upon their policy'.

The Labour Representative Committee – later the Labour Party – was born, and the conference agreed unanimously that Ramsay should be its secretary.

CHAPTER 6

July 1900–July 1904
'Our mammie away
from us'

The executive committee of the new party, the Labour Representation Committee, met in the tiny back room in the flat in Lincoln's Inn Fields – sometimes with one of the members perched on the coal-scuttle. As secretary, Ramsay had no vote and would often sit through proceedings without speaking, waiting for his opinion to be asked. Within nine months the party was faced with the challenge of an election, and the secretary became more and more absorbed in political work. In the next four years Margaret produced three more children. She decided to have her second confinement in Lossiemouth, and Ramsay became somewhat tetchy, anxious at the separation and resentful of the 'Grimalkin' who demanded so much of her attention. Their son cried a lot and exhibited Gladstone rather than MacDonald features. Margaret, realizing that Ramsay needed her undivided attention for some time at least, agreed to leave the two little boys with Grannie, and went off on a long trip with him to South Africa. The next arrival came 'in hat, hatpins and petticoat' to Lincoln's Inn Fields, followed only fifteen months later by their third child. David was born in Lossiemouth just when Ramsay, always concerned about his health, was recovering from an appendix operation. He had nurses and Margaret's sister Flo and her uncle George to look after him, but he felt abandoned nevertheless.

In July Ramsay was busy in Leicester, and his mother came to London for a rare visit to Lincoln's Inn Fields.

〰 Ramsay to Margaret.

> 3 July 1900
> St Mark's Vicarage
> Belgrave Road
> Leicester

My dear Lady,

Such is the effect of my crucifiers & my Madonnas-Lady! And being in this haven of sanctity & sacrifice [a vicarage] I am all the more deeply grieved that my family should sulk when its gee-gees and puff-puffs are galloped and engineered by other hands. I am very good-gooder than ever. As an example of my goodness I am to give up all newspapers where the news of preaching & religion is jumbled together under the general heading "The Churches", because such a thing shows an aggressive disregard for my feelings and an impertinent assumption of superiority which should be visited by the only punishment which the ordinary subscriber can inflict. That is but an item in my new creed . . .

〰 Margaret to Ramsay.

> 29 July 1900
> Lincoln's Inn Fields

My dear Sir

I am having an awful trouble with your mother & son. The latter alone is bad enough, but at any rate he confines his vagaries to the daytime. When you come home, ask your mother what public place she was drinking in at 10.30 p.m. on Saturday night, and why she made me give her my latchkey at 9.30 on Sunday night, so that she might go out walking with a man I never saw before. I am dreading tomorrow evening: she is going to gallivant again, I know.

The LRC put up fifteen candidates for the 'khaki' election in October. The country was caught in a fever of anti-Boer jingoism, and not surprisingly, only two Labour men were returned, Hardie and Richard Bell of the Railway Servants.

∾ Annie Ramsay to Ramsay.

Tusday [October] 1900
The Cottage
Lossiemouth

My dear Ramsay

A good many of the Fishermen asked me to writ you to say they hope you will win the battle on Thursday and none is more interested than old James Hay so by the tim you get this the wirk will be near the end of the last meating i hope Margaret is none the wirse of hir wirke i sent the male yesterday wich i hope will rech all safe My cold is beter or geting beter now but the wether is so cold i have not much nues i never go far frim hom i will expect to here soon frim you both and ever thing go well with both frim your Mither

A Ramsay

Ramsay was defeated at Leicester.

The Midland Free Press
6 October

LEICESTER'S CHOICE
BROADHURST AND ROLLESTON
"UNNATURAL ALLIANCE."
KHAKI AND OTHER DODGES OUST HAZELL

Mr. Henry Broadhurst (L.) 10,385
Sir John Rolleston (C.) 9,066
Mr. Walter Hazell (L) 8,528
Mr. J.R. Macdonald (I.L.P.) 4,164

The election of two Parliamentary representatives for the borough of Leicester in 1900 will be writ large on history's page, seeing that the result of a short and sharp contest was arrived at on Tuesday as given above. Polling in earnest from 8 a.m. to 8 p.m., no fewer than 20,812 Leicester electors recorded their votes, out of a total number on the register of 24,760, and by a curious mixture of favours for which a certain section were responsible that solidarity of Liberalism for which the borough has long distinguished itself has been upheaved.

Margaret often went out of London to attend meetings and speak on behalf of her women's committees . . .

꙰ Ramsay to Margaret.

Wednesday 1900
The Speedwell Commercial Hotel
Portsmouth

Our dear Mammie,

We are having, oh such a fine time . . . Then one of us had to go away &
left the other with Gurling & since then we have not seen each other, but we
are going to. We both understood that we were to be away until next
morning.

The one who went away had a very good meeting, but as his lecture was
sandwiched into the middle of a concert of sacred songs & comic
recitations, it was rather trying. But we are both trusting that the mammie
will uphold the reputation of the family on the platform.

We are pitying our poor mammie away from us. She must be having a
lonely time & we are enjoying ourselves so much. "Back again, mammie".
But we hope she is not forgetting us altogether & that she is reminding her
friends "from all parts of the country" as the papers are saying, of our
existence by a liberal distribution of our regards and love. "Back again,
Mammie"

Thy Two

꙰ Ramsay to Margaret.

30 January 1901
Wellington Hotel
Manchester
(Trades' Council)

Thine Own to Mine Own

Here I am solitary and alone. The others have gone to the Pantomime & I
am waiting until eight o'clock summons me to the Trades Council. How is
my widder and my orfan boy? I expect they are getting on wonderfully well
despite their bereavement. They have a way of buoying themselves up in
anticipation of coming meetings. I hope you are counting the hours that lie
between us and Leicestery. It is so nice for me to think of my "property".
Perhaps my "property" is darning or sewing on buttons. I am looking after
the affairs of state. We have talked a lot & done some business. The NAC
(or such members as have been present) do not like the ILP resolutions put
down on the Labour Repres: Conference Agenda:

239

Has Little It said "Blessie Daddie"! and did he sleep this morning? How did you succeed with the ladies who love darkness rather than light in Hornsey?

> Ever thine
> You know whom.

Margaret decided to go to Lossiemouth for her second confinement.

~ Annie Ramsay to Margaret.

> Sunday morning [? July] 1901
> Thee Cottage
> Lossiemouth

My Dear Margaret

i have a Mackintosh sheet a good sise so do not bring wun up nor nothing hare then you have as i have so much here and if we want any thing better to get them as it is all wun to you They will be kept all right to you and i have such a houst of things. i do not now about spilling Alister i never spilled a child and i will try and do to him your way only he will have liberty here Dear little boy i am looking forward to do my best to you all i hope you will be well and have a good jurny here and i will be glad to met you at Elgin and spek fir a cab at Lossie to met there . .

> Frim your Mither
> AR.

~ Ramsay to Margaret.

> 24 July 1901
> 3 Lincoln's Inn Fields

I hope you will tell me how you got up & whether Little It was a goody boy, or whether he or the old lady was the more talkative, & if anyone got into the carriage, or if you had all for your ticket & a half. Then you will have to tell me about mother, the house and the garden. With many so & so thoughts for you & Little It and the others, and the usual dutiful message to mother.

> Every thine
> R

〜 Ramsay to Margaret.

26 July 1901
Labour Representation Committee

My Dear Wandering Sheep or Ewe Lamb

Nightie-Nightie! Blessie (interval of 7½ hours) Morning! Blessie! But there was no little They about so I got up and had my solitary hot water for breakfast on the advice of Dr Munro.

But when I got home I found your nice little card awaiting me. I hope you are all fit and fair this morning. Tell Little It that his poor Daddie is thinking of him – and of nobody else . . .

Ever R

〜 Ramsay to Margaret.

27 July 1901
L.R.C.
3 Lincoln's Inn Fields

Dear Madam

Your little letter was so late in coming today that I thought Selina [the expected baby] had taken time by the forelock. I posted an *Echo* to you yesterday but it refused to go away. I have persuaded it this time, I think.

I am not leaving on Wednesday but on Saturday because Lawrence wants me to work out the week at the *Echo* & if I am to go up with the ordinary tourist ticket, I may as well make five guineas here and go up three days later. Besides I shall stand you and Little It a drive to Elgin. I shall arrive at 1.7 by the Highland Railway on Sunday & you might drive up and meet me in some dog cart affair if it be fine, but at any rate you might arrange to have me met. If it is not fine you might come up in a cab. The great thing for you in Lossiemouth is to keep decent. John Moir is all right & Robbie Ried, but confine your attentions to a few & let them be aged. London is different. Here one can use liberties . . .

Nightie! Nightie! Morning! Morning!
Thine
R

I wrote you ever so many nice things & hope you have had them.

〜 Ramsay to Margaret.

> 31 July 1901
> L.R.C.
> 3 Lincoln's Inn Fields

My Dear Missus,

Oh yes I read the long letter. How could I do otherwise? Business first (1) You need not ask Cousin John for money, just at present (2) If you do not go to the kirk what was the use of my getting a new surtout? (3) Do you know of anyone who will play golf with me on Monday?

I have bought a hat and got my hair cut. How the money goes. Now I must buy a pair of light golfing shoes so that I need not take up the heavy ones on Saturday.

I think this is all but Mrs Tipping has come back.

> Bringing home her Tommy
> Whilst my family all-alack
> Have skeedadled from me.

The usual endings are all here attached.

> Ever thine
> R.

〜 Ramsay to Margaret.

> 2 August 1901
> L.R.C.
> 3 Lincoln's Inn Fields

Ma Chère Marguareet,

I have an appointment with a young girl on Sunday, so if I do not turn up at Elgin you will understand. I suppose you will not mind very much as the drive will do you good and we shall meet later at any rate.

Supposing I put in an appearance on Sunday morning. Please take with you:-

1) Brown's Family Bible-10 vols — I want to read it on the way down.
2) Last week's washing. I want to see how it is done.
3) Some pens and ink and paper. I want to write poetry.
4) The garden. I want to see how it looks.
5) The washtub. I want to see if it will do as a bath.
6) Dr Fairbairn. I have an introduction to him.
7) The Golf House. I want to arrange for a partner.

There are one or two other small things but you might manage to put these under the seat. But at any rate don't hire another conveyance.

With kisses all round and many gratitudes for Timothy's most readable epistle.

> Thine
> R.

∾ Ramsay to Margaret.

> 10 August 1901
> 3 Lincoln's Inn Fields

Mine Own Onnie

Somebody went away'way with an ache from the two who came to see him off at Elgin, and all the way along the hills looked so sad, that somebodys ache was very bad. He left something behind him for long four weeks. It wasn't nice at all to leave Mammie and Little It. But the journey hasn't been at all bad as journeys go.

I am sending you the *Daily News* and the *Labour Leader*. No more just now, but I hope my onnies are very well & had a nice day at the Cathedral yesterday.

With love and kisses to you all including Isobel Allan and Malcolm John alias Selina [all names for the imminent arrival].

> Ever thine
> R.

∾ Ramsay to Margaret.

> 12 August 1901
> 3 Lincoln's Inn Fields

My Dear Onnie

Morning to Mammie! Morning to Alister! Morning to the others! I had such a nice day yesterday out at Tottenham. Fortunately no one was at home except Alice and we had a very pleasant time. This is one of her new tales of women and their ways. Scene Southampton last Spring Miss Petty being a visitor at the house of a Dr Roger there. Enter Miss Mee, 60 years of age and a proper conservative. They discover a mutual friend, Dr R. And there is another mutual friend. Miss Petty knows Mr MacDonald – you remember, Miss Mee, the man who was the terrible radical.

Miss Mee. Oh! Don't mention it, my dear doctor. He was an awful person. Surely Miss Petty does not know him, or if she does I hope she does not agree with him.

Miss Petty. Oh! We know him very well. He is not at all so bad as you think he is.

243

Miss Mee. Well! I think there <u>was</u> something peculiar about him. Wasn't he the Radical who married a lady?

With many kisses to you all,

Ever thine
R.

∾ Ramsay to Margaret.

13 August 1901
3 Lincoln's Inn Fields

My Dear Missus

Morning again to you all. And with the morning comes your very nice letter. I am getting through such a fine lot of work & shall be able to go to Leicester, I hope, in some peace of mind, though these lectures are a great fag.

I am reading about American diplomacy and so you may understand that I am up to the tricks of the trade. I am glad that Providence has shown himself once again to be no papist in Scotland.

I wish I were in Lossie but I am not, but still I can send little and big kisses to you all round – thems that are and thems that are not.

Ever thine
R.

∾ Ramsay to Margaret.

14 August 1901
3 Lincoln's Inn Fields

My Dear Missus

Yours came tripping in just like a Lossieite, raw and blooming. It would take off its coat itself and in the tussle I had to split it open with my thumb. It said it did not bargain for such usage and did not think you would have approved. But in its pocket there were a note from you which was pleasant, one from Bella which was laconically like her ending with a sniff, & another with an unfulfillable prophesy at its top. But in all those letters there is a little wizard who jumps out, waves a wand & says to London:- "Hey prest! be gone. This is Lossiemouth". Funny, isn't it? I must report to Effie [Johnson] and the Psychical Research. There's something uncanny in it. I struggle along & hope to be pretty well on before I leave for Leicester on Saturday. Did you get the Factory Inspector's Report? Coates is doing Box and Cox tricks again. I have not sent the Consolidating Bill. It seemed so useless and it was so easy to follow in the newspapers. I'll send it when it gets printed as it went through the Commons last night. That will likely be tomorrow or the next day. Now I have written you a very long letter and like a sow return to my wallowing in the mire of American diplomacy and English History.

With love and kisses to you all
Thine R.

Washing has not been sent for. Can you write? Give me a better idea of what biography you want.

✎ Ramsay to Margaret.

16 August 1901
3 Lincoln's Inn Fields

My Missus Dear,

There is nothing at all today except love. Let it be Isobel or Isabel and if Allan let it be A not E. I do not know that Malcolm is the best burden we could place on his back if it be his. Can't you write a list of tolerable names and send them on? Mrs Harris[1] and I shall vote on them! . . . And perhaps call in Wynne should there be a tie! Why don't you accept all you get – Hammocks etc., Thank Providence, and think well of your husband? Have finished & am now posting my review and am today looking up Wisdom for Leicester gassifying. Little It as the Apostle Paul is rather secularising the scriptures.

Now all love & kisses & blessies & nighties

Ever thine
R.

✎ Ramsay to Margaret.

17 August 1901
3 Lincoln's Inn Fields

My Dear Inmate of a bed of sickness.

The monkey [baby] was in a beastly hurry. Did it come on the street or at a fashionable tea-party? Your letter and its telegram came together this morning. How does Alister take it? And now I must pitch the news at Mrs Harris' head. Perhaps it is better as it has happened for a telegram reaching me in the middle of a peroration at a street corner might have upset my chances. I suppose there was no tag upon it with a name. Is it like Alister,

---

1. His landlady in Leicester.

or you, or Billie, or Aunt Agnes, or any of the departed ones? I suppose in time I will have all the particulars. Meanwhile take the Lossie air lying quietly in bed. The next good news I look for is that you have got up and have flopped into the hammock. I am now waiting for further news of your well-being. There are three persons now who have to draw upon my store of Mornings! Nighties! Blessies! and those little X X X's. Distribute these commodities fairly and send me reports in due course.

Ever thine
R.

❧ Ramsay to Margaret.

18 August 1901
Leicester

Up in my room the staircase echoing & re-echoing the billing and cooing of the Harris turtles. My matronly one How is it? – the cradled it and the bedded it and also the She. Mrs Harris blushed visibly and Mr Harris was not at home to keep her in countenance & when he came home I blushed and we all blushed and went on eating as fast as we could. Cox came with flowers thinking you might be with me, but none of us screwed up courage to tell of the unfortunate accident. We shall content ourselves by announcing it from the platform this evening so that, Little –? may have . . . a fair start.

Tell us all about the monkey, if it has teeth & hair or can walk or squalls or smiles or what; and with my usual daily allowance of good things to you all,

I am, Thine ever
R.

❧ Ramsay to Margaret.

19 August 1901
Leicester

My Dear Mammie multiplied by two, Mrs Harris and I are having very nice times, & I am only sorry that we are only to be a week under the same roof. We both think of being in your bed of pain & sickness and sympathise with you as one human being ought to sympathise with another, and we both take the moral view of hoping that you may be blessed to feel the compensations which always accompany pain if we could only see them. We have not seen your special compensation & Mrs Harris thinks that she will remain faithful to Alister, but she thinks Malcolm would be a pretty name and might have the effect of endearing the bearer to her heart. But we are benefiting by your absence. Cox came on Saturday with a fine boquet of sweet peas and presented them to Mrs Harris in your absence; and then yesterday, one of the most gorgeous boquets ever invented appeared at the meeting and the poor man was so disappointed that there was no stout little missus to receive it. But we consoled him so here we are sitting in bowers of flowers & the atmosphere laden with the perfume. The meeting yesterday was magnificent . . . But alas! my poor throat today is truly awful & I do not [know] what is in front of me. I spoke for just over an hour and the collection was the record for the Square, £2.5.0. We also made converts.

And now with the usual enclosures, I am

Thine ever. R.

∾ Ramsay to Margaret.

20 August 1901
L.R.C.
3 Lincoln's Inn Fields

My Dear Missus,

The news has gone around like wildfire. Envious people of all kinds come up to congratulate you on the triumph of the "blinking laddie" but I ask them to wait and give personal delivery. No letter has come from you this morning yet, so I do not know how you are getting on. I send two things which are evidently the first perquisites of a Times Advertisement.

Good meeting last night, but very hoarse.

Am sending post.

The usual enclosures.
Yours Ever
R.

TELEGRAM

Handed in at: SPEEN AUGUST 19 1901 @ 11.23. Received 12.42 pm.

To:- Master MacDonald Junior Lossiemouth
Hearty welcome from the great Aunts.

∾ Ramsay to Margaret.

> 21 August 1901
> L.R.C.
> Lincoln's Inn Fields

My Dear Missus

As you seem to be so interested in your Littlest It and white fish I shall not trouble you with a long letter. We all sympathised very much with Little It compelled to pass a sleepless night with a teething infant and we all agree with him that it should have been put down in the kitchen under the table or somewhere else where its howls would not have been heard. When Alister can endure life no longer under such conditions Mrs Harris says he may come to her. You will be interested to know that Mrs Shirley is sufficiently interested in me to make advances for an introduction. She has got so far as Amos Sherriff, so she is not far off now.

The Mission is very well, thank you, but the missionary is sadly hoarse. Yesterday at a garden party at the house of the wife of Robert Raithby, I had to hint to a nice young lady dressed in white – boots and all – that she had not heard my sweet voice. I send the papers. They speak of "Fair" meetings. The fact is, we never had such meetings even at the General Election. Last night again there must have been a 1000 present on the open space by the West Bridge – the bridge we cross to Raithby's. The crowd went out into the street and, what is more, it stood for an hour and the collection was over 12/-: If Malcolm was a decent person, let the crittur have it.

> Ever thine
> R.

∾ Ramsay to Margaret.

> 22 August 1901
> L.R.C.
> 3 Lincoln's Inn Fields

My Dear Image of the Second Son,

Be thy kingdom everlasting and thy hammock speedily used. We had another fine meeting last night & I am holding out very well though hoarse, the Harrises being fairly good to me. This afternoon I am going to a tea party of ladies at Gee's to discuss the holding of a big bazaar next year with big guns to open it, e.g. Lady Kelvin, Countess of Warwick & Mrs J.R. MacDonald (Family permitting) on the third day. I hardly think the Liberals will meet us and we shall have to consider what is to be done in that event.

The conference will be held most likely in September. Poor little Malcolm John – so unlike the beautiful Alister. His lot will be hard, however sweet his disposition may be. Squealing like a cat too! Does he squeal more than Alister? Will you be able to meet me in Elgin leaving Gimcrack [Malcolm] behind us as we shall have plenty of luggage? But we shall see about these things later on. Kindest regards to Dr Brander[1] etc., love to the household and the usual enclosure to the family.

Ever thine
R.

~ Ramsay to Margaret.

23 August 1901
L.R.C.
3 Lincoln's Inn Fields

My Dear Real Lidy

I am afraid another Selina has come as I have had no letter from you this morning. . .

~ Ramsay to Margaret.

24 August 1901
L.R.C.
3 Lincoln's Inn Fields

My Dear Missus

The mission is now practically finished and it has been thoroughly successful. We expect a big crowd in the Market Square tomorrow evening. Tchonnie [Malcolm] I suppose does not interest himself in these things yet. I gather from your letter that he does howl more than Alister and . . . that there is another feature he has in common with the other side of the house.

Tell Alister that his heather is very nice and refreshing and that his Daddie appreciates it very much. I am going to see the Harris's palace this afternoon. It is a few doors from their present gate nearer the station, and Mrs Harris is specially proud of it. But there is not much chance of you seeing it for a long time as you are not to be invited because Tchonnie is not like me.

Yours ever
R.

---

1. The doctor who delivered the baby.

❧ Ramsay to Margaret.

> 26 August 1901
> L.R.C.
> 3 Lincoln's Inn Fields

My Dear Missus

Only a short note again as I have to go out & may not be back before 6pm. Have got back to London, Mrs Harris falling on my neck and weeping as I left. Everything went well in Leicester. It poured from 5 until 6.15 but after that about three or four thousand came out & the fishermen collected £13. Total in Leicester £32. At 8pm we had our meeting and about 1000 stopped through rain.

With the usual

> Thine ever R
> GAVIN is a good name.

❧ Ramsay to Margaret.

> 27 August 1901
> L.R.C.
> 3 Lincoln's Inn Fields

My Dear Missus

I am settling down in my own nest like a cuckoo after elbowing Timothy and his brother Grimalkin out into the cold world. But so long as Mrs Gurling is pleasant and ministers faithfully to my wants, I see no reason to repent of my sins. Nor have I time for affairs of conscience. There is much to be done before I take my departure for Swansea.[1] There is no letter from you up to the time of writing. And how is Grimalkin's little squeal? Is he going to be as good as his predecessor or is he not to be one of whom you can boast? Mrs Gurling sent off a mysterious parcel yesterday the contents of which she would not divulge. I hope you got it. Are Mother, Kitty and the rest behaving with propriety, and does the village observe due decorum? Or is it like a hen with a hatched egg in the middle of many addled ones? How the days draw on to the end of my very pleasant holiday.

Give them all my love & kiss the proper ones for their Daddy and her sir. Hope you can come up *unencumbered* on Friday week with Little It to show you round and protect you generally. Do you want me to take up any books or anything short of London or the household furniture?

> Ever Thine
> R.

1. To the Trades Union Congress.

∞ Ramsay to Margaret.

> 28 August 1901
> L.R.C.
> 3 Lincoln's Inn Fields

My Dear Missus

The whisky is here & when you get up today you can drink it in imagination until you grow a sixth finger and an inability to count it. Malcolm no doubt has memories and however unbounded his generosity might have been had we been in his own house, he had to keep himself severely in check in the midst of strangers. Didn't you notice his Daddie's spook dancing round about? You don't mention it. It is there but perhaps was not so forward as to obtrude and intrude. Of course I answered Miss Irwin & all the other ladies except Jennie who having been so mean as to come when I was away will have to be content with a note from her own sec.

I hear this morning that N.E. Lanark is likely to be fought by us. What price holiday then? I ought to be there. The place ought to be fought, however. But you will know more than I do as you see the *Scotsman*.

With all the usual mornings! blessies! and nighties! to the Wiffie and the increased family and love and regards to the nurses and the more remote friends.

> Yours ever
> R.

∞ Ramsay to Margaret.

> 29 August 1901
> L.R.C.
> 3 Lincoln's Inn Fields

My Dear Missus

I saw Mead last night. He has just returned to town and is full of interesting interviews with all kinds of people on the Continent which all go to confirm the sad fact that we are getting more and more detested and despised. But when I was returning I had a much more interesting meeting still – the fair Miss Dodd on the stairs going to the post. I am going up tomorrow evening and hope to drink coffee with them and gossip. Presumably the *Daily Chronicle* wants you to write in its controversy on the decay of domesticity and if you have anything to say, it might not be bad. It is of the greatest importance at the present moment to keep before the

251

public and the discussion seems to be well carried on so far as the principal writers are concerned. The *Daily News* was the only paper I saw with comments on the Leicester campaign. Now I am off to the B.M. for my lectures. I am forging ahead with them & shall bring them to Lossiemouth practically finished I hope.

With much love to you and the brethren.

Yours ever

R.

∾ Ramsay to Margaret.

30 August 1901

L.R.C.

3 Lincoln's Inn Fields

Mine Own Missus & Poet

I fear we must put up with it. Grimalkin's hunger is but another link between him and the other side of the house[1] where appetite is a strong point. This is my last day here and work is far from finished. I must finish a full syllabub for the lectures together with a bibliography before getting to Scotland. The Leicester Mission was really a very great nuisance coming as it did.

Then the *Echo* marches in again with a smiling face but a troublesome proposal. Lawrence came here yesterday to ask me to be their special correspondent for the Congress which means an article wired up every night and £1 an article. But that means me staying at Swansea until Friday at any rate. I am to hear more definitely to day. But I cannot see how I can refuse the job in the present state of finances. Further he was sounding me out about regular work. "If Hammond goes, would I write the first article every morning at about £2 per week?" It would only be twenty minutes work at the outside. "Or would I go in three days a week at a pound if that were arranged?" If the former arrangement is accepted it would be on the condition that I have frequent Monday mornings off as he is anxious that my lecturing work should not be interrupted, and other breaks could always be arranged for e.g. long holidays & N.A.C. meetings. All that I could say was that I wanted more work and that any offer they might make would be carefully considered. I mentioned our desire to return to America once more before age came & we could not enjoy things and seeing things and taking in new . . . impressions, and he said that the arrangement would be between friends in that respect & that I might give them quid pro quo. So

---

1. Malcolm is a Gladstone!

there it rests. You will know at the beginning of the week when to expect me.

Love to you all

> Thine ever
> R.

⁓ Ramsay to Margaret.

> 1 September 1901
> Hotel Metropole
> Swansea
> Trades Union Congress

My Dear Missus

I have had a very nice breakfast with Ben Pickard.[1] We were very friendly and he told me all about his meals. He has had a very bad appetite this morning and was quite in the dumps because he could only eat a sole, a chop and two or three peaches, toast, coffee & a large soda and milk. We also talked politics and I find that whilst he is personally very favourable he is not well inclined towards us collectively.

With love to the boys & their guardian and parent.

> Ever thine
> R.

⁓ Ramsay to Margaret.

> 3 September 1901
> T.U.C.
> Swansea

Mine Own Missus

. . . Ben Pickard has been telling me all about his dead missus. He hates Hardie and will have nothing to do with us. The Congress is rather dull up to now and it is more evidently than ever bossed.

The feasting is worse than ever. Mrs Dilke's[2] tea party is now going on and there is a banquet tonight. Sir George Newnes gave a garden party yesterday and gave silver watches, marble clocks etc., to his constituents as prizes.

"Letters for the North" says Boots

> Yours ever
> J.R.
> Love to boys.

---

1. Miners' leader and Lib-Lab MP.
2. Daughter of Sir Samuel, and a close friend of Margaret.

∾ Ramsay to Margaret.

4 September 1901
Hotel Metropole
Swansea

Mine Own Onnie

The die is cast and I must remain. There is to be a great debate on Labour Representation either on Thursday or Friday, My holidays vanish for I am pretty certain to be wanted in North East Lanark. We are having a good time . . . and a busy one, and among my other interests is button-holing delegates and trying to get them to vote for Leicester for next Congress.

I enjoy your hammock doings and wish I were up. Is Timothy quite black & gypsy or only so-so? Is Grimalkin a sint or what? Give them all my love & my kisses, keeping some of both for yourself.

Yours ever
R.

∾ Ramsay to Margaret.

5 September 1901

"In the hall"

. . . very busy and have to remain here watchful. I did not write to you this morning because I wanted to see the docks and though I have been here since Saturday I have hardly seen the town at all.

Love to the boys.

Yours ever
R.

∾ Margaret to Agnes King.

18 September 1901

[Malcolm] is like a crab with goggle eyes. He is supposed to look like me.

After her return home to Lincoln's Inn Fields she took the children to visit her King aunts. . .

254

❧ Ramsay to Margaret.

19 October 1901
3 Lincoln's Inn Fields

Mine Own Missus

I hope that you and the little flock of sons got down alright. You had hardly gone when Uncle George came demanding to view the new arrival [Malcolm] and he was very disappointed to find the nest empty. We gossiped about the war, however, and under the circumstances had a good time. Otherwise, nothing has happened worthy of standing between you and your aunt's gossip for a single minute.

Ever thine
R.

The Evening Express 26 Nov 01
A MORAYSHIRE MAN ON LONDON COUNTY COUNCIL

The London correspondent of the "Aberdeen Daily Journal" writes:- Mr James Ramsay MacDonald, who has just been returned to the London County Council for Finsbury, is a north country man hailing, I believe from Elgin. He is not to be confused with Mr James MacDonald, the secretary of the London Trades Council, who may be remembered by your townspeople as an active worker on behalf of Mr Tom Mann a few years ago. Mr J.R. MacDonald is a very different personality. He was a school teacher in the north until 1888, when he came to London as a private secretary to Mr Thomas Lough then Liberal candidate for West Islington. He afterwards joined . . . the Fabian Society and became a fellow-worker with Mr George Bernard Shaw. Like Mr Shaw he became a vegetarian and at one period he endeavoured to convince people that they would be healthier and happier if they would abjure chops and steaks and live on fruit, pies, and fruitcakes. He actually embarked on a business of this kind but it failed. He also held extraordinary ideas regarding dress, and used to attract a good deal of attention as he walked along the street, owing to his peculiar attire. Some years ago he married a Miss Gladstone, and since then he has dressed and behaved like ordinary mortals.

∾ Annie Campbell to Margaret.

> 28 November 1901
> Tenby Cottage
> West Pilmuir Forres

My Dear niece Margaret

I am much pleased with good news in your letter allow me to congratulate you both on Ramsay success. I hope he may be the means of improving the condition of the inhabitants of Central Finsbury by his service I think it is something he will like to do I wish him all success. I am glad to hear of the welfare of the bairns God bless them Kiss them both for me.

I intend to go to Lossiemouth in a few days I trust Annie and I will be helps to each other in the short dark days. I cannot do much but Female like I can talk.

With much to you all

> Your loving Aunt
> Anne A Campbell.

I.L.P. Leicester
Programme for 1901

3 February
> Mrs J.R. MacDonald to talk on
> Commercialism and Child Labour.

∾ Ramsay to Margaret.

> Sabbath 25 May 1902
> Imperial Hotel
> Wolverhampton

My Dearest Missus

Just a line in haste to say that you and he looked very nice yesterday morning.

That's all except love to you all & that meetings are good.

> Ever thine
> R.

∾ Alister & Malcolm to Margaret.

[after July 20] 1902

Our Dear Mammie,

We are very angry with Daddie as we did think of your birthday & told Daddie what to get for us for you. Many birthdays.

Your obediant servants especially when one of us has the bokkle

Alister

xx   Malcolm   xx

In August Margaret and Ramsay sailed off to South Africa, while the children were sent to stay with their grandmother in Lossiemouth.

South African News August 20th 1902

Labour Politics in Britain.
Arrival of Mr J.R. MacDonald, L.C.C.

Among the arrivals by the *Scot* are Mr J.R. MacDonald and Mrs MacDonald. Mr MacDonald's name will not be new to readers who follow British Labour politics, nor that of Mrs MacDonald to those who concern themselves with the various associations of women's workers of Britain. Mr MacDonald is a well-known literary man & a member of the London County Council. He is upon two of the most important committees of that body – the Technical Education Board and the Asylums Committee. He is also a member of the National Executive of the Independent Labour Party and Secretary of an association which he remarked in the course of a conversation with a representative of the *South African News* "represents the most interesting departure in Labour politics in Britain in recent years".

This is the:- Labour Representation Committee, which was formed in 1900 as a result of a vote taken at The Trades Union Congress the previous year. An attempt was made to unite co-operators, Socialists and trade unionists for the purpose of Parliamentary action. A conference was held for this purpose. The co-operators failed to take any great interest in the movement but the Socialists and the Trades Unionists put in considerable representation and the committee was started. The growth of the movement has been phenominal. Some of the older Trades Unions predicted that it would not number 5000 members at the end of five years. As a matter of fact it has a membership in about two years of three quarters of a million.

〰 Annie Ramsay to Margaret.

> Thursday morning (21 August] 1902
> Thee Cottage
> Lossiemouth

My Dear Margaret

We are geting on very well the children his had colds but i do not now how thay have gotten them i never let them visit with any wun because we have not 2 howers like wun worm and the next bitter cold. i had a letter from your Aunts non from Flo and a paper frim Hardie M.P. with much love frim your mither

> A Ramsay

〰 Annie Ramsay to Ramsay & Margaret.

Wendsay 1902

My dear Ramsay & Margaret

i am sure you will be thinking long to here from me the children are all well and happy Alistiar is in his glory only we have cold wether we war on the sands yesterday but today we wear not out of the garden the wind so cold in the afternoon with love from your Mither

> A Ramsay

〰 Margaret to Annie Ramsay.

> 26 September 1902
> St George's Hotel
> Maritzburg

My Dear Mother

We have been seeing so many Lossiemouth friends since we last wrote that I must just tell you shortly about them, and leave further accounts till we meet. At Johannesburg we saw James Denoon, and spent an evening with William Denoon & his wife and James Denoon took us round to see Miss Reid's sister, Mrs Lowe, one morning. It was just our last day there and we were sorry we had not known where she was earlier so that we might have spent a little longer with her. Then we saw George Denoon and his wife and baby at Pretoria & had tea with them in their pretty little new house there. Now we have just come from Durban where we spent part of a day with Mr and Mrs John Galt out at Mount Edgecombe where he has been station-master for six years, but which he is leaving shortly to try for work in the Transvaal. We went over a sugar factory there and Mr Galt got the foreman to give us some white sugar in a bag which we had seen made ourselves, & you must tell Alister we are bringing it home for him and Malcolm & will tell him how we saw the sugar cane growing in the fields and the black people cutting it and taking it to the mill where the juice was crushed out in a big machine with rollers and then boiled and purified till at last we saw it put as a sticky mass in a round pan and whirled round very quickly for a few minutes and then when the machinery stopped there was nice white sugar which we are bringing him.

We saw some of the Armstrongs too at Durban. Ramsay says you will know which ones if I say it was Jimmy Armstrong's family that used to be in the lane; old Mr & Mrs Armstrong & their son Willie & his wife and child and a younger son who was born out here. Some of the others we had not time to see. Of course they were all very pleased to hear about Lossiemouth and sent their remembrances to you and other friends there.

We have had two letters from you and Alister since we last wrote: One of the English Mails seems to have been delayed, as we got both your letters & those from London a week late. We are glad to hear that you are all keeping well & hope that the children have not had colds again. Please thank Alister for his letters and for the forget-me-nots he sent, & thank you too for the newspaper cuttings.

I am glad Malcolm's teeth are not troubling him. We feel as if we were on our way back now, as more than half our time here has passed. We have found it very interesting and have been very fortunate in our weather & we have both kept quite well. We expect to have some more driving before we get home, as we have arranged for carts across part of the Orange River Colony & hope to see some more of the farmers; but both there & especially in the Transvaal it is very difficult to get about as the country is so destroyed that there is no accommodation or food. The people who are going back to their farms have to live in tents till they can get their buildings which have been burnt covered in, and the cattle & the means of transport and the food of all kinds are very difficult to get. In the towns it is almost as difficult to get lodging and food as the people are crowding in and everything is very dear.

Now I must put some kisses for Alister and Malcolm. We saw the sea, of course, at Durban and now we shall not see it again till we get to Cape Town as we shall be up country all the time. Here is a picture of the little carriage which the Zulus draw here in the streets and which many people use instead of cabs or trams; they are called rickshaws. I am afraid I haven't drawn the man who is pulling the rickshaw so that you can tell he is a man.

In Durban many of them wear big ox horns on their heads and deck themselves out in all sorts of bright coloured feathers and flowers . . . . .

On 6 October John Gladstone died; Margaret and Ramsay came home a few weeks later.

∾ Lily Montagu to Margaret.

4 November [1902]

My Dear Margaret

I fear it will be a sad home coming for you, but I should like to be one of these to wish you & the God-Son a welcome. This note is my deputy. Your father's death which all workers would desire & I am sure that for him you can only rejoice. But separation from that friend must be hard to bear and you must face a severe wrench with much happiness connected with life which has so beautifully ended. It is I expect a great deal though to feel wanted & you are dreadfully wanted, not only by the obvious people J.R.M. and the stalwart sons but by heaps and heaps of creatures who, some perhaps without having seen you have learned to know you as a friend.

Life has been very full for me & I have many hopes for the year. It is not the slightest use beginning to tell you about schemes for they are too numerous – one day I will send you book to read – people were kind enough to put me on the NUWW Executive so I shall see you occasionally on committees and that's so inspiring.

Goodbye dearie. I am very glad you have come [?home]

Love to you both from your friend
Lily M [ontagu]

∾ Bessie to Margaret.

10 November 1902
191 Rue de l'Université

Dear Maggie

I suppose you will soon be at home again now; and unfortunately you will find a great change. One can hardly believe even yet that Papa has gone to a better world & that our old home is closed for ever. It was better for him that he should have been called away suddenly; but it is hard for you to come back & find all the past finished and done with – though it would not be forgotten. We shall appreciate Papa's character more and more as time goes on; what he lacked chiefly was the power of putting himself into right contact with his fellow men and making his influence felt.

I was over in England for nearly three weeks, helping Flo in the first pressure of work. But much remains to be done. She will have much sorting out of letters & family papers in which you can help her; she will also have much to do settling into her new house [Chepstow Villas].

> I remain
> Yr affect^{ly}   .
> E.A. Bach

∾ Wilfred M. Hunt to Margaret.

> 25 November 1902
> 6 New Court
> Lincoln's Inn

Dear Margaret

I was very sorry indeed to hear of your father's sudden death and I must express to you my sincere sympathy with you in your great loss.

As to business matters; the annuity of £300 per annum, payable by your father to you under your marriage settlement, ceased on his death.

Perhaps, I should also give you a word of warning on one point viz. not to launch out on new expenses during this the 1st year after your father's death. Under his will (a copy of which you [have] no doubt seen), £15,000 is payable to your settlement trustees and when paid you will be entitled to the interests & dividends thereafter produced thereby. But the executors need not pay this sum for a year after your father's death . . .

> Your affectionate cousin
> Wilfred M. Hunt

∾ Annie Ramsay to Ramsay.

> 4 February 1903
> thee cottage
> Lossiemouth

My Dear Ramsay

I am soory to sea by yu letter this morning of Margaret having Measels thay are verry traying in old but it will be a winder if som of the cheldren dis not toke them I will be verry anxious to here of you all. we have verry strong wind here fir som day and every thing blin out of the ground I have sent a few frish eggs . . . I hope thay will not get briken Margareet might enjoy som of them I could not get fish and the Hadek is not good but if the boats is out I will tray and get whitens My leg is geting strung now and I am feeling much better only I cannot do much at the Misheen nor I may never with my back

> With love frim Mither
> A Ramsay

✑ Ramsay to Margaret.

> Thursday 1903
> 3 Lincoln's Inn Fields

Missus,

Does the measly children mean that we cannot go to Pembridge Square at Christmas?

I suppose a cold welcome will await me when Mrs Collins will howl "She's gone with another".

✑ Annie Ramsay to Ramsay.

> 1 February 1903
> The Cottage
> Lossiemouth

My Dear Ramsay

I have been down at Mrs Stuarts and I do not feel my leg any the worse Mrs Stuart wants me if I can come down to mirrow to the serves at 1 oclock thay are to be luft at 2 I shall be plased to tray and go down in saterday that though[t] Mrs Stuart was to be frist but she is a little better now but is stil in bed. . . she will tray to be lufted to sea his remains to night when the house is quite thay spoke of wiring you but that could get no right answers frim hir but it wis night before thay sent me word so i did not now then if thay sent word or not he was so ill for days thay could not get him keep down but he feel quite & slapt away he is just like wun in his Slep the church was taken last night and Mr Roberson his all the Elders and dickens to tea to nigh Mr Allan cam over to sea if I hard any thing ring fir the Provist and James Doonen was running about so much this morning I do not think thay are any feer of it but I will tak no hand in it fir I am not able to bothr any way will do me With love to all frim yu Mither

AR

❧ Ramsay to Margaret.

> 18 February 1903
> Norfolk Hotel
> Newcastle-on-Tyne

Mine Own Missus

Just a line from my exile to say that I got into it alright, that a crowd of us went up, that we played cards all the way, that we had a poor meeting at Jarrow and that I am thinking of you and the little onnies.

> Ever thine
> R

Margaret was pregnant again, and was thinking of spending the summer after her confinement in Lossiemouth.

❧ Annie Ramsay to Margaret.

> Monday (?) 1903
> Thee Cottage
> Lossiemouth

My Dear Margaret

Your letter to hand this morning I am verry glad you think of cumming hom I am far better plased as I have all my things at hand and I shall get a string gural if possible fir the work and Magie Shand fir the children that is Janies sister I had with me when I was ill she is so quite and nice do war you think best I shall be plased Mrs Read is not moved yet but she is cleaning and expect to get the house let but little keeps hir bissy I do not now wat she will do with ludgers only I must get wun that will do all the work or nearly so fir July & August i will do my best No fear I will be glad to have you all here I am geting Kettie in to help cleaning next week everything will be down I can fir yu with love from Mither A Ramsay

My Dear Margaret

Many thanks i got my teath down but they do do not fit so i must go back i will not pay him till they fit they tell me how my face is so like Ramsay's with them in i send you 1 night gown and will bring the next with me . . .

> from your Mither with love to the rest
> A Ramsay

Ramsay to Margaret.

> 1 March 1903 Friday
> 88 Telford Road
> Inverness

My Dear Missus

I got up alright just in time to see the last of poor old Aunt [Annie Campbell]. I was over half an hour late & got in just before Dr Black. She had of course shrunk away a good deal and her smiling lively face was sadly changed.

Mother is here & the consequence is I can hardly get a word in edgewise about anything. For the twentieth time she is now telling about everybody and everything – all their ailments and manner of death.

I came back here about 5.30 with Uncle and John Fraser and when Fraser went I tried to get some information from Uncle about her last days, but it was really no good. So soon as he began Mother chimed in.

She has not left a silver sixpence – that also being a rather mysterious circumstance as she ought to have had a pound or two. Her funeral will cost seven or eight pounds & I have promised to stand in with Willie Duncan, Uncle and perhaps Sandy Campbell for the sum. Sandy Campbell did not come up to the funeral.

How are the little Onnies & how is school? I am hoping for much news when I cross the deep & reach Belfast.

> Ever thine
> R.

Ramsay to Florence Gladstone.

> 2 March 1903
> 3 Lincoln's Inn Fields

My Dear Flo

As is usual with us the express from heaven with its solitary passenger (this time in hat, hatpins and petticoats)[1] came some days before its advertised time, and we had not got rid of the already arrived encumberances. We were wondering if you could take them for a day or two until we get them carted further afield & if so whether we could send them to you or how?

---

1. Their daughter, named Ishbel Allan.

At the ILP Conference in April Ramsay was re-elected on to the executive, polling 116 votes to Hardie's 128. He addressed the Conference on the subject of the Railway Nationalisation Bill.

〜 Ramsay to Margaret.

[April] 1903
Crown Hotel
Knaresborough

Here Shallard[1] and I are at the first stage of our tramp. We have had an excellent conference but Bruce [Glasier] has been as bad a chairman as usual.

We stayed at a fine old hotel at York with rambling passages & upstairs and downstairs; & as there was a crowd of us together (something like Leicester) we have had a very merry time of it. But it is all over once more and I have come away laden with enquiries after you and wishes that you may be able to go to Cardiff next year. At half past one this morning the innocent Jowett[2] was shouldering the fire irons & marching round the room singing "We're all brothers", but as Mrs Hardie was there and Mrs Pankhurst had only just gone to bed, it was not quite true.

. . . And now how are our own little onnies from the drunkie onnie upwards? Give them all a likkle kiss for me & say I am longing to see them all so much. The same to yourself.

I hope my mother is enjoying herself and that the Oratorio was a success. Love to you both

Your person
R.

〜 Ramsay to Margaret.

? May 1903 Friday
The Hill Inn
Chapel le Dale

More moth eaten stockings have come but as we are wet through up to the knees small holes by the calves of the leg are as nothing. What a glorious day we have had! To begin with I slept last night from 9.30 pm to 7am & rose refreshed like a daisy. We started at 8 & walked over a hill between

---

1. George Shallard, a member of the ILP.
2. F. W. Jowett, later a Labour MP.

Keptlerwell & Arncliffe then up the valley, and over Pen-y-gent & down its precipices to Horton then over the spurs of Ingleborough here, arriving at 5.30. The wind has been biting cold and the snow has been whirling about our ears. But the day has been most successful – our best day hitherto.

Tell Alister how dutiful I think him to think of sending me his head, and how glad I am it was not necessary as I like best to see his head on his shoulders where I hope it will be when I see him on Tuesday. Kiss him and Malcolmie and tickle Ishbel for me. I hope Mother is also enjoying her stay in London & not getting homesick.

Love to all
Ever thine R.

In August Annie Ramsay was taken ill and went into hospital in Inverness. The whole family went up to Scotland.

  Ramsay to Margaret [in Inverness].

15 August 1903
Lossiemouth
Elgin

Dear Mrs MacDonald

We have had another very good night & have read a book on American Railways & another on the Manchester School, and are now about to turn to the Settlement of Wages, Local Government in England & Fox's Journal & Sir W. Molesworth's speeches. The rest of us are out in the garden enjoying ourselves. In consideration of our grannie's appetite we have been down at Mr Watt's & bought a box with 3 or 4 dozen farthing wine biscuits; it will go to Inverness today. If it is not delivered you will find it at the station.

We are all very glad to hear that Grannie goes on so well. There are many enquiries about her here and we answer them in proper style. Mrs Reid does very well for us and our washing has gone. We prefer our Daddie as a dispenser of good things rather than our Mammie – we esteem our Mammie nevertheless for the sake of her connections & the elephants they are to bring us. We are thankful. We close with kisses to Ishbel, Mammie, Grannie & Aunt Kate & we subscribe ourselves to be

Your affectionate
Fambly

New Year was spent in Lossie.

∽ Ramsay to Florence.

6 January 1904
Lossiemouth

The youngsters have been in great form and want Christmas weather and chocolate presents of which we had rather many (one very gorgeous one from George Cadbury) to last for ever. I am very glad we came up as it has done us all so much good . . . Last night we had a great function at which the town and its wife turned out — the opening of the Free Library to wit! I had to do the speechifying as "our respected fellow townsman". It was like the joy in heaven . . . when we got home a drunk wife — on invalid port — had called to congratulate Margaret on having such a husband, and in the emotion of her heart had let a jar of jam fall on the step. We were up to our ankles in jam!

Sometimes Ramsay 'babysat' while Margaret attended to her work.

∽ Ramsay to Margaret.

1903/4
3 Lincoln's Inn Fields

My Dearest Missus

I suppose you have been having a great petticoat day & that the leafy rustle of dresses has been soothing the piercing screams of the Creighton debate. Did they sit upon you unmercifully? Are you as thin as a pancake? Are you flattened as your latest hat? Are you snuffed out like a candle? are you silenced? the last one alone I think to be impossible and having thought of such a towering climax as proof positive that I am still a man of wild imagination. You will also see that you have smitten me with family mania (on your side) of asking questions. So put your arm in mine and let us stroll along. How do the girls look? (Flo, Lily and the rest I mean) What do you talk about? Which of the waiters has captivated your hearts? Whose bonnet do you envy most? Put those questions to an open vote & declare the result to me.

The family here seems to jog along with bottles, trains and jugs. It is always at home at meal time and always last at table. What more encouraging news do you want — except that it sends kisses and love to you and Flo & requests me to do the same (?) as by their presents.

Ever Thine
R.
XXXXXXX these Ishbel gave out.

In February Ramsay and Keir Hardie went to the Riviera for talks with Kruger (the former Boer president of South Africa) and to meet Italian socialists.

❧ Ramsay to Margaret.

> February 1904
> Hotel St Petersbourg
> Paris

My Dear Old Missus

Are you having a gay old time of it like me? Nobody in Paris can talk a word of English – especially the officials, but I daresay I shall plough along. When I got to the Strand I remembered that I had left the Paris guides behind me, but there was no time to return for them. So I came here as innocent as a child. Last night M. something or another of the Ministry of Commerce called and gave me the necessary introductions & today I start on my travels. I spent the evening with Bessie [Bach] in her panelled walls & in the midst of 17 Pembridge Square furniture. They are all well & had a little dinner party of one gentleman and two ladies – petit bourgeoisie et Alsace parsons. I think they talked mostly of their bellies and Bessie's greatness. Bessie however, was very nice, very nice indeed & it was quite a pleasure to look in. Henri is more my gentleman amongst his flock than ever. Harry is shaping into a nice boy. There now, what more do you want? . . . Now I must away to my early interview with M. Robelin. How are the onnies? You are just bathing them, for I have got up early & have had breakfast. The post has not yet come. Perhaps there will be something from you, perhaps not. But whether there is or not I enclose the usual things as under.

> Yours ever
> X X X X X X X XRX X X

❧ Ramsay to Margaret.

> March 1904 Thursday
> Hotel Engel
> Luzern

My dear Missus

Snow is falling and Pilatus is lost in clouds & snow storms. It is very cold. We get on very well though Hardie cannot do much walking. I have your very indecent card. When Hardie saw it he thought it came from Paris. Unfortunately after I started, I found my camera was broken and wouldn't work and after due consideration of pros & cons & an attempt to get it mended in Zurich, I bought another – a folding one which goes into my pocket. I have also bought a little French-English Dictionary which I hope will improve me. We have had no difficulty with language yet, however.

I have been looking around for something soft and safe to send to Miss One Year Old for Wednesday, but can find nothing so far. If nothing arrives on Tuesday buy her a bunny or something from me & give her the promise of my photograph when Mrs Wallis sends me one.

I have been sending little pictures to the Ònnies & shall do so till the end of the chapter.

I think the trip may do me some good though I am loth to be away at this time, and I am longing already to get back. I hope the fambly continues to be harmonious and goog.

> Ever thine
> R.

◆ Ramsay to Margaret.

> Saturday 27 February 1904
> Hotel Victoria au Lac
> Lugano

My Dearest Wifie,

Here we are in Lugano at last. When I woke this morning the sun was shining on the tops of the mountains in front of my window and great black clouds lay low upon the lake & up the slopes of the hills. As the day goes on, the sun becomes stronger & by & by I shall take a few photographs from my bedroom window.

We went to the Apollo the first night, & whether the play was really very funny or purple we know not, but I have never known such a continuous outburst of laughter. I think it was a mixture, perhaps I watched a respectable looking lady with her father & possibly, young cavalieros in a box & sometimes she laughed visibly and sometimes up her sleeve. So I knew when the naughty bits came.

I have come across nothing that I could send to the littlest onnie for Wednesday. But I have been thinking that it would be nice . . . to give her a cheque for £10 and give it to her annually.

Don't send too much but if there is anything worth sending – e.g. the LCC elections this day week, let me have them. What is your Aunts address? I might stretch a hand across the bay to them.

Did Alister or Malcolm or Ishbel or yourself send me the big fish which came sailing under my window this morning? I thought that perhaps they came with kisses or telliwags, because they wagged their tails a lot before they went away. Now I am going out & I shall post this, buy a few cards, post them and have a look about town. In the afternoon we may go out upon the lake. Adieu to your own self & the family

Ever thine
R.

The fish came back.

[He drew a picture at the bottom of the letter.]

The line at the top is the lake & the wiggly lines are put in to show that it is water. The round beady little things are the kisses rising to the top and the tail is turned up funny to show it is waggling.

~ Ramsay to Margaret.

1 March 1904
Hotel Londres & Metropole
Firenze

My Dear Missus

I am quite bewildered here & wish I had not come. It is a place for at least a month's stay. Some day we must try and get over this ground together. I shall only peep in here and there tomorrow. I manage to get on fairly well & my broken English is getting excellent. I am also sleeping a little better but still far from well as I should like. I hope you gave my love to Sir Owen Roberts and the other friends of mine whom you met in Southampton. Have you told your aunts that I am in their neighbourhood? If you send me their address I shall wink at them across the Mediterraneum. Also to Flo if I knew where to find her.

I heartily wish the Elections were come and be done with. All this delay & rumour is most troublesome. So far as I can make out there has been an election here and the socialists have been badly beaten today or yesterday, Could you send me a list of the candidates nominated for the County Council Election?

I am glad the chickabiddies like my postcards. I would have sent some today on my way here but they are not sold in Italy as they are in Switzerland at the Railway Stations. I send my kisses this time by Railway train.

ever thine
R.

 Ramsay to Margaret.

February 1904
Casa Fanshawe
Bordighera Italy

I am going over to Menton this afternoon to see Kruger. It is glorious country & if we could only manage a fortnight's walking in the Maritime Alps . . .

The result of the County Council Elections is better than I thought it could have been, but I suppose the Moderates had no alternative policy. I bought a London Sunday paper yesterday at San Remo and it gave all the results except the city. I have been reading novels almost exclusively since I came out. This morning I go to see if I can lay my hands upon some pottery which I can bring back with me. I have already bought two jolly little ashtrays for the sum of one half a penny each, and if I can buy a mug for you it will be my present & thank offering at your shrine. I have not been able to get anything I fancy for the youngsters yet, but when I get to Avignon I suppose I shall be impelled by the necessity of making up my mind. This place though full, is quite quiet and it is easy to cut yourself away from the mediocre English Currents upon which the Duke of Leeds & the Lord (knows what) Strathmores are floating like gaily glittering bubbles on the top.

I think I told you that there is a Socialist majority in the commune here. The Socialists wanted to give Hardie and me a spree, but I declined. Hardie, however, is sure to accept.

And now I turn to the little flower garden that is sprawling about you. How are all the lillies & roses? Flourishing I hope, in spite of all the winds and rains & fogs which I see are your lot. I shall be home for tea on Monday.

(My young lady has come)
She has a dog and a stick and I cannot wait.

Love to you all
Yours ever
R

271

∾ Ramsay to Margaret.

February 1904 Monday
Casa Fanshawe
Bordighera
Italy

I have been kept so long by the Socialist Mayor of this 'ere little town that I have lost the post & I wanted so much to write to you today. I got here on Saturday & have had two letters & a *Labour Leader* from you. Mrs Berry is not at all what I imagined she might be – very stout, very energetic, very much of a leader of Bordighera life from Cruelty to Animals to Church going. She keeps Berry [an old friend of Ramsay's] in good order and is altogether a most likeable person. I thought he would have had a turning dropping lily, but he has chosen a good, big independent red, red rose.

I have heard from Mrs Steyn and shall see them at Cannes. She has also written to President Kruger's secretary & I shall go to Menton on Wednesday to see if I can meet the old man.

Ever Thine
R.

∾ Ramsay to Margaret.

March 1904 Saturday
Avignon

My Dear Wiffie

. . . I found a sheltered spot on the top of the hill where the Pope's palace is built & I sat down in the sun and read your letter & the two papers. I think I shall always let you do the Labour Column. Did I see Ishbel's hand in the barmaids? or was it all your own? The *Leader* is miserably poor, Hardie's article is particularly so & to make it worse his manuscript seems to have got mixed up. . . Glasier's maudling is not even tolerably well written. And everybody is as long winded as they can be.

Well, I feel at the threshold of 3 Lincoln's Inn Fields again & I am very glad we have tried to cover too much ground; but I am coming back with enthusiasm for the Riviera. It is sickening that such a glorious coast is becoming more & more only a rich man's paradise. Someday we must walk it. After leaving Bordeghera, where I fell in love with Mrs Berry's little sister of 22, I went to Cannes for a night, taking Monte Carlo in on the way. It was not so devilish as I had imagined it, and evidently a good many people were there "for the fun of the thing". The gold tables, however, gave me the notion of the real thing. I have taken away the impression that women, not men, are the gambling sex. I found President Steyn at Cannes,

sitting in the "stoep" so like to his pictures. He, his wife, his wife's brother
& his commandant made a fine family group. Mr Steyn is more splendid
than I had quite taken in. How rich the memories of these people are!

Kiss all for me and help yourself to one.

Ever thine

R.

8 April 1904

ILP Conference at Cardiff

Appointed to NAC

S–Chairman   F.W.Jowett
Keir Hardie   Isabella O.Ford
Bruce Glasier   Mrs Pankhurst
J.R. MacDonald

Ramsay had an appendix operation in early May.

❧ Ramsay to Annie Ramsay

10 May 1904 Saturday

3 Lincoln's Inn Fields

My Dear Mother

You will see by this that I am getting on very well. All the inflammation
is about out now, and so there will be no danger about the operation. We
are glad to hear that you had Jessie Ramsay[1] with Jane and Jamie Falconer[2]
seeing you. I suppose you will have seen a great difference in Jane. We
shall very likely see them when we get up. The box you sent has come
alright and the flowers are very fresh. They are all about the room, now. We
had a letter from Aunt Katie today telling us about her visit to you, but we
have not yet heard anything from Bella. Margaret will not have to alter any
of her plans on my account. The operation will take place in about ten days
and though I shall not be allowed to rise for about three weeks afterwards,
there will be no need for her to wait on.

With love from all of us

Your affectionate son

J.R.MacDonald

---

1. Daughter of Alexander Ramsay.
2. Annie's sister and brother-in-law.

༆ Margaret to Ramsay.

[May] 1904

I found when I got in tonight that Hardie had been in a few minutes before & left this card with Elsie. I trotted off to Nevill's Court at once in chance of catching him but the place was shut up and deserted; and a young man who met me as I was coming away said he thought he could find Mrs Shields for me (at her daughter's across the way) found that Mrs Shields was not there, but they thought Hardie had gone off to Scotland; the young man (I suppose a lodger or a son Shields) thought he had not been at his room last night (unless very late).

I am sorry to have missed him, but am sending a p.c. to Gurnoch tonight.

I left one pound with Miss MacDougall to cut your hair and shave you (7s6d) & buy you bandages and the rest.

Miss Alloway [his nurse] says the doctors usually like to see some relative and pow-wow with it after the operation while they gently pocket the fee. So she advises me to come about 10.45 on Tuesday. Meanwhile I must try to find out from Dr Abel what the fee is to be as I don't see the joke of drawing a huge cheque without previous notice. The anaesthetist also expects to be paid on the spot. Miss Alloway says.

I hope you will like your new room tomorrow.

I think I should prefer it to the one you are in.

Au revoir
M.E.M.

༆ Margaret to Ramsay.

19 May 1904
3 Lincoln's Inn Fields

My Dear Sir

I have been planning much gossip and benedictions to impart to you but they must go by wireless telegraphy or wait till tomorrow afternoon as the fields are filling with the sounds of champing bits which warns me that the fashionable world is about and it is time for me to retire. We had the band at six o'clock. I let Alister and Malcolm sit up to listen to it for a little while as they were so excited about it and we were all very sorry that you were not there to enjoy it too.

Ishbel came into the bedroom at bedtime waving her hands with most jubilant ta-tas to greet you, but was disappointed to find your place tidy &

vacant, though she persisted for some time in energetic ta-tas to you. However she was not dull when the others came over to bed and had great frivols.

Au revoir & nighty-nighty & good morning.

M.E.M.

24 May 1904
Telegram

Handed in Oxford St. 11.34. Received Lossiemouth 12.32

To:- Ramsay

Operation over very satisfactory doctors pleased

Margaret

∾ Margaret to Ramsay.

Postcard

I hope you are having a good night after the bowers of flowers and the barley water nectar and other good things. The children were all asleep when I got home, but Alister woke up sufficiently to hear you had had his messages.

If any special messages need to be sent earlier the number here is 4850 Holborn (Natl) or 4114 Central (Par)

Yours M.E.M.

∾ Margaret to Ramsay.

5 June 1904
Lincoln's Inn Fields

Mr Dear Sir,

All the little ones are sleeping in the sunshine – it comes streaming into the back bedroom and is making Malcolm quite sunburnt – whilst Alister asked not to have the screen up after he was in bed (I will put it up when I retire) as he likes the band and the sunshine. He was very pleased with his first day up, and if the weather keeps warm and bright I expect he won't feel the tedium of being in one room so very badly. He is more lucky than you in being able to look out. He was pleased to hear of all the gathering of the clans at your bedside. I hope it was not too big a party for you. If I am able to keep coming to see you we had better try to keep 4 to 4.30 clear usually or we shall never have any time to ourselves as I can't reach you much before 4 with Alister ill. It will save sixpences as you say. I hope you will think I was right deciding not to get off this week. I did think it over a lot, & it seemed as if it would of course be simply a waste of effort if the children were not on the point of sickening.

I wish I could do more to help you with the *Labour Leader*, etc., but I don't see much chance at present. I might manage the German story (translation) in a few days time, as I can write comfortably and quietly in the evenings & do my tidying up of clothes, books, etc., during the mornings . . .

Yours

M.E.M.

Malcolm seemed very much at home when I got to Chepstow Villas. They were both in Flo's room.

Ishbel began to sing to me when I tried to change my dress in here, so I had to adjourn to the other side for my toilette.

I will come tomorrow afternoon. Au revoir.

M.E.M.

Margaret decided that her fourth child should be born in Lossiemouth.

✍ Ramsay to Margaret.

June 1904 Friday
19 Chepstow Villas

My Dear Missus

I got your telegram yesterday and we were all (Basil [Holmes, Margaret's brother-in-law] included) glad to hear of your safe arrival. We hope you are now enjoying yourself. Of course I had a very happy day with Billson at the Reform Club and all my nurses at 10 Montagu Place. They all came to kiss me, but as you can well imagine I drew the line at one. Miss Alloway was also there, very much expanded, and rather tell tale about the many heroes which Miss MacDougall had nursed. My nose did rather feel out of joint even although the young lady vociferously protested that the tales were all made up. It all finished up by my having Electricity and promising a photograph to Miss Alloway for her best room gallery of celebrated victims.

I saw some old friends at the Reform Club including Birkett, Sidney Lee, & Herbert Paul. Bannerman was glad to hear that I had consented to lunch with Billson & the pow-wow was very friendly & I gave assurances to be conveyed to Bannerman that we detested Rosebery & would not start wildcat amendments to the address if the Liberals would give us definite assurances that they meant business so soon as they settled down to legislation.

I am enclosing you some letters which I have not answered as you will no doubt like to do so yourself.

Today I am going to try to see Donald at the *Chronicle* & then have a talk with Hardie and finally at 5 o'clock have tea with Dr Abel.

Yours ever

R.

Labour Leader 10 June 1904

Our Own Outlook
Our Invalids Our readers will be glad to hear that J. Ramsay MacDonald is recovering rapidly. The operation appears to have been most successful and already the patient is able to receive friends and interest himself with the news of the political world.

❧ Ramsay to Margaret.

11 June 1904
From the window

My Dear Missus

Dr Abel was here yesterday & we discussed plans. I am to be allowed to have my shoulders off the flat tomorrow in bed as I have my belt on now; on Monday I shall sit up a little more & on Tuesday I shall get up on the chair. I have also seen my wound for the first time and it looks in great condition. It hardly has a scar. Nothing apprently will prevent my leaving this on Thursday morning. When you send my clothes you might put a cheque book in my inside pocket, as I shall have to pay for my belt & I can also pay Miss Alloway & save you the trouble.

Ever thine R.

❧ Ramsay to Margaret.

25 June 1904
19 Chepstow Villas

My Dear Missus

I am afraid that Thursday will be practically impossible for me. The committee is to be long and contentious.

I saw Dr Abel yesterday afternoon and have been wiped off his list.

This is not a very good day. It poured all night and is now cold. If it improves I am going to the Licencing Bill Demonstration in Hyde Park and then Flo and I are to dine at the Earl's Court Exhibition. On Monday if it is fine, we are going to a Society of Arts evening reception at the Botanic Gardens. Tomorrow we dine with Mrs Hertz. So you see we are gay enough.

I am seeing a lot of folks now and being free I am walking out several, Miss Alloway, for instance, who has become quite skittish.

My love to you all
Ever R.

❧ Ramsay to Margaret.

26 June 1904
Chepstow Villas

My Dear Missus

I have had a very happy day and I am going to have an equally happy evening. The reason for the first statement is that Polly and I have been to see the children and Ishbel was equal to the dignity of hostess whilst Malcolm seemed quite well though evidently pining for his family.

Flo and I had a good spree at Earl's Court last night, the usual sights and sounds. I very nearly bought some Venetian glass as a marriage present but did not quite know how to dispose of it in the meantime.

The Temperance demonstration in Hyde Park was a great success. Uncle George Gladstone and I went to the National Liberal Club to see it march off, but I had to leave him before it had all gone, it was so long.

Tomorrow I am going to the Botanic Gardens with Flo in evening dress, to a Society of Arts blow out; so you see I am quite established again.

I hope you enjoy yourself. Couldn't you see Mr MacDonald [his old schoolmaster] about Alister. The only thing he wants, I think, is an hour's regular work at reading etc., every day.

Love to you all
Yours ever R.

~ Ramsay to Margaret.

June/July 1904 Monday
3 Lincoln's Inn Fields

My Dear Missus

I am sending you the rent account. The housekeeper's fee is correct as in the book. I shall pay in all the money I have today, amounting to about £110. But I am to draw £17 odd for Dr Abel. I find that first class return to Inverness is over £7 & so I shall not take it as it is out of all proportion to its value for me. I may be able to write you tomorrow saying when I can get up. Meanwhile I am glad to hear you are having such excellent weather. It is good here too.

Love to you all
Yours ever J.R.

~ Ramsay to Margaret.

27 June 1904 Monday
3 Lincoln's Inn Fields

My Dear Missus

There is a little girl just waked up in the corner rubbing her eyes because she thinks she may be dreaming, and a little other person at my elbow telling me about a tiger wearing little Sambo clothes and 'brella. I am going to a meeting of Birkbeck Governors and have looked in on my way to see how the family is getting on & to write you a letter from your old home.

I improve as usual and now nothing remains of my invalid days – except that I am still a feather-weight.

We had a nice dinner party at the Hertz's last night. Ormond Cross; Harris the Positivist, a German & an Austrian who had just returned from the Congo, all with ladies to match. I took in Mrs Hertz as being the most distinguished guest – "the man of greatest promise" as she announced to the table.

At this point the Kings have come in. Ishbel is on Aunt Elizabeth's knee playing peep-bo. She holds up her own pinafore. Aunt E. is funny without her teeth. They send love. Aunt E. wrote you yesterday she says. Now I can only add my love to mother, you and Alister and Close

Yours ever
R.

❧ Ramsay to Margaret

28 June 1904
3 Lincoln's Inn Fields

My Dear Missus

I got your long epistle this morning and Flo and I joined in fraternal prayers of gratitude that you are enjoying yourself. Flo thinks that your references to flirtation are to her, and blushes when I read them. So be careful or you will rouse false hopes. I haven't seen Hardie since Friday, but I expect to see him tomorrow, as Parker,[1] he and I are to talk over the business of Thursday's L.R.C. meeting.

Yours ever R.

Ishbel and Malcolm went up to Lossiemouth to join their mother at the end of the month.

❧ Ramsay to Margaret.

2 July 1904
19 Chepstow Villas

My Dear Missus.

My three days committee are over. Things have gone very satisfactorily, and now I must clear off the business which "arises out of the minutes", send a few things to the printers, leave some instructions regarding machinery to be put into operation should there be an election & then off. I am going to Amsterdam as delegate from the LRC along with either Shackleton or Henderson, and I am also told off to go to the Trades Union Congress at Leeds and the Railwaymen's Annual General Meeting in October. But I think I shall be able to leave London this coming week, so you may expect to see me soon.

I was very glad to hear that the little things had got up safe and sound.

Thine ever R.

David was born on 4 July 1904.

---

1. James Parker, a colleague on the LRC.

TELEGRAM

Handed in at Notting Hill 9.29
Received Lossiemouth 9.57

To:- MacDonald − Cottage − Lossiemouth

Glad to hear all goes well
Welcome from Flo and other

Ramsay

~~ Ramsay to Margaret.

5 July 1904
London

My Dear Missus

And so Georgie's train has been as usual more than punctual. The news was quite unexpected and waited my return from the Auntie's Dinner Party. I am glad, however, it is over and that you and It progress favourably. May it continue. I suppose you will send a description of the person in due course. You may inform him that his arrival (on the Elgin Holiday) was announced with toll of bell, barking of dogs, blowing of cats at Chepstow Villas.

I had tea with Miss Marshall yesterday & then went to Mrs Bradley's where I saw the dear George Gooch, Emily, several Boers, including Mrs Williams & the gay bouncing daughter etc., etc., There is nothing but personalities to report − no special news − no nothing. The feeling now abroad is that the election is once more postponed. All this waiting & these false alarms is worse than midwifery. I hope to get up next week for certain, but I have not had time to see to anything relating to the house yet. On Thursday I shall be able to turn my attention to that, however.

Mrs Cummings has arrived at the Bedford Hotel at the head of 14 ladies & wants to see you. Her card has just come. I shall answer her and send it on to you.

This seems about all. So with renewed welcome to the stranger and hopes for both your health & strength; love to you all round,

I am
ever thine R.

∾ Ramsay to David.

5 July 1904
19 Chepstow [Villas]

My Dear Nameless No 3

I have come in just in time to catch the post with a rush. Have been out all day and am tired. Have bought paper for the bedroom, linoleum etc., been to the office, lunched with Masterman who sends his love and Hammond, met Miss Nettie who sends ditto also Mr Husband & Mr Matheson etc., etc., I shall write you or somebody else definitely tomorrow when I am leaving to see you. Possibly Saturday, Sunday or Monday. Meanwhile today I have bought a campbed for the garden & it will arrive in due time. Tell mammie what it is for so that she may not appropriate it.

You seem to be very anxious about your name but you have not described yourself at all to me. You might be George Washington because you came on Independence Day or you might be Georgie King, or George Ramsay or David Thompson, David King, or David any mortal thing. Or you might be William Kelvin, or Kelvin King or Kelvin William or Davie Jones or Roger or Geof. If your Mammie likes David, David let it be. You will see or your mammie will for you, that I have captured the *Daily Chronicle* for N.E. Lanark. It was a job but the loss of my tail did not make such difference.

Your Auntie Flo is out or she would no doubt be sending messages.

Now I must close. Tell us about yourself when you write next and accept the love of your daddie and distribute it around the family.

∾ Ramsay to Margaret.

11 July 1904
19 Chepstow Villas W.

My Dear Missus

It is nearly six o'clock so I must hurry. Besides there is little news. Flo has been at Lincoln's Inn Fields today & so I have not been. She and I have been at the New Gallery, but except for [Walter] Crane's Sicily pictures the show is not particularly good. I cannot say yet when I may be up – sometime next week I hope but there are some things to be done here lest an election may come suddenly, and as I am feeling very well I shall finish things here before deserting my post . . .

Yours ever
R

🙐 Ramsay to Margaret.

July 1904
3 Lin: Inn: Fields

Dear Missus

Nothing new since I last wrote Squaky [David]. I propose to leave on Monday morning & shall break my journey either at Edinburgh or Perth & shall come on Tuesday. That will enable me to travel third. I shall send a telegram saying when I am to arrive. Flo and I are going to the Egyptian Collection at University College this afternoon. I hope you all enjoy yourselves and that all traces of the measles have now gone. Chertsey is not bad but apparently the Liberals played it very low down.

Love to you all
Yours ever
R.

🙐 Margaret to Florence.

19 July 1904
Lossiemouth

My dear Flo

Very many thanks for your letter – for the £1 cheque from Aunt I – and for the box which arrived for Malcolm on Saturday evening. The latter however was too soon for his birthday as that is in August not July. I saw what it probably was & just looked inside & then put it away where he can't reach it in any exploring expedition. I expect we shall keep his birthday rather before the time as Ramsay will be in Amsterdam on August 17th, so we will produce the box then. Alister when he got his card from you was very pleased to be let into the secret of the birthday present and to caution people against reading that part of his card aloud to Malcolm. Malcolm has great stories of your farm – Auntie Flo has 2 cows and a sheep etc., etc., all very circumstantial (I forget the numbers) but I presume it was only a toy one and that you have not started any livestock to rival Geoff and the cat in your garden.

It is disappointing about Wilfred if he really cared about the Navy; I wonder what he will do instead. I am sorry about Bessie's poor health, but was very glad to think she was out of Paris when we read the account of the great heat there.

I hope you will have a nice time at Ketley. It is very dry here & very broiling in the sun, but there is a nice [?]. Ramsay's camp bed is very nice out on the lawn & we have garden chairs and hammock in addition, so are quite rural.

David commonly called Goliath sends you his love with a snort . . .

Yrs MEM

283

CHAPTER 7

August 1904–October 1906
'A ballot box
full of kisses'

This was a happy, busy period for the MacDonalds, and there was not much time or occasion for writing letters. In their second-floor flat overlooking the trees in Lincoln's Inn Fields, on the big black dining-table, page after page of socialist propaganda was produced. The four children – now six, three, one and a baby – shared their nursery with the Labour Party offices and were expected to join in the informal political soirées when Margaret served bananas and bread and cheese. She told Annie Ramsay that they were so desperately busy that Annie had better consult the pages of the *Pioneer* and the *Labour Leader* for news of what she and Ramsay were up to.

Ramsay was welding the Labour Alliance, putting up socialists and working men for Parliament and formularizing a theoretical basis for his new party. He wrote in *Socialism and Society* in 1905:

Throughout our lives we are but as men feasting at the common table of a bountiful lord, and when we carry the dishes for the feast . . . we pride ourselves on our wealth and the magnificent reward which our labour has brought us . . . man is moved by his head as well as his pocket . . . Economic needs may give volume and weight to the demand for change, but reason and intelligence, the maturing of the social mind, ideals of social justice . . . give that demand a shape . . . A consciousness of class disabilities may be either a motive for reactionary sycophancy or for revolutionary indignation. A man's poverty may make him a Socialist, but it is as likely to induce him to sell his birthright for a mess of potage . . .

Socialism marks the growth of society, not the uprising of a class.

When the Unionist Prime Minister resigned, Ramsay's pact with the Liberals secured an astonishing result in the 1906 election. There were now twenty-nine Labour men in Parliament – Jerusalem was in sight.

Meanwhile Margaret, taking a break from child-bearing, turned back to her own work. She involved herself with every women's question which was a matter of public discussion: the condition of barmaids, child-neglect, the problem of sweated labour, women's suffrage, the feeding of schoolchildren and the training of nurses. Rhetoric was not her forte; she disliked showing off, and enjoyed collecting facts. Her scientific background and love of statistics equipped her admirably for her work with the Women's Industrial Council (she had been a member since before her marriage), which carried out a unique series of investigations into the conditions of working women. Thirty-five trades were examined in detail, and Margaret researched seven of those single-handed. In 1906 she helped to put together an exhibition about sweated labour, in an attempt to show middle-class ladies what it was like pasting together cardboard for boxes and carding hooks and eyes for a couple of pence per hour. She scribbled and searched, collected and collated, and at the same time befriended her cases.

The National Union of Women Workers (NUWW) was a similar organization to the WIC, but seems to have been more a manifestation of the Edwardian lady at play. Their annual conference at Lincoln was reported in *The Queen* (October 1910):

In the evening a brilliant reception was given in the County Assembly Room by the Countess of Londesborough. Lady Londesborough wore a transparent tunic of black ninon deeply fringed over black satin and her headdress was a very becoming black tulle turban with a black osprey. A beautiful touch of colour was added by her bouquet of pink orchids . . .

On the Thursday evening the Conference concluded with an ethical meeting at which Mrs George Cadbury gave an address on the need of a spiritual awakening entitled 'Whereunto' and Canon Masterman, vicar of Coventry and sub-dean of St Michaels, spoke on magnanimity and how to develop it.

Tuckwell Collection, TUC Library

The professed aims of the NUWW were to promote the social, moral and religious welfare of women workers. There were a lot of bishop's wives and perhaps Margaret did not feel completely at home, but they had taken up the cause of barmaids, which was close to her heart. Critics accused her of being an ignorant busybody who knew nothing about pubs except what she had seen from the top of a bus. Better a bus than a private carriage! In fact, the exploitation of young girls was something she genuinely abhorred, and worked tirelessly to ameliorate.

In spite of her dislike of forms, and her suspicions that the organizing of good works was in fact a dehumanizing process, Margaret was an excellent committee woman. She was not particularly inspired, either as a writer or as a speaker, but her force of personality, her commitment and her industry kept her in the forefront of the organizations to which she belonged. She was elected president of the Women's Labour League, a body set up soon after the 1906 election on the suggestion of a docker's wife. It was an organization of Labour women, working towards the securing of independent Labour representation in Parliament. Two years later it was directly affiliated to the Labour Party, and by December 1908 there were eighty branches throughout the UK.

In August 1904 Ramsay was sent as the Labour Representation Committee delegate to the Congress of the Second International in Amsterdam. Margaret accompanied him, and the children went up to Lossiemouth.

ↄ Alister to Margaret (in Amsterdam).

> 16 August 1904
> Lossiemouth
> postcard

Tusday. My Dear Mammie we are all well I[shbel] & M[alcolm] & David is in bed when I am writing we are glad to get the cards this morning and glad to sea of them you were all well Gan and Malcolm and I are going to the Flower Show tomorros and the gurals in the afternoon if the day is fine – but it is cold now here we got flags made to day so we are very happy we are going for a country walk to sea the reapers cutting down the corn we will be looking for a letter soon now with love from all to Mammie and dadi Grani is bettr only hir hed is still sore and we are geting well from Alister.

After a few weeks back in Lincoln's Inn Fields, Ramsay was soon on his travels again.

◈ Ramsay to Margaret.

> 5 September 1904
> Electric Light
> Trevelyan Hotel
> Leeds

My dear Missus

This is just a line (5 minutes before post) to say that I am not on to speak until Wednesday & so cannot get away until Thursday. I am awfully sorry but it cannot be helped. Great crowds here and many enquiries about you and yours.

> Love to you all
> Yours ever
> J.R.M.

◈ Ramsay to Margaret.

> Sabbath 11 December 1904
> The Albion Hotel
> Piccadilly
> Manchester

Dearest Madame

Lest I may not be able to pour out my heart to you tomorrow, I do it today. I found your card on my arrival this afternoon & I am sorry it contained no messages from the divers [children]. I am sending many messages to the divers, but I shall not pack them up here but shall send them tonight so that they may reach the divers when dreaming . . .

. . . I really hope that your Leicester visit is not quite impossible. Could you not get Mrs Collins to sleep with them on Saturday night so that you could come up that evening & attend the Trades Council tea & the Sunday meetings? You might try.

We had excellent meetings yesterday & I had a delightful drive at night about nine miles to catch a train . . .

> Every thine
> R.

Leicester Evening News:

December 1904

LABOUR SPEAKERS ON THE UNEMPLOYED QUESTION

Mr. James R. Macdonald's speech at the Leicester Palace yesterday on the unemployed does not clear the air. It was a pretty oration. As an essay it might have charmed the student of language. As a contribution to a serious social problem its value is not apparent. It smacks too much of the study and not at all of the hard realities of the slums . . . Mr. MacDonald said he "wanted to lay down one simple proposition with regard to the unemployed . . . It was this. In society, as it was organised today, the spiritual things of life were absolutely subordinated to the material things of life." It is a peculiar characteristic of the average Labour orator that, though he vigorously denounces what he calls the inactivity of Parliament, no one is more given to word spinning than he. And surely the opponent of Sir John Rolleston and Mr. Broadhurst can say something more businesslike than this we have quoted . . .

∾ Ramsay to Malcolm.

13 December 1904
98 Regent Road
Leicester

My dear little Malcolm

I am coming up to see you tomorrow & I expects you will be diving but Alister will have gone to his school before I get up. Mrs Billson likes your photographs with Ishbel very much. Tell Mammie there is no news but I have told Mr (?) Lumley that she is coming to drink tea and eat buns and cake with him on Saturday. It is a fine frosty day here and the road is white. I hope that Alister and Ishbel and you and David are all very good.

I am sending a diver to pick up a big box of kisses I was sending you but it fell into the sea. He will pick them up for you and you can hand them round to Mammie, & Ishbel & Alister & David and take some for yourself.

With love to you all

Your affectionate
Daddie

Ramsay spent the New Year of 1905 with his mother and Margaret stayed at home with the children.

❧ Ramsay to Margaret.   29 December 1904
                                                        Lossiemouth

My dear Missus

I was so hurried this forenoon after golf that I could hardly write you. It is simply divine up here with a magnificent moon in the morning and wind and rain in the evening with bracing dry hours in the middle of the day. We go calling for an hour every evening – Yesterday to John Stewart's & this evening to the Provost's. Poor John is very bad. Jane and he talk about parting in the most comical way and you would laugh outright if the thing underlying it were not so very touching. He was very glad to see me again. We are going to the "Templer's Tea" on Monday & shall shortly pay a grand visit to Mrs Ramsay[1] in Elgin. I hope to put in a lot of work before getting back. This is the place for that . . .

Send on Malcolm's clothes & say how longer arms & legs should be. Ditto my drawers. I bought two little things from Mrs Webster (Bazaar) which I may or not send on . . .

Ever R.

wind blowing kisses

❧ Annie to Margaret.
                                                        Monday? 1904
                                                        Lossiemouth

My Dear Margaret

I was so sorry to here of the cheldren[2] only if they are slight they will soon get over it but I do hope you will get here for the change will do all good evey thing is looking well and this one was the frist Holly day so we was to go to the hills fir a day and the rain cum but it is dowing mor good them we would have got and it is poring I am so glad Alister . . . (?) the fish and I feel for you only I am Redy to do wat yu wish I am prity well and my ankel is better Jane and Jamie[3] is looking much better sinse they cam to Lossie and we are verry happy here I do wish you will be able to get on. I am so glad to here of Ramsay and hope he may have better helth now and take care of him self remember me to Auntie Flo it is so kind of hir we all just in Love to all the cheldren and all of yu My Love to Ramsay and my though are on yu night and day

From yur Mither
A Ramsay

---

1. 'Aunt Katie'.
2. They had measles.
3. Her sister and brother-in-law.

〰 Ramsay to Margaret.

30 December 1904
Lossiemouth

Mine Own Missus

A guid New Year tae ye and the Bairns. I hope you continue to enjoy yourself. (Mother has come in and she will talk) I am sending my Labour Column because I believe posting on Monday here will secure but an uncertain delivery. Will you see that it gets to the *Echo* at the proper time? . . .

The Aberdeen papers are still full of me and my "portrait" – "how iver a daecent woman mairrit that chiel I dinna ken" is the comment on my comely self. But it has brought all the drunken fishermen in the place to shake hands and ask to see my "leddy" but my "leddy" is not here. I nearly lost the train this afternoon becaue a "fou" fisherman wanted to know why I always used Parliamentary languidge. I had at last to tell him that it was the only way to keep Teetotal. "Faith my lad" said his leddy "ye warna' born yesterday". Sic a trainin' at answerin' back them meetings gie ye!"

Now mother insists upon my taking supper so I comply and subscribe myself Ever thine R. With all a Daddies' love to his little onnies.

〰 Annie to Ramsay.

Saterday 1904
Lossiemouth

My Dear Ramsay

I am so glad to here about you and it is so kind of Margaret to writ Me so every day . . . I sent som Flawers yesteray to Margaret and I hope she will soon be down every thing here are verry dull and all the bots are away we are having the dreans put down and they are up at the street and nothing but sand fir 10 feet . . .

fru Mither
A Ramsay

〰 Ramsay to Margaret.

2 January 1905
Lossiemouth

My dear Miss Gladstone

A very rude and forward lady [Ishbel] wrote me a New Year's day letter trying apparently to win my affections from you but I write you these few lines to let you know that I remain true as steel as the poets say and that I have been playing in the New Year's tournament & won a prize which I took in the shape of 6 2/- Haskell balls so as to save money in view of our coming marriage which will be a very expensive blowout as I want it done decent as a lot of the fishers are doing here just now, and as the Temperance tea to which we are going tonight which is to take place after the usual New Year's procession through the town which is very sober as all the public houses are closed showing how far ahead of England Scotland is . . .

Ever Thine
R.

∽ Ramsay to Margaret.

3 January 1905
Lossiemouth

My dear Missus

The time flies. This day week I shall be in Inverness and on Thursday night I shall be back on the branch of the tree where my nest is built, and where the fledglings cock their heads. I hope Ishbel enjoyed her Christmas tree . . . We really did not sit out the Old Year as we were both rather tired, so we had hot bottle like little David. I hope he will not continue the habit.

We have been at Mrs Dean's tonight and I did not get in more than half a dozen sentences edgeways. Mother has got all my vices of quoting conversations only hers took place forty years ago and are repeated in vast detail with many parenthetic scandals . . .

I am afraid I shall not be able to half finish my work before leaving. These visits take an awfully long time & the morning's golf with Fleming, who is slow, is about three hours from here back again.

Is there a decent clean red tie knocking about? The one I am wearing is filthy & I have no change with me. Don't trouble about the drawers. Are you always sure you get the things back from the wash? My drawers seem to have a way of disappearing.

Sorry to hear of Ishbel's vanity but rather expect it . . .

With many kisses to you all. We are rushing off to catch the train to call upon Mrs Ramsay.

Thine ever R.

291

〰 Annie Ramsay to Margaret.

Tuesay ? 1905
Lossiemouth

My Dear Margaret

Many thanks for your letter and papers I do like a paper and I realy do grug my self papers I always get the nights paper I saw a bit about Ramsay in last Saterdays Gaziette . . . I am not taking any hand in the church as it is no use the 2 ministers is away up to Edinburgh . . . I saw John Stuart on Saterday he was verry ill with his breath and pain he asked kindly fir you all and sad they are verry kind but I could not speek to them altho they were here I did not here any word of Mr Ramsay Marrage only I wrote him and got a wans back She is so young only he must plase himself he will be about 59 and she 27 yu were asking me about my back I am rubing it with oil and turpentin so it may get som better by & by I do not now how much wool I will ned only I will sea when I finish the rent is paid about the 28 of this month Now I hope David is geting on With love to all I may try and get some frish to send soon from Mither

AR

〰 Ramsay to Margaret.

25 January 1905
Hotel St George
Lime Street
Liverpool
(L.R.C. Annual Conference)

My dear Missus

Just another line to give you Mrs Pankhurst's love, Miss Ford's & a gentleman's . . .

My kisses to you all are below

Ever thine
R.

〰 Edward Carpenter[1] to Ramsay.

Thursday 26 Jan 1905

Dear MacDonald

I called yesterday on the Kropotkins[1] at Bromley and though I did not see him, he sent a message to me through his wife – which I now forward to you.

---

1. Edward Carpenter was an anarchist and sage of the Simple Life.
2. Prince Peter Kropotkin (1842–1921) was a Russian geographer and revolutionary.

He is very anxious that the Trades Unions of England should now come forward – as soon as possible – to the help of the Trade Unions & strikers in Russia and especially in St Petersburg. He hears that a great number of men in St P. are unable to return to their homes for fear of being arrested and are spending the nights in holes and corners wherever they can, and the days in wandering about the city in a destitute state. Anyhow to help the Russian workers now will be a grand thing for the cause of unionism and for the solidarity of the workers, every where. He does not doubt the British unions will be anxious to move in the matter.

There is a difficulty of course about transmitting any funds that may be collected. It certainly would not do to send by post; but the Kropotkins make no doubt that they could get some one to go in person from here for the purpose – that is if the fund were sufficiently large.

I called on you as being in touch with the Trade Unions; and now I find that you are at Liverpool in L.R.C. Conference – so your wife suggests that you might be able to put the whole matter before them tomorrow. It is important of course that no time shd be lost – and it would not be a bad thing if a telegram could be sent saying that funds would follow; as this could inspire confidence & also perhaps make others in Russia & in Europe generally more ready to help.

Kropotkin is still very ill – some form of pneumonia; but his wife seemed to think there was a change for the better. Tho' very weak, he cannot be kept from reading the papers & letters about the affair.

Kropotkin's address (in case it is wanted & not at hand) is "Viola", Crescent Road, Bromley, Kent.
and my address for the next few days will be
4 St. Mary's Terrace, Paddington, W.

Fraternal greetings to yourself and all friends at the Conference.

Edward Carpenter

Your wife asks me to call on Monday evening next & see you – so I will do so!

In case anything appears in the Press about this, I am *not* sure whether Kropotkin would wish his name to be mentioned esplly if he shd be a channel for the transmission of funds. it might possibly not be wise. But if a Trade Union Committee is formed, their names will be sufficient.

3 February 1905

Sir – the delegates attending the annual conference of the L.R.C. representing 900,000 members of labour organisations, instructed us to appeal to the trade unions and the public of G.B. & Ireland for subscriptions in aid of the Russian strikers and those who suffered from the massacre of Sunday Jan.22

   etc.etc-

> D.J. Shackleton – Chairman
> Arthur Henderson – Treasurer
> J.R. MacDonald – Secretary

27.1.1905

Labour at Liverpool p.527   *55th Annual Conference*

The reading of the Annual Report gave rise to several interesting questions and answers. In regard to the figures, the Secretary (Mr JRM) reported that owing to the initiation of a compulsory and retrospective levy for Parliamentary candidates several societies had withdrawn, the figures now standing at 900,000 as against 969,000 last year.

Second Day.

J.R.M. said there was a movement on foot at present which would lead, it was hoped, to a consolidation of Labour forces the like of which had never before been attempted.

Last business of the day

The new Executive – JRM unopposed.

Other Meetings

L.R.C. Demonstration.

Mr James Ramsay MacDonald said it had too long been the custom to go cap in hand to beg for something from men whose interests were opposed to the petitioners'. They had got plenty of pledges in the past and also plenty of apologies for not fulfilling these. They had now made up their minds to do their own business by their own men in Parliament. Speaking of the charge of isolation brought against the Labour Party, he declared that the real isolation was alliance to a party which prevented progress. The policy of independence was the direct opposite of isolation.

❧ Ramsay to Margaret.

> Monday 27 February 1905 8.15
> 98 Regent Road
> Leicester

My dear Missus

I hope you are having a very nice breakfast and that the little birds are all on their boughs enjoying their early worms. I have had a nice bath and a nice breakfast. The weather is atrocious . . .

There were great meetings yesterday. 150 at 9 a.m. instead of the usual 70. 250 at 3 p.m. instead of about 30 & in the evening the Shoe Trade Hall was packed out . . .

How is everybody? Love to everybody

Ever thine R

[see picture]
There's a cannon firing a ball full of kisses to you all

Labour Leader

10 February 1905

JRM at Derby.

Further on in his address, Mr MacDonald said they had been told that by including Trade Unionists, Co-operators and Socialists under one head they were letting in the middle classes. He had nothing but contempt for that body of men who were styled middle class . . . but there were sections of the thinking middle classes who were, he was proud to say, the heart and soul of the movement. They were Socialists who had been thinking deeply over these great problems, which were now about to be solved when many of the working men themselves were paying no attention to the matter at all. In time he prophesied that all the members of the parties of true progress would be under their banner and the only parties in the country would be representative of capital and labour.

17 February 1905

A new branch at Islington – I.L.P.

Mr James Ramsay MacDonald in a powerful speech emphasised the excellent principles of the party and dealt with the unemployment problem. Referring to the attacks upon the L.R.C. he said that the action of the capitalists in the Taff Vale attack upon the Trade Unions were now being supplemented by the attack of Liberal professed friends of Labour.

17 February 1905

Labour demonstrations at Norwich.

Wednesday night. The I.L.P. entertained Mr James Ramsay MacDonald to dinner and held a great demonstration to give Mr S.H. Roberts a good send-off on his second — and it is to be hoped, successful, campaign as Labour candidate for Norwich.

Thursday night

Demonstration in St Andrew's Hill.

Mr James Ramsay MacDonald also supported the resolution (of confidence in Mr J.H. Roberts and pledging to use every endeavour and secure his return) and on rising received a great ovation . . . they were told they were Ishmaelites by those who did not know who Ishmaelites were. But if they would turn to Genesis XVII, 20, which he as a Scotsman knew — (laughter) they would see. Behold I have blessed him and will make him fruitful and will multiply him exceedingly. Twelve princes shall he beget and I will make him a great nation (applause). The I.L.P. had become fruitful, it had been blessed and it had multiplied (applause).

❧ Ramsay to Margaret.

n.d.
276 East Park Road
Leicester

My Equally Beloved Missus

The dawning of Tuesday brings us joy. Thursday alone will soothe my pained heart . . .

Mrs Hubbard[1] & the Lady help are good but what are they to thee? A backyard rockery to a glacial morraine! Wages Boards to Licencing!

The mouths of many whispered thy praises last night; the tongues of many wagged sorrowfully that they were not to grasp your palm. Mrs Banton, Mrs Carter, Mrs Cox and the rest were there; there also were their men of war, their protectors & councillors . . .

---

1. With whom he was staying.

What I have written, you may read; what I have left out you may put in; and you may add what you think will be an acceptable offering to the Goddess of Knowledge.

Then let the song be typed & let it await me.

Selah! Kiss them all & yourself for me.

> Ever thine
> R.

∾ Ramsay to Margaret.   3 March 1905
                                               Leicester

My dear Missus

I shall try to catch the 11.11 a.m. train on Sunday. You had better not wait for me, but if I get home in time I shall follow you to Flo's and take my chance of scraps.

We had another good meeting last night. I hope you got home all right and that none of you are any the worse for having eaten birthday cake [Ishbel's].

> Ever thine
> R.   a ball full of kisses
>   [a drawing]

Campaign in Leicester.

                                    Labour Leader
                                    10 March 1905

Mr J.R.M. concluded a week's highly successful mission at Leicester on Friday evening last by addressing a large meeting at Emmanuel Schools. The great meeting of the series was on Wednesday.

Margaret and Ramsay spent Easter in Ireland.

Ramsay . . .   Easter 1905

We walked from Killybegs round the shoulder of Donegal to Dunfanaghy through Carrick and Glencolumbkille – over the mighty cliffs which rise up into Slieve League, which we tried to cross in a mist, but from which we had to retreat, up on to Horn Head where we spent a day watching the myriads of birds on the cliffs, screeching, flying, fluttering, swooping, and the sleepy sea below placidly dreaming of wrath and fury.

                                  Margaret Ethel MacDonald

Labour Leader

28 April 1905

L.R.C. Russian Fund

Sir, We would be much obliged if you would insert the following announcement in your next issue –

The L.R.C. Russian Fund has now reached £950 and will be closed on Saturday 29th inst. etc.

J.R.M.

Any contributions thereafter remaining in hands of collectors to be sent to the Friends of Russian Freedom: 40 Outer Temple, W.1.

Labour Leader

5 May 1905

Mr James Ramsay MacDonald at Belfast.

Mr James Ramsay MacDonald went from the I.L.P. Conference at Manchester to Belfast, where the L.R.C. congress is to be held in January 1906. He said the movement was not associated with the Conservative and Liberal party. They stood for more than the Liberal party ever stood at its very best (Applause). They were not tied to any party.

Labour Leader

16 June 1905

Mr James Ramsay MacDonald on the Unemployed Bill in *Saturday Leicester Pioneer*

Takes a much less optimistic view of the bill than K. Hardie and fears that its amendment would be a hopeless process. He holds that the unit of administration should be a rural area, plus towns within it.

Labour Leader

30 June 1905

An article by James Ramsay MacDdonald on the 'Labour Party' forms the twelfth of Mr Stead's series of "Coming Men on Coming Questions". The article gives a fresh and most interesting account of the genesis of the Labour Representative movement, and discusses the political position and practical aims of the new party.

On the cover of the pamphlet there is a new portrait of Mr MacDonald that presents him in a highly poetical light. We shall hope some of these days to receive from him verses for the *Leader* worthy of his poetical pose. The pamphlet also contains a sketch of Mr MacDonald's career and a complete list of up to date L.R.C. candidates. Its price is a penny and it may be ordered through the I.L.P. head office.

~ Ramsay to Margaret.

29 August 1905
Amalgamated Society of Carpenters
& Joiners
Belfast

My dear Missus

I am afraid this is to be a troublesome business.[1] I shall get home by next Friday & we shall go down to the country for the week end, but I shall have to get back again on Monday. There is no-one here who can be trusted & who knows the business of an agent. The fight seems to be pretty hopeful . . . So, I fear, I must sacrifice myself once more. It is a fearful nuisance but I cannot get out of it. Nothing from you today, yet. I had a nasty crossing yesterday & was just on the point of being sick though I lay down.

Now I must return to work.

With much love
Yours ever
R

~ Margaret to Florence.

30 August 1905
3 Lincoln's Inn Fields

My dear Flo

I hope you have a clearer sky today than we have. It is cloudy and rainy & looks rather bad for any chance of clearing up within the next two or three hours. Ramsay is on his way to Belfast, where there is a bye election with a Labour candidate. He has got snow spectacles with him, which we got in Switzerland & which ought to do nicely for looking at the sun if there is any to be looked at: & Malcolm & Ishbel are preparing to do great things with the other pair of spectacles at home. Malcolm is rather vague as to what is likely to happen; he has just been asking "when are we going to the sun?" Alister will see it at the Harley's if it is to be seen. Mr Harley seems to have given him and his children a careful explanation of it yesterday.

---

1. A by-election in Belfast. The Labour candidate was William Walker.

You seem to have an interesting set of people with you, and are sure to have a nice time, I should think. I hope Marion's [Holmes, their neice] relish for her meals soon returned. Please thank her for her letter received in Lossiemouth. We enjoyed our stay there & were very energetic bathing every morning before breakfast. Alister's arrangements that he would learn to swim were rather interfered with by a slight attack of mumps, which he transmitted to Ishbel. Neither of them were at all bad with them & only stayed in the garden for a few days with their heads tied round with flannel. It did not even seem to hurt Ishbel to eat & Alister ate perfectly well with a little grumbling that it was sore.

I have written to Florrie Underhill to ask her to come here. The B Ass: seem to be having a good time.

Love to Uncle, Marion & yourself and kind regards to the Miss Storeys and anyone if they happen to be about

> Your affectionate sister
> Margaret E. MacDonald

〰 Ramsay to Margaret.

> Sabbath n.d.
> Robinson's Temperance Hotel
> Belfast

My dear Missus

Would I were at Chesham Bois[1] & not tied down here all day writing etc.

We are having an uphill fight and are suffering from lack of organisation and concentration of authority – and also from drink. By the end of the day our Committee Room smells like a whiskey barrel. The canvass so far has gone excellently but it is too soon to make forecasts.

I have just finished the Faurés MSS & shall send it off. . .

Now I must turn to manifestoes and other devilish devices.

> Ever thine
> R.
> A messenger with kisses.

---

1. They had just bought a country retreat, Linfield.

❧ Ramsay to Margaret.

2 September 1905
North Belfast By-Election 1905
Mr William Walker's Candidature

My dear Missus

Now that I am hearing from you the floods of divine blessedness are pouring down upon me & I am happy . . . Our chaps broke up a meeting in the Orange Hall last night & carried a resolution against Dixon. Such a thing has never been known in the history of Belfast before.

You have all my love and felicitations. I shall send all my returned newspaper cuttings to you and you can keep them until I return. I shall send them separately so that you need not open the packets.

Ever thine
R.
So sorry to hear of the invalid but hope he is better!

A likkle Irish pig full of kisses and standing on a big kiss.

❧ Ramsay to Margaret.

10 September 1905
Robinson's
Commercial Temperance Hotel
Belfast

. . . I am sorry I came, for a Belfast election is rather an American affair. The Corrupt Practices Act is completely suspended & intimidation is everywhere. Every paid man on my staff will vote and almost everyone who votes for Dixon will expect to be paid. The Belfast workman is really a good sort at heart and, under good leadership, would be a tremendous power. But Walker is bent on winning & has insulted Catholicism in order to appease Protestants and is afraid to fight any of the controversial points of the day. The other side is attacking me more than it does Walker, & with my name posted on every hoarding I am much more notorious than Election Agents usually are . . .

〰 Alister MacDonald to Annie Ramsay.

2 December 1905
Postcard of

Dear Grannie

think you for your letter. I am making things for Xmas. I will send some. Malcolm thanks you for your letter.

Alister

Early in December the Conservative Prime Minister, Balfour, resigned, giving Ramsay and the LRC a chance to test the strength of their pact with the Liberals in an election. They put up fifty candidates. Ramsay combined his new-year visit to his mother with campaigning in the north.

〰 Ramsay to Margaret.

Sunday [January 1906]
The Albion Hotel
Manchester

My Dear missus

All serene. Hodge[1] thinks he is sure of a majority between 3000 and 5000.

Hope you are all in grand style and that the youngsters are not heckling you too much.

My love to you all.

Ever thine
R

Ballot box full of kisses
[a drawing]

〰 Ramsay to Margaret.

n.d.
Lossiemouth

My Dearest Missus

We are glad to hear of the safe arrival [in London] of the five of you and we send our very very sad condolences to the little curly head that was sick going to Aberdeen. We are all sorry you are not up here now. The Weather

---

1. John Hodge, steelworkers' leader and Labour candidate for Gorton (Lancashire). He won by 4,000 votes.

has never been so fine since the creation, the links are balmy, and I began bathing this morning. The water was perfect.

We had a call from an old flame of mine but you need not trouble. I could not get a word in edgeways. I gave up the competition and sat admiring in silence.

I am afraid I must go to Liverpool at once, but if I leave I will send you a wire. It looks as if my stay will be long as they have apparently appointed an agent who does not know his work and I have had an alarmist wire from Hill[1] this evening . . .

Have not Parliamentary papers in wrappers been sent to me? The pink papers will be in these. You are to send me the list of slides I need at Leicester for the Tour lecture . . .

❧ Ramsay to Margaret.

[January 1906]
The County Hotel
Newcastle-on-Tyne

My dearest Missus

I am enjoying myself immensely and I am just beginning to take to the life. Last night we had two crowded out meetings of electors and it is expected now that Taylor may win. The fight began badly, but it has woke up within the past day or two & is now going with a swing. This is my last day campaigning & when I get to Motherwell I hope to hear from you all.

You might send me a pair of sleeve links to Lossiemouth. I have come away without them . . .

I'm afraid from what I can hear that the leadership of our Party is going to give rise to trouble. Henderson[2] is desperately ambitious to have it & will sulk if he does not get it, whilst if he does get it, the more active sections will lose a good deal of their confidence in us.

I hope the offspring flourishes. Kiss them all from me & the same to yourself.

Yours ever
R.

At Ramsay's own adoption meeting in Leicester a 'tremendous gathering of supporters . . . filled every nook and cranny of the Temperance Hall'. According to the *Pioneer* 'he led them through

---

1. John Hill, Labour candidate in Liverpool.
2. Arthur Henderson was in fact chosen to be Chief Whip and became Chairman on Hardie's resignation in the autumn.

many intricate subjects . . . they seemed to follow him with an almost breathless eagerness . . . when the final climax came and the speaker had added the last link to his chain, there was such a round of cheers as could only have come from the throats of the British working men'. In the election twenty-nine Labour candidates were successful, most of them trade unionists. In Leicester the Conservative polled 7,504 and the two radicals, Ramsay and the Liberal Broadhurst, polled 13,999 votes each. Ramsay was now a Member of Parliament, and could not wait to go in triumph to Lossiemouth.

❧ Ramsay to Margaret.

29 January 1906
Lossiemouth

My dear Missus

Fine cold showery windy day, golfing under difficulties but splendid for bracing up . . .

. . . I am going to feast with Jamie Duneen. I hear there are preparations being made for a great banquet on Monday . . .

Love and kisses all round

Ever thine
R.

this one is sick
/

Mammy	Alister	Malcolm	Ishbel	David
xxx	xx	xx	xx	xx

❧ Ramsay to Margaret.

n..d.
Lossiemouth

My dear Missus

I was very sorry to hear that these colds are troubling the youngsters again. Do they not hang about in the mornings bathing and dressing far too long without a fire? I hope however, they are all right again . . .

〰 Ramsay to Margaret.

28 January 1906
Far and Sure
The Moray Golf Club
Lossiemouth

My dear Missus

The weather here is simply glorious . . .

. . . We paid state calls on Jane Stewart who has a cold in the stoomack
that entered her back above the kidneys; Mr Mitchell, who was out; tailor
Smith; Misses Reid, who were out; Mrs Shirley; & Dr Brander who gave us
tea. Lossiemouth is aflutter of pride . . .

I hear that there is a great log rolling going on about the leadership of the
party, and I am rather afraid that personal jealousies combined with Trade
Union Exclusiveness may produce nasty feelings & unfortunate results.

We must just do our best however. I am sorry that [Tom] Barnes is
talking so foolishly. Some people seem to imagine that their size depends
upon their bragging & their threats. Taylor's fight was simply splendid. We
can take nearly every country division in Durham now. There will be a
fearful amount of work now adapting the machine to the new circumstances,
but so soon as our members settle down and hold their tongues, things will
move all right I hope . . .

〰 Ramsay to Margaret.

26 January 1906
[Lossiemouth]

My dear Missus

Got home all right last night, the town being excited. No luggage come as
yet. I shall wire you this forenoon if it has not then arrived. When did you
send it off? There are no trousers either. I hope you sent them off by Parcel
Post . . .

When I return I shall give the Home Secretary notice of a question about
the wording of the Home Work sections of the Factory Act, in order to find
out what the Sanitary inspectors are really doing. Is Miss Irwin coming
up? . . .

The prescription came.

Mother is wonderfully well. Willie Duncan did me much honour etc. I
hope everything goes well. I can get no golf till my things come.

In haste to catch post.

Ever thine
R.

The new Parliament met on 13 February. For the recently christened Labour Party, led by Keir Hardie as chairman and with Ramsay as secretary, it was a disaster. There was squabbling among the leaders, and the trades union member spoke hardly at all, spending most of their time in the smoking-room.

[Margaret]. Was appalled when she discovered how easy it ws to undo what had been built up by years of patient toiling, and how the most absurd revolts found passionate followers. She used to say she never understood Moses and the Children of Israel until 1906.

Margaret Ethel MacDonald

Ramsay's maiden speech was an attack on the education of factory inspectors and on the notion of a 'general education for administrators' . . .

5 March 1906

[The] purely academical and theoretical university and collegiate syllabus was putting a premium upon book learning, and making it impossible for a man with a practical knowledge of factory theory to compete with young men just leaving Oxford and Cambridge. He might say that when he was in Johannesburg he met almost the whole of Balliol University (sic), and the only justification given him was that under circumstances such as existed there, the administrators were said to require a very general knowledge and a general education. Every single one of those gentlemen had been an absolute failure (Cries of "No, no!"). Perhaps there was one exception, but with one exception the whole of the Balliol kindergarten in South Africa had been a failure. The Right Hon. Gentleman was proceeding on precisely the same lines as those responsible for the Transvaal acted upon immediately after the war, and he ventured to prophesy that if the experiment was conducted for three or four years the same disastrous results would have to be recorded at the Factory Department of the Home Office. These men when appointed were handed over to subordinates, and the time of the subordinates was taken up looking after them. These very men, who had not the opportunity of becoming full inspectors, had to coach the men who were appointed to the full inspectorships . . . Decent employers of labour should make a strong protest against this attempt to use the factories as schools for university men who received appointments as inspectors. There never was a happier hunting ground provided by the ratepayers for people who were able to send their sons to be educated at Oxford, and whose idea of respectable occupation was that they should turn their attention to the Civil Service . . . He and his hon. friends of the Labour Party held that capital should not be unnecessarily harried by untried men of no experience, amateurs who had merely passed literary examinations; they held also that workmen should not be exposed to the dangers of their calling by the imperfect knowledge of inspectors.[1]

In June it was Margaret's turn to step into the limelight when she addressed the inaugural conference of the newly formed organization of Labour women, the Women's Labour League, as follows:

26 June 1906

We want to show the wives of trade unionists and cooperators, particularly, what they have not yet fully discovered, that the best way of looking after their homes is by taking an interest in the life of the community . . . that to improve their condition it is necessary to take up their cause with earnestness on the same lines as men have done and if it is to be anything the Labour Women's Movement must be international.[2]

൦ Ramsay to Margaret.

3 August 1906
House of Commons

My dearest Missus of whom distance does not lend enchantment to the view even when ancient butlers and overgrown page-boys are in the background, unto thee Uncle George & sister Flo greeting. I have seen of your speechifying. 3/4 of an hour! Has woman ever curtain-lectured the B.A. so thoroughly. I shall tell Mr Gladstone today that both sides of the family are in league against him.

There is nothing doing here, but ordinary work, work, work! I have now roused the fury of the women's suffragists for not having referred to woman's suffrage in what I said about the Transvaal constitution. Sister [Isabella] Ford has written saying she is to take action and demanding an explanation first of all. She has got it, poor thing!

The enclosed letter has come from Mother. Don't gallivant too much &

1. Quoted in Lord Elton, *The Life of James Ramsay MacDonald*, pp.139–140.
2. Quoted in Lucy Middleton, *Women and the Labour Movement*, p. 26.

don't hold Bowley's hand in public. Remember your decent maiden aunts, to one of whom I have sent my love this morning.

Now I have to go upstairs & listen to the Trade Disputes Bill debate. I have been photographed this morning in grand style.

> Ever thine
> R.

Ramsay. . .

September 1906

[At the end of the session] came another long absence from home. [Margaret] was tired and wanted to get away. Australian politics allured her, and the long sea voyage still more. She longed to sit on the deck on a calm sea 'just feeling happy'. Her old hungering after being, as well as doing, had come upon her. It seemed a prodigious holiday, but she said that the world could well spare us for a few months. People in active life must go away into the wilderness at least once in four years, she thought. 'I am going away', she wrote to a friend, 'with an easy conscience. I only wish you could all go in the same way. Our only chance of having three meals a day together and of discovering really how nice people we both are (sic), is to run away altogether from you. I think we can tolerate four or five months of our own dear selves and then – Charing Cross, the Customs, and you.' We went through Canada and were disillusioned. Our old Rat Portage had vanished into another name. The islands on its lake no longer kept in silence the bodies of departed Indians; vulgar chalets were built upon them and instead of white ragged streamers, Stars and Stripes and Union Jacks flew over them; annoying motor-boats had taken the place of delightful canoes. We went westwards to the mountains seeking the seclusion we had found further eastwards only a year or two before, and they gave us peace. Long walks through their woods and by their lakes brought us into the serene world of being.

Then came the Pacific with favours of calm weather and sunny days in Honolulu and Fiji, and finally Australia and New Zealand with their keen-hearted, hospitable people, their wonderful and weird places, like the deserts with Broken Hill and Kalgoorlie and the geyser regions with Rotorua and Tokaano; their beauties, like the Wanganui; their domesticity, like Adelaide. She investigated the operations of Wages Boards and compulsory arbitration, she went to see the land settlements created from the break up of the great estates, she counselled the women regarding the formation of Labour Leagues but she always said: 'I am here for a family party , not on a mission.' Of the friends she then met none found a warmer welcome in her heart than Mr. Price, the Premier of South Australia, a genuinely simple and unassuming good man, the type of the best which Labour can give to the State . . .

The voyage home pleased her greatly. The weather was perfect. A day in Ceylon with the night at Kandy, brought her under the allurement of India. She returned happy and buoyant longing for the yoke of work.

Margaret Ethel MacDonald, 255.

〜 Annie Ramsay to Margaret.

26 September 1906
Lossiemouth

My Dear Margaret

I am glad to say we are all flourishing and looking well We were down at the harber after Malcolm cam out of school to day and saw the James Combie and Ishbel asked me if it was the boat Mammie and dadie was in if Alistar had been down I should have go on board as the pillot was thear and she was loading water we went on to Inverness on Saterday as it was the Holliday . . . and went on to Aldarn and the children romed about till after 4 so happy and they were verry kind so the train was late and we got the 5 down so we got hom all right . . . we are geting on verry well I am doing my best to make the children comfortable and I am standing out pritty well but I am very tired by night May Ann is doing very well the boys is doing well and every wun seems so kind to them I had a letter frm Aunt Bella she is well thank you for papers and letter I have written evry week will send on a paper of last week David can speak now so plain and Ishbel is such a dear gural I am making sum warm things for them Alister had to get New Trowsers for the 2 pars was down but I get navie Sarge and Shand mad them so Malcolm will get the sam and I think they are groing They realy are very good I got Skarves for the 2 boys Alister will writ yu now I must close with love to both. The cold is only slight — a little in the head from

Mither

〜 Alister MacDonald to his parents.

October 1906

Dear Daddy and Manny
I am glad to say I am better and at school.
I got wors and Grannie sent for the doctor. he gave me medcin and sounded

me and ordered cod liver oil. We had a letter from Auntie today they are home again tomorrow is Haloween we are going to Cpt Charles Makenzie to spend the evening whith Colin and to Miss Grants on Saturday afternoon It is cold here love and kisses from all

from Alister XXXX XXXX

❧ Annie Ramsay to Margaret and Ramsay.

My Dear Margaret & Ramsay

I am glad to say that Alister is better It was pain in the stomoch it must have been cold and he spok on the hol night and nothing but Milk and soda water I send for the Doctor he sad he had a cold but it had no cach of the chest but his throat was verry sore and festered he has a little coff yet but I do hope he will progress all right . . . I have a real lady now Ishbel is so prod that she can step with any lady now we are all very good we have a walk evry afternoon unless it is weet I do feel tired only I must give them a walk . . . David is a strange boy he can say evry word and speks so nice now I must close with love to both from Mither Ishbel is such a little dear and thayer play going to Met Mammie & didi but noone is so often in the play as Aunt Bella Thay go often to sea Aunt Bella in a motor car We had it wet today but the boys is at school with love from the children fru

Mither

CHAPTER 8

January 1907–December 1909
'Just a hurried line'

This was a frantic time. The hours spent on work built up with a relentless momentum, consuming them both. Ramsay was living on his nerves, as secretary of the Labour Party, chairman of the ILP, writer, propagandist, agitator, father and husband. He was 'even more conscientious than Disraeli' in his attendance at the House of Commons, often working into the small hours on party business, dashing off to Leicester or to address rallies and conferences. The traumas and stresses were beginning to affect his temper. Margaret had children of nine, six, five, and three, but still made time for research, meetings, writing and talking. 'To our parents', wrote Ishbel, 'children were all in a day's work'. And when another one, Joan, arrived in April 1908 she did not prevent Margaret from going to Leicester, but was 'bundled up in mother's arms and taken everywhere'.

The MacDonalds were quite extraordinary parents for Edwardians. Lucy Herbert told a story of a friend from overseas who spent some time in the company of the four oldest children and was astonished that they expressed themselves so clearly, and had so much savoir faire. The friend asked if they were typical English children. 'Oh, no, they are the MacDonalds' children', was the reply. For in spite of his punishing schedule and continuous exhaustion, in spite of his compelling need to prove himself publicly and to crusade for a new world, Ramsay spent much more time with his children than most of his contemporaries did. Ishbel remembered, '. . . we bathed in a flat round bath on the linoleum under the supervision of a shaving father who laughed to hear us gulp when he now and again squeezed an unexpectedly cold sponge down our backbones'. Every time he spent a weekend at Chesham he took them all bird-nesting, and there were many occasions when Margaret left him to babysit while she worked. To lighten the load, or perhaps simply because he enjoyed their company, he would sometimes take one or two of the children with him on his travels. David accompanied him to the Newcastle by-election in 1908.

Both Ramsay and Margaret were especially concerned that they should not be an encumbrance or embarrassment to their children. 'Don't you think that our children have some rights against us?' she once said in a conversation about the Education Bill. 'For instance, don't you think they have a right to be protected against the silly prejudices of their parents – mine and yours both?'

Perhaps because of her own motherless childhood, Margaret was particularly anxious to keep the children with her while she worked. (How different was her attitude from Beatrice Webb's: 'I had laboriously and with many sacrifices transformed my intellect into an instrument for research. Childbearing would destroy it, at any rate for a time, probably altogether'.[1]) But it was not always possible and they were frequently left in the charge of others. Ishbel wrote: 'We had hard working, much engaged, busy parents and were left very much to the tender mercies of the charlady and nursemaid . . . our clothes were quaint and embarrassing to wear. Yet our souls and spirits were fed with such happy understanding that we were made immune for ever from cynicism . . . We were encouraged to be as independent as possible.' Alister, at eight, was certainly considered quite old enough to take Malcolm and Ishbel (four) for a walk along the Embankment. It was a spartan, bizarre household, full of love, life and responsibility. Ramsay read to them a great deal, and every Sunday evening, just before going to bed, they would all gather around the piano and sing 'plantation songs', finishing up by marching round and round the large table singing *Onward Christian Soldiers*. Ramsay wrote about Margaret, 'Her ideal of a mother was she who was the dearest of the friends of her children'.

---

1. *Diary of Beatrice Webb* ed. MacKenzie (London, 1983) 193.

Labour Leader

18 January 1907

We join in welcoming back Mr & Mrs J. Ramsay MacDonald from their tour in the Colonies. They have been away nearly 4 months and have visited Canada, Australia and New Zealand. They have both, we understand benefited greatly by their holiday – they come back laden with information regarding the most recent developments of labour and social legislation in these new lands, populated chiefly with our own Anglo-Saxon and Celtic kinsfolk.

To Mrs MacDonald the *Leader* is deeply indebted for her series of articles descriptive of the tour.

We shall defer printing the substance of certain criticism which Mr MacDonald's remarks concerning the policy of the Canadian Socialists have evoked until after the Labour Party Conference at Belfast.

Labour Leader

25 January 1907

Letter: Good Luck To the Party
      Greetings from Chairman of ILP.

Dear Mr Editor – We are home once more and doing our best to emerge from a pile of arrears which awaited our arrival. But let everything else perish. I must send you a scrawl by way of Hip-Hip?Hurrah! for the way things have been going with the ILP this winter. There seems to be a new spirit abroad from North to South for wherever we have wandered we have met men and women professing the Socialist faith and they have all had a lilt in their manner as though they felt the stars were with them . . . The Socialists in the Colonies need help badly & we shall never realise our great hopes for an international brotherhood until the Labour parties in the Colonies get into much closer touch with our spirit . . . Well! Well! What do I want to say to you and the branches and the comrades is Bravo and again Bravo.

～ Ramsay to Margaret.

> 23 January 1907
> Grand Central Hotel
> Belfast

My Dear Missus

Your budget came all right this morning. We flourish. Hodge wants us to dine with his Society on Friday Feb: 8th. It is "Old English Poetry" evening, and I am loth to give it up, but perhaps we ought.

Love and kisses to the kids etc.,

> Ever thine,
> R.

Ramsay in the *Labour Leader*.

> 1 March 1907

. . . The socialist in Parliament is like a circus rider trying to bestride two horses . . .

> 8 March 1907

. . . the spirit of all the sinister devils was in possession of the House of Commons last Friday, and my little Bill which proposed to feed the school children of Scotland was the occasion.

On 15 March Ramsay and Margaret went together to Aylesbury; he spoke on the Labour Party in Parliament, she on Labour politics and women workers. Then in early April Ramsay attended the ILP Conference in Derby. He followed this with a tour of Wales and the West Country, while on 18 May Margaret took the chair at the Women's Labour League Conference. Her dear friend, Mary Middleton, was elected secretary.[1]

The Conference discussed the feeding of schoolchildren and sent messages of congratulation to women labour representatives in Australia and Finland. There was a resolution to add to the objectives of the League, while a clause about the 'education of working women in the principles of socialism' was withdrawn so that it might not offend the trade unionists among the membership.

---

1. Mary Middleton worked with Margaret for the Women's Labour League; she and her husband, Jim Middleton, assistant secretary to the LRC, were close friends of the MacDonalds.

From May to July Margaret was pouring out articles for the *Labour Leader*, attacking the legal minimum wage. She wrote for the *Women's Industrial News* a report on an inquiry into the conditions of work in laundries, a factual analysis of an appalling state of affairs, where women worked up to within minutes of their confinements, up to their shoulders in steam and ankle-deep in water. The end of June saw her and Mary Middleton canvassing and promoting the WLL in Jarrow. A month later she went to Stuttgart for the First International Conference of Women Socialists.

Meanwhile her husband travelled endlessly round the country . . .

∽ Ramsay to Margaret.

15 September 1907
Liverpool

My dear Missus

I have had parcels of books & letters sent here but the pressure of getting up steam for this week has been too great to enable me to look at anything very carefully.

I was sent for in a hurry because things began a bit slow, but I think they are now alright & I am going back to Lossiemouth on Tuesday morning. The meetings are only fairly good but they are getting better and the enthusiasm is undoubtedly working up. The men on the spot say that they have begun far better than they did with Conley, but the place has a queer smell of North Belfast to me.

I am glad to hear you are all well. I hope the scholars are growing in wisdom & the non-scholars increasing in grace. I am going out for a walk this afternoon with an old tramp, but I shall not trouble to go and see any friends. My voice after four open air meetings is gone and wants a rest today, for there are three meetings tomorrow.

Ever thine
R.

MY BALLOT PAPER! [drawing]

315

∾ Ramsay to Margaret.

> 17 September 1907
> Stork Hotel
> Liverpool

My dear Lady

I am going back to Lossiemouth tomorrow morning.

Books come but I have no time to breathe & I can not carry them up with me, so I am sending them back.

In great haste,

> Ever thine
> R.

∾ Ramsay to Margaret.

> 18 September 1907
> Lossiemouth

My Dear Missus,

Just back to the scene of my leisure after a very prosperous time at Kirkdale.[1] It is too soon yet to say whether the place can or cannot be won. It has begun well. I think that a first class candidate would win. Hill is a bit too solid.

I have been looking through my slides. Australia is practically unrepresented. Could you send me any that look well. I want most particularly the Piper receiving us at Freemantle. Also send the panoramas that are in a parcel – eg. the ones I have already used. I also notice that I have no slides after Ceylon except one. The missing tail must be in the other box. I had better have them.

I return *l'Humanité* & a few other things. The little pile of Australian cuttings should be stuck on sheets by Miss Connelly. They deal with the Tariff Bill & Preference and are good.

I really cannot remember what the Printing Trade Books were to cost us. If they are to be sold @ 2/6 Johnson had better have them at ordinary trade terms. He knows now we supply Simpkin Marshall. We were out of pocket about £70 and we ought to try and get some of it back. We ought to get at least 6d or 9d per volume . . .

---

1. John Hill was defeated in Kirkdale by-election by 4,000 to 3,330.

Poor Mildred! And she was a nice kind of Amurrikan too. I know Stitt Wilson.

Miss Connolly had better return to help you . . .

M.s.s. has been woefully delayed for a week and I have now two days' correspondence waiting me. I'll send it as soon as I can.

I cannot remember when my B.A. paper was left. But I cannot possibly get at it here now, so it does not matter . . .

Could you send the slides at once as the lecture is on Tuesday and I must get some frames made for the panoramic ones.

All well

> Ever thine
> R.

∿ Ramsay to Margaret.

> Lossiemouth
> 21 September 1907

Mine Own,

Kirkdale is upsetting everything. I go back on Wednesday morning for meetings that night and Thursday & it is hardly worth while returning here for three days. It will be much better to keep my return ticket & use it for the New Year. I shall, in consequence, travel up to London from Liverpool either on Friday or Saturday.

There isn't much news. Everybody is going . . . A gale of wind & rain has been on the boards today & I went out in the morning. It was too fine to miss. I returned and ate a bullock for dinner. Mother's head continues to trouble her, & so does the Doctor who will not give her an account. In reckoning up our obligations I think we forgot that item. I had a cheque for £15 made out for myself & so I gave her that but I shall give her another £5 before leaving.

You will of course send me nothing here after Monday as I leave on Wednesday before any mail arrives.

Enclosed are two chapters for Miss Connolly. My work has been much upset, but my four days in Kirkdale lifted the place & I suppose I had better go back. My place is there however much I may regret being in its toils.

We shall not see each other for months this autumn. It is going to be a fearful campaign, but it is the right thing just at present both for the movement and myself.

If you come to Liverpool put up at the Stork Hotel in, I think, Queen's Square. I shall go there on Wednesday night, and if you get there before me you can arrange accordingly. I arrive about 7.30 . . .

Ever
R.

❧ Ramsay to Margaret.

25 October 1907
Commercial Temperance Hotel
Keighley

My Dear Missus

Just a hurried line. I am afraid there is no time for getting photographed again. The printing at this time of year is a very slow process. You must ring up the photographer and consult him. You will find the photographs in one of the books I have sent back in a parcel. Please send to me at the Albion Hotel Manchester immediately on receipt of this "Walter Crane" & "Pioneer Humanists" The latter is upstairs on my desk. I hope you have found the children all well. I motored from Scarboro' to York yesterday with Dr and Mrs MacDonald. They were asking about you & others are doing the same – the Roes last night.

Give kisses to the children from me and take some for yourself

Ever thine
R.

❧ Ramsay to Margaret.

27 October 1907
The Albion Hotel
Manchester

My Dear Missus

I enclose some MSS for typing. The opening sheets are lying on my desk upstairs. Together they form about half an article, the other half being upon Wages Boards. Get Miss Connelly to have them ready for my return. She might also get together the reports etc. from which I can fill in the blanks. They are lying about somewhere. Tell her to type them on foolscap sheets with a two inch margin on the left hand, an inch space at the top and an inch and half space at the bottom. They should be numbered at the top. I hope to finish the second part before I return.

Now I am off to Oldham. Tremendous meeting last night, in Huddersfield. At least 2,500 present and hundreds turned away. Grayson was very friendly & all the Colne Valley people ditto.[1] Did you go to the cottage on Friday? or were you kept in London by the accident?

Love and kisses to you all

> Ever thine
> R.

ᖗ Ramsay to Margaret.

> 28 October 1907
> Albion Hotel
> Manchester

My dear Missus

Only just a line. Awfully busy. Meetings greater and greater. Packed out at Oldham last night both afternoon and evening. Writing article for *Daily Mail* first of Socialist series. Glad to hear of success of sale. Oldham wants W.L.L. You ought to organise for women's candidates next November.

With much love and kisses.

> Ever thine
> R.

Labour Leader

> 1 November 1907

Mr MacDonald's campaign schedule last week: Huddersfield, Saturday; Oldham, Sunday; Middlesbrough, Monday; Briarfield, Tuesday; Crewe, Thursday; And tonight Chester.

ᖗ Ramsay reported in the paper:

> 22 November 1907
> Derby

the Socialist movement [is] stronger, more intelligent, more determined, better organized, more feared than ever before.

In December the whole family headed north. Ramsay to work, Margaret and the children to visit Annie Ramsay.

---

1. See pp. 326-7, April 1908.

The letter below shows Ramsay at his most obscure; perhaps his wife understood it!

∽ Ramsay to Margaret.

Scottish Council for Women's Trades
[December 1907] Glasgow

My Dear Missus,

I am just home from hearing Dr George Adam Smith on the Brit: Ass: Religion, Women's Labour, Socialism, the Hebrew Prophets & a few other things. It was really very fine and in marked contrast with the last Brit: Ass: Sermon I heard – that in Dover by Mona's papa.

Miss Irwin is gaily floating like a waterlily on the pond of the proper and the festive, dug and filled in welcome of the B.A. My ladies are coming to see me and hear me go for Cree tomorrow on "Wages, Supply and Demand". But I shall not be there. Indeed, I fear that beyond my cousin of that Ilk and my beloved sisters & their chaperon Sir Willie I shall see nobody of the pond. Miss Irwin thinks Sir W. gallant and bases her opinion on his great kindness to ladies – ladies being a generalisation of the one lady Flo. Of course I opened no cupboard doors to show the wardrobes of the family, but assured my hostess that the Mint has long been famous for hospitality and chivalry & that the meanest petticoat which aids the University janitor in dusting the Gilmore Hill establishment is held in reverential honour and can command the chivalrous fuss of the Honorary Secretary.

I came straight here yesterday & did not go to the Union Restaurant and this morning in the Clarion I have found the place of the 4°/clock meeting. Miss Underwood & Tom Jones come to lunch at 1.30, so I shall not be deserted altogether and I shall try & see the inside of the Windsor between that and 4p.m.

I hope the family enjoyed the clowns and the donkeys & then saw the sunset which was very fine from the train over the Sidlaw Hills.

Miss Irwin is disappointed with me because I have no wedding garments to entitle me to go to evening functions and I am telling her that I feel I am her guest under false pretences.

Now I must close. I hope Mother's cold is better & that Grimalkin's [Malcolm's] goolies are more tolerably decent than they were. Miss Irwin is anxious to send love etc., etc: and I enclose it as I have got it. My own to you all goes with it.

Yours Ever
R.

〰️ Ramsay to Margaret.

Edinburgh
4 December 1907

Mine Own Ladye

I am here again and have found 10 bundles. My correspondence is simply fearful and is making all other writing impossible. Many friends ask about you and I am going with Allen[1] tomorrow afternoon to the Glasgow Women's Liberal Unionist meeting to support him in his defence of Socialism.

I did not know you were returning on Saturday and after changing I began to hunt for my letters. When it looked as if I was going to miss my train I started to find Mr Barber and my eye caught your note to Mr Harris.

I am not sure that many Labour members are strong enough about barmaids & the Women's Trade Union League pronouncement will influence them. Hodge ought to sign and Richards[2], Wilkie,[3] and Jenkins[4]. I am not at all sure of them really.

On Friday 24th there is an NAC meeting. It will probably be held in London & so I could speak at a meeting that evening. You had better find out from Johnson however, if we are to meet in London. Tell him I think that only London will suit me.

Yes, the children might accept the 21st. We shall probably be very busy that weekend. I really should like to be out of London, but do not see that it is possible.

December 19 would do me for an At Home. It is the last day of a Labour Party Executive Meeting & some of the members might remain overnight though they will no doubt try to get home.

I hardly know what to do with the enclosed from [A.H.] Reynolds.[5] It means that our £100 is gone, The loss of the *Pioneer* would be a great blow, but I fear that if we gave them a loan of £50 it would go with the rest and our young people will be more and more expensive to us for the next 20 years now. If you think we can spare it you can send a cheque but let him understand that we would like repayment as a first charge – that we cannot take shares etc. I have not replied to Reynolds, so you might write to him

---

1. J.A. Allen, owner of the Allen line, a Glasgow business-man who was trying to rescue the *Leicester Pioneer*.
2. T.F. Richards, trades-unionist and Labour MP.
3. Alexander Wilkie, trades-unionist and Labour MP.
4. J.A. Jenkins, trades-unionist and Labour MP.
5. A.H. Reynolds ran the *Leicester Pioneer*.

immediately on receipt, let me know what you have done, and send back the letter.

With love to you and the chickabiddies.

Ever thine

~~ Ramsay to Margaret.

Sabbath. December 1907
The Cross Keys Hotel
St Andrews

My Dear Faire Ladye,

I could not write you in time for today's post as I have been at Church with the Herkless's, lunch, tea, the Principal's, and doing things generally. Have you ever been here? The place has vanquished me. I have never seen such a shrine of a town. I wish our youngsters were brought up here. I have only returned from the Herkless's for an hour to write a letter or two. There is to be a meeting of professors & some of the senior students at their house after supper & I have to discourse upon Socialism. Bosanquet,[1] who I met at the Gifford lecture yesterday afternoon, will not come to defend himself. The Master of Elibank[2] is also here and we had a long talk last night at the Club about the political situation. Before that I had a fine game of golf in a perfect afternoon with Herkless. Alas! I leave tomorrow . . .

I had a great meeting at Dundee. 1400 people all of whom paid for admission. I turn my back upon the old land with sorrow and reluctance – except that in five days the grand campaign will be over. Elibank says the Liberals are amazed at our activity and do not understand how we can do our work. He is rather angry with us, however, because he says we are frightening people away from the Liberals.

Now I must cease. Love & kisses to you all.

Ever thine
R.

---

1. Bernard Bosanquet (1848–1923), author and Professor of Moral Philosophy at St. Andrews.
2. The Government Chief Whip.

❧ Ramsay to Margaret.

n.d.
In the train to Dundee.

My Dear Missus

I was glad to have yours this morning. For the last two days I have been in a great rush and yesterday afternoon and this morning I have been particularly so. I went to a grand Women's Lib: Unionists meeting in a drawing room & heard Mrs Snowden quoted with great gusto by the Anti's. I replied that the book had been adversely reviewed in the *Lab:Leader*, & that one who was near and dear to me & who had more experience of middle class ways than I was glad to say I had (sniffs from the ladies) had exclaimed to me, after reading the book: "Why, Mrs. S. wants us to do under Socialism the same silly things & live the same silly lives as we middle class women do now." (Consternation) The two Hendersons were there & asked after you.

I'm afraid poor Allen is going to pay for his Socialism. He told me privately – and it must not be repeated – that one firm has withdrawn £700 worth of traffic from the Allen line, and he will have to clear out. He has also over-spent his limit at the Election & having refused to sign a false declaration, he is liable to a fine of £100 & five years disenfranchisment. Geordie Hardie seems to be advising him to do all sorts of silly things and a deputation which saw me this morning expressed some concern about what may happen if Geordie Hardie retains Allen's confidence. Hardie wants him to run for Parliament & they fear that [George] Hardie may get Allen committed before he knows where he is.

Ever thine
R.

Good meeting last night again 1500 to 1700.

❧ Ramsay to Margaret.

10 December 1907
Newcastle on Tyne

My Dear Ladye,

Your billets doux have come in all their portly massiveness, & I rejoice to hear of your well being.

Can you find out for Miss Irwin the facts she wants to know & have them ready for my return?

Mother's letter is disquieting.[1] The winters become worse and worse for her, & I fear she is seriously breaking up. It is quite out of the question thinking of her for Easter. Have you thought about things?

I find I cannot get back here on Thursday night, so please send my letters on Thursday up to 6 o/clock to the Post Office, Bishops Auckland. I have to leave London for Blackburn on Sunday morning and as I am coming up on Saturday from Middlesbrough, there will be no time to go into the country. Were you going down? If I go, can I get by Gt Central to Blackburn by about 4 o/clock on Sunday afternoon? I am free for Saturday night in any case, either to do this or go to Flo's. You can decide.

With much love to the rampagers and yourself with kisses.

> Ever thine
> R.

∾ Ramsay to Margaret.

> 11 December 1907
> Clarendon Hotel
> Newcastle on Tyne

My Dear Missus

The post to hand. You have not sent me the book I asked for. If you have not done so please send it at once to Mrs Coates Haslem's (?) address. Nor have you sent last week's *Pioneer*.

All serene. Love and kisses to you all.

> Ever thine.
> R.

> 12 December 1907

My Dear Missus

I enclose two cheques which I have forgotten to send for some time.

My train on Saturday is due at King's Cross at 1.40 I think I will have lunch on board so as to save time. Great meeting in Gateshead again last night. The Town Hall was packed, about 1500 having paid for admission.

Off to Bishop's Auckland.

With love and kisses

> Ever Thine
> R.

---

1. Annie Ramsay had been ill.

∾ Ramsay to Margaret.

13 December 1907
Talbot Hotel
Bishop Aukland

My Dear Ladye

Every thing to hand. I am not very keen about going to Ealing[1] for Christmas, though if the children would like it, I am willing.

From a business point of view the *Contemporary* is not a good investment. That kind of Review is rather on the decline. Its income is precarious for two main reasons 1) Its advertisements come from old fashioned firms which are gradually undergoing changes and 2) Its connection depends largely on the personality of its Editor. No expert valuer would ever dream of putting these shares at par. They pay six per cent I think & they are certainly not worth more than from 6–10 years' purchase. I know a very much better literary property than the *Contemporary* which changes hands on a ten years' purchase basis. I doubt if the XIX Century is valued at par as Knowles life is running out. These personal things are of the nature of life insurances. You might extract this for Basil's[2] information.

Was there much discussion on the Home Work Bill at the W.I.C.?

With love and kisses to you all.

Ever thine
R.

Ramsay's anxieties about his mother's health proved to be unfounded, and she was out and about again by the new year, falling over on the icy ground and happily picking herself up again.

Annie Ramsay to Margaret.

January 1st 1908
The Cottage
Lossiemouth

My Dear Margaret

A happy New year to all I hope you are all well I am much better but we cannot look out for frost and the roads like glass evry wun falling I got such a tumble right on my back but I was none the worse only by back som sore I

---

1. To Margaret's half-sister.
2. Basil Holmes, Margaret's brother-in-law.

was glad to be able to help Miss Allen I did all fir Charlie with Mrs Fazcers help so every thing went on all right so I managed to go over to day and sea Annie she is so helpless Miss Garnel is with hir we are to have a Christmas tree fir the Sunday school this year Tell the boys fir me wear sorry last year we had not wun last year did you get all right I have just got Kettie Anderson in it is verry kind of hir to cum down for a fue howers She wishes to be remembered to you all Kettie Stewart was over this morning with a par of Slipers for the house for me She is verry kind and so is them all Now I must close with love and a good New Year to one and all frim

Granie

January 20th 1908
The Cottage
Lossiemouth

My Dear Margaret
Thanks fir your kind letter I am not so strong as I ust to be only I will do watever you like It is not my way you now I always trays to do my best for you all if it had been here I would not fear but I will do wat you like you can think over it and let me now when you go hom I am keeping much better now Magie is still here only I think by the eand of the Mounth I shall do nicle aline if I am tide I had a letter from aunt Kettie they are keeping better only my brother his a bad coff yet wun of the fisherman here was cumming frow (?) Week hom to berry his Father and was killed and thron out of the train I never saw such a larg Furnal The Father and son went both to the Cimematry yesterday he his left a wedow and 3 children the youngest only 7 weeks

You can writ me and let me now wat we will ned & I will get them any way My love to Ramsay and do not over do your self I still expect to here frim you and you can say wat you want and I shall sea to it frm

Mither

Ramsay's work-load was as heavy as ever. Margaret wrote to her mother-in-law on 20 March: 'It is not often that he is home for any meal.'

In April the family went off to Lossiemouth while Ramsay chaired a turbulent ILP conference in Huddersfield. The tender Labour alliance was threatened by the return to Parliament of Victor Grayson, a young socialist rabble-rouser. Grayson had become the mob leader of the unemployed in Yorkshire, and although he was a member of the ILP, the executive decided not to support his candidature at the Colne Valley by-election the previous June. To their astonishment and horror, he succeeded without them. His return to Parliament was dangerous to the new party; it was a symbol of revolt, and for the alliance to survive it had to retain the support of the moderate trade-unionists, the ordinary working-men who might be frightened off by too much explicit socialist theory.

Ramsay handled the rebels with consummate tact and skill, although he was evidently incensed, and they were outvoted. He received a standing ovation.

〰 Ramsay to Margaret.

> n.d.
> Huddersfield

My Dear Missus

The special Conference is over in grand style. I ruled like an autocrat and we finished by 5 o'clock. The Colne Valley crowd is swamped. Of course the Grayson position does not come up directly until tomorrow, but we gave the opposition faction such a thrashing on the Labour Party's relations to us that it did not challenge a vote.

How are you? etc., etc., and Mother? Just off to a meeting . . .

> Ever thine
> R

〰 Margaret to Ramsay in Huddersfield.

> [April] 1908
> [Lossiemouth]

I hope this represents your attitude towards the comradesses. I am sending on lots of papers and proofs and things. Mrs Dean sent Ishbel some Easter eggs & gorse blooms for drying, so Mother has done them to send off by the post to Wroxham. We also have a lot of daffodils & wallflowers from the Lossie garden to make us look springlike. Going to tea with Flo and the Rogerses tomorrow. Hope you have had some holiday today . . .

〰 Ramsay to Margaret.

21 April 1908

Things gone well, excellent conference sung for I'm a jolly good fellow. . . Been a terrible time of strain and have had 3 meetings tonight at Dewsbury. Shall wire you my address tomorrow. Going to Whitby

Ever thine
R.

〰 Ramsay to Margaret.

In train-End April 1908
Beginning with Sights Station.

My Dear Missus,

I was knocking about so much all day that I missed the last post. . . You are very dilatory. [She was about to give birth.]

Huddersfield went very well, but my particular job was exceedingly difficult. They were very good, however, and allowed me to rule them with a rod of iron. Sam Reeves wanted to know how I was managing to cheat them so well. The delegates saw quite clearly that the agendas were far too much for them and that somebody had to cut down things for them and shorten speeches and discussion. Poor Kitty and Bruce [the Glasiers] had to sit up all night to do the *Labour Leader*. I heard that the W.L.L. Meeting went very well, but an important meeting of the N.A.C. prevented my attending it.

Florrie's[1] hooking is very exciting. When is the Wedding to take place. I suppose she thinks herself the happiest & the most fortunate of all the girlies now. Has she acquired a scottish accent yet?

I had a dutiful letter from David but otherwise I have heard nothing from [anyone] except from you. I suppose the Wedding came off all right, but the weather must have been disappointing. Yesterday was an awful day & today, though summer has given us both hail & snow.

I think I had better get back to London on Saturday after my meeting at Heywood. I do not know when I shall arrive but probably early in the afternoon. It is hardly worth while going to the cottage with aliens in possession.

I am afraid I cannot tell you who all send their love to you. They were many & a vote of condolence was nearly passed on you by the Conference.

---

1. Underhill, Margaret's friend.

Mrs Glasier, Mrs Moore, Mrs Campbell, Mrs Middleton and a few others constituted themselves a kind of column of heralds of Peter, however, and the universal anxiety became allayed. But I was very sorry & lonely kind not to see my wiffie sitting below ready to submit to my tyranny.

I am going through glorious hill country covered with snow & the train is very shaky, so I shall close.

I hope Mother keeps well and with much love to both, I am

> Yours ever
> R.

THE TIMES
LONDON, APRIL 28 1908
BIRTHS
MACDONALD – On the 28th inst. at 3, Lincoln's-inn-fields, London, W.C., the wife of J. Ramsay MacDonald, M.P., of a daughter [Joan]

When Joan was born her father was euphoric after his triumph at the conference. But soon the frantic nerves of the prima donnas of the ILP were jangling again. Hardie, Bruce Glasier, Snowden and Ramsey himself – all were driving themselves relentlessly. They neither ate nor slept enough; they were always on the move, going from one mass assembly to another and churning out propaganda in spare moments between meetings. Not surprisingly, there were spats between the four of them – Ramsay, much more organized and efficient than Hardie, found it increasingly irksome to be in his shadow, and had frequent bouts of despair in which he talked to Margaret of giving everything up. Both of them were exhausted.

~ Margaret to Aunt Elizabeth.

> 17 July 1908
> [Linfield, Chesham]

I want to be here for R. and the children as it is about the only time he has any leisure just now.

Ramsay wrote:

. . . hungering and thirsting after domestic privacy and quiet . . . made [Margaret] long for family week-ends in the country, and when we found that it was our destiny to be drawn into the maelstrom of public life and that

London was to give us no peace, we chose a little house on a spur of the Chilterns for our retreat. There were commons and woods and field-paths near, there were historic shrines and old churches and hospitable inns all round. In hot summer days we strolled amongst shady trees; when the ground was hard in winter, when the hedges were bursting into green in spring, when the woods were golden and shedding their leaves in autumn, we tramped mile upon mile, revelling in each other's companionship, discussing many projects which remote leisure might enable us to carry out, and singing praises in our hearts to the Providence who decreed that our paths through life were to meet and merge. She enjoyed this so much that when we were not there ourselves she always tried to get someone to use our house, lest happily the peace and joy it gave to us might fall on them too.

Margaret Ethel MacDonald, 13.

The Chiltern summer of 1908 drew to a close. Ramsay went north to oversee the by-election in Newcastle, taking David, who was four, with him. The left wing of the movement, the SDF (now calling itself the SDP), upset the apple-cart by putting up their own candidate when it had been decided not to challenge the Liberals. What annoyed Ramsay and Snowden most was the fact that the local ILP supported the SDP candidate.

❧ Ramsay to Margaret.

9 September 1908
Newcastle

My Dear Ladye

I got here all right. The meeting decided by 21 to 7 to fight [the by-election] & its resolution has to be confirmed or otherwise tonight. I have seen one of the fighting stalwarts to-day, however, and he has changed his mind. They will undoubtedly accept the recommendation to fight, tonight, but I think there will be no contest all the same as they will not get a candidate. I have summoned a meeting of the Executive at Nottingham for tomorrow (Thursday) at 3 & shall go on to London afterwards.

Enclosed are puzzles & a Women Soct. with some things in it which you ought to see.

With love to you all

Ever thine
R.

Puzzle: What is this?

<pre>
    X X X
    X X X
      X X
</pre>

Weather divine . . . Likkel chatterbox [David] & I have solemn afternoon walks & many parcels are being made up for Londing. We all send our love and kisses which you can distribute not forgetting yourself.

Ever thine
R.

After the by-election, father and son went on to Lossie.

〰 Ramsay to Margaret.

[Sept. 1908]
Lossiemouth

My Dear Madam

Yours with artistic enclosures has come. I'll try and get a belt, but I may not be in Elgin. Lewis Montagu and his wife & children are here. I had tea with them yesterday. & I am dining with them tomorrow. I shall not touch Wages Boards till I return.

I am much troubled about Newcastle, etc. A crisis is coming. I really cannot remain in the Party if this sort of thing is to be habitual. It is S.D.Fism [like the SDF!] of the worst kind. I have induced Snowden to write an article for the *Labour Leader* this week. I hope my letters to N.A.C. went without delay.

With love and kisses to all

Ever thine
R

〰 Ramsay to Margaret.

[Sept 1908]
[Lossiemouth]

More rain again. Lossie holiday. Louis Montagu charmed. Jane Bullen greater than ever on the stomach. General advice: "Tell yer Missus tae keep traivlin' about or her stomach will trouble her and the glut will nearly choke her." I've telt ye.

Mother is pretty well.

Love and kisses.

❧ Ramsay to Margaret.

[September 1908]
Lossiemouth

Mine Own

Just a line. The holidays are ended. Am playing with Sutherland & Provost Archibald of Buckie today. You are a landlady or fellar. I offered £5 and got the thing. Whittet[1] comes down today for some final matters. The plan is now much improved. Large bedroom for mother WITH FIREPLACE. She wanted it very much. I have a wild article on the Newcastle disgrace in the *Leader*.

Love and kisses to all. Likkle David is very incited. He is coming round the course with me & then lunches with us at the Hotel.

Ever thine
R.

❧ Ramsay to Margaret.

24 September 1908
[Lossiemouth]

My Dear Lady,

I had two letters from you yesterday which made me especially wealthy, and as I dined with the Montagus and walked over the hill with Miss Grant you can understand what a red letter day it was for me. The Montagus leave this morning. They are charmed with Lossiemouth. So am I. But we too leave on Tuesday. Mrs Martin Haddow is to meet us at the station and [carry] off David for an hour or two. I shall then pick him up and travel back overnight. I think, on the whole, that is the best arrangement.

The W.I.C. presents a problem. I should be unwilling to leave it, but if it agrees to support Minimum Wages officially, I do not see how I can remain a member. I was hoping it could have remained neutral whilst the agitation for legislation was going on, and after a bill had been passed it could have treated that as it treats all other laws. Whatever happens, I do not think we should whisper one word of resignation until the Council has taken its decision. If you happen to see Miss [Clementina] Black you might point out to her that we have always concentrated on work which did not divide the members except on one unfortunate occasion which was very special & which nobody would want to repeat. I always feel that to talk of resignation as a reason why one's opponents should not do something or another is

---

1. The builder of the 'Hillocks', the house Ramsay had erected for his mother.

objectionable. Of course, if the Council committed itself to Wages Boards, I should most certainly resign. It is bad enough to have Wages boards accepted by Parties to which one belongs for reasons of great far reaching principle. One belongs to the W.I.C. for its practical and detailed work.

How go the likklie onnies? And how are the new schools suiting the old scholars?

With love to you all

Ever thine
R.

Have sent tears to Flo.

The Daily Mail

January 1909

Alexander Ramsay, a guard on the Highland Railway, and uncle of Mr. J. Ramsay MacDonald, M.P., secretary of the Labour Party, was killed at Boat of Garten, Inverness, on Christmas Day, says the *Labour Leader*, by slipping when entering his van and falling between the platform and the moving train. He was sixty-seven years of age, and left a widow and family.

Ramsay went home to be with his mother.

❧ Ramsay to Margaret.

4 January 1909
Lossiemouth

My Dear Missus

Another glorious day. The sunrises and sunsets are wonderful. Tonight I speak here and I am very busy. Had another nice round of golf and a look at the chimney on my way over the hill.

We were up at Mrs Coull's & Miss Mustard's last night & Mr & Mrs Wellwood were in for tea.

Mother is great. Everybody's mother, married sister, and tenth cousin are being traced out with wonderful detail, but noone else gets in a word edgeways.

I am having many messages for the youngsters especially to David from Miss Mustard.

Willie's boy has been taken home apparently all right again. It seems a queer kind of thing. The doctor gave them no hope & behold the child got

333

better. I thought it might be meningitis; and even now I should fear something.

Uncle's £50 has been traced. He deposited in a bank, but there was no obvious trace of it. I shouldn't wonder if some ? escape us. I think we might have another talk with Aunt Bella after I return.

Give my love to the young and rising generation and so and so to your self.

> Ever thine
> R.
> X   X   X   X
> x   x   x   x
> x   x   x   x
> x   x   x   x

∾ Ramsay to Margaret.

5 January 1909
Lossiemouth

My Dear Lady

Glorious morning again. Nothing ever like this weather. Reporters are coming this afternoon to get tomorrow's speech, so I must hurry up. Good meeting last night. Mother seems very much better but complains about her nights. I said the *Pioneer* proposal was very dangerous & that at any rate I could give nothing this year. You enclosed the wrong sheet of L'HUMANI-TÉ.

I am back in London on Thursday (?) week as I am to leave Belfast at 9.15pm on Wednesday. Reynolds is coming up to see me in London.

Poor David! Poor, Poor David! What DID his Daddie often tell him? Want no rules and regulations whatever.

Send letters to me on Friday and Saturday to Albion Hotel Manchester.

The house gallops up. They are now at the bottom of the second chimney.

I am trying to have some MSS ready for typing. If I send it without any note tomorrow (I must go early to Elgin) you will know.

Now with love & kisses to all I must close.

Yours ever R.

334

ᕙ Ramsay to Margaret.

10 January 1909
The Albion Hotel
Manchester

Mine Own,

Here I am hundreds of miles nearer to you. My address for Monday evening's letters will be:-

Blytheswood Hotel, Glasgow.

Tell Ishbel and David that the Postcard drawings, and puzzle were very good, but I think Mammie is more beautiful and has a better nose. Grannie in bed was excellent. I think I found David's man on the road between the two other men.

The M.D.C. seem to be in high feather. But you must dress down its headgear. Glasier came here last night & kept me up till about 3a.m. He is optimist. Kitty and Ethel are reconciled. Ethel seems to have written honourably whilst her wreath of American boys was still green on her brow. I hope you gave Alice my love.

I left Lossiemouth in a glorious morning. The men were again at the house and would probably have finished the second chimney if the day kept fine. On Friday evening I looked up to see the Dr. He and his sister were in great fettle. She had been in Elgin & had heard about the meeting. I have not yet made up my mind about how I shall cross to Belfast, but you will have due notice.

Love to you all & my usual offering of kisses

Ever thine
R.

Thanks for Fabian information. It is interesting. Can you motor to Southampton on the Monday from Portsmouth? I go there. Is it Miss March Phillips who has resigned the W.I.C.?

ᕙ Ramsay to Margaret.

Sunday February 1909
The Wellington Hotel
Rochdale

My Dear Missus

Just off to Cleckheaton after I have seen Glasier, who is due here in a few minutes. Give the cuttings about my resignation to Miss Connolly & admire the one about yourself. Great meeting at Todmorden last night. Party seems

335

to be changing for the good. I am beginning to believe that Edinburgh will be like Portsmouth.

Riley says that Colne Valley will not discuss Grayson for any thing. They seem to be sick & sulky.

No more at present

Ever thine
R

A
Sack
Full
of
kisses

Leicester Daily Post

15th Feb. 1909

THE FEEDING OF SCHOOL CHILDREN

Mr J.R. MacDonald, M.P., and Mrs Macdonald were among the principal speakers, last evening, at a demonstration under the auspices of the women's Labour League in the Trades Hall. Its object was to promote the movement for transferring the feeding of underfed children from the Canteen Committee to the Education Committee, and its cost from the Christian willinghood to the rates. Mrs Cox, the President of the League, embodied the demand in a resolution which characterised the present management as inadequate and unsatisfactory, and demanded a "system of meals organised and financed by the local Education Committee." Mr. MacDonald, in supporting the motion, remarked that they had the starving children. If so, it is clear that the parents are primarily to blame. They know perfectly well that they have merely to appeal to either the relieving officers or the Canteen Committee to obtain the requisite relief. If a mother knowingly permits her child to remain half famished while the indispensable nourishment is to be obtained for the asking, she incurs a very grave and most unenviable responsibility. All are thoroughly agreed that the necessitous children must be fed properly at all costs, and that utterly irrespective of the character of the parent. The only great issue is the most effective and satisfactory method.

In March Ramsay took the children to Lossie while Margaret went on business to Glasgow.

❧ Ramsay to Margaret.

Saturday 6 March 1909

Hope you flourish and prevail over your enemies. I was to take the children and the Middletons to Maskelyn and Devants today but the day is horrid and Malcolm is not at all well. For the rest everything seems to be alright.

Kindest regards to Miss Irwin and the other Glasgow friends. More to yourself.

R.

He then returned to London and to high-powered negotiations with members of the Government while the family stayed with Grannie.

❧ Ramsay to Margaret (in Lossie).

[Spring 1909]

My Dear Missus

I got all your messages and am glad that the little mannie is doing so well. I am sending him a card today. What are you proposing to do? Masterman[1] has been seeing me about India. It is the wish of the powers to be that I postpone my visit, on account of eventualities. They would be glad if I could see my way to stay here during the autumn & I have to see Mr Asquith and Lloyd George today or tomorrow. They are making preliminary arrangements for an election in January. This of course is very secret and must on no account be told. I have not made up my mind & gave Masterman no grounds to suppose that I would change my plans. [Lloyd] George appears to have made up his mind that the Lords are to throw out the Budget.[2] Pike Pease[3] said to me last night that I ought not to be away after the New Year & *The Daily Telegraph* representative offered to bet with me that I would not go at all. One of the habitual sudden changes seems to have come over the scene. You might let me know if you have not done so already what your plans are in regard to the scarlet fever . . .

---

1. Charles Masterman, a Liberal MP.
2. The famous 'people's budget'.
3. J.A. Pease, a Liberal minister.

I am glad you found the rest of the herd in good fettle. Mother must be worrying a bit & no doubt doing too much. Is she isolating herself? I hope she is keeping well. What about my going up?

But I must wind up. The Speaker has got in the chair & I must go into the House. You will gather other items of news from what Miss Connolly will send you.

Give my love to them all and please do me the honour of putting on your hat and accepting the same blessing yourself.

Ever thine

R.

At the ILP conference in April Ramsay delivered his final address as Chairman – a stirring defence of parliamentary socialism.

There has been just that slackening in our hold of the workers which ought to remind us in these days of industrial depression and Capitalist failure, that Socialism is not to come from the misery of the people . . .

I know that there is a belief still fairly prevalent amongst one school of Socialist theorists that the more Capitalism fails, the clearer will be the way to socialism, that from the misery of the people the Socialist future will arise. I have never shared that faith. For with depression has not come more strenuous thinking, but more despairing action. Poverty of mind and body blurs the vision and does not clarify it . . .

It is not a society unnerved with panic and distracted with hunger that advances towards Socialism, but one in which a certain success in satisfying physical needs has awakened mental desires and made easy the exercise of the social instincts and the community consciousness of the individual . . .

Are we to accept the aims and methods of democratic government? Hitherto we have been a little too content with answering those questions by words and phrases the meanings of which were not always specific or definite. We have for instance, declaimed against Party government whilst doing our very best to form a new Party with a written constitution. At one moment we have proclaimed the eternal justice of majority rule; at another, we have demanded that a Socialist and Labour minority should determine the work of the House of Commons. Many criticised the action of the Labour Party on the Licensing Bill without having spent an hour in considering the conditions of political advance as we in all honesty ought to have done. Even our great watchword "Independence" has not always been sufficiently defined . . . But we seem to have been rather averse to discussing "Independence" as a method of Parliamentary action, and under Parliamentary conditions. If, for instance, we held the balance of power between two parties, how would we use it? Would we turn one out in preference to the other, or would we turn out the first one and then the other and make government impossible until we ourselves were wiped out for the time being by a series of General Elections that were regarded by the country as being nothing but a great nuisance?

The left-wingers were unmoved, and a vote in favour of a motion put by Victor Grayson prompted the angry and humiliated NAC members, Ramsay, Snowden, Glasier and Hardie, to resign.

At Whitsun a group of Labour MPs visited Switzerland.

Ramsay to his mother.

[May 1909]
Top of the Rigi 5.905 ft above the Sea.

We started from London on Friday night, crossed from Dover to Belgium during the night & travelled all yesterday through Belgium & Germany to Switzerland. Late in the afternoon we got to Bale, a very old town & famous for its connection with the Reformation. Here we had three hours & saw the town and then we went on to Lucerne which we reached a little after 11 o'clock at night, having been travelling for about 25 hrs. This morning we woke up in the most splendid of old towns and after having spent an hour or so looking around we got on a steam boat & came along a bit of the Lake of Lucerne a beautiful piece of water surrounded by high mountains. One of these we have climbed. The walk up took us four hours & here we are refreshed after tea sitting at a point which is one thousand five hundred feet higher than the highest point in Scotland. We are going down again presently & are to go tomorrow back to Lucerne for the night. Tomorrow we start on a four day's walk amongst the mountains in the course of which we shall be very much higher than we are now. Margaret joins in love yr

JRMacDonald

Ramsay to Margaret (in Lossie).

5 August 1909

My Dear Missus

I was glad to have your telewag yesterday and your card today. I hope the wedding went well & that you said the proper things to the young adventurers.[1] I wish I were up with you too, but it has been such a pleasant change in the weather that even London has been tolerable.

It looks as though there was to be no difficulty in our getting away to India. H[ardie] yielded to the view about the Osborne case which I mentioned to you & agrees that it need not keep me so I have asked for the 10th or the 17th boat which means we can leave (if there are any places) on the 10th, 17th, or 24th. You had better make your arrangements with mother accordingly. Do you like the house [The Hillocks]? Is the furnishing all right – the carpets etc.? I have sent the insurance form as it had better be filled up on the spot. The risks ought to be covered.

There isn't much news. I dine with Flo on Friday as I cannot very well get from Amersham to Oxford on Saturday night, however I get back on Monday morning.

I hope the fambly is well and likes its new surroundings.

Love to mother and all the friends.

Ditto, ditto to yourself & yours.

Ever thine

R.

❧ Ramsay to Margaret [in Lossie].

2 September 1909

My Dear Missus

I have just received your telegram, but I fear that it is impossible to get up to Lossiemouth this week end. At any rate I could not leave till tomorrow night. We are to be up all night this sitting.

David [who had been ill] seems to be having a good recovery, but the real danger is yet to come. He must be carefully kept from cold and otherwise nursed. Miss MacDougall will be very necessary. Leaving her up there will give us some peace of mind. I must send up something to amuse the lively invalid, but I hardly see a shop now.

The opinion all round at present is that the Election is to be in January. That means that we shall be back in time for the actual fighting, but that before we arrive all the active skirmishing will be over, and all the preliminary preparations made. It will be most awkward and probably do us considerable harm. I am breakfasting with Lloyd George tomorrow to talk things over. Elibank told me yesterday that he wanted me very much to go to India, but admitted that the time had turned out to be most awkward for

---

1. He is referring to Florrie Underhill's wedding.

myself. It is troublesome but early next week some more definite information will be available. There is a meeting tomorrow of the chief Liberal agents. Estimates of Election results will then be presented and considered.

I hope Mother keeps well and is not over-taxing her strength. The crowd seems to be in great style. May they keep it up. I send my love to them all and abudance of the same good fortune to yourself.

Ever thine R.

I will give your instructions to Mrs Gurling.

❧ Margaret to Annie Ramsay.

8 September 1909
Lincoln's Inn Fields

I have been busy all day and had a number of sewing ladies this afternoon . . . found Ramsay asleep as he had been at the House till about 3 a.m.

> On 17 September the MacDonalds set sail for India, leaving the younger children with Grannie. Margaret told Lily Montagu that she hated leaving them, but she felt Ramsay needed a rest, and she wanted most to be with him.
>
> David was not well while they were away.

❧ Annie Ramsay to Margaret.

[Sept 1909]
The Hillocks

My Dear Margaret

We are geting on very well I have got my blanks dray and I felt very tired yesterday but my bilor is redy fir to do the close you left David is geting on well I think the Doctir will be here to day Nurse seems put out at he weet his bed twise last night but I sad nevr mind it would be worse if not any He is quite happy and Miss and I are very happy I shill tray to do all in my power to make his so she keeps a big fire on I now the coll will be hevy only that will be aallright I lufted the carpep on the top loby and I think I will do the sam to the stars and . . . with . . . I found Nellie did not put Alister ready clowes all on I send hir (?) . . . and both together this letter cam frim Mrs Howie so I took no noties of it I had a letter frim Hillen hir Brother died the morning before Willie was going on to the furnel on Saterday I had a letter frim Aunt Bella she is so sirry for us all but I have no fear if but we will do the best we can with love frim the cheldren Tell Alister how I miss him and theyt Joan was singin and saying two on two and tata at 2 this morning how she woke up I do not now she is all right and walk som steps yesterday alone

With love
from Mither

The Mail

13 Dec. 1909

SIX WEEKS IN INDIA

LABOUR MEMBER'S REVIEW OF AN EMPIRE.

Mr. Ramsay MacDonald, secretary of the Labour party, arrived in London yesterday to take part in the electoral campaign after a brief visit to India. He had travelled from Calcutta practically without a stop. "To-morrow," he said yesterday, "I am in the saddle again at the head of the Labour organisation and ready for anything."

CHAPTER 9

1910
'The sun darkened'

Parliament was dissolved at the beginning of January, and by the time
the MacDonalds were back from India, the election campaign was
well under way. Ramsay set off at once for Leicester, where he was
re-elected after a fairly easy fight. The Liberals scraped home, and
the Labour Party managed to get 40 seats, thanks to their entente with
the Liberals. Asquith and Lloyd George embarked on a series of
reforms which were mutilated by the Lords, and a constitutional crisis
was precipitated about the right of veto. In an attempt to get a bigger
majority and a vote of confidence in his policies Asquith dissolved
Parliament and another election was held in December. This time the
Labour Party did better, managing to take three seats away from the
Liberals.

But there were problems within the party. Its very existence was
threatened by the Osborne judgement of the previous year which had
declared it illegal for any trade-union to raise funds for political
purposes by a compulsory levy. There was also trouble with the
leadership. After the January election Arthur Henderson resigned as
chairman, having fulfilled his two-year stint,[1] and George Barnes was
appointed in his place. Barnes proved to be, in his predecessor's
words, 'a conspicuous failure', and the job was offered to Ramsay. He
was hesitant because he thought that he exercised his real powers in
the party through his secretaryship.

---

1. He became secretary of the Party the following year, and held the position for
twenty-three years.

But for most of 1910 politics were not uppermost in Ramsay's thoughts. While the battle for the working-man went on, the flat overlooking the trees in Lincoln's Inn Fields and the sturdy grey villa in Lossiemouth were wreathed in a fog of private misery.

❧ Ramsay to Margaret.

> [January 1910]
> In the train to Leicester
> [for the election campaign]

Mine Own

We had two excellent meetings last night & the withdrawal of the two old members brightens the prospects for us. But Goldstone[1] is not a good candidate. He cannot grip his audience. He will probably win in any event but a good man would lift the place quite easily. Hamar Greenwood will help him in.

You might put in a couple of tins of Sanatogen amongst the treasures which the young lady is to bring to Leicester on Monday. They might be useful.

How are you and how are the chickie-biddies?

Kiss them all for me & ditto yourself.

Thine ever R.

> Annie Ramsay had been taken ill, and could not write herself, so sent her good wishes through a neighbour.

❧ To Margaret.

> 12 [January] 1910
> The Hillocks
> Lossiemouth

Dear Mrs MacDonald

Grannie wishes me to write and let you know how she is getting on She had a better night last night, than she has had yet, and feels a little stronger to day

Grannie hopes everything will succed with you at Leicester when the election comes on with kind love from Grannie to the children, Mr MacDonald and yourself from

> Mary

---

1. Frank Goldstone, NUT Labour candidate for Sunderland; MP till 1918.

My Dear Margaret

I had a better night and I think a little better this morning My eyes is bad I cannot do much with love to you all

I get the papers red

ˋ   from
                    Mither

〰 Ramsay to Margaret.

19 January 1910
The Albion Hotel
Manchester

My Dear Missus

Three meetings last night & asked to take one in the open air, WHICH I DECLINED. Much fresher this morning. Hope you are surviving. I left word at Earlstown last night to send your letter at once, so hope to get it in time for post tonight. Glad Alister has gone up. I am thinking of knocking off the three cornered Scottish meetings.

Yours ever
R.

〰 Ramsay to Margaret.

20 January 1910
The Albion Hotel
Manchester

My Dear Lady and Slave

Things are going not so very badly. Hardie's poll [at Merthyr Tydfil] was wonderful but if he had released his outside supporters for a place like Sunderland & had accurately gauged the progress of his own fight I would have thought better of it. It isn't cricket.

I got piles of letters at Wigan last night.

I got an income tax paper but did not know what it meant. If you have paid it – all right. If not ask for an explanation but pay it if it seems proper.

Glad to hear of Malcolm's success. I expect they will find they cannot chaff him with impunity. Also glad to hear of Alister's goal. Give him congratulations from me. I am sorry to hear of David. Why these throats?

I am toiling with India [he was writing *The Awakening of India*] & I am not answering congrats. What about a secretary? Could you see the Bureau people and have someone ready for me to see? Or have you any other ideas?

My present intention is to be back on Sunday night. I am not to help Tories to get in.

As soon as the election was over Ramsay went to Lossiemouth to visit his sick mother. He had only been there a few days when an anxious letter arrived from Margaret about their seven-year-old David, who had been taken into hospital with suspected diphtheria.

❧ Margaret to Ramsay.

27 January 1910
London

Dear Sir

Before you get this you will have had a telegram about David as he is not so well today & I am to telegraph progress to you tomorrow morning. I rang up at 2.30 & a man said he had just got a report & that it was "Not so well". "Parents to see Doctor". I went up at once and saw a different Doctor, the one who saw Dr Abel – nicer than the other one, I thought. He said David's throat had cleared up alright but the danger now was the poison in the system which was very virulent.

He is vomiting again & they are having to feed him with injections. He hopes he may improve during the next 24 hours, and advises my writing to you to warn you & telegraphing tomorrow morning if their report was that you had better come home. I went up and saw David for 10 minutes: he looked very comfortable but quiet. He had your card & sent his love to you and Grannie. He also was much interested in an operation to the eye of Auntie Flo's dog and told me about the description she had given him of that. He has a nice bright Scotch nurse, but very cautious & wouldn't give me any opinion – refered quite properly to the Doctors. She seemed very fond of David – said he was very good & she was so glad to have a Scotch boy as she comes from Edinburgh. I wonder how mother is today. I sent you lengthy telegrams. It is most important – I wish I could come up to you but of course with this news about David, it is out of the question for a few days. I don't know what to write to mother as I shall have to explain why I can't come up. So I am getting the children to write.

The Doctor will give me further news if I telephone between 8 & 8.30p.m. I do hope it will be encouraging. I think his constitution is pretty strong. He has a nice room and a nice nurse.

I suppose you will have to get someone in to look after Mother, who will be a companion & nurse combined. It is very difficult to think what we can arrange. I hope you can throw some light on it.

Alister & the others are all very blooming still. I can't make out about Alister. Dr Abel says he is sure he has had it already. If so it must be as far back as July as he has had no bad throat since. I don't know whether he has been disseminating poison ever since, nor how David happened to get it from him when they were only together an hour or so, and Alister says he didn't kiss him. However unless Alister gets worse he is to stay here: he has been for a solitary walk this afternoon. The M.O.H. agrees & will wait to disinfect us till next week. Dr Abel was rather better today.

I hope before you get this you will have better news about David. If not I supopse you would like to come home and see him in case of anything happening.

Your loving wife.

∾ Ramsay to Margaret.

28 January 1910
Lossiemouth

My Dear Missus

I hardly know what to write. Mother is mentally very ill & is suffering from delusions. Miss Grant, Mrs Mustard & others whom she describes as Tories are persecuting her. They are offering her plates & other things and trespassing on our grounds. We have also deserted her and she has tried to tear down my photographs. She was considerably soothed by your letter. Write her again and get the children to do so too. I will wire you tomorrow if I think you would do good by coming up. Mr Denoon met me at the station and Mrs Dean is here and has been for two or three days. This will just let you know how the land lies.

She was glad to see me but immediately wandered away into the land of delusion though she knew all the time she was speaking to me.

Everything is under snow here. Hope to hear of David in an hour or so.

Ever thine R.

∾ Ramsay to Margaret.

[January] 1910
Thursday night
The Hillocks

My Dear Lassie

WE are very very frail & this is the most heartbreaking experience I have yet had. I am sitting with Mother & the poor thing is glaring at me with wild

347

eyes telling me of the terrible things that have been done to her. They have ill-used her and beaten her and there are now evil persons about and holes in the wall through which light is coming. Death is terrible, but nothing like this. I have been trying all day to find someone to come in, but I cannot find one, and the horror of having to send her away is growing upon me.

God knows what is to happen. I will send you a telegram tomorrow.

I have written to Aunt Bella asking her if she could come up for a fortnight. By that time we might have managed something. At any rate she can not be left now, even if I have to remain here myself. Your telegram came and I suppose it means that you cannot come up. For some reasons I am not sorry. This is too pathetic. As I watch, I see signs that she is weakening, but they say she is better today since I came up. The night is always a trying time however, & when the morning comes she may be calmer and more rational. I wish there were a good doctor here. If I had only Mott or Jones of Claybury! But that cannot be.

Friday morning.

Mother has had a bad restless night & is very weak this morning. She did not know me at first & then told me that she was dying now. I thought it better to send you a warning telegram, but will send you another later on when we see how she gets on. It really looks this morning as though she will not get better.

It is fearfully cold here and is snowing. I poured out some water to wash myself this morning and then shaved. When I had finished I found the water in the basin almost solid. I have just had a morning walk and have returned for the doctor.

He has gone. She is much weaker and he will come back in time for me to write you to come tonight, if necessary.

Love to all.

Ever thine
J.R.M.

You did not send the MSS sections?[1]

---

1. *The Awakening of India* was being typed in London. It was published in 1910.

∾ Margaret to Ramsay.

28 January 1910
London

My very Dear Sir

We are certainly passing through very deep waters. Poor Mother, I would give anything to be with her and you. I am sure she must miss me even if she is not very sensible She always used to talk about nursing her own mother and said she hoped she would have someone to do it for her and now it seems terrible that I cannot come. Can you tell her the children are a little seedy or something not to worry her but to make her feel that I would come up if I possibly could. I am so glad that Aunt Bella can go up. I was sorry I had to give you anxious news about David. I have just come from seeing him. You might write him something each day – anything will do & I shouldn't say much about Grannie being ill in case he worries. His nurse says he looks forward so to his letters. The Doctor thinks he will pull through this attack but he is handicapped having so much albumen and he says that is left over from scarlet fever. I have [called] up Nurse MacDougall since & she says they were most particular about that. She kept sending specimens. You might mention it to Dr Brander & see what he says. At any rate we shall have to be very particular for the next 6 months to do everything to get rid of it or it may become chronic. I think both the Doctors here are very capable and careful & they seem to be very well up in their business. They let me telephone two or three times a day & I can go up each afternoon. David sends his love to you and Grannie. I took him some toys from the children today and he was very pleased in his solemn sort of way. As I say the Doctor did not think there is any immediate danger though they are a little anxious. I saw on the chart that he had not been sick since 8 a.m. I don't suppose I can wire tomorrow but will do so early on Monday. The others are all bouncingly well. Dr Abel did examine their water you know & found it all right. I think David's constitution is quite good & we must get all the best advice and attention. I told you the throat part was out of danger now – it is other complications in which the vomiting puts him at a disadvantage but I see on his chart his heart is sound.

I am sending you the MSS Miss MacDougall sent and also Miss Stone's. The last little bit is to be done by Miss Stone on Monday, he has not read this over. I think it is all there but she is not here herself today.

Wallace Carter rang up – He had made an appointment for Monday 12.30 but I said I didn't think you would be back – we are to ring him up when you are. Everybody who knows is very good about enquiring about our various invalids. I hope you are getting some sleep. One must keep up &

eat & sleep for the sake of other people. Dr Abel has not been nor rung up today. Of course he knew I would ring him up if anything was wrong.

I should hardly like to go North before last train on Wednesday, even if David gets on quite steadily I think the others ought to be past suspicion then if they do escape. How I wish I could come up to you both. I nearly wired to you to send for a specialist, Mott or someone. Would it be worthwhile?

Yours MEM

On Thursday 3 February David died in the London Fever Hospital. Among his mother's papers is a list in an unfamiliar hand.

David MacDonald

5 vests
1 shirt
2 nightgowns
3 sleeping suits
2 pr. stockings
1 felt slippers
1 dressing gown
1 waistcoat
6 handkerchiefs
1 brush and comb
1 vase.

Ramsay to his mother.

Telegram
3 February 1910

Hillocks Lossiemouth
David cremated Golders Green Hampstead 2.30 Sunday.

Ramsay

A week later, on 11 February, Annie Ramsay died. She was buried in the desolate Spynie Graveyard just outside Lossiemouth. After the funeral Ramsay returned home to London, and Margaret and the children seem to have stayed up north.

∾ Ramsay to Margaret.

no date

Mine Own

I am very sad and lonely. The house is very empty & I am crying over two who have left us altogether.

I wouldn't come back next week at all, but perhaps it is better to go through with it & see if it will end. Tell me how you got on. No more but heaps of love to you all.

I am saying "Blessie" because you ought to be just starting from Aberdeen.

Every thine
R.

Life went on for the bereaved parents.

∾ Margaret to Katherine Bruce Glasier.

no date

These statistics of mortality among children have become unbearable to me. I used to be able to read them in a dull scientific way . . . It is not true that other children can make it up to you, that times heals the pain. It doesn't; it grows worse and worse.[1]

∾ To Ramsay

The Dundee LRC Annual Meeting instructed me last night to send you an expression of their deepest sympathy in your double bereavement. They desire me to say that whilst it may be impossible to restore to you those who have departed, they can and do offer you their heartiest support and loyalty in your life's work.

In May a party of Labour MPs went to Germany; Ramsay was among them.

---

1. quoted in Lucy Herbert, *Mrs Ramsay MacDonald*, 22.

❧ Ramsay to Margaret.

> 6 May 1910
> Bahnhof Hôtel
> Dusseldorf

My Dear Missus

I am just back from a day in Solingen and am leaving for Berlin tonight, but I must send you a Billet doux. The rain has rained all day and has upset my plans but we have had a pleasant time with some Trade Unionists in Solingen & have got a good deal of information. But you can see all that in the *Daily News*. I am sending my first article with this post.

And how are the children? The little Onnie who has left us makes me very anxious about the others.

Now, there's a heap of kisses for you all

I say "bless 'em all" every night

> Ever Thine
> R.

Margaret joined the party.

❧ Ramsay to Margaret.

> [10 May 1910] Tuesday
> Hotel Elite
> Berlin

Mine Own

I do not think that a letter after this will find you before you start so here's to a good journey. I am off to Söneburg "where they make the toys" in a few minutes, thence to Nuremburg and Munich.

I hear the King is to be buried on Tuesday. That is a nuisance.

Now all good things attend your journey and with love and kisses to you all

> I am ever thine
> R.

David was never very far from their thoughts.

❧ Ramsay's diary . . .

4 July 1910

My little David's birthday but no little people were calling when I awoke "Happy birthday" Worries and sorrows multiply. Sometimes I feel like a lone dog in the desert howling from pain of heart. Constantly since he died my little boy has been my companion – especially on my railway journeys.

> In his despair Ramsay – perhaps missing the religion of his youth – turned to astrology for comfort.

T.D. Benson[1] to Ramsay.

22 July 1910
Eccles

My Dear MacDonald

I thought that as you had an idea that I did not tell you any thing about your horoscope because there was something bad coming, that I would go into the matter at once. Provisionally I have taken your time at 7.30 in the evening which seems to fit in with some of the events in your life that I know of. The first thing in the Horoscope that strikes me is the impossibility of your ever saving any money. No matter what you make it will vanish. I should say that if you ever save money it will be during the next five years and I can assure you that you will need all you can save for the following five, so take note of that, for it will come true as sure as you live. The next five years will be the best part of your life up to date. You are entering on the *steadiest* part of your career and also I should say one of the most brilliant parts. In 1912 the feminine element will enter largely into your life and you will receive considerable help from members of the opposite sex. Everything will then go well with you. The last twelve months must have been very trying and things will have gone wrong with you, but the period is drawing to an end. I should think this must have affected your health, among other matters. However you are as I said on the verge of a big change and things will go as well as they have gone badly. I see no trouble of any great moment till 1915[2] and then it seems to refer mainly to money matters.

The two noticeable features in the horoscope are, if I have the time any where near correct, difficulty in regards to money matters and health. You have two evil stars in the house of money and five stars in the house of health.

---

1. An ILP Treasurer, on the right wing of the party.
2. In 1915 *John Bull* exposed his illegitimacy!

I do not think however that either one or the other will bother you to any great extent for five years. You will have a couple of sharp knocks about May or June next year, but they will be quickly over and the generally good prevailing conditions will modify them. One of them I should say will refer to the loss of money, the other is an aspect of Mars and might mean legal or other matter like a fever or an operation, so be careful not to overdo matters about that time. These are the two worst signs I see for the five years and they are within a month of one another. I congratulate you on the coming years. They will be all you could desire in your most ambitious moments. [They were.] Looking back in your horoscope I should say that 1892 and 1893 must have been pretty black for you and that from 1900 things have gone well.

You were born if the time is correct under Gemini the sign of brotherhood and one of the intellectual signs. You have the curious star Nepture as the most elevated planet. It is curious but I have noticed several other socialists have this star high up in the heavens. I have, George [Barnes] has, and others. Astrologers do not understand its meaning as yet, but it is I think, responsible for our being apparently out of touch with the times and believing what people think are delusions like socialism.

Kindest regards from

Yours sincerely
T.D.B[enson].

≈ Ramsay to Margaret.

15 September 1910
Sheffield
Trades Union Congress

Mine Own

The Congress is fairly dull & disorganised owing largely to the poor chairman who muddles feebly along. It would be a grand meeting if the chairman were a strong man who could keep the reins tight. The Osborne debate (see introduction, p.000) was quite good but slightly spoiled by a small row between Walsh and Shackleton and an ordinary S.D.P. howl by Gribble. But the vote was simply magnificent and quite unexpected in its overwhelming majority.[1] It would ease the position and frighten the Government.

---

1. The Congress voted 1,717,000 to 13,000 for legislation to reverse the Osborne judgement (see introduction p.000)

We are just off for our offical teetotal tea & thence to our meeting. I'll send a card to Ishbel tomorrow and a letter in the morning if I can, and if there is any news.

Love and kisses to you all
Ever thine R.

〰 Ramsay to Margaret.

21 September 1910 [Wednesday]
Lossiemouth

Mine own

Hurry to get to Mr Hay's funeral yesterday made me overlook the letter on W.L.L. notepaper referring amongst other things to Leicester & I sent a telegram today. Give my apologies liberally to everyone. Price of Central Edinburgh came back with me from the funeral and lunched. He and I go to Elgin today to an Industrial Exhibition which Sunderland is to open.

The weather here is very cold & blowy but splendidly bracing and the ships are blazing away in the Firth. There are four off the harbour, one being a Dreadnought. I had a game with the dominie last night & we play again on Saturday afternoon.

Tell Ishbel that I was glad to hear the story of her going to school. I hope she likes it very much and that she is to be a great scholar . . . It is a pity I was not at home to see her start. I would have enjoyed it . . .

Ever thine R.

〰 Ramsay to Margaret.

23 September 1910
Lossiemouth

My Dear Missus

I could not write to you today as I did not get back from Inverness in time . . . Aunt Katie appears to be alright again but is getting old. Her deafness is increasing & so is her stiffness but she appears to have got over her special illness . . .

Aunt seems to have told them [her children] that our house was painted to the door and papered like a palace and that it was not at all likely that we should allow Jessie's rough colts to batter it with their hoofs. She gave me that enlarged photgraph of grandmother. She was very pleased to see me. Finding my name so often in the papers keeps her pride up and she was sad that so many of the others have gone before they too saw it. She was hoping that Grandmother knew all about it. It was a very nice visit & I was glad the hotels were full.

I saw the lawyer and the banker and found everything right. The stone for Uncle [Alexander Ramsay] is troubling them.

Aunt insists upon a "decent one". A mean one would be a reflection upon all of us. It is the service we can now give to him and it must be at least £25–£30. I think I have devised a scheme that will work . . .

Ever thine R.

〰 Ramsay to Margaret.

[October] Tuesday 1910
Victoria Hotel
Wolverhampton

My Dear Own

Another wearisome morning with correspondence. Many last night sent love.

I am shocked to hear of poor Mrs Johnson's death. One's quieter moments get fuller and fuller of thoughts of the dead one's. We are getting old and our own friends are thinning out now.

The Barnes message[1] is a difficult one to answer. I am not to take the leadership of an anarchistic party . . . If Lloyd George's last speech really means the beginning of a new policy I am going to help carry it out. Our best men seem to be very doubtful of the future & as I can influence things in other ways I am not going to cut myself off from them by becoming the victim of our folks. I have written a private letter to Shackleton asking him to tell me what he proposes to do. Barnes has certainly made a mess of things – even a greater mess in the country than in Parliament. Hardie too seems to be plotting and planning and will probably put himself at the head of some movement. He has told Benson that he is to stand for the N.A.C. If it had been after consultation with some of us, that would have been alright, but as usual it is off his own bat. He wants to be Chairman again. Then the Secretary-ship of the party is involved. I cannot be Secretary outside & Chairman inside.

With the usual to you all. Thank Joan particularly for her love. I send her a special lot in return.

Ever thine R.

---

1. This was a message from George Barnes relinquishing the chairmanship of the party and offering it to Ramsay.

Public and private anxieties were taking their toll, and when Ramsay went to his constituency for the election campaign in November he was suffering from one of his bouts of illness. Margaret was unable to go with him as she was eight months pregnant, but their two sons, aged twelve and nine, went along to some of the meetings.

❧ Ramsay to Margaret.

November 1910 Sabbath
Leicester

Mine Own Dear

I hope the children got home quite safely last night. We thought Alister and Malcolm looking rather pale and that hollowness about their eyes was back again. Are they being properly fed? They will have told you all about the meeting. It was most satisfactory. They tell me I was never better. A Leicester audience was certainly never better. I am really very fit again. Every bad symptom has gone but when I get back I shall go to either Ronald Ross or Jamie Cantlie and get a series of blood examinations. It was a pity that doctor in India did not tell me that it might be Malaria. I should have had it out of me by now . . .

Now as to my return. I have been trying my best to get off everything but I find I am rather fixed at Sheffield.

Balfour is there on Monday at the Albert Hall & the same place has been taken for me on Tuesday night to reply to him. Some thousand tickets have been sold & the Liberals are consenting to accept my reply & are going to turn out. The polling is on Wednesday. Pointer is very shaky in his seat. I MUST go & I shall take the greatest care. I shall return on Wednesday.

The elections yesterday are pretty much of a drawn battle. But I have an uncomfortable feeling that things will end too close to be effective unless a supreme effort is made by Liberals to poll their last men tomorrow.

I am afraid both our vote and majority will be reduced here. I did not get in in time; the Liberals are working harder than we are & I am told, are getting better meetings. On the other hand the Tory candidate has not done much. Oddly enough, we are all suffering by Lloyd George's vulgarities. I hear of several people who are to abstain or vote Tory this time & who are giving his speeches as an excuse. I met one last night . . .

Ever thine R.

∾ Ramsay to Margaret.

26 November 1910
Leicester

My Dear Missus

I have got a bit of feverish cold & didn't sleep last night so I sent for "Charlie" & he came & looked at my tongue etc. & gave me 'tuff. He is to look after me as a friend during the election. I am to be kept indoors all tomorrow & Thursday morning.

We have had various (?) consultations today & things seem to have started alright now. There will be the usual trouble over the polling cards, but that will come out all right. Everybody is sorry you are not to grace the Committee room.

Sunday.

No word from you. I am much better, and hope to be quite fit tomorrow. The nomination meeting last night was most satisfactory Reynolds says. No polling cards & no dissension of any kind.

I have a pile of stuff to get through and thick head to do it with.

Love and kisses to you all

Ever thine
R.

My Dear Ishbel

It was a nice card. I suppose the people went way along the road. Tell me if I am wrong.

With love from
Daddie

My Dear Malcolm

Thank you very much for your nice card. The knight was good but the castle seemed falling over on its nose.

With love from
Daddie.

෴ Ramsay to Margaret.

November 1910
Leicester

My Dear Missus

All your letters, mandates etc. have duly come. Today I am fit and thoroughly better. Everything nasty has gone. Drs. Peak and Bond came this morning & I waited in bed for them. They come again at 6p.m. and are to decide how many meetings I may take when I return to London I must get examined for Malaria as apparently it was that. I have to go away for recruiting purposes. A warm place was suggested but I said that there was no place on earth like Lossiemouth. We shall see.

I suppose you are getting the *Post & Mercury* daily, I have asked Gracie (who is most successful) to see to it.

Your absence, I hear, is much commented on.

Tell Joan that I got her message & that I liked the letter all the more that she posted it. I am sending her an extra kiss.

I have been admiring Malcolm's other grand sketch.

Blessie all.

Thine
R.

෴ Ramsay to Margaret.

28 November 1910
Telegram

handed in 5.55pm Leicester
received 6.16 pm

Am all right fever gone

Ramsay

The Times

8 December 1910

BIRTHS

MACDONALD – On the 7th inst., at 3, Lincoln's Inn-fields, W.C., the wife of J. RAMSAY MACDONALD, M.P., of a daughter. [Sheila]

〰️ Ramsay to Margaret.

[December]
Leicester Labour Party
General Election 1910

My Dear Missus

My two meetings last night bucked me up as no medicine has done. I speak for about 25 minutes at each & then drive home & am imbibing Mr Billson's soup by about 10.10p.m. and get to bed ten minutes afterwards. I am getting off some meetings next week. Originally I intended to return to London on Saturday & travel back on Sunday night, but we have taken the Temperance Hall for Saturday afternoon and I am meeting the workers in the evening. I shall return on Monday though, I think. It will be hard if we drop Pointer. I hear he is having a stiff fight. I must look in on Gorton on Friday. Bond is well satisfied with the care I am taking of myself, so do not worry.

How do you flourish? Will you go to bed on Monday & not wait for the result or shall I try and get through on the telephone? Probably the best thing would be for you to arrange with the *Daily Chronicle* to ring you up (if you are sitting up) so soon as the result comes in. Wilshere is a poor candidate, but my meetings dropped to insignificance as soon it was known I was not speaking. Last night they pulled up and were as good as last January.

I am recieving a Suffragette deputation tomorrow headed by Miss Pethick whose fine has been paid as she is wanted here. . . They are fools.

Love and blessie to you all
Ever thine R.

With the election out of the way, having secured Leicester for himself he took his sons to Lossiemouth for the New Year.

〰️ Ramsay to Margaret.

Tuesday night 28
December 1910
Lossiemouth

Mine Own,

Every body has gone to bed, but I am writing to you because we are going to Elgin tomorrow. Katie Anderson is dead & I am going to her funeral. How sad it all is.

The day has been divine but I have not been out since the golf round in the morning. Some sleet has fallen but tonight it seems to be frosty. The hills are white especially away to the north. The boys have been paying a round of calls & Malcolm has been introducing folks to his clown. We have been reading "The School of the Woods". It is admirable. We have also been playing with Flo's dominoes & they have given us all much pleasure. Miss Mitchell is flourishing but I am afraid this is too near Johnnie Mackillyan. He is giving her presents of the Elgin Cathedral in its glory etc, etc. . .

Your letters duly came & I was glad you had enjoyed the luxury of a bath & that you saw your toes alright. Did Joan point them out to you? Morley keeps properly friendly.

Could you get at once & send up to me Hunter's *Socialism* (or *Socialists) at Work*? I want to use it & forgot to get it from the *Times* before I left.

The bed has come but I have not touched it yet and now I shall not be able to do anything with it tomorrow.

Give my love to all the littlie ones and take some to yourself.

Ever thine
R.

❧ Ramsay to Margaret.

[30 December 1910]
Lossiemouth

Mine Own

I went up to Elgin yesterday to Katie Anderson's funeral. . . Her age was only 43. She was most alarmingly like Mother as she lay in her coffin.

I have seen nobody here yet, but I must go to Mrs Dean's tonight. The days are so short. The new bed is up this morning & it looks very well.

I bought a beautiful little mirror in Sherraton (sic) style yesterday & gave £2.50 for it. I thought I had better get something pleasant to look at & I could get nothing worth buying under about 30/-.

The weather keeps delightfully wild but clear with only passing showers & the youngsters are in fine fettle.

They came to Elgin yesterday & on their way to the station were waylaid by Whisset and taken home by him. They spent the day with his children. I have bought warm jerseys for them & they have hoops with which they career on the roads.

If tomorrow be fine, I may go with Cameron to Dingwall in a motor. I can hardly spare the time, but the run will be bracing and do me good. We shall return in the evening. If we go, you will have no letter from me on Saturday.

I am glad you found Mrs Middleton lively & that the journey passed off all right.

With heaps of love to you all.

> Ever thine
> R.

❧ Ramsay to Margaret.

[1910 Dec]

Have been in Elgin & Spynie & no time for more before post. Just back. Packing squaring up etc. today. Alas! book not finished but not very far off. Another week here would have settled everything nicely. All well, Hope you same.

> Ever thine
> R.

Self	X	X	X	X	X
Ishbel	X	X	X	X	X
Joan	X	X	X	X	X
Sheila	X	X	X	X	X

CHAPTER 10

1911–37

'A lone dog in the desert howling from pain of heart'

1911 was a momentous year for the Labour Party. The Parliament Act which limited the veto power of the House of Lords was passed; payment of MPs and a national insurance scheme were introduced. The way was paved for the modern welfare state.

Ramsay, who was by now acknowledged as a fine parliamentarian, had been effectively leading the party for some time, with the loyal support of Arthur Henderson and the powerful and lucid Philip Snowden. Keir Hardie was troubled with ill health, and was beginning to take a back seat.

The new year started for the MacDonald family, as it usually did, with a trip to Lossie. This time Margaret stayed at home with the girls and the new baby, Sheila, while Ramsay took the boys on the long train journey north. He spent a few relaxed weeks playing golf, visiting old friends and building up his strength for the burdensome months ahead.

Ramsay to Margaret.

> The Hillocks
> Monday night [January 1911]

Mine Own

I could only scrawl a very hasty note to catch the post today as I had been out all the morning playing in the tournament and had to hurry back to claim the reward of my labours. I came out third and got a most beautiful travelling rug of Elgin make. It will warm Sheila's feet and the cockles of your heart when you see it.

I have at last managed to pay a few calls – Brands, Moirs, Bill Stewart and tailor Smith as well as Mrs Dean. I wanted to do more, but they all insisted upon tea and at last I had to give up my programme as another cup of tea and another crumb of shortbread would have bowled me over. So I took the boys home to read to them whilst the liquid and the stuff were assimilated. I saw Mr Denoon this morning as I wanted his signature for my election accounts, and at the golf house I have also seen a number of the old cronies including the Dominie.

Alister and Malcolm have gone to John Denoon's to tea and are going to a cinematograph show at the cross afterwards. They are much better for their holiday and are enjoying themselves greatly.

I am enclosing a chapter [of *The Awakening of India*] for Miss MacDonald to type. She might return it as soon as she can. I doubt if I can send her much as I have a great deal to write and require the whole thing by me.

I saw the newspaper interviews. If you had only allowed me to write on porrich it would have been both fame and fortune to the W.L.L.

Tuesday morning.

Ishbel's very nice note has come. Thank her for it. The boys are writing to her. The clown went to the show last night and performed between the acts I hear.

Give Nurse my parting greetings and thanks.

This is the finest day we have had. Cold, frosty, sunshiny, with the steady roar of the sea filling the air.

Love and kisses to you all.

Ever thine
R.

〰 Ramsay to Margaret.

The Hillocks
5 January 1911

My dear Missus

There is nothing to report today. I am working as hard as before and things are moving, but I do not get out except for my one round of golf. The boys are to make some calls on their own account today.

Amongst other letters enclosed is one from Henderson on the eternal worry [the leadership of the party]. I have replied reciting the reasons why I see nothing but worry and vexation ahead if I took on the Chairmanship & also why I do not think that present circumstances offer me much chance of really getting the party in to shape. I should not wonder however if the job were forced upon me for the simple reason that noone else will take it & noone else is so obviously valuable that he will be pressed to put the halter about his neck. The 1911 will be a happy year!

With my love to you all & the usual kisses.

Ever Thine

R.

∾ Ramsay to Margaret.

The Hillocks

Thursday [Jan 1911]

My Dear Missus

Now we're having it. Yesterday, it was almost impossible to get out & today the ground is white & the snow is falling whilst the wind is high. I am so sorry: Spynie [graveyard] now seems impossible. I do not believe that Elgin man has done anything & it seems useless to go back to him. I may go up myself tomorrow weather or no weather, but there is still much to do with the book. You might read the chapters Gracie is now doing.

Malcolm's latest: If an Annie goat [anecdote] is a short story, is a Billy goat a long one? Malcolm went out in a plaidie.

I am going over to the golf house to keep an engagement as a matter of duty but there will be no play. I'll have a short walk & then back to a day's work.

Hope you all flourish.

Ever thine

R.

We arrive Euston 8.5 Sunday morning.

∾, Ramsay to Margaret.

Lossiemouth
10 January 1911

My Dear Lady,

Your nice letters come in most orderly array between sunrise and dinner, and dutifully in their train come those of the little daughter. She really must have an extra kissie for them. They are all most cheering.

The boys are just back from a long spin. They ran up past Mr Wellwood's out on to the Elgin Road and home. The day again is simply gorgeous, cold, windy, threatening snow & a new coat of white is being worn by the lower hills.

I am playing with Dr Clark at 2. John Sim and I played yesterday. I am trying to get to Spynie and Elgin tomorrow, so you may well not hear from me. I am toiling away however like a slave. The *Review* has been an irritating interruption during the past week & that is perhaps why I have written a "whacking" outlook.

Among the enclosures is a letter from Barnes. Please return it.

We shall bring up oatmeal and dresses, and shall arrive on Sunday morning. You did not send me the *Labour Leader* & so I have not seen it. I wanted to see my letter.

Duncan has sent me a bill for over £3 most of which Mother owed him & I have paid it. You might pay in the enclosed cheque.

Malcolm with the fresh air & the better food has turned out a most extraordinary rascal. He cannot sit quiet for a moment and is as lively as a mouse. He is now composing poetry & is contemplating some mischief for the soirée tomorrow. His rapartie (sic) is worthy of a Union debater & of course he is the darling of every woman in the place. I am so glad that this holiday has gone off so well. It will keep them going, I hope, till Summer. Sometimes the place is very sad with reminders of both of them who have left us.

I am glad Sheila gives little trouble. We are all looking forward to seeing her on Sunday.

We all send boundless love and piles of kisses,

Ever thine
R.

Ramsay arrived back in London and plunged immediately into party affairs. Arthur Henderson had written to him on 2 January urging him to rescue the party from George Barnes and on 17 January

The Times reported that he had decided to offer himself for the chairmanship. He was the obvious choice.

> 10 February 1911
> *Leicester Pioneer*

The unanimous election on Monday of Mr Ramsay MacDonald M.P. to be Chairman of the Parliamentary Labour Party will mark a new epoch in the history of the party.

Margaret had misgivings about Ramsay's elevation.

We are the martyrs of life. There will be more publicity, more attacks, more claims upon you . . . But we are doing the work of our destiny, and how silly it is of me to weary of the labour. I am not really weary; but it is heavy

> *Margaret Ethel MacDonald*, 8,9.

But the 'heaviness' was not just the burdens of Ramsay's office or the demands of her own work — Margaret was also exhausted from her latest pregnancy and drained by the loss of little David. There was no longer any granny to help out with the children, and the final straw was the illness of her friend Mary Middleton. The two women had worked in harness for the Women's Labour League and had become very fond of one another. Margaret went daily to Clapham to help nurse her, and when Mary died at the end of April aged forty-one – the same age as herself – Margaret did not have the reserves left to sustain this loss. She kept on working, planning for the family and worrying about Ramsay but the life had gone out of her.

❧ Margaret to Aunt Bella Ramsay.

> 19 May 1911

Did Ramsay tell you we were planning to go to India this November and December? He is rather bound to go on political business and I think a break and holiday will do him good. – He never gets a real one in England. I shall not like leaving the children especially as things have altered so since last time, but I also do not like letting him go alone . . .

In June Ramsay escaped to Lossiemouth to arrange for a new housekeeper for 'The Hillocks'.

∾ Ramsay to Margaret.

The Hillocks
Tuesday [June 1911]

My Dearest Mrs MacDonald

The world is very hot & the golf links very hard, the country is parched, but the whins & broom clothe it in a glorious mantle of yellow. It was hot yesterday but hotter today. Gourlay is coming up tonight and a postcard which is very indefinite says the Billsons are leaving Leicester at 1.25p.m. (presumably today) whilst another from Mr Wanderson says he cannot get round so far.

I have been talking over domestic affairs with Miss Mitchell.[1] I think she beams. The man is a manager of a distillery. They met at the fatal wedding at the new year & he seems to be unwilling that she should stay on here. I gather that she wants to go as soon as possible. Her mother is opposed to drink coming into a respectable family in any shape or form. Miss Mitchell does not think that Miss Cowie will do at all. She recommends a Mrs MacDonald who is a widow & is trying to dressmake here; or a Miss Elder who lives at Fortrose now but who kept house for a brother in London. I am not sure that the latter is the better, though there may be a difficulty with her about money. Mrs MacDonald was a cook or something in America, but she is a daughter of people who lived below us once & the sister of Mrs Bruce who died – Bruce the Milkman's wife. I shall see her without delay.

Sky and sea and far away land are simply glorious and the golfcourse is full of the scent of whin blooms. But everything still tells us first of all about the two who are not here now, Davidie & Mother. If they were only with us, how they would enjoy this day.

At eleven o'clock last night I was reading fairly easily without a light, & when I went to bed I could see every house from the end window as though it were but afternoon.

You will have had my letter today. You would have got nothing yesterday no matter when I had written it as it was Whit Monday. I am glad you had a nice week end I hope the young ones are well.

Love and kisses to them all & the same to you.

Ever thine
R.

---

1. She had been looking after 'The Hillocks'.

 Ramsay to Margaret.

The Hillocks
7th June 1911

My Dear Missus

Mrs Gourlay & I send love. It is a nice day again & we have been golfing & are now hastening to dinner as Cameron is motoring us this afternoon from Elgin up to the Findhorn. It is windy today and looks like rain but I hope it will hold till night & then come down as much as it likes. Gourlay seems to be enjoying himself.

The tablecloths etc. have not come yet. I hope you are all having a good time at Leicester.

Am returning some letters with notes on them for Fidus Alister.

I hear by the gossip of the town that Miss Mitchell's gentleman is a widower with two or three children. She has not said so to me but an innocent reference by me to the wiles of widowers was received in silence & cold suspicion gripped my heart.

There's the ting-a-ling for dinner, so there is just time for love and kisses to be enclosed in abudance to you all.

Ever thine
R.

I have seen Miss Elder. She seems very capable [of looking after the children]. Would you please write to her at Fortrose (that is the only address) giving her the details of the engagement – financial, coals etc. When we are up, servants & so on, as she would like to consider it. She is not afraid of the children & is fond of the tribe generally. I think we had better not press Aunt.

J.R.M.

 Ramsay to Margaret.

Dunfermline
Monday morning [June 1911]

My dear Missus

There was no post yesterday and as I was very full with kirk, family prayers, walks, visits I did not write. I have had a pleasant week end and I have packed my bags & baggage though it is not seven in the morning yet.

The weather is splendid though on the hottish side. This morning it seems to be cooler and there is a breeze blowing, but there is not a cloud on the sky.

But the domestic clouds were gathering, while the country simmered and frothed with lightning strikes and sabotage and Germany threatened war. Ishbel, who was eight, remembered:

One Sunday morning at the end of the summer term mother said she felt too stiff to walk to Amersham station and was afraid she must have to bother father to get a pony trap . . .

Ramsay remembered:

On Thursday, the 20th of July, [Margaret] went to Leicester with a member of the Home Office Committee appointed to investigate the management of Industrial Schools; on the morning of Friday she attended a meeting of an Anglo-American Friendship Committee; a little after noon she joined me at the House of Commons to lunch with one whom she had desired to meet ever since she read his pathetic book on the negro, Professor Du Bois; that afternoon we went to the country for a weekend rest. She complained of being stiff, and jokingly showed me the finger carrying her marriage and engagement rings. It was badly swollen and discoloured, and I expressed concern. She laughed away my fears; "It's only protesting against its burdens!" On Saturday she was so stiff that she could not do her hair, and she was greatly amused by my attempts to help her. On Sunday she had to admit she was ill and we returned to town. Then she took to bed.

For six weeks and a half she lay never murmuring, always hoping, never asking about herself, sorry when, in the earlier days of her illness, she saw a friend and feared she had not been cheery enough.

*Margaret Ethel MacDonald.*6,7.

While his wife lay fighting the poison in her blood Ramsay, the new leader of the Labour Party, was called in by the Prime Minister and Lloyd George to save the country from industrial collapse. 1911 was the year of the great strikes. The Osborne judgement, price rises, and the constitutional crisis over the House of Lords veto had created a feeling of frustration and irritation with the parliamentary system. What was the point of the Commons introducing reforming legislation if the Lords were to throw it out? The Labour members did not seem to be achieving much, and direct industrial action was the obvious alternative. There were a series of strikes and in Liverpool troops were called in to 'shoot down, kill and maim, inoffensive citizens, who have been goaded on by their dire and pitiable conditions to revolt'.[1] On 15

---

1. This is quoted from a letter Ramsay received from Charles Gray in Melbourne.

August the four great railway unions decided to call their men out, and for three days Ramsay was locked in negotiations. At 11.15 on the third day agreement was reached and on 25 August the *Labour Leader* published Ramsay's explanation of the new settlement. A week later the *Leader*'s bulletin about Margaret's condition was depressing:

1 September

Mrs MacDonald's condition is very serious. Reduced to a state of extreme weakness she has had another relapse and the greatest fears are expressed as to her recovery. It seems unbelievable, impossible, that she should be actually fighting for her life. That this radiantly strong woman who never knew the meaning of a headache should be so suddenly brought down to the edge of the valley of shadows.

Hundreds of well-wishers sent letters of encouragement and support.

Alexander Grant:

. . . tell her she cannot be done without. Dear Old Chap, I wish I could do something to help. I am not what you would call a religious man but from my heart I say God be with you.

W. Joynson-Hicks:

May I as one who does not often agree with you but who is influenced by dictates of our Common Humanity, send you a line of personal sympathy.

H.M.King George V. (Telegram):

The King regrets to hear that Mrs MacDonald is so ill and hopes that she is progressing favourably and that you may soon be able to give a better account of her condition.

On 8 September she let go of Ramsay's hand for the last time:

I asked her if she desired to see anyone who would speak to her about what was to come. 'That would be a waste of time,' she said, 'I am ready. Let us speak of what has gone past. God has been very good to me in giving me so much work'. . . She was convinced that she was going on a journey and that when she ceased to hold my hand she would exchange my clasp for that of those who had gone before her.   *Margaret Ethel MacDonald*, 46.

Malcolm, who was then ten, later wrote:

At a single blow my father was transported from infinite happiness to inconsolable sadness. I can never forget the terrible anguish which he suffered at her departure.

People and Places (London, 1969) 16.

Ishbel said:

The funeral started for Golders Green crematorium. The kerbs in Kingsway were lined with people standing limply to watch us pass. It did not impress me at all, I knew my mother had hundreds of friends . . . Daddie . . . was a changed man. Everyone was frightened and overawed by his silent grief . . . Instead of the boyish father who, at Amersham and Lossiemouth sat on the top step and while we piled on his back then (sic) carried us off downstairs hanging to his shoulders, and who tickled us till we didn't know where to turn for escape; I found a quiet intensely loving overthoughtful and maternal father.

A memorial was put up to her in Lincoln's Inn Fields, and the Kensington Baby Clinic was set up in her memory. But Ramsay's book was the best tribute. In his grief he turned to his pen as he had done before, and spent the three weeks after her death in writing a memoir. This was to become his most popular work, going into many editions.

❧ Ramsay to his half-sister, Florence Gladstone.

29 September 1911

I have finished my little tribute to Margaret . . . If I remember aright her Mother is buried with her Father at Kensal Green and if there is room ought not her name go upon the stone that is there already? . . . I was to begin another book this autumn but would far rather do this, my difficulty being that our marriage and my own work come so essentially into her life that it would be almost impossible for me to write some of the chapters. I am writing to a library friend who knew her well both at home & in the world & if he is free to cooperate the thing might be done. The blank gets more and more vacant. It was another sorrow to write the last sentence of my tribute. It seemed to dot the I's & stroke the T's of the fact that she is dead and I would gladly linger with thoughts of her until the market places become more familiar again.

Back in the market-places, filling his days with fiery words, often in the House until midnight, walking home through the fallen leaves, the blanks grew more vacant still. For time did not heal Ramsay's wounds; there were twenty-six solitary years ahead. He did not marry again, and it was a long time before he began to seek out the company of women. One can only wonder why this handsome widower, with five small children to care for, could not bring himself to love again. Perhaps the blessing of his marriage – the companionship, the cause and the children that they shared – was such that he neither dared nor cared to try and recreate it with another. Within the space of a few months he had buried his mother and his six-year-old son. Now, a little over a year later, his lassie had left him, and he withdrew into himself. There were complaints that he was cold and aloof, and Emanuel Shinwell said he was unable to make even 'a show of comradeship'. When any problem arose in his political career – even when he was Prime Minister and there was some hard decision to be made – he would escape from London and travel north to his mother's house in Lossiemouth for shelter and solace.

The family carried on living in the flat in Lincoln's Inn Fields. Ramsay felt a great sad tenderness for his children, but he could not share his grief with them, and after the first anniversary of Margaret's death never spoke to them of their mother. He took his paternal responsiblities very seriously now, writing to the children when he was away, reading to them whenever he could and interrupting many committee meetings by telephoning home to make sure they were all right. Friends rallied round with words of comfort and practical help. The baby, Sheila, was whisked off and cared for by an old friend of Margaret's, and an efficient Dutch housekeeper was installed to keep things in order. There was enough money for them to be comfortable; with the £800 a year from Margaret's Trust fund and Ramsay's salary as an MP.

The three elder children went back to school and Ramsay threw himself with desperate energy into the business of leading the party. Thirteen years after his wife's death he achieved what would have seemed incredible in the early days of their life together – he formed the first Labour government. Three times he held the highest office in the land, in his intense loneliness persevering in the cause to which they had devoted their marriage. When he became Prime Minister of the first national government, he arrived in Lossiemouth to be presented with a bunch of red roses. A friend noticed them dying, and

Ramsay said he had intended to take them to Margaret's grave. Through the trials and anxieties of the Great War, when he was attacked and reviled for his refusal to condone the slaughter, through the bitter crisis of 1931 when his old comrades in the party could only shout 'traitor', he must have thought of Margaret's words to him just before she died . . .

'When I go, I may plead to be allowed to be with you . . . and if in the silences of the night or of the hills you get consolation, say to yourself that it is I being with you.'

Afterword

After fifteen years of radiant love, comradeship and achievement, my father was left a widower with five young children, to face a further twenty-six years of life without Mother. Alone he rose to take the highest office in the land. But the story of our parents' partnership does not end with her death. Such was its strength and magic that it lived on in the hearts of the family, of friends, of political colleagues, and it continued abundantly to mould the development of the Labour Party and the political scene. This then is an epilogue, not an epitaph.

I am the youngest of their children. I never knew my mother, and Father was so deeply saddened that he could scarcely bring himself to talk of her. But my memory goes back to the days of 3 Lincoln's Inn Fields, and to Lossiemouth which is still our family home.

Lossie lay at the core of our father's being, and throughout his life he would return there for inspiration and for renewal of his spirit. It is a strangely beautiful place. As I write this, seated at his desk, the fiery scarlet and black of the sunset sky is softening to the pale pinks and mauves of a dying twilight, reflected in the Lossie river and the sea. It is a place steeped in romantic Scottish history and heroic story. We used to walk over the blasted heath where Macbeth met the witches, and picnic overlooking the castle where the Wolf of Badenoch, son of King Robert II, rampaged against Court and Church. Magic there was as well – witches' stones, kelpies, fairy knolls, and geologically the surroundings are fascinating – it was here that the local Hugh Miller studied the evidence for the antiquity of the earth.

Lossie is a simple place, and life had no frills. Porridge and herrings, plus-fours and kilts, bare feet, long rough walks, reading aloud in the heather, singing Scottish songs. This simplicity continued to the end. It was to the quiet of Lossiemouth that Father withdrew when faced with the task of constructing the first Labour government, communicating with his colleagues by telegram, and drawing up his list of Cabinet appointments by the light of a green-shaded oil lamp. For there was no telephone nor electricity at The Hillocks.

From the moment our mother met our grandmother, Lossie became her home too, and a place where the pressures of the world could be shut out. Malcolm and David were born here. When our parents were long away, they sent the older children to live with Grannie and attend the local school. Here our mother was buried and here 'Her dearest Sir' rejoined her in 1937.

Lincoln's Inn Fields – their home in London – brings back vivid memories. I was conscious of constant comings and goings, of lots of people gathering round the big black dining-room table heaped with papers, talking and talking. I remember the discomfort of being bathed in a tub on the kitchen table, for lack of a bathroom. The future policies of the Labour Party were greatly determined by all the research, the discussions and the practical planning that went on for many years around that table in the midst of our family life. One proverbial family story tells of an evening when, after the large weekly 'At Home', our guests went to gather their coats, only to discover a very small Malcolm asleep in bed under the pile. On another occasion at a Women's Labour League Committee baby Joan was crawling around perilously near the fire, to the consternation of all the members – except the chairman! This mixing of family and work must have been very disconcerting at times, though it never seemed to disturb Mother. Forty years later I learned firsthand of the extraordinary impact these gatherings had made. When I accompanied Malcolm on his appointment as British High Commissioner to Canada we were greeted with the greatest cordiality by the prime minister Mr Mackenzie King because – he said – as a lonely colonial student in London he had been made so welcome by our parents. War-time Canadian-British relations were strengthened as a result.

Life in 'No 3' was far from serious – our parents delighted in fun and teasing. Father would give us elephant rides round the room – thus introducing us early to his love of India! My last memory of living there is of the night of the first Zeppelin raid. Our housekeeper had shepherded us down from our top-floor flat to the entrance hallways, where we huddled, bewildered. Suddenly, in through the revolving glass doors hurtled Father, having fled the House of Commons to see if we were all right. Another time he rushed out of the tube station, regardless of the Alert, and overheard the guard saying, 'It's no good. You can't stop Ramsay. He's got children at home.'

Our mother still watches over Lincoln's Inn Fields. On her memorial seat there families dally to enjoy the sunshine, and at night dossers lie down to sleep tucked into their cardboard boxes and newspaper wrappings, protected beneath her outstretched arms.

I turn now to the beliefs and the human causes which brought our parents together and governed their whole lives, and to which on her death Father continued to dedicate himself for a further twenty-six years.

They were part of a splendid company of progressive-thinking people of varied viewpoints, all trying to solve the problem of how best to bring Utopia to Earth. They themselves were practical idealists and believed in gradualness and fraternity. Neither of them was bound by class-consciousness. Her world had not been confined by her surroundings and he had moved far beyond his lowly beginnings, helped by his Scottish democratic temperament, and by his marriage. Of course, they were unstinting in their efforts to improve working-class conditions and social justice. But to them the fraternity of man covered class, race and nationality alike, as their Lincoln's Inn gatherings testified.

Anxious for solid progress, they rejected militancy and violent action as forces bound to destroy more than they built. At the 1899 National Administrative Council meeting Father introduced a delightfully phrased Resolution that 'the TUC independent action should not be too defiant'. This was passed by a large majority. Complaints that such attitudes would 'postpone the Socialist millennium till Doomsday' were countered by their reply that 'resistance to change is much more quickly and surely overcome by persuasive and educational means'. However, there was one essential condition to this pragmatic approach – there must be no disavowing of principles in the process. From the earliest days the battle was on (and still is) between moderates and extremists, and it is said that through his insistent rejection that communist ways were socialism Ramsay MacDonald did more than anyone to save the British Labour Party from succumbing to the communist involvements of continental socialism.

His objections to militancy caused him to disagree with the bulk of the Labour Party in 1914 and utterly to oppose the War, because he considered that the country had drifted into militarism, not for the protection of civil liberties and the quality of life, but owing to long-standing status and commercial jealousies between the Powers which could, and should, have been settled around the conference table. Undeterred by isolation and vilification, he devoted himself to the campaign for a negotiated peace. I experienced an example of this. In 1921 Father was fighting a bye-election in Woolwich (the arsenal of military production) against a Tory candidate, advantageously entitled Captain Gee V.C. He took us daughters to the eve-of-the-poll rally. We drove in an open car through the streets lined with an uproar of yelling people shaking their fists, and passed trams bearing huge placards: 'A Traitor for Parliament?' There must have been cheers too, for he lost by only 683 votes. That night I saw two very different sides of politics – unfettered emotion in the electorate, and the power of a courageous stand. To our father, when principles were at stake, concern for his own advancement and comfort were as nothing. Courage and reason were to triumph. In less than three years, the Labour Party became the responsible government of the country, only twenty-four years from the formation of the Labour Representation Committee – a remarkable performance achieved by a truly remarkable band of people. Father became Foreign Secretary as well as Prime Minister. The international basis of socialism and our parents' early years of foreign travel proved an invaluable preparation for the job. Their hearts and minds had been set on harmony. They saw first-hand in New York the less-known squalid side of American life. In India they were to feel ashamed of the prevalent British attitude of superiority. Their book *What I Saw In South Africa* was an indictment against colonial repressiveness. For us children their enthusiasm for travel also opened up fascinating horizons. Young Alister went with them to Amsterdam for a meeting of the European Peace Movement. Father took us daughters to Ceylon to introduce us to some understanding of the East. The Passion Play at Oberammergau was a regular pilgrimage. Father's authoritative grasp of the international scene, coupled with his unorthodoxy and patience in negotations, certainly shook up world affairs. For example, in 1924 the Labour government recognized the Soviet Union. Its ambassador Mr Maisky was frequently frigidly received. So sometimes he would drop into 'No 10' informally to forget politics and drink a cheery cup of tea with the family. Another example happened in 1929 when Father decided that a personal discussion with President Hoover would be the only effective way to break the Naval Treaty deadlock. This was frowned on by some of the Foreign Office mandarins who thought that such a move would demean Britain's paramount status. But anyway, away he went with Ishbel, to this first Summit Meeting with the United States.

Our parents' attitude towards colonialism was also vitally important. Faithful to their belief that the world is the inheritance of all, they never felt that other people were inferior by nature. Why should Britain force their minds 'into grooves they won't fit'? With the advantages of experience and wealth we should be using our resources to help them use theirs to develop their own organization and 'way of life.' It is generally agreed that, despite strong opposition, Labour was able to follow these principles of colonial policy which were then continued by the National Government. How fitting it is that Malcolm should have contributed a unique role in the transition from Empire to Commonwealth.

Returning to their theme of realistic ideals – 'The heart is good for inspiration but not for guidance' – where *did* they look for practical guidance? Not surprisingly, they turned to scientific methods. After all, her father had been the youngest Fellow of the Royal Society and Lord Kelvin was her great-uncle. As for Father, it was in order to pursue his ambition to become a scientist that he had originally set out south from Lossiemouth. Quite logically, therefore, it was they who in 1905 suggested to the Annual Meeting of the British Association that it should create a Political Science section; and that the dining-room in Lincoln's Inn Fields was witness to such an incredible amount of research and planning. I well remember an occasion when I apologized to Father for not producing a book he wanted, with the excuse that I had thought it was on the shelf but it wasn't. He answered quietly, 'Don't think. Know.'

They were also passionately concerned with the provision of education for all. In a democracy it is little use confining knowledge to an élite. This opinion was to be expected of them. Mother's father was a liberal educationalist. Our father had been saved from a life of digging potatoes and herding cows by education. However, they regarded academic distinction as secondary to making the best of whatever qualities one had. Every day we poured milk on our porridge from a jub embellished with a portrait of W.E. Gladstone and his maxim 'Effort, honest, manful, humble effort, succeeds by its reflective action upon character better than success.' Honours too were extraneous. Father refused a Marquisate on the grounds that the title Mister had served him all his life and that Mister he would remain. Unfortunately, the expected transformation of society through education was misjudged. We are still awaiting much. But Father never allowed himself to lose faith in human nature. He remained an optimist to the end.

This 'Singular Marriage' was achieving great progress as a champion of human causes when, in 1910, tragedy struck. Father's mother, their young son David, and Mother's dearest friend and co-founder of the Baby Clinic, Mary Middleton, all died within a few months. Then in 1911 our mother died. Father was heartbroken. For the next twenty-six years he carried on, following the path of life they had planned together, inspired by her example and the Labour cause. She was always in his thoughts. After crossing the threshold of No.10 Downing Street for the first time as Prime Minister he wrote in his diary, 'Ah, were she here to help me. Why are they both dead – my mother and she?'

Father had a complex nature. He was a shy and private person, reserved and over-sensitive, apt to become downcast. These characteristics doubtless arose from his illegitimacy, and they never entirely left him. With the coming into his life of Mother, his full personality flourished, as this book shows. The complete acceptance of him by both her father and herself gave him a much-needed confidence in himself and his abilities. She was a wise counsellor as well as a devoted wife. Her affection and wisdom kept his despondencies at bay. He wrote in his memoir of her: 'To turn to her in stress and strain was like going into a sheltered haven, weary and worn, buffeted and discouraged. My lady would heal and soothe me with her cheery faith and steady conviction and send me forth again to smite and be smitten.' She managed to break down his early withdrawn reserve. She had a gift for friendship with all kinds of people and this helped to establish greatly that trait in him. He had a magnetic personality and was as happy in a fisherman's cottage as in a laird's castle. His close personal friendships ranged over an unusual variety of people. One day he would be supping with an old Labour colleague; the next day I would be making tea for Max Beerbohm, Harriet Cohen, Wilson Steer . . . He appreciated stimulating conversation and learned talk. He delighted in entertaining banter and the liveliness of attractive company. He used to chuckle over an episode in 1916 when, having been seated at dinner next to some elegant woman, she thanked him for his company, commiserating: 'It must be terrible for you to have the same name as that despicable traitor Ramsay MacDonald.' But always he longed for his Margaret. At the height of his career someone asked him why he had never married again. He replied, 'Because I buried my heart in 1911.'

Mother's richness of interests joined with his to make their life together tremendously rewarding. Much of their exhilaration and stamina sprang from their delight in the beauty of nature – its freedom, wildness, and changing moods. Until his last years Father would take us every summer to the Cairngorms for two days of hill-walking. When he was in office it was rumoured that his detective was chosen for his walking, rather than his professional, prowess. Books were always a special delight to both my parents; Father started buying them with the few pennies he managed to earn while still at school. His reading aloud to us, which he did regularly, was one of our most cherished family moments.

Often people describe Father as a romantic. This is quite true; they both were. Romanticism pervaded his spirit, born of his Scottish inheritance and the history, literature, scenery and myths which gave him his roots. Theirs was a singular marriage; it was also a Romantic marriage.

On her death loneliness seized him – and lingered. Nevertheless, his life till 1931 was charged with much joy and vigour. He had the exhilarating spur of Labour's political mission, the happy companionship of friends, colleagues, and family, refreshing travels, a lot of fun – and golf! Nevertheless, his early despondencies began slowly to creep up on him again. His Aberavon election agent sometimes despaired of his occasional moods of depression. More and more he grossly overworked himself, and his health deteriorated.

Then came the 1931 crisis. I was at No. 10 with him throughout. I well remember the atmosphere of tense anxiety, the constant callers, the emergency Cabinet meetings and Father working almost to breaking-point. However, his practical vision and courage never faltered. On the advice of his senior officials and the Chancellor of the Exchequer, and despite his own Keynesian leanings, he concluded that it was necessary to pass severe short-term measures which went against orthodox Labour policy, in order to ride the international financial crisis and to preserve national stability for the progress of Labour in the long-term. As he told me one morning at breakfast, he was utterly at variance with those powerful sections of the Party who, in his opinion, put their interests before the country's: 'Never will it be said of me that I allowed national sectional interests to dictate Party decisions.' He tried desperately to bring agreement both within the Party and with the other parties. The Cabinet at last accepted the stringent cuts, then changed its mind, and prepared to resign. I started to pack our bags and prepare our house for our home-coming. However, he was immediately pressed to form a National Government. He had intended to support the emergency cuts from the back benches but he decided to forgo the lure of semi-retirement and take up the challenge of running this momentous experiment.

August 1931 almost shattered him. He was expelled from the party which had nurtured him and which he and our mother had nurtured. Close friendships were broken. He was weary. But he was uplifted by the sureness that what he was doing was right. He loved a critical challenge, and he responded with his usual resilience and took up the cudgels with vigour.

He had intended to stay in office for only a short while over the crisis, and it would have been better had he kept to this intention. But the Indian Round Table Conference was looming and he was eager to be in charge. And policies kept arising which he was able to influence in a progressive way. Yet, despite enjoying new successes and new friends, he always felt alien to the political ambience of the other two parties. His health started to worsen considerably, and his gloom and irritations to descend more frequently, bringing a serious and sad decline in his effectiveness. But his old spirit would still flare up. 'Given time, I would convert this whole Government to Socialism. But I no longer have the strength.' Alas, nor did he have his 'sheltered haven' to turn to any more. She would have given him peace of heart and calm of mind and the wise counsel which he needed to tackle his task. In 1911 he had written of her political effect: 'Noone, not even I, can ever tell with accuracy how much of what steadiness there is in the Labour movement is due to her.'

He finally retired from public life and immediately planned a voyage to unfamiliar places – to Central and South America. Off he went with me, full of boyish excitement and curiosity, on his last adventure. He died five days out at sea. On the last morning of his life he played a game of deck quoits, then started work on the revision of his book *The Socialist Movement* to bring up to date the practicalities of the ideal.

Sheila Lochhead
July 1988

INDEX

THE FAMILY OF JAMES RAMSAY MacDONALD
(A guide to the relationships in this book)

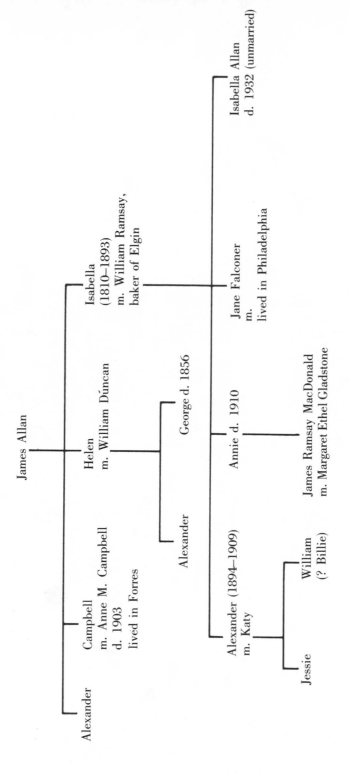